"Willson brings heart and wisdom to his inquiry into the skills and sensibilities necessary for a truly reflective planning practice. He offers an original framework for reflection, derived from well-chosen first-person accounts by practitioners. An immensely valuable text for students, novices and seasoned planners alike."

Leonie Sandercock, Professor in Community
Planning, University of British Columbia

"Willson challenges us to embrace reflection and incorporate this practice into our everyday work life. Using his experience, both in academia and professional practice, he builds a case that planning is rooted in observation and reflection. He accomplishes this by using a series of case studies that allows the reader to see how experience and context shape judgement. We can learn more about our profession and ourselves by looking both inward and outward, using the practice of reflection."

Kurt Christiansen, FAICP, President,
American Planning Association

"My colleague, Donald Schon, would have been delighted to see how carefully Richard Willson has expanded the idea of reflective practice. Drawing on seven cases, Willson has conducted a learning experiment to better understand how to empower reflective planners. He offers a conceptual framework which goes beyond Schon's description of double loop learning by highlighting how emotions, intellect and moral values come together in making practical judgments in an uncertain and contentious world."

Bish Sanyal, Ford International Professor of Urban Development &
Planning, Massachusetts Institute of Technology

"Students and practitioners of spatial planning take heart. Richard Willson and some talented compatriots show how practical judgment shapes the plans we make. Truly comparative cases offer useful insights about the conduct of our craft. We can learn to anticipate and invent the future together in many ways. Must read for practitioners and students of spatial planning."

Charles Hoch, Urban Planner and Professor Emeritus,
University of Illinois at Chicago

"This book helps us understand the grounded complexity of planners' work; it will stimulate debate about refining planners' reflective practices and their deliberative practices too."

John Forester, Professor, Department of City and
Regional Planning, Cornell University

"For planners, moving from naiveté to novice to expert requires experience. The challenge is how to mimic that in the classroom so students gain experience, but within low stakes environments. This book's framework, cases, and reflection techniques get students' feet wet with the 'swampy lowlands' of planning practice, minus the crocodiles."

Bonnie J. Johnson, FAICP, Director/Associate Professor,
Urban Planning Program, School of Public Affairs and
Administration, University of Kansas

"Rick Willson has written a thoughtful, engaging and practical book that guides the reader to understand planning in a manner that incorporates past and current thought as well as the realities of complex practice situations. This book is useful for planning theory courses, studios and practice-based seminars as well as for practitioners who seek greater insight and effectiveness in their work."

Barry Nocks, Professor Emeritus and Lecturer, City &
Regional Planning Program, Clemson University

"Planning depends on a public process of reflection, and, as Reflective Planning Practice makes clear, individual planners will flourish when they reflect effectively. Reflective Planning Practice expects the planning excellence required of the 21st century, and reveals useful tools for planners to achieve ambitious goals."

James Brasuell, Manager Editor, Planetizen Chris Steins,
Founder, Planetizen

Reflective Planning Practice

Reflective Planning Practice: Theory, Cases, and Methods uses structured, first-person reflection to reveal the artistry of planning practice. The value of professional reflection is widely recognized, but there is a difference between acknowledging it and *doing* it. This book takes up that challenge, providing planners' reflections on past practice as well as prompts for reflecting in the midst of planning episodes. It explains a reflection framework and employs it in seven case studies written by planning educators who also practice. The cases reveal practical judgments made during the planning episode and takeaways for practice, as the planners used logic and emotion, and applied convention and invention. The practical judgments are explained from the perspective of the authors' personal experiences, purposes, and professional style, and their interpretation of the rich context that underpins the cases including theories, sociopolitical aspects, workplace setting, and roles. The book seeks to awaken students and practitioners to the opportunities of a pragmatic, reflective approach to planning practice.

Richard Willson is Professor in the Department of Urban and Regional Planning at California State Polytechnic University, Pomona (Cal Poly Pomona). Over his career he has worked to link planning scholarship and practice. Dr. Willson is the author of *A Guide for the Idealist: Launching and Navigating Your Planning Career* (2018) and extends this interest to the American Planning Association Blog Series *Launching Your Planning Career: A Guide for Idealists*. Dr. Willson is also an expert on transportation planning, parking supply and management, and climate change planning. His 2013 book *Parking Reform Made Easy* provides a method for reforming minimum parking requirements. *Parking Management for Smart Growth* (2015) provides a strategic approach to parking management in the context of a sharing economy. Dr. Willson began his planning career as a practitioner and maintains a transportation consulting practice with regional agencies, local cities, and developers of urban infill projects.

REFLECTIVE PLANNING PRACTICE

Theory, Cases, and Methods

RICHARD WILLSON

Routledge
Taylor & Francis Group

NEW YORK AND LONDON

First published 2021
by Routledge
52 Vanderbilt Avenue, New York, NY 10017

and by Routledge
2 Park Square, Milton Park, Abingdon, Oxon, OX14 4RN

Routledge is an imprint of the Taylor & Francis Group, an informa business

© 2021 Taylor & Francis

Library of Congress Cataloging-in-Publication Data
Names: Willson, Richard W., author.
Title: Reflective planning practice: theory, cases, and methods/
Richard Willson.
Identifiers: LCCN 2020019784 (print) | LCCN 2020019785
(ebook) | ISBN 9780367258696 (hardback) | ISBN 9780367258689
(paperback) | ISBN 9780429290275 (ebook)
Subjects: LCSH: City planning.
Classification: LCC HT166 .W5354 2021 (print) | LCC HT166
(ebook) | DDC 307.1/216–dc23
LC record available at https://lccn.loc.gov/2020019784
LC ebook record available at https://lccn.loc.gov/2020019785

ISBN: 978-0-367-25869-6 (hbk)
ISBN: 978-0-367-25868-9 (pbk)
ISBN: 978-0-429-29027-5 (ebk)

Typeset in Bembo and Gill Sans
by Deanta Global Publishing Services, Chennai, India

To Robin

Contents

Figures

Tables

Boxes

Contributors

Richard W. Willson is a Professor in the Department of Urban and Regional Planning at California State Polytechnic University, Pomona (Cal Poly Pomona). Over his career he has worked to link planning scholarship and practice. Dr. Willson is the author of *A Guide for the Idealist: Launching and Navigating Your Planning Career* (2018) and extends this interest to the American Planning Association Blog Series *Launching Your Planning Career: A Guide for Idealists*. Dr. Willson is also an expert on transportation planning, parking supply and management, and climate change planning. His 2013 book *Parking Reform Made Easy* provides a method for reforming minimum parking requirement. *Parking Management for Smart Growth* (2015) provides a strategic approach to parking management in the context of a sharing economy. Dr. Willson began his planning career as a practitioner in Ontario, Canada, and maintains a Los Angeles–based transportation consulting practice with regional agencies, local cities, and developers of urban infill projects. Dr. Willson holds a bachelor's in environmental studies in planning from the University of Waterloo, Canada; a master's in planning from the University of Southern California; and a PhD in planning from the University of California, Los Angeles.

Four colleagues wrote cases for the book that broaden the case material, planning approaches, and perspectives that are represented. They are:

Lisa K. Bates is an Associate Professor in the Toulan School of Urban Studies and Planning at Portland State University and is a nationally recognized scholar in housing and community development on issues of gentrification and displacement. Her collaborations in Portland include working on the implementation of anti-displacement measures in the city's Comprehensive Land Use Plan and community development strategies in North/Northeast Portland. Dr. Bates has participated in this work through research partnerships and serving on technical advisory and oversight committees with the City of Portland, and maintains deep engagements with community-based organizations working toward racial justice and housing rights. She received the 2016 Dale Scholar Prize given by the Department of Urban and Regional Planning at Cal Poly Pomona in recognition of research that links theory with practice. Dr. Bates holds a Bachelor of Arts in political science from George Washington University and a PhD in city and regional planning from the University of North Carolina, Chapel Hill.

Ana Gelabert-Sánchez is Principal of Gelabert-Sanchez LLC, a planning and design consulting firm. She has over 25 years of experience in the planning field. In 2010, she was awarded a Loeb Fellowship at Harvard University, and she served as planning director for the City of Miami from 1998 to 2010. Gelabert-Sánchez led the Miami 21 initiative, a form-based zoning code that took a holistic approach to land use and urban planning to achieve a more sustainable, pedestrian-friendly and better-planned city. Miami was the first major U.S. city to adopt a form-based zoning citywide code. Miami 21 won numerous awards, including the American Planning Association National Planning Excellence Award for Best Practice in 2011. She has also worked as an urban planning and design critic at the Harvard Graduate School of Design, was named Top Public Official of the year for 2010 by *Governing* magazine, and received the Congress for New Urbanism Groves Award on Leadership and Vision in 2011. Gelabert-Sánchez holds a BArch from the Rhode Island School of Design and a master's in landscape architecture from the Harvard Graduate School of Design.

Kameshwari Pothukuchi is Distinguished Service Professor of Urban Studies and Planning at Wayne State University. She is also the founding director of SEED Wayne, a campus–community food systems collaborative dedicated to building student leadership in sustainable food systems in Detroit. Dr. Pothukuchi's research examines food systems' linkages to public health, economic development, social justice, and ecological sustainability. She has published papers on urban agriculture, grocery stores, food planning and policy, and university leadership in food systems. Recent projects explore urban growers' ability to obtain city-owned land for agriculture in Detroit and Cleveland, the impacts of fracking operations on rural communities, and community partnerships in food systems education. She is a member of a work group convened by the City of Detroit to inform the development of the city's urban agriculture ordinance. The ordinance, its history, and future prospects are discussed in a book chapter published by the American Bar Association. Among other roles, Dr. Pothukuchi has served as a cofounder and first vice chair of the Detroit Food Policy Council, co-chair of the American Planning Association's Food Planning Steering Committee (2006–2014), and a two-term board member of the Community Food Security Coalition. She co-authored, with Jerry Kaufman and Deanna Glosser, the *Community and Regional Food Planning Policy Guide*, which was adopted by the American Planning Association in 2007. SEED Wayne's projects include the Wayne State Farmers Market and three campus vegetable and herb gardens (2008–2016); Earthworks' passive solar greenhouse development at Meldrum and St. Paul; and Detroit FRESH: The Healthy Corner Store Project (2009–2013). Dr. Pothukuchi holds a Bachelor of Architecture from University of Bombay, Mumbai, India; and a Master of Planning, Master of Architecture, and a PhD in urban, technological, and environmental planning from the University of Michigan, Ann Arbor.

Laxmi Ramasubramanian is a Professor and Chair in the Department of Urban and Regional Planning at San Jose State University. She is an architect and urban planner. Dr. Ramasubramanian is the author of two books – *Geographic Information Science and Public Participation* and *Essential Methods for Planning Practitioners: Skills and Techniques for Data Analysis, Visualization, and Communication* (co-authored with Dr. Jochen Albrecht) – and numerous peer-reviewed book chapters, journal articles, and conference proceedings. She received the 2019 Dale Scholar Prize given by the Department of Urban and Regional Planning at Cal Poly Pomona in recognition of research that links theory with practice. As a scholar and educator, Dr. Ramasubramanian is committed to preparing thoughtful and engaged planning practitioners who can work collaboratively to address critical technical and societal challenges while simultaneously addressing issues related to diversity, equity, and inclusion. In her current research funded by the National Science Foundation, she is working with educators and practitioners to empower academic women in the geospatial sciences. Dr. Ramasubramanian holds a master's in city planning from the Massachusetts Institute of Technology and a PhD in environment-behavior studies from the University of Wisconsin-Milwaukee in addition to degrees in architecture from her home country, India.

Acknowledgments

This book is born of the observation that planners too-seldom discuss the underlying assumptions, methods, and theories that shape the practical judgments they make while planning. Through structured reflection on these elements, I hope that planners find paths to effective practice. My commitment to reflection stems from experiences as a practicing planner and a professor, and all that I have learned from mentors, supervisors, consulting clients, community members, elected officials, academic colleagues, and students.

I am grateful to the four contributors who joined me in this enterprise. Each took up the reflection framework and wrote insightful case studies: Lisa Bates, Ana Gelabert-Sánchez, Kameshwari Pothukuchi, and Laxmi Ramasubramanian. I learned much from their accounts of practice and am grateful that their voices and experience broaden the scope of the book. Their biographical sketches are provided on the previous pages.

The book includes other voices in the form of short commentaries from academics and practitioners. Thank you to Serena E. Alexander, Christopher Auffrey, Dan Carmody, Linda Dalton, Raphaël Fischler, Galid Ganish, Paul Niebanck, Danilo Palazzo, Jose Pillich, Tom Rothmann, David Salazar, Patrick Siegman, Martin Wachs, and Tad Widby.

Many colleagues offered advice and encouragement along the way. I am grateful to Dina Abdulkarim, Howell Baum, Soraya Coley, Ed Cornies, Linda Dalton, John Forester, Elizabeth Gallardo, Andrea Garfield-Castro, Robert Goodspeed, Charles Hoch, Annette Koh, John Lounds, Morgan Lyons, Linda

McIntyre, Patricia Moore, Paul Niebanck, Barry Nocks, Leonie Sandercock, Patrick Siegman, and Martin Wachs.

Thank you to my wife and fellow planner Robin Scherr who offered encouragement, insights from a career in community development, and editing throughout this project.

Lastly, I am grateful to Routledge for its interest in this project and especially to Editor Kate Schell and Editorial Assistant Sean Speers.

Chapter 1

A Roadmap for Reflective Practice

Effective city planners build reflection into their practice. More than just look-ing in the mirror, reflection is a dynamic activity that involves looking through and around the mirror at context factors and the interplay of thought, emotion, and action. Planners *reflect-on-action* in examining past actions for insight, and they *reflect-in-action* to support practical judgments in the midst of planning episodes. This book helps you develop a roadmap for reflective practice.

Reflective practice is widely acknowledged in the professions, but there is gap between acknowledging it and *doing* it. This book takes up that challenge, offering a reflection framework, reflection-on-action case studies, and prompts and ideas for incorporating reflection in daily practice. Reflection mills dis-crete experiences into practical wisdom that is needed in the dynamic context of planning.

My emphasis on reflection has two origins. The first source is my direct experience of the benefits of reflection during a hybrid career as a professor and a practicing planner. Reflection helps me clarify my personal values in relation to the profession, increases my ability to understand and influence context, enhances my collaborative capacity, and improves the quality of my practi-cal judgments. The second source is scholarship that supports this approach, including Donald Schön's seminal work (1983), that has continued in academic and professional interest in reflection, emotions in planning, and mindfulness

(Baum 2015, Ferreira 2013, Fischler 2012, Hoch 2006, Lyles and Swearingen White 2019, Osborne and Grant-Smith 2015, Willson 2018).

Reflection is essential because of planning's complex socioeconomic and political context, its demand for ethical reasoning, and its multidisciplinary nature. While all professions benefit from reflective practice, allied professions such as architecture or engineering tend to have more clearly defined aims, techniques, and clients. Said simply, planning does not allow for a straightforward application of technique – it requires practical judgments about how to proceed, what knowledge to employ, and whose interests to serve. The cyclists on the front cover are a useful analogy for planning practice: attention to the long view is required, there are choices of paths, and balancing requires sensing and reacting, moment by moment.

Reflection helps planners navigate the space between theory and practice. In a recent review of theory-practice tensions, Forester (2019) identifies four generations: (i) theory responses to wicked problems, (ii) the emergence of argumentative planning, (iii) attention to meditated multi-stakeholder negotiations, and (iv) consideration of the moral infrastructure of deliberation. Of the current moment, he argues the following: "The pragmatic imperative to act in fluid, complex, and contested settings requires creative and practically situated improvisation" (Forester 2019, 1). This last generation demands that planners reflect and learn from others.

The book is also motivated by my love of a profession that has design, economic, social, and environmental betterment as goals. Over 40 years of practice, I find planning to be an enterprise worthy of devotion, and an antidote to despair, alienation, and cynicism. As my friend Paul Niebanck says, "Planning is interesting, exciting, complex, messy yet orderly, humble yet powerful, challenging yet fun, and worthy of investing oneself in" (personal email communication, September 26, 2019). In the face of local and global challenges such as climate change or poverty, planning is *something we can do*.

The framework for reflection offered here includes elements of planner-as-person, emphasizing individual values, aims, and ways of working, and assessment of context. My practice experience in transportation, land use, and environmental planning is a part of a broad diversity of activities that makes it difficult to pin down a definition of planning. Urban and regional planners make plans, design built form, regulate development, program infrastructure, solve problems, develop and implement programs, organize and empower communities, and conduct many other tasks. The profession's topics of concern include those just mentioned, plus economic and community development, equity and social justice, housing, public health and human services, and urban design/placemaking. To address this variety, the book's core method is seven case studies written by me and four other planners who share their understanding of past planning episodes. Their voices are joined by commentaries from other practitioners and scholars.

Case Studies as a Method for Understanding Practice

As an academic who also practices planning, I observe that planning education and professional conferences seldom explain how things *really* work. Rather than "looking in" on planning from a detached academic perspective, the book's case accounts are experiential and explained from the inside out, recognizing the inherently personal dimension of planning practice.

Fischler (2012) describes reflective practice as "a form of professional activity in which the practitioner assesses her own experience critically and submits it to the scrutiny of others" (314). In the cases, each planner assesses their own experience; the scrutiny of others is achieved through text box commentaries and by inviting the reader to consider and critique the account.

Case studies offer richness of detail, specifics, and grounding that is essential to understand practice. The moment a planning conversation moves from a theory to a case, all the contingencies of planning action are introduced, including shifting context; the relevance of many theories and forms of knowledge; and the planner's habits, aims, and many ways of working. Cases come to life when they reveal how the planners synthesize the multiple elements of planning and make critical practical judgments about how to proceed.

My approach is appreciative of previous reflective accounts of planning such as *Making City Planning Work* (Jacobs 1980), *Making Equity Planning Work* (Krumholz and Forester 1990), *Advancing Equity Planning Now* (Krumholz and Wertheim Hexter 2018), and case-building efforts by the Lincoln Institute of Land Policy. The book provides first-person accounts because two planners in the same situation will practice differently – using acquired habits and intuition, acting out of their own values, reading context, applying knowledge and skills, operating consciously and unconsciously, and drawing on experience. This is why the writers of the American Institute of Certified Planners (AICP) professional certification examination questions are challenged to determine the correct answers to planning scenario questions. The exigencies and conflicting perspectives of practice call for improvisation, intuition, and collaboration.

The cases address mainstream and equity planning, public sector, consulting, and nonprofit settings, and a range of places. They vary from famous (the

Miami 21 form-based code) to seemingly mundane (an entitlement decision on a single project in Hawthorne, California). Case writers, and those who provide commentaries, offer a diverse set of voices.

Show-and-tell was a feature in my grade-school education. Students brought a favorite object to class, showed it to their classmates, and talked about their relationship to it. The difference between *show* and *tell* distinguishes this book from research that *tells* by arguing for particular procedural theories of planning, asserting certain causal relationships that draw on substantive theories in planning, or claiming particular planning solutions based on various forms of evaluation. Instead, the book *shows* what the case authors thought, felt and did in the hope that these reflections will help other planners consider and improve their practice.

A Framework for Reflecting on Practice

The case studies are *reflection-on-action* – authors consider what they thought, felt, and did in hindsight. Reflection-on-action is not just history for its own sake, however, as it provides insights for *reflection-in-action* in the midst of future planning episodes. The cases show how practitioners made decisions about how to proceed in a diverse set of planning contexts.[1]

Planner's actions are framed by their personal commitments and identities, hence the *planner-as-person* component. The approach is reflexive in that case authors are self-referential, seeking to understand and reveal their position as an individual planner and person.[2] Practices are shaped by personal values, and wide-ranging formal and informal theories about human nature and change processes, as well as past experiences. Intuition, habit, and unconscious factors shape the synthesis of these factors in action.

The *context* element acknowledges that planners act within economic, market, political, administrative, and cultural frameworks that are broader than the particulars of the planning episode. Further, their actions are shaped by values they have adopted as members of a profession. Planning, therefore, takes place in a tension between human agency (planner-as-person) and structure (context). Planners don't respond to this framework passively, though, because they influence context through their work. For example, a planner's refusal to participate in or reproduce discourse that demonizes a particular group of people, and/or their resistance to it, may influence politics by delegitimizing that discourse, encouraging others to speak up, and therefore changing context.

The *planning episode* occurs in the space between planner-as-person and context. It is an assignment that leads to the development of a plan, policy, or program; recommends a decision; or implements a plan or program. During the episode, planners think, feel, and act in ways that transcend single theories or practice prescriptions, so the interpretive lens used here uses two pairs of elements: logic and emotion, and the application of convention and invention. *Logic* is a core commitment of the profession: planners use it in developing knowledge that supports decisions, clarifing relationships between ends and means, and designing implementation mechanisms. Yet logic alone is insufficient. *Emotion* is a profound dimension for the planner and for those engaged in the planning episode. Engaging both logic and emotion, planners act. Regarding convention and invention, one form of action is shaping outcomes so they meet community norms, best practice, research findings, or the guidance contained in plans. In this work, planners identify and apply *conventions.* Other times, planners solve problems in novel ways, facilitate new visions, create plans or programs, or disrupt the status quo. This is the *invention* aspect of practice. Often, planners apply conventions and invent at the same time.

Figure 1.1 provides a visual representation of the framework, which is shown in more detail in Chapter 5, Figure 5.2. While planners may well find a different or modified framework is useful for reflecting on their practice, my purpose is to support structured reflection, improve practice discussion among planners, and support comparisons of approaches. The framework is a tool intended to be used, modified, and transformed.

This book emphasizes individual reflection because that is the starting point in interacting with others, as planners work and reflect in social and

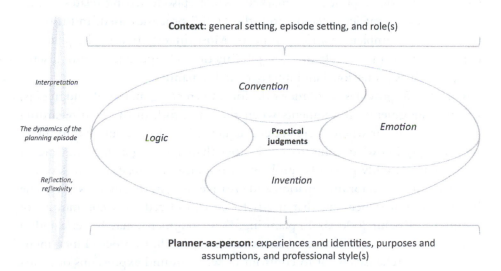

Figure 1.1 Reflection Framework

political networks with other planners, other professionals, community members, decision-makers, developers, and so on. Much important work on these interactions has been completed in recent decades. In discussing Schön's focus on inquiry, Laws (2010) reminds us that "inquiry is a social process involving behavior and interpretation constituted with respect to others whom we need because they can observe our behavior without fully sharing our interests and assumptions. This makes others useful; talking with them can help us get access to the elusive theories that are shaping our behavior" (601). Indeed, many of the case observations describe those interactions. The cases provided here show *how* individual planners improvise, and subsequent chapters seek to build the reader's capacity for doing so, in hopes to improve reflection in those networks. Even though no one plans alone, planners make practical judgments as individuals participating in larger processes.

Map of the Book

Following this introduction, Chapter 2 provides notes about the planning profession, the roles of planning theory, and reflection. Chapter 3 then explores planner-as-person at three levels: *experiences and identities*, *purposes and assumptions*, and *professional style(s)*. In any planning episode, the planner-as-person is core to the action.

Chapter 4 introduces context in three structuring elements: *general setting*, *episode setting*, and *planner's role(s)*. General setting includes elements such as society, institutions, politics, or markets, while episode setting relates to history, interests, conflict/collaboration, the "talk" processes used, institutional dynamics, and implementation prospects. Most directly tied to the planning episode is the planner's role or roles: job function, charge, and level of discretion, as well as professional and interpersonal dynamics.

Chapter 5 provides a framework for interpreting practical judgments. Practical judgments are moments when there is a fork in the road regarding how to proceed or where there are consequential choices about how to interpret or apply knowledge and to act. Rather than applying a rule, they are "a response to a highly particular problem, a response that reflects and develops character, that calls for imagination and creative insight, that evolves over time in light of experience and that needs to be considered by a community of inquirers" (Koehn 2000, 3). In planning, these judgments may be reflected in decisions to take a qualitative or quantitative approach, to proceed incrementally or comprehensively, or to confront or work around expressions of xenophobia or science denial. Further, practical judgments are made about whether to accept an assignment as given, seek to reframe and redefine it, or refuse it. The episode reflections organize the elements employed in making practical judgments in four categories:

- *Logic.* Planners add logic by seeking ends–means coherence, informing choices with substantive theory, providing data analysis and forecasting, evaluating alternatives, organizing methods of argumentation, thinking through sequence, interrelationships and strategy, and/or ethical reasoning.
- *Emotion.* Planners engage, manage, and transform feelings, working with emotions such as altruism, hope, care, or curiosity, or sadness, guilt, or fear. They transform apathy or harness exasperation to fuel planning action. They use models of facilitation, reconciliation, healing, or alternatively, tap anger about injustice to motivate a constituency to fight for change. Planners' own emotions are involved in responses to events in bureaucracies, politics, and communities.
- *Convention.* Planners shape outcomes based on conventions such as precedent, practice habits, protocols, community norms, best practice, plan and policy guidance, and/or legislation. Convention also includes shaping outcomes based on experience or constraints, relationships, and ethical commitments, as occurs when practitioners seek to "balance" stakeholder interests.
- *Invention.* Planners create. They foster innovative visions, plans, and regulations; reframe issues; and engage in mutual gain negotiations to find a win-win. Invention includes harnessing imagination and play through a design charrette, experiment, or pilot project; undertaking a collaborative effort; or welcoming accident or experimentation. Planners also organize disruption or insurgency that generates the new.

Figure 1.1 shows the planning episode in the space between planner-as-person and context. Those realms, however, are uncertain, changing, and negotiated. Uncertain about their interpretation of context, and perceiving ambiguity about what is sought, planners often move through assignments in a provisional, experimental manner. They also encounter incongruity between their values and the choices made by decision-makers.

Chapter 6 is the first of two plan-making cases, exploring the development of a climate action plan seeking to make Cal Poly Pomona, a comprehensive university in Southern California, carbon neutral by 2030. Climate change was a new issue on campus. Working without precedent, the case required practical judgments to proceed with analytic uncertainty, advocate for cost-effectiveness analysis, and pose critical questions about the scope of the plan. I wrote the case based on my experience in a dual role, as a faculty member and a consultant to the university.

Chapter 7 explains planning and pedagogical practice in developing a vision plan undertaken by a graduate capstone studio in Hunter College's planning program. The case writer is the professor who initiated and taught the class, Dr. Laxmi Ramasubramanian. The topic is climate resiliency for Mamallapuram (also known as Mahabalipuram), India. The case explains the planner/professor's practical judgments to facilitate rather than regiment the process, prioritize an engagement in cultural competence over product, and allow for disappointment while pursuing ambitious ends.

Plan-making and implementation are linked together in many planning episodes, as discussed in Chapters 8 through 10. Chapter 8 addresses efforts to address racial equity in Portland, Oregon, with the development of an inclusionary zoning ordinance for housing. Written by Dr. Lisa Bates, it shows how a planner and communities working for empowerment and advocacy must engage in implementation as well as policy-making. The case illustrates practical judgments to push equity using political action, advance knowledge and analytic frameworks in an advocacy context, and rebuild relationships to move forward. The case writer was a member of the Planning Expert Group and a paid consultant for the effort.

Chapter 9 illuminates the development of an implementation tool for carrying out and influencing the vision of a comprehensive plan. The Miami 21 form-based code was the first form-based zoning code in a major U.S. city. Form-based codes shift the focus of zoning from separating land uses to managing building form and its relationship to the street. The case illustrates practical judgments to address vision and implementation simultaneously, use a bottom-up community-based engagement process, and respond to political support for action. The case author, Ana Gelabert-Sánchez, was the Director of Planning for the City of Miami during this period.

Chapter 10 shows planning under conditions of entrenched disagreement in which the way forward was talk, not technical analysis. The case is the development of parking policies and programs for Dana Point, California, occurring after previous proposals generated community controversy. The case describes a role as a parking "whisperer." It reveals practical judgments to prioritize talk over technical analysis, "nudge" and "frame" rather than argue, and work on a "first-world" problem of inconvenience that nonetheless addresses larger issues. I wrote this case based on the experience of being a consultant for Dana Point.

Chapters 11 and 12 concern efforts that emphasize the implementation and administration roles of planning – program development and implementation, and an entitlement decision that implements a general plan. Chapter 11 chronicles experimental, entrepreneurial planning. Written by Dr. Kameshwari Pothukuchi, the case describes an effort led by campus and community partners to assess and increase the availability of fresh produce in corner stores in selected impoverished Detroit neighborhoods. It explains practical judgments to navigate the planning episode, step by step; address a part of the overall problem in a focused way; and extend the familiar to develop innovations. The case writer was the manager for the grant-funded project as part of her academic role at Wayne State University.

Chapter 12 addresses planning regulation and the land use entitlement process: the evaluation of a real estate development proposal seeking revisions to a community's comprehensive plan and zoning. This case is a proposed multifamily housing development adjacent to SpaceX Headquarters in an industrial district in the City of Hawthorne, California. The case discusses practical judgments to accept a limited, downstream consulting role, tailor recommendations to political realities, and ignore broader planning issues outside the scope of work. I wrote this case based on my experience as an independent consultant to the developer.

Chapter 13 synthesizes and reflects on the key practical judgments and planning takeaways from the cases, examining commonalities and differences, and exploring implications for planning education, professional development, and mentoring. Chapter 14 then explains how planners can bring reflection into their practice. The chapter provides methods for acquiring information to support reflection, looking outward and inward, and reviews interpretive reflection methods. It offers a series of reflection question prompts that build on the framework.

Chapter 15 concludes by addressing the feeling of being "lost" that a reflective planner can experience in a multi-paradigmatic profession and a society that emphasizes the individual over the collective. It draws on pragmatist and existentialist philosophy to suggest how to practice in such a condition. Neither theory dogma or purely intuitive practice offer a way forward. Structured reflective practice is the answer.

And Now to You: How to Use the Book

My intent is to stimulate you to consider your past, current, and future practice in reflective ways. Since the book's approach is personal, you may be wondering who I am. Box 1.1 provides information on my professional background; the case authors provide their introduction in the case narratives that follow.

Box 1.1 Where I'm Coming From, Professionally

I started my career as a land use planner in public agencies and consulting organizations in Ontario, Canada. All my degrees are in planning – bachelor's, master's, and PhD. After practicing land use planning in Canada, I moved to California to obtain the master's degree, and later worked as a transportation planner for the Community Redevelopment Agency of the City of Los Angeles. A member of the American Institute of Certified Planners (AICP) since 1987, I support the aspirational principles and rules of the AICP Code of Ethics.

I became a professor in the Urban and Regional Planning program at Cal Poly Pomona in 1986. This was an unexpected career turn, spurred by dissatisfaction with the planning job I held as well as the rare opportunity of becoming an academic without a PhD in hand. Cal Poly Pomona's commitment to pragmatist John Dewey's conception of learning by doing in education resonated with me (Dewey 1938). I began a PhD program after I started an academic career, which shaped my interest in linking theory and practice. My PhD dissertation was a mixed-methods examination of employer parking policies that included a multinomial logit model of travel mode choice. Along with this work, I sustained an interest in communicative action in transportation planning, academic management, and pedagogy. This movement from practice to academia led me to appreciate Donald Schön's and others' work about reflective practice.

Early in my academic career, I formed a consulting firm in transportation planning that operated in parallel to my teaching and research career. The interplay between research, teaching, and practice informs my outlook and approach. As shown in the cases I author, my research and planning practice address parking requirements, parking management, transit-oriented development practices, and climate change planning. I work for transit agencies, cities, developers, and nonprofit organizations as a solo practitioner and a member of larger consulting teams.

The arc of my academic interests traces a path starting with technocratic transportation planning, expanding to planning theory and practice, and finally the role of planner-as-individual. Positions in academic administration, including department chair, interim dean, and academic strategic planner, have shaped my thinking about planning practice. Along with planning consulting, these experiences grounded me in the processes of making change in organizations and communities. I've written two books on parking reform, and my latest effort is *A Guide for the Idealist: Launching and Navigating Your Planning Career* (Willson 2018). This book continues my focus on planners' effectiveness. In supporting their professional development, I conduct practice workshops, teach *Planetizen* online courses, and write a blog series for the American Planning Association called *Launching Your Planning Career: A Guide for Idealists* (www.planning.org/idealistblog/).

The book has a beginning, middle, and end. Reading it from front to back will present the interpretive framework, seven case studies, and methods and conclusions. Or, you could start with a case that interests you and then go back to consider the framework from the perspective of a case. If you are interested in connecting planner-as-person to practice, start with Chapter 3. If insightfully reading context is your concern, see Chapter 4. Or jump around. This advice on using the book is consistent with the pragmatic approach of the book – just like planning theories, use the book in ways that work for you.

Discussion Questions

Each chapter concludes with discussion/reflection questions to help you further consider the information in terms of your own practice. These questions can be taken up individually or in group discussions.

1. Do you incorporate reflective practices into your professional work? How? Do you see opportunities to increase the role of reflection?
2. Reflection requires a level of vulnerability because it may lead to you to reocognize error. How can a tolerance for this type of reflection be created in workplaces, community settings, and professional organizations?
3. The book calls for recognizing the role of planner-as-person in understanding practice. Are there limits to this perspective? Are there instances when planner-as-person should be pushed to the background?
4. How should planners find the right approach to responding to context and seeking to change it?
5. Regarding your approach to a planning episode, which elements are generally most important? Logic or emotion? Convention or invention? How would your practice change if you modified your emphasis?

Notes

1 These concepts were developed by Schön (1983 and 1987).
2 The idea of reflexivity is further explained by Howe and Langdon (2002).

References

Baum, Howell. 2015. "Planning with Half a Mind: Why Planners Resist Emotion." *Planning Theory & Practice*, 16(4): 498–516. doi: 10.1080/14649357.2015.1071870.
Bertolini, Luca, David Laws, Marilyn Higgins, Roland W. Scholz, Michael Stauffacher, Joan Ernst van Aken, Thomas Sieverts and Luca Bertolini. 2010.

"Reflection-in-action, still engaging the professional? Introduction Practising "Beyond the Stable State" Building Reflectiveness into Education to Develop Creative Practitioners The Transdisciplinarity Laboratory at the ETH Zurich: Fostering Reflection-in-Action in Higher Education Donald Schön's Legacy to Address the Great Divide Between Theory and Practice *The Reflective Practitioner, Revisited: The Notion of Deep Understanding* Concluding Notes." *Planning Theory & Practice*, 11(4): 597–619. doi: 10.1080/14649357.2010.525370.

Dewey, John. 1938. *Experience and Education*. New York: Macmillan Company.

Ferreira, António. 2013. Emotions in Planning Practice: A Critical Review and a Suggestion for Future Developments Based on Mindfulness. *Town Planning Review*, 84(6): 703–719. doi: 10.3828/tpr.2013.37.

Fischler, Raphaël. 2012. "Reflective Practice." In: *Planning Ideas that Matter*, edited by S. Sanyal, Lawrence J. Bishwapriya Vale, and Christina D. Rosan. Cambridge, MA: MIT Press, 313-332.

Forester, John. 2019. "Five Generations of Theory-Practice Tensions: Enriching Socio-Ecological Practice Research." *Socio-Ecological Practice Research*, 2: 111–119. doi: 10.1007/s42532-019-00033-3.

Hoch, Charles. 2006. "Emotions in Planning." *Planning Theory and Practice*, 7(4): 367–382. doi: 10.1080/14649350600984436.

Howe, Joe and Colin Langdon. 2002. "Towards a Reflexive Planning Theory." *Planning Theory*, 1(3): 209–225.

Jacobs, Alan. 1980. *Making City Planning Work*. Chicago, IL: American Planning Association.

Koehn, Daryl. 2000. "What Is Practical Judgment?" *Professional Ethics, A Multidisciplinary Journal*, 8(3–4): 3–18. doi: 10.5840/profethics200083/420.

Krumholz, Norman and John Forester. 1990. *Making Equity Planning Work*. Philadelphia, PA: Temple University Press.

Krumholz, N. and K. Wertheim Hexter. 2018. *Advancing Equity Planning Now*. Cornell, NY: Cornell University Press.

Laws, David. 2010. "Practising 'Beyond the Stable State'". *Planning Theory and Practice*, 11(4): 598–602. doi: 10.1080/14649357.2010.525370.

Lyles, Ward and Stacey Swearingen White. 2019. "Who Cares?" *Journal of the American Planning Association*, 85(3): 287–300. doi: 10.1080/01944363.2019.1612268.

Osborne, Natalie and Deanna Grant-Smith. 2015. "Supporting Mindful Planners in a Mindless System: Limitations to the Emotional Turn in Planning Practice." *Town Planning Review*, 86(6): 677–698. doi: 10.3828/tpr.2015.39.

Schön, D. 1983. *The Reflective Practitioner: How Professionals Think in Action*. New York: Basic Books.

Schön, Donald. 1987. *Educating the Reflective Practitioner Toward a New Design for Teaching and Learning in the Professions*. San Francisco: Jossey-Bass.

Willson, Richard. 2018. *A Guide for the Idealist: Launching and Navigating Your Planning Career*. New York: Routledge.

Chapter 2

What We Know About Planning, Theory, and Reflection

This chapter reviews issues in planning, theory, and reflection that set the stage for the framework and case studies that follow. In the last half-century, planning has developed a significant literature on theory and practice, supported by insights in the broader professional reflection literature. After exploring definitions of planning, the chapter addresses planning theory in the context of reflective practice and the literature on reflection and reflexivity.

What Is Planning?

An overarching notion of the profession is that planners use reason to manage change in cities and regions. The word *reason* is used in a broad sense to mean making sense of things. Planning has evolved from conceiving of plans as "blueprints" for physical development to incorporating a broad range of plan processes including comprehensive, incremental, equity, and communicative approaches. The profession's substantive foci include physical, economic, environmental, and social aspects of communities, cities and regions. Regarding process, planners employ technical, design, and communicative reason in widely varied practices. What differentiates planning roles is that sometimes planners serve broad public interests, while in other instances they advance justice and equity for specific groups. Some planning work is proactive (vision- or goal-seeking) and sometimes is reactive (problem amelioration). Lastly, planners engage in a complex interplay of client-driven and value-driven activities.

Friedmann defines planning as linking "scientific and technical knowledge to actions in the public domain" (Friedmann 1987, 38). This action orientation distinguishes planning from most social and phsycial sciences, and aligns it with professions such as medicine, architecture, or engineering. Brooks (2002) describes planning as an attempt to shape the future, while Levy (2017) emphasizes it as working with interconnectedness and complexity. Reflecting on planning's modernist roots, Beauregard (1989) explains planning's traditions as bringing reason and democracy to bear on capitalist urbanization.

The promise of technical rationality lies in urban planning's roots, but Rittel and Weber (1973) describe the nature of "wicked problem" challenges: problems lack a definitive formulation, solution, criteria, or testability. Many planning problems are one-time events, interconnected with other problems, and solved in collaboration with other interests and professionals. Usually, there are many possible solutions and the stakes are high. Moreover, Hopkins (2001) explains challenges to the notion of planning as predictable control that are found in planning problems: (i) interdependence, e.g., housing markets affect social outcomes; (ii) indivisibility, e.g., an infrastructure project can't be half-built; (iii) irreversibility, e.g., a capital investment can't be undone; and (iv) uncertainty, e.g., multiple, plausible scenarios exist. Even if a plan could get a grip on those factors, technical rationality does not encompass the rich forms of meaning and interpretation, cultural dimensions, and political and ethical questions that animate experience and decision-making. Planners find their way through messy and complex problems, embedded in institutions and responsive to multiple interests. Schön (1983) called this territory the "swampy lowlands."

Recognizing the need for communicative and deliberative dimensions in planning, Forester (1989) sees the profession as the guiding of future action in which planning analysts are "selective organizers of attention to real possibilities of action" (14). Using the term socio-ecological practice, he describes planning in three processes: "(1) formulating significance or value … , (2) assessing what is known and yet to be studied … , and (3) negotiating what can be done" (Forester 2019, 19).

The American Planning Association (APA) is the professional practice organization in the U.S. For the APA (n.d.), "The goal of planning is to maximize the health, safety, and economic well-being of all people living in our communities. This involves thinking about how we can move around our community, how we can attract and retain thriving businesses, where we want to live, and opportunities for recreation. Planning helps create communities of lasting value."

On the academic side, the U.S.-based Association of Collegiate Schools of Planning (n.d.) indicates that "planning is a systematic, creative way to influence the future of neighborhoods, cities, rural and metropolitan areas, and even the country and the world."

Taking these notions together, a number of key ideas emerge: reason, rationality, public interest(s), equity and representation, justice, interconnectedness and long-term thinking, uncertainty, process, engagement, listening, negotiation, and action. Perhaps a simpler thing to say is that planning brings a hopeful attitude about the future. While not ignoring good attributes of the present, planning has reform in its roots, in movements concerned with housing and living conditions in cities. Following this reform impulse and drawing on pragmatist philosopher Richard Rorty (1999), I see planning as a movement from unsatisfactory elements of the present to a better future. The work has moral, technical, communicative, and political dimensions.

Sanyal et al. (2012) define four major planning ideas that "matter:" livability, territoriality, governance, and the subject of this book, professional reflection. For them, the challenge to the profession is to be "self-reflective, participatory, but also critical of the status quo" (Sanyal et al. 2012, 21). This book takes up that challenge by focusing on structured self-reflection. This is not a new topic, but a timely one. Fischler (2012) explains that "reflective practice has become a very familiar idea among planning scholars and practitioners, but ... the concept is at once popular and marginal" (313). "What makes reflective practice a powerful idea is also what makes it difficult to accept and to apply: it holds the promise of improved collective action in the future by *imposing a burden of individual responsibility in the here and now*" (Fischler, 2012, 326, italics added).

The book's case approach is built on a view that understanding the artistry of planning practice requires attention to the micro level of personal case studies, focusing on practical judgments. Hoch (2019) describes the value of the case is to "avoid the analytic separation of rational and emotional dimensions of judgment, describing their integration in the context of practical judgments" (27). Of course, planners work in collaboration with other professionals, community members, and decision-makers, but each planner makes practical judgments as an individual as they engage in group processes.

Notes on Theory

Most planners encounter planning theory in their education. While this is not a theory book, theories are addressed by the case writers as they explain their actions. Theory is taken to mean an abstraction or generalization from particulars that allows for explanation of phenomena, including systematic reflection on guiding assumptions. It implies an ability to extricate oneself from a situation and understand the big picture as if we are spectators at the theater, discovering explanatory or predictive power. Those seeking an overview of planning theory may find one of many readers in planning theory useful (e.g., Fainstein and DeFilippis 2016).

In examining their actions, the case writers in this book discuss how they employed procedural theories (how to plan), substantive theories (how cities work), and ethical theories (what is the good). In some cases, theories are *descriptive*, e.g., this causes that, and in others they are *prescriptive*, e.g., indicating desirable process or outcomes. A descriptive theory might reveal the factors that explain travel patterns in cities; a prescriptive one might define the qualities of a good city.

I shared a draft of this chapter with a former supervisor and planning director who practiced in Canada and internationally. His reaction to my discussion of theory was, "I can't think of a time when I was influenced by a planning theory. Is there really such a thing as a generally accepted planning theory that guides planners? My advice and recommendations were guided by various forms of conventional wisdom, which changed many times over the course of my career, as well as the views of the people I worked with and those that were consulted as part of the process" (Ed Cornies, personal email communication, July 4, 2019).

My supervisor is not the only planner who is skeptical about the value of theory.[1] When my graduate students interview practitioners, they often hear the view that the "real world" isn't accommodating of theory. In a planning practice blog I write for APA, the most-viewed post in 2018 was titled "Planning Theory – What is it Good For?" Yet, in discussing theory and practice, Levy (2017) argues,

> One difference between the practical person and the theorist is that the former takes these ideas for granted, whereas the latter thinks about them consciously and makes them explicit. But when one acts, one inevitably acts on the basis of some theory about how things work.
>
> (431)

My view is that planners theorize as they work, and that they use theories as they offer practical help. One practitioner told me that theory is a backdrop for the action, a point of reference (David Salazar, personal email communication,

December 13, 2019). Supporting this view, Whittemore (2015) finds correspondence between scholarship in procedural planning theory and the writings of practitioners. The key difference is that academics often develop a single theory, while practitioners employ and develop multiple theories in response to complex practice settings.

It is easy to reject theory as inadequate for the "real world" because it cannot fully anticipate the planner as an individual who reads context and the particular dynamics of the planning episode. Rather than reject theory because of this, the book takes a pragmatic approach to theory, focusing on how theories can support the planning episode and promoting reflection as a way of understanding explicit and tacit theories in use. Along these lines, Hoch (2019) argues that professionals should draw on multiple theories to *guide* practical judgments rather than use theory to *justify* them, with an orientation of coping with complexity rather than controlling it.

Consistent with the aforementioned views, many planning theorists observe or interview planners to understand their practice (Forester 1993, Hoch 1994, Tasan-Kok et al. 2016, De Leo and Forester 2017). This book is aligned with those efforts but uses experiential, first-person structured reflection by planning educators who practice.

The planning profession has particular qualities that impede the development of a singular theory. It has loose boundaries (i.e., what is and isn't planning) and includes many activities. Planners have varied professional educations as shown by the degrees held by the case writers. The field is interdisciplinary. It addresses both value-related ends and technically-related means. In practice, planners are often stumped, realizing that the particulars of the case place them in a condition of unknowing. Understanding these conditions, Schön (1983) describes how professionals develop a "theory-in-use" that is tacit and therefore hard to explain. For example, a theory-in-use might be a particular way of forging a compromise in response to assumptions about conflict in organizations. Planning scholars who study practitioners by interviewing or observing them can be misled if planners articulate an espoused theory that obscures an underlying, perhaps unconscious, theory-in-use.

Rorty's pragmatist ideas have helped me understand my own planning practice. He described his general approach as replacing a "yearning for certainty, with hope" (Rorty 1999, 32). If the early eras of planning were built on a yearning for certainty, as found in rational, technical comprehensive plans, new planning approaches allow for complexity, uncertainty, and interdependence, such as scenario planning. A better future is at the core of the effort. Also, *expecting* that an overarching theory of planning exists is a form of yearning for certainty; engaging in a complex, unpredictable planning exercise is a hopeful enterprise.

John Dewey (1938) described the goal of pragmatism as achieving a "warranted assertability" that arises out of respect for context. Planners seek warranted assertability in making recommendations rather than establish proofs. And context includes *me* as a human agent. The cases I wrote for the book show my evolution from a view that data and models point to optimal solutions that will be adopted by rational decision-makers, the yearning for certainty part, to a communicative practice in which evidence is used in moving toward incremental improvement, the hope part.

Practitioners who disavow theory may in fact use it implicitly, operating in the background, as "ways the world works." They may also use it when they are stuck, as "another way to formulate a problem, a way to anticipate outcomes, a source of reminders about what is important, and a way of paying attention that provides direction, strategy, and coherence" (Forester 1989, 137). My practice improves when I explicitly consider theories, their efficacy, interrelationships, implications for action, and blind spots.

One additional issue that requires attention is the distinction between two significant historical periods: modernism and postmodernism. These terms mean different things in epistemology, ethics, aesthetics, and cultural theory. For planning, *modernism* refers to the enlightenment tradition of knowledge secured by reason, extended in planning to endorse rational comprehensive planning and embedded in notions of a universal public interest, a guiding narrative of progress, and technical rationality. *Postmodernism* refers to the challenge to singularity in values or political loyalties, valuing of diversity, and skepticism about truth claims. Eagleton (2003) describes postmodern as a "movement of thought which rejects totalities, universal values, grand historical narratives, solid foundations to human existence and the possibility of objective knowledge. Postmodernism is skeptical of truth, unity and progress, opposes what it sees as elitism in culture" (13). Since planning practice is embedded in broad trends, it must respond to changes in the underlying assumptions and theories about society and knowledge.

As the hold of modernist ideas has lessened, a planner can no longer assert a universal public interest as the basis for their work. At one time, freeway building was seen as serving the public interest; today most planners feel differently about such a prescription. The planner's technical expertise is frequently challenged, for good if the challenge exposes embedded values that create bias, and for bad if climate change scientists are not believed. Recommendations based on norms are thought to be oppressive because they do violence to individuality. In short, there is more focus on differences than commonalities. This societal shift has created a crisis for traditional notions of planning theory.

Planning can no longer claim legitimacy based on the planner as "scientist" of the city. Multiple conceptions such as technical rationality, communicative rationality, humanism, and others coexist in varying degrees. Hopkins (2001) described planning as paddling a canoe in a moving current; sometimes practitioners feel like there isn't even paddle.

To illustrate the complexity, my transportation planning consulting practice reflects multiple theories: tenets of modernism (technical, quasi-scientific planning), economics (utility maximizing travel behavior), neo-liberalism (pricing concepts), and humanism and communicative action (seeking local knowledge and context). I use data and maps, technical models, and rational planning methods to evaluate dynamic parking pricing proposals, yet I seek individuals' qualitative experiences of transportation systems and their engagement through discourse. Complexity abounds – economic ideas of Pareto optimality (the greatest aggregate good) may be in conflict with a commitment to a Rawlsian theory of justice (Deakin 1999), which prioritizes opportunities for those with the least. In other cases, they are mutually supportive, such as when an equity objective of improving bus service for transit-dependent populations is also more economically efficient than building light rail transit in lower density areas.

Transportation models reveal this complexity. Traditionally, they considered the aggregate performance of transportation options in ways that do not consider environmental justice. The Pareto optimality approach exacerbated inequality by leading to plans that widened highways instead of improving transit service. Contemporary transportation planning seeks to correct that bias but faces complex questions about whether aggregate efficiency and equity are complementary, or if they are traded off against one another. If there are trade-offs, what exchange or sacrifice is appropriate? Furthermore, economic methods may be complementary with justice, for example, if they critique proposals that appeal to voters but are grossly inefficient.

Planners are hunter-gatherers in the theory realm. We use what works, adapting and developing theories on the fly. We draw on best practice for guidance but consider context and applicability carefully. We embed various theories in our work, but may do so in a way that often makes them invisible, either to ourselves or our planning consituents. We are on the move, responsive to the environment, and know how to follow a trail. To extend this comparison further, we avoid a "Neanderthal" planner approach that seeks to bludgeon each planning challenge into submission, armed with a single approach, theory, or paradigm. These planners face extinction.

To summarize, effective planners practice without a single theoretical foundation, among multiple, sometimes contradictory theories in personal, context-dependent, contingent, and political situations. Practice is like plowing a field in the dark; we don't know if the lines are straight until the sun comes up. The "sun" is the complex set of reactions and interdependencies that cannot be known a priori. Taking a reflective approach to practice, as discussed next, can help planners see by the dim light of the moon. Moving theories from an implicit level to an explicit one increases our vision so that we can guide the plow as it moves.

Notes on Reflection and Reflexivity

Reflection may seem natural for planning scholars, as their job is to observe, step back and ponder explanatory factors, and develop theories. But the situation for practitioners is different. Developing theories is not in their job description. Rather, they take action. The pressures of the moment, the need to "put out fires," and the requirement to draw on intuition means that the cards are often stacked against reflection. I acknowledge this reality, but it is not necessary to "stop the world and think" to incorporate reflection in practice. The cases and concluding chapters show ways to incorporate structured reflection in ongoing practice. Readers seeking greater insight on reflection in the professions may find utility in Bolton and Delderfield (2018).

Reflection supports single-loop learning, in which practice is refined by reflecting on what happened, and double-loop learning, which examines what happened with a critical focus on *why* questions, including the practitioner's assumptions and beliefs (Argyris and Schön 1974). Reflective planners assess actions, consider what worked, understand their own position and views in relationship to others, and deepen their ability to recognize the consequences of approaches taken. Ed Cornies, previously quoted about theory, said this about reflection: "I, as well as most everyone I ever worked with, constantly reflected on what we had done and how to become more effective in the future" (personal email communication, July 4, 2019). The best types of reflection are bound in action; they are not static, self-justificatory accounts but rather located in context and structures in which the planner works. Reflection encourages thinking about values, and works through engagement with others.

Meaningful reflection requires a willingness to look at practice close-up and acknowledge missteps. It requires vulnerability, if only with oneself. But its full value is only realized if it is part of a learning process with others. Reflection may reveal and challenge assumptions, habits, biases, inequalities of power, and issues with personal behavior. Importantly, encountering the limits of our personal views can stimulate interest in learning from others. This book takes inspiration from Donald Schön's work on reflective professional practice, narrowing the lens to planning. Raphaël Fischler studied with Schön at the Massachusetts Institute of Technology (MIT) and has written on his legacy. Box 2.1 provides his interpretation of Schön's work and influence.

Box 2.1 Donald Schön and *The Reflective Practitioner*
Raphaël Fischler, Dean, College of Environmental Design,
Université de Montréal

Although he was trained as a philosopher (and as a musician too), Donald Schön had little patience with abstract theory; as a student of Pragmatism, he aimed to understand how people behave in practice, how they make decisions, and how they learn. He worked as an innovation consultant for many years, before being named Ford Professor of Urban Planning and Education at MIT in 1972. He was a respected contributor to debates on the theory and pedagogy of design and planning. But he owed his fame to his work on professional practice and on organizational learning.

The roots of *The Reflective Practitioner* (1983) lie in Schön's doctoral dissertation, which was an attempt to understand how people think in action, how they try to make rational decisions in the face of uncertainty. He analyzed in particular how people strive to transform "problematic situations" into discrete problems to be solved, a translation in which metaphors can play an important role (in an infamous example, defining urban blight as a cancer to be removed by means of urban renewal). In his thesis, Schön anticipated some of the work done in planning theory and policy studies over the following decades. He contributed to these fields until his untimely death at the age of 67, for instance in his 1994 book, written with Martin Rein, on the framing of public problems (*Frame Reflection: Toward the Resolution of Intractable Policy Controversies*).

Schön contributed to a radical rethinking of prevailing thought on professional action. Unlike fellow scholars of the 1960s and 1970s, he did not critique political systems but epistemological ones; his aim was not to right social wrongs but to understand how people and organizations can make better decisions in the face of fast-paced change, uncertainty, complexity, and conflict. In unique, ill-defined, and fluctuating situations, he argued, scientific knowledge and technical know-how are insufficient; effectiveness can only come from professional learning from experience, entering into a dialogue with the situation and with peers in order to figure out how to proceed, reflecting on their actions in response to failure and being open to questioning their assumptions and theories.

Schön's theory of professional practice, his emphasis on intellectual and emotional nimbleness, and his appeal to lifelong learning from experience are hallmarks of contemporary thought on the future of work. The pace of societal change that Schön noted in the 1960s has greatly accelerated and the complexity of situations that decision-makers face has only increased; conflicts over values have deepened and uncertainty has worsened. As time passes, Schön's call for reflective practice grows only stronger.

Like everyone else, planners want to maintain their dignity as they work in rough-and-tumble political and community environments in which we are sometimes blamed unfairly (Baum 1987). Similarly, as planning built its credibility as a profession it was more common to make authoritative claims to expertise than reveal what looked like an unscientific, exploratory process. But reflect we must.

Reflection is both a professional development tool and a state of mind (Bolton and Delderfield 2018). They define reflection and reflexivity as follows:

- Reflection is an in-depth review of events in which the person reflecting "attempts to work out what happened, what they thought and felt about it, who was involved, when and where, what these others might have experienced and thought and felt about it from their own perspective. Most significantly, the reflector considers WHY?, and studies significant theory and texts from a wider sphere" (Bolton and Delderfield 2018, 9).
- "Reflexivity is finding strategies to question our own attitudes, theories-in-use, values, assumptions, prejudices and habitual actions; to understand out complex roles in relation to others" (Bolton and Delderfield 2018, 10).

Without reflection, planners avoid taking responsibility for personal and profession identities, values, actions, and feelings. Indeed, the alternative to reflection and reflexive practice is to grow a hard shell and adopt a defensive posture. It hurts to admit that I used an analytic technique that was unsound, or that I neglected important values, or that I made unwise political compromises. While it is natural to protect oneself, the hard-shell approach leads to rigidity, burnout, and cynicism. It is not conducive to learning or professional growth.

The case study reflections are personal and of course are not free of self-justification. They are not the full story; other participants have their own accounts. The case writers cannot avoid unconscious motivations that shaped their actions but escaped notice, and cannot be free of implicit assumptions that generate biases and in turn affect what was noticed and filtered out. Drawing on research in human cognition, Hoch (2019) reminds us of the complexity of looking backward, and the possibility that we "author our past selectively to make sense of current practice" (69). The case writers do not disagree with that, but have sought to be aware of selective authoring in writing the cases. Some case writers entertain whether they might have done things differently and why. To evaluate alternatives in past action is the concept of a counterfactual, a thought process of creating alternatives that are contrary to what actually happened.

It goes without saying that the cases are interpreted differently by others involved in the planning episode and differently by someone observing from outside of the planning episode. The cases address the risks of subjectivity, unconscious bias, and selective memory by offering different voices in five authors, and second opinions offered in commentary boxes that accompany them. In addition, the cases are written with enough detail that the reader may disagree with the approach the case author took.

The reflective case approach proceeds with the aforementioned caveats because if the caveats are taken too far, planners *could not* reflect about their work. A strictly objective, outside-in approach to studying planning practice gives researchers all power of interpretation; such practice negates the reflective voice of planning practitioners and their own human agency and ability to reform their practices. Planners who reflect about their practice benefit themselves, their profession, and communities with which they work.

And Now to You: Backward, Forward, Now

The planning profession's characteristics, as discussed here, make it particularly suited for reflective practice. Lacking unambiguous methods, the field requires you to make practical judgments in the midst of planning episodes. The more these judgments are informed by reflection-on-action and reflection-in-action, the more effective your practice will be. If you develop habits of reflection based on a shared framework, as discussed in the next three chapters, then you will be able to understand and explain your judgments, and compare notes with other planners and learn from them.

Discussion Questions

1. What was your conception of theory before your read the chapter? Has it changed? If so, how?
2. If you practice planning, does theory primarily operate on an explicit or implicit basis, or some combination? Or, is it irrelevant to your planning practice? What theories do you draw on, if any? Why do you take the approach you do, either using theory or not?
3. What are the practical implications of planning lacking a single theory to guide practice? Is that an advantage or disadvantage for the profession? How does that affect our legitimacy with elected officials, the public, and other professionals?
4. Does reflexivity make you nervous? If yes, why? If no, why?

Note

1 With notable exceptions, planning theory is not discussed in the meetings of professional organizations such as the American Planning Association (APA), and practice is not prominently positioned at academic conferences such as those of the Association of Collegiate Schools of Planning (ACSP).

References

American Planning Association. n.d. "What Is Planning?" Accessed March 11, 2020 at https://www.planning.org/aboutplanning/.

Argyris, Chris and Donald Schön. 1974. *Theory in Practice: Increasing Professional Effectiveness*. San Francisco, CA: Jossey-Bass.

Association of Collegiate Schools of Planning. n.d. "What Is Planning?" Accessed March 11, 2010 at https://www.acsp.org/page/CareersWhatis.

Baum, Howell. 1987. *The Invisible Bureaucracy: The Unconscious in Organizational Problem Solving*. New York: Oxford University Press, Inc.

Beauregard, Robert. 1989. "Between Modernity and Postmodernity: The Ambiguous Position of US Planning." *Environment and Planning D: Society and Space*, 7(4): 381–395. doi: 10.1068/d070381.

Bolton, Gillie and Russell Delderfield. 2018. *Reflective Practice: Writing and Professional Development*, 5th edition. Thousand Oaks, CA: Sage Publications, Inc.

Brooks, Michael. 2002. *Planning Theory for Practitioners*. Chicago, IL: American Planning Association Press.

De Leo, Daniela and John Forester. 2017. "Reimagining Planning: Moving from Reflective Practice to Deliberative Practice – A First Exploration in the Italian Context." *Planning Theory and Practice*, 18(2): 202–216. doi: 10.1080/14649357.2017.1284254.

Deakin, Elizabeth. 1999. "Social Equity in Urban Planning." *Berkeley Planning Journal*, 13(1): 1–5. doi: 10.5070/BP313113027.

Dewey, John. 1938. *Logic: The Theory of Inquiry*. New York: Henry Hold and Company.

Eagleton, Terry. 2003. *After Theory*. New York, NY: Basic Books.

Fainstein, Susan S. and James DeFilippis (editors). 2016. *Readings in Planning Theory*, 4th edition. Chichester, West Sussex: Wiley Blackwell.

Fischler, Raphaël. 2012. "Reflective Practice." In: *Planning Ideas that Matter*, edited by Bishwapriya Sanyal, Lawrence J. Vale, and Christina D. Rosan. Cambridge, MA: MIT Press, 313–332.

Forester, John. 1989. *Planning in the Face of Power*. Berkeley, CA: University of California Press.

Forester, John. 1993. "Learning from Practice Stories: The Priority of Practical Judgment." In: *The Argumentative Turn in Policy Analysis and Planning*, edited by F. Fischer and J. Forester. Durham, NC: Duke University Press / Cambridge, MA: The MIT Press.

Forester, John. 2019. "Five Generations of Theory-Practice Tensions: Enriching Socio-Ecological Practice Research." *Socio-Ecological Practice Research*, 2: 111–119. doi:10.1007/s42532-019-00033-3.

Friedmann, John. 1987. *Planning in the Public Domain: From Knowledge to Action.* Princeton, NJ: Princeton University Press.

Hoch, Charles. 1994. *What Planners Do: Power, Politics, and Persuasion.* Chicago, IL: American Planning Association.

Hoch, Charles. 2019. *Pragmatic Spatial Planning.* New York: Routledge.

Hopkins, Lewis. 2001. *Urban Development: The Logic of Making Plans.* Washington, DC: Island Press.

Levy, John. 2017. *Contemporary Urban Planning.* New York: Routledge.

Ritttel, Horst W.J. and Melvin M. Webber. 1973. "Dilemmas in a General Theory of Planning." *Policy Sciences*, 4(2): 155–169. doi: 10.1007/BF01405730.

Rorty, Richard. 1999. *Philosophy and Social Hope.* New York: Penguin.

Sanyal, Bishwapriya, Lawrence J. Vale, and Christina D. Rosan (editors). (2012). *Planning Ideas that Matter.* Cambridge, MA: MIT Press.

Schön, D. 1983. *The Reflective Practitioner: How Professionals Think in Action.* New York: Basic Books.

Tasan-Kok, T., L. Bertolini, S. Oliveira e Costa, H. Lothan, H. Carvalho, M. Desmet, S. De Blust, T. Devos, D. Kimyon, J.A. Zoete, and P. Ahmad. 2016. "Float Like a Butterfly, Sting Like a Bee: Giving Voice to Planning Practitioners." *Planning Theory and Practice*, 17(4): 621–622. doi: 10.1080/14649357.2016.1225711.

Whittemore, Andrew H. 2015. "Practitioners Theorize, Too: Reaffirming Planning Theory in a Survey of Practitioners' Theories." *Journal of Planning Education and Research*, 35(1): 76–85. doi: 10.1177%2F0739456X14563144.

Chapter 3

Planner-as-Person

It might seem odd to lead off the chapters describing the reflection framework with a discussion of planner-as-person. Aren't planners supposed to be objective professionals who set aside their personal views to serve the public good and respond to political and client direction? Frequently, the practice settings of planning often communicate such an idea.

Picking up on these cues, planners often present themselves as fair-minded analysts rather than partisans. After all, what they recommend should be good for the broader community, not just personal opinion. Professional conferences and planning research support this view by emphasizing planning techniques, best-practice approaches, and theories over the personal dimension of practice.

The views outlined previously are ones in which planners act as technical professionals. When I started my planning career in my 20s, I uncritically accepted the idea of planners as objective, rational analysts who determine the best means to achieve ends (goals) established through political processes. Yet many planners chose their career for altruistic reasons stemming from personal values about making the world a better place. In addition, being a professional implies a level of autonomy and self-regulation that might bring planners in conflict with political or client direction.

For me, being a planner means having normative views about the ends that planning serves. Furthermore, I and other planners are individuals who did not forsake our humanity and personal agency when joining the profession. These two realities, professional autonomy and personal agency, elevate the importance of planner-as-person elements. Rather than ignore the planner's personhood in favor of professional technique, I argue that effective practice requires that planners stay engaged with personal dimensions, and employ reasoning to navigate differences between the personal and planning context.

The idea that professional practice can be detached from one's personhood does not stand up in the messy, complex arena of planning. My earlier technocratic view of the profession changed based on practice experiences, as I gradually acquired self-knowledge and sought authenticity in my practice. Planners' values, experiences, and points of view are inevitably and appropriately part of their practice. They don't have the right to *impose* them on the public, of course, but neither can they act as if their personhood does not exist. The best approach is to have a reflective and dialogic approach to those values and inclinations so as to assess their appropriateness for a given planning situation. Taking ethics as an example, a recent study confirms that planners' personal ethical frameworks are at play in their practice. Planner interviews "revealed the difficulties in resolving ethical conflicts between the ethical frameworks in their personal lives and those they felt they should use in their professional practice" (Lauria and Long 2019, 402).

Planner-as-person reflection is inherently psychological, engaging emotions, but Hoch (2006) complains that "practitioners and analysts learn to treat emotions as a source of bias and distortion" (367). Furthermore, Baum (2015) shows that planning's traditions ignore emotions by emphasizing the rationality of planning activities and denying the possibility of dark, irrational forces. The separation of planning action from emotions and psychology does not stand up in the contemporary setting of planning – both for the planner and for those with whom they plan.

When planners "own" their emotional state they practice more sensitively. Awareness of my emotional experience makes me more conscious of the emotional lives of others. Acknowledging my emotional state means avoiding thinking of it as something external to my planner persona. Emotions are part and parcel of planning practice. Recognizing emotion does not suggest that planners should engage in psychotherapy or any other psychological practice unless they want to, but it does recommend that they reflect on the emotional dimensions of their work, in themselves and others, and consider appropriate *uses* of emotions in planning.

Regrettably, the number of first-person perspectives in the planning literature is overwhelmed by the number of objective studies. Surprisingly few planner autobiographies are available. Notable exceptions include Allan Jacobs as planning director of San Francisco (Jacobs 1980) and Norman Krumholz as planning director of Cleveland (Krumholz and Forester 1990). Even so, those books do not emphasize the origins of the writers' emotions, beliefs, and approaches as discussed here.

The professional as individual is of interest beyond planning, including professions such as law, medicine, education, counseling, and other helping professions. Previously, Chapter 2 introduced the concept of reflexivity in professional practice. Reflexivity is an ethical response to the reality of the personal in professional practice. Rather than pretend that the personal does not matter, or does not shape practice, a reflexive approach leads to a critical evaluation of *how* a planner's personhood affects their professional actions. This occurs from the standpoint of learning about oneself and others, and provides the ground from which a planner can assess the ethics of practical judgments in a planning episode. It could be looked at as gaining access to the theories that guide our actions, explicitly and implicitly.

Reflective Practice

Wise incorporation of the personal into planning practice is based on self-knowledge that develops moral character and emotional maturity. This self-knowledge helps identify motivating factors and underlying assumptions so that a planner understands them and can consciously choose an approach. It helps the planner explain why they favor one position over another, to themselves and others. Moral character and emotional maturity help them decide what to do.

Some – perhaps many – planners do not have the time or the inclination for planner-as-person reflection, either before, during, or after a planning episode. For many, reflection is seen as something that takes time and an appropriate setting, which are often in short supply, and it requires honesty, vulnerability, and a willingness to change. Reflection requires self-confidence because it may threaten a planner's self-image as a dignified, rational professional, or as a selfless change-agent lacking any unconscious motivations. Further, sharing personal reflections with others, even trusted colleagues, requires careful discernment about whether sharing is appropriate, and if it is, the courage to do so.

A valid objection to reflection is that it can be a narcissistic endeavor, a form of confession intended to discharge responsibility. As mentioned in Chapter 1, reflection is more than looking at one's reflection in the mirror. Bolton and Delderfield (2018) use the idea of "through the mirror" reflection to denote looking beyond one's own reflection to understand context more fully. This critical reflection questions understandings and assumptions, and considers the individual in the context of others.

My experience with creative planners is that they engage in critical reflection, on past practice and in real-time. Reflection practices are helpful in situations in which technical approaches are insufficient, such as when goals are in conflict or there are different hierarchies of values. Similarly, reflection is helpful when the issues at stake are unclear or there is insufficient information. Reflective planners are willing to experience "surprise, puzzlement, or a confusion in a situation which [they] find uncertain or unique" (Schön 1983, 68). Schön refers to action experimentation as a response to the external context for practice, but I argue that this concept also applies to the personal dimensions of planning. Planners can practice in an experimental way in which they learn about themselves and their relationships with others.

This focus on the personal in planning practice *does not* endorse a conception of a self-actualized hero-planner saving the world on their own, telling others what to do and how to live, as was common when utopian planners made all-encompassing prescriptions for cities. Those prescriptions were largely developed in the utopian planners' own heads, oversimplifying social, economic, and political life. On the contrary, planners work in complex social and political networks and cannot think well without understanding and engaging others. So while the planner does not work alone, it is equally true that personal factors shape a planner's judgments.

Elements of Planner-as-Person

The interaction of an individual planner with other planners and stakeholders explains much of what occurs as a planning episode unfolds. Table 3.1 provides a framework for considering planner-as-person elements in three categories: experiences and identities, purposes and assumptions, and professional style(s). While the last element, professional style(s), can be observed and studied, a planner's experiences, identities, and underlying purposes often operate in tacit, unobserved, and subtle ways. Planners rarely discuss these issues at conferences or among colleagues despite their influence on practice. Instead it is common to meet up with those with similar affinities, missing opportunities to learn from those with different core assumptions, values, and dispositions.

The planner-as-person elements listed in Table 3.1 are wide ranging. Accordingly, this discussion is necessarily a sketch because fully addressing each element requires an encyclopedic treatment of what is known about the

Table 3.1 Planner-as-Person Reflection Categories

Element	Reflection Categories
Experiences and identities	• Nature/nurture/choices • Identities • Cultural identifications • Skills and inclinations • Personality type • Spiritual or religious understandings • Unconscious elements
Purposes and assumptions	• Guiding values and personal ethics • Theories of human nature • Theory of knowledge (epistemology) • Theory of change • Theories of justice and equity
Professional style(s)	• Concept of profession • Preferred techniques • Communication style • Professional ethical commitments • Sedimented experience • Level of ambition and career stage

human being. That range, however, does not diminish the need to understand these elements. The very nature of professional activity is to be aware of one's subjectivity in order to appropriately engage it.

Experiences and Identities

Planning attracts people with a wide variety of experiences, inclinations, and identities because of the diversity of activities and settings that constitute the profession. Unlike more narrowly defined fields such as civil engineering, planners are a diverse group that includes those attracted to analyzing data, designing, disrupting, implementing, organizing, political deal-making, problem-solving, reforming, regulating, and visioning. Yet a unifying theme is a commitment to a notion of the public good, variously defined, and a desire for a better future.

A common view is that a person's characteristics are influenced by a combination of nature (genetic predispositions), nurture (family life and socialization), and the choices they have made. Let's assume that some combination of these factors explains who a planner *is* in terms of their core identities. Accordingly, each planner brings evolving personal, family, and social identities to their work. By identities, I mean a person's overall constructions of self, with characteristics that are seen as unique and distinct from others. Identities also relate to membership in groups and can be seen as an adaptation to the social world. Elements of identities include aspects such as gender, cultural affiliation, class, ethnicity, nationality, race, religious affiliation, and occupation. In cultural affiliation, for example, identities shape social behavior and norms.

Planners also possess different skills and inclinations. Among a team of planners, those with acute spatial perception and a good drawing hand may be inclined to prepare site plans, renderings, and concept diagrams. Those who find satisfaction in numbers and computation may be drawn to analytic, data-driven approaches. Across planning teams, design-oriented and quantitative planners may experience tensions among one another in process, reasoning, habits, and favored solutions. Given the range of roles available in the profession, planners sort themselves out by seeking a fit with their skills and inclinations.

Getting to the heart of experiences and identities requires an extended treatment of philosophy, religion, psychology, sociology, anthropology, and many other fields. A simple way to capture differences among planners is to consider how these elements are summarized in personality types. The idea of "types," or archetypes, is found throughout human literature. Jung (1980) explained them as deep instinctual sources that produce archetypical images. The idea of types was operationalized in the Myers-Briggs Type Indicator personality assessment and variations of it that address work style in groups and leadership roles. There are valid questions about the scientific validity of type definitions, so I do not argue that they accurately describe a person. Rather, they are useful tools for self-reflection. Many people find value in the idea of types for reflecting on preferences, strengths and weaknesses, and tendencies in interactions with others.

Reflecting on personality type is helpful in planning education, in mentoring, and in professional practice. Self-awareness about how personality type shapes my thinking and action helps me better understand myself, my planning colleagues, and members of the public with whom I engage. Myers-Briggs–type tools (Myers 1962) use four categories to describe a "type":

- General attitude toward the social world: extroverted or introverted.
- Preference in perceiving information: sensing or intuition.
- Preference in processing information: thinking or feeling.
- Acting based on that information: judging according to a rule-based approach or perceiving in a more improvisational way.[1]

With even this brief sketch, connections between these dimensions and a planner's approach can be explored. Planners adopting a rational analytical approach may have type elements of introversion, sensing, thinking, and judging. Planners adopting a political approach may have type elements of extroversion, intuition, feeling, and perceiving. Awareness of these dimensions can help explain why two planners facing the same assignment approach their work in a different manner.

Planner-as-person also includes spiritual or religious understandings or identities as they pertain to planning practice, as discussed in Box 3.1 (next page). Since the core motivations of these traditions concern repair and betterment of human and natural systems, it is natural that there is a connection to planning. Planners who view the profession as a calling, for example, may be motivated by spiritual or religious commitments. Yet traditionally, a secular planning approach is adopted: "preserving religious freedom from constraining regularities of *public action* … and preventing religious forces from regimenting the *public sphere*" (Manouchehrifar 2018, 655). A traditional modernist approach is to relegate religious views to the private realm, but that requires planners who have spiritual and religious commitments to separate a part of themselves from their practice. In the last two decades, scholars have been exploring the idea of the post secular city and the complexities of planners working with religious expression in diverse and plural societies (Habermas 2005, Beaumont and Baker 2011, and Berking et al 2018).

Of course, focusing on an individual's known motivations ignores the role of unconscious factors in professional behavior. This occurs at a personal level, in choice of field and way of practicing, and at an organizational level. Baum (1987) explains how unconscious dimensions unfold in the rituals of professional performance and organization settings, showing that the "reasons why" things turn out relates to these factors. Reflection can move some of the unconscious elements of a planner's practice to a conscious level, improving self-awareness.

Purposes and Assumptions

The interpretive framework offered in Table 3.1 conceives a planner's purposes as building upon personal qualities, experiences, and life choices. Coherence between experiences, identities, and purposes is, of course, loose and provisional. But most planners select purposes and make assumptions based on their experiences and identities. Clearly, finding alignment between planning work

Box 3.1 Spirituality and Religion in Professional Practice

Spirituality and religion are challenging self-knowledge topics for planners. In secular states, religion must not be a part of planning decisions; the rational technical model of planning, existing in the roots of the profession and in day-to-day practice, is an antithesis to spirituality. In keeping religion out, however, appropriate senses of personal spirituality have been excluded. Sandercock (2006, 65) says it this way: "I must ask myself, and my profession: are we not missing something important by not talking about this thing [spirituality] that lies at the heart of planning and marks us all as at least closet utopians?" Most planning practice is based on hope and a faith that the collective action can lead to a better future. Sandercock (2006, 66) goes on to say:

> I think of spirituality as a way of being as well as a way of knowing, informed by certain values that then underpin ways of acting. The values can be named as respect, caring, neighborliness; a concern with building connections between people, building a caring human community from whatever fragile stating point; a notion of service to others.

Ahorn (2006) identifies a series of values associated with spirituality: connections, holism, recognizing multiple ways of knowing, mystery, mysticism, valuing pluralism, and self-awareness. Planners can harness spirituality in planning by considering what these values may bring to their planning practice. Rooting planning practice on these values provides resiliency through challenge and failure. It can offer the planner self-nourishment, renewal, and recovery from disappointment. Most important, it engages a reality for many people that is a powerful element of planning and a new way of building connections with others.

I cannot separate my spirituality from my planning practice, while at the same time I restrain any religious dogma I may hold. I grew up attending the United Church of Canada, left it all for Eastern meditation, and then landed in Reform Judaism. My religious practice is a weekly touchstone for me to consider my purposes and the appropriateness of my actions. It is the single most important explanation of my aims and actions, yet is often off limits for discussion among planners.

My personal practice goal is to move toward alignment between spiritual values and planning practice. Following Sandercock's example, the most important effects of my spirituality that are relevant to my planning practice are as follows: a regular practice of reflection; an orientation to advancing metaphysical notions of love, justice, truth, and beauty; a commitment to repair brokenness; humility about truth claims, but seeking truth anyway; and a realistic notion of human nature.

and any planner's purposes is an imperfect process and is perhaps a lifetime goal.

Professional experiences also *influence* a planner's purposes and assumptions. When I reflect on my career, I see how professional experiences shaped the dynamic unfolding of my identities. An example is my approach to conflict. Early in my career, economic approaches to planning interventions appealed to me. In reflecting on that, I realize that the "invisible hand" idea of economics offered a way out of messy human interactions found in political conflict, community engagement, and even collaborating with others. *Lord of the Flies* (Golding 1954) was a book that resonated with me as a child; a fear of mob mentality was an early influence. Over time, though, planning experiences broadened my approaches beyond economic ones, part of a quest to know myself and align my work with emerging identities and purposes.

A defining element of a planner's approach is the *guiding values* that motivate them. Drawing on philosophical and religious traditions, I previously wrote about four values that may shape a planner's practice: love, justice, truth, and beauty (Willson 2018). Of course, there are many interpretations and meanings assigned to each term, philosophically and personally, and a survey of planners would surely indicate a wider variety of motivating values. I simply use them as markers of core commitments. For example, a value of love might be articulated as deep connection, mutual expression of care, or experience of being seen and appreciated. Justice might represent a respect for due process and evidence, reward according to effort, or redressing past injustices. Truth might indicate a commitment to evidence and warranted assertability. And, beauty might be expressed in attention to physical spaces that evoke reverence, connection, and resonance in the soul.

While a fit between values and practice is not assured, planners who seek it practice with authenticity. A focus on love, for example, might lead to "people" work – developing human capital, healing community conflict, remedying damaging histories, building communicative capacity, or enhancing collaboration. A focus on justice might lead to equity work, fighting corruption, addressing structural racism, promoting fairness, and/or empowering communities. A focus on truth might lead to technical and evidence-based work in the science and social science traditions, as found in environmental planning, transportation modeling, or land use planning. Finally, a commitment to beauty could lead to efforts in urban design, placemaking, and livability. Undeniably, these four value motivations are not the only possible ones, and they are not mutually exclusive.

These values, and others, affect planners' actions as they are embedded in *personal ethics*. For example, a planner whose personal values emphasize truth may translate that to a personal duty or obligation to following rules and procedures, in both technical studies and the planning process. This is a deontological, rule-following approach to provide insightful information based on professional expertise, recognizing the democratic legitimacy of decisions. A planner who values justice may focus on distributional aspects of a decision and assert them in deliberations. And as discussed later in this chapter, personal commitments may be consonant or in conflict with the desires of planning supervisors or clients, and/or professional ethical commitments such as the American Institute of Certified Planners (AICP) Code of Ethics. In a study of planners, Lauria and Long (2019) found that "most of our interviewees espoused different ethical frameworks in their personal lives than they would use in their professional lives" (402).

In additional to fundamental values, planning practice is shaped by what I call personal "theories of." These are understandings of how the world works, more specific manifestations of some of the ideas previously described. Here, I discuss theories of human nature, knowledge, change, and justice.

Let's begin with theories of the human nature. One view is that people are inherently communitarian and cooperative. Another view is that self-interest motivates behavior. Still another is that humans have a latent potential for evil. My personal view, developed through experience and in my religious tradition, is a hybrid: that humans seek the good and the good seeks them, but they also have a broken, destructive side that can produce harm. My personal goal is to pursue the good, and outsmart and outmaneuver my destructive side. That view influences how I think about those with whom I plan, as I warily seek the good in them.

These views of human nature connect to a planner's approach and instincts. Assumptions of communitarianism, for example, lead to grassroots and collaborative approaches, while assumptions of self-interest lead to using market mechanisms to channel individual selfishness toward social good. A planner's view on human nature explains much about their approach to planning, yet we rarely discuss these fundamental assumptions. One's own theory may seem self-evident, or perhaps it is invisible, so discussion about it doesn't normally ensue.

A second element is underlying theories of knowledge. These theories address what constitutes valid knowledge and different ideas about how knowledge is produced. For example, one view is that knowledge is "found" – that it exists independent of its discovery, and that science and social sciences can approach accurate understandings of that true reality (often considered Platonic or neo-Platonic thought). This idea is reflected in the traditional, deductive process of social science statistics, in which the basis of knowing is the process of hypothesis development, statistical testing, refutation of false relationships, and building of theories. This is the "high ground" of theory and technique that Schön (1983) discussed that emphasizes a pursuit of truth (Simon 1969, 1996). A "knowledge is made" view, on the other hand, reflects a pragmatist view that valid knowledge is socially created, not found. In that view, operationalizing knowledge in its context is a prerequisite for its validity, generated as part of designing what can be (Simon 1969, 1996).

Using these two views as an example, we can see that they lead to different planning approaches. In preparing a local economic development plan, for example, the "knowledge is found" approach might emphasize collecting and analyzing economic data to reveal relationships affecting investment and sales. A "knowledge is made" perspective would build understanding out of the situated, lived experience of local merchants, using collaborative workshops, pilot projects, and evaluations to engage in action/knowledge generation.

The next element, theory of change, was invisible to me in my early career. I took for granted that providing insightful analysis would lead to better decision-making, therefore assuming that the impediment to change was an information deficit. If decision-makers lacked good information, then my work was developing insightful plans and policy proposals with strong analytic justifications. This is reflected in the ideas of the rational comprehensive planning process, which call for a long-term, comprehensive view and logical connections between ends and means. Information-deficit thinking also underlies policy analysis, which advances robust problem definition and rational evaluation of methods to address problems. It naively assumes that decision-makers are waiting for an insightful recommendation.

An example of my work under an information-deficit theory is exposing unwarrantedly optimistic rail transit ridership forecasts. In contrasting rail investment with the benefits of more flexible and socially equitable bus services, I critiqued politically attractive but wasteful strategies (e.g., ribbon-cuttings for wasteful projects that please constituents or issuing capital projects contracts that lead to campaign contributions). I hoped that evidence would carry the day.

In many instances, evidence did not carry the day, which created dissonance with my implicit theory of change. My view shifted through these experiences as I became more realistic about the politics of planning. Another shift occurred when I spoke with a relative who obtained a PhD in evolutionary biology. He became a nature filmmaker instead of a researcher. I asked him why he did not follow a traditional research career. His theory of change was based on a "deficit of care" concept. For him, scientific evidence on species evolution was less important than inducing viewers of his films to care about the species, nature in general, and to understand webs of interdependence. Planners can ask themselves similar questions: Will better spatial analysis lead to improved cities, or will education, community engagement, and/or organizing do more?

Theories of change are obviously not limited to an information/care duality. Other theories of change are discussed in the following:

- *Clever solutions*. In this view, change is impeded by the lack of a clever solution. Workplace parking subsidies, for example, encourage solo driving and worsen congestion, pollution, land use efficiency, and equity outcomes. But since most people receive them, they naturally oppose proposals to take them away. Shoup's (2005) proposal for parking cash-out (offering commuters the cash value of renting a parking space if they commute by another mode and therefore don't park) introduces an opportunity cost to parking without taking away free parking. Planners working with this view search for innovative, politically acceptable solutions to complex problems.

- *Deliberation and learning*. Theories of communicative action hold that there are better and worse ways to structure communication, and planners can be attentive to and improve conditions for dialogue by addressing the structural setting and processes for that dialogue (Forester 1989). As groups learn how to deliberate, planners adopting this theory of change may direct attention to accuracy (is there evidence to back a claim?), legibility (can others understand?), sincerity (do you mean it?), and legitimacy (is there an experience basis for the claim?). These planners lean to collaborative efforts, mutual learning, and incremental steps. A practical manifestation of these ideas is mutual gain negotiation theory, which focuses on finding and trading joint interests so that all parties are better off.

- *Implementation*. Plans sometimes fail because of flawed logic or a weak empirical basis, termed "theory failure," but sometimes the problem is "program failure." In this perspective, better implementation design, follow-through, and evaluation hold the key (Patton, Sawicki, and Clark 2013). For example, carbon trading mechanisms are an economically efficient way to gradually reduce greenhouse gas emissions because they incentivize emitters to reduce emissions in ways that produce the greatest benefit for the lowest cost. But flaws in implementation sometimes undermine those programs, such as when a seller of credits fails to reduce emissions or gains credit for reductions they were going to do anyway. Planners with this view focus on aspects such as legal language in law and agreements, project management, administrative capacity, and compliance monitoring.

- *Political and community deal-making.* Planners adopting this view know that many good plans and ideas are proposed but fail to be implemented. Their theory of change is based on assembling a powerful coalition to support change. This is accomplished by plans and projects that offer something to each interest group, enough to induce them to join a coalition that supports adoption and implementation (Banfield 1961). The strategy is to win broad loyalty and support for a plan or project that does something for most interests. This theory of change is often found among redevelopment planners and entrepreneurs for infrastructure investments.

- *Power for underserved, disenfranchised, and discriminated groups.* This theory focuses on the distribution of political and economic power. For example, homeowners have more power than renters, who in turn have more power than unrepresented future residents. This imbalance supports not-in-my-backyard (NIMBY) policies that benefit homeowners seeking to reduce development impacts and increase the value of their homes. This theory of change leads to advocacy planning to increase the voice and power of renters, those outside the community who want to live there, and to demand a long-term regional perspective in local policy (Davidoff 1965). Equity planners with this theory of change prioritize gains for the group(s) they represent.

- *Process compliance.* This theory understands that following established processes is a way to ensure good outcomes (the deontological approach mentioned earlier). For example, planners documenting impacts for environmental impact reviews base their work on the notion that accurate and transparent disclosure of those impacts will result in appropriate choices by decision-makers. Compliance with the process is seen as leading to good decisions by creating transparency, supporting democratic practices, and preventing corruption. (Alternatively, some planners hold a theory that the process is the problem: that bureaucratic processes paper over harms, and so they seek to *disrupt* the process for systemic political change.)

Theories of change are rarely discussed in staff meetings or in the deliberations of decision-makers. Yet it is fruitful for planners to consider the theories of change that animate their work, understand others' theories of change, and reflect on other theories that provide insight. When a planner explicitly identifies and articulates their theories of change, and encourages others to do so, it improves deliberation.

Lastly, varied theories of justice underpin practice. These flow from guiding values and personal ethics discussed earlier. Justice in planning generally involves *social justice*, informed by philosophy and religion, and *procedural justice*, informed by law. Multiple theories of justice may apply in a single episode, and they may be in conflict. A classic distinction is concern with outcomes (utilitarian) versus concern with duty and process (deontological). These various theories of justice are then embedded in professional codes. In planning, for example, certification as a member of the AICP means agreeing to comply with the AICP Code of Ethics (Code). Because AICP membership is not required for practice, deciding to seek certification and agree to the Code is a personal, voluntary decision.

The Code asserts that members shall "work to expand choice and opportunity for all persons, recognizing a special responsibility to plan for the needs of the disadvantaged and to promote racial and economic integration" (AICP 2019). Adherence to this outcome-oriented statement means, for example, working to reform exclusionary housing policies that might be favored by a local government. Among many philosophical positions that support this view is that of Rawls (1999).

A procedural justice example is found in the Code statement, "we shall avoid a conflict of interest or even the appearance of a conflict of interest in accepting assignments from clients and employers" (AICP 2019). Adherence to this provision involves avoiding personal gain, or the perception of it.

The primary issue in social justice is core ideas of fairness, about which there are many conceptions (Taylor 2017). One idea is that each person should be served by planning programs in relationship to their level of contribution through taxes. This is reflected in arguments that taxes should be paid in relationship to public benefits received, as in user fees such as gasoline taxes or supplying parks in relation to the tax receipts from a neighborhood. A second idea of fairness is that benefits of planning programs should result in equal opportunity for all. This could mean that benefits are not proportional to contribution, since areas with greater service needs would receive more benefits. Park space expenditures might be greater in low-income communities because there is less public and private open space in those neighborhoods. For example, spending on parks could be allocated so that each neighborhood achieves a 10 acre per 10,000 residents ratio. And a third idea is that the benefits of planning programs should be distributed in a way that produces *equal* outcomes.

For example, park space could be distributed in a manner that seeks equal public health and recreational participation outcomes. Planning debates in the U.S. most often vacillate between the first and second view.

There is another aspect to fairness, of course, concerning the group that is considered for fair treatment. Is fairness compared for spatially defined areas (e.g., a neighborhood or a city), interest groups (e.g., youth, immigrants, or transit riders), or according to the individual?

Planners, community members, and decision-makers frequently talk past one another when they have different underlying notions of justice. A planner supporting utility maximization would prioritize the greatest overall good, called Pareto optimality, while a planner supporting redistribution would be concerned with improving the conditions for those with the least opportunity.

Lastly, there are also competing views at the level of individual planning action. Is the judge of proper action the *intent* of the person? Or should it be the *outcomes*, regardless of intent? Or do both apply, and their application should vary according to circumstance? The AICP Code of Ethics contains both systems of thought and leaves it to the individual planner to develop a justifiable position.

These personal "theories of" are not presented to suggest that planners are *defined* by one or more theories, but rather to suggest that a planner can understand their own choices and actions better by explicitly acknowledging the assumptions that underlie their practice. Dialogue and reflection that moves these theories from an implicit to explicit level creates insight, opportunities to compare practice, and openings to develop new forms of practice. Many planners may find that experience changes their "theories of" over time. And as planners read context, as described in Chapter 4, they may draw from multiple "theories of."

Professional Style(s)

The personal dimension closest to planning practice is professional style(s). Some planners may not agree that they have a professional style, arguing that they carry out assigned job duties without injecting their own personal approach. I do not seek to *prove* that planners consciously adopt a style. Some contexts, as discussed in Chapter 4, impose highly defined tasks, codes of behavior, and expectations. But usually, the planner has choices.

One professional style is as a neutral public servant, an "ask-then-answer" technical professional. Levy (2017) describes this as providing "how to" and "what if" advice rather than "should" or "should not," while Catanese (1974) calls it an apolitical-neutral role. In my experience, many planners espouse this role but do not fully practice it – they do not maintain a firewall between their analysis and their personal views.

A common planner role is covert activist – presenting themselves as a neutral technician to the public but acting politically in working toward preferred values or means (Catanese 1974). For example, many transportation planners advocate for active transportation modes, seek to build support for certain plans or solutions, and act in entrepreneurial ways to implement projects. Yet they work for public agencies or as consultants serving public agencies, where their job is primarily to advise and respond to the direction of elected officials and clients.

A third role is overt activist, in which the planner makes their values clear and works openly for particular kinds of change (Catanese 1974). This could include activism for planning ideas such as Vision Zero programs that seek to eliminate pedestrian and cyclist deaths. Or a planner could act as an advocate for low-income renters being displaced by gentrification. They could also act as an agent of radical change, supporting movements that seek to change economic structure, political systems, or underlying relationships to environmental systems. This work is usually done in the nonprofit sector or in civic space, or by being elected to office.

Planners have different understandings of the powers they possess. Planning power relates to specialized knowledge, authorized roles, participation in networks, and regulatory responsibilities, which affect the choice of the roles noted earlier. A planner with a highly regimented role is likely to function in an apolitical-neutral model, whereas a public agency planner who possesses organization power and independence may follow the covert-activist model. A nonprofit, foundation-funded planner or a planner/real estate developer is likely to follow the overt-activist model.

Professional style emerges in the choice of roles discussed earlier and manifests in elements such as concept of the profession, technique, communication strategy, and ethics. It is also seen as related to sedimented experiences and level of ambition.

Let's examine the planner's concept of the profession. For some, planning is a calling or vocation to serve the public good, fueled by an idealist conception of their mission (Willson 2018). The idealist conception may operate in different ways – truth-seeking modelers, livability-seeking designers, or power-fostering community organizers. Other planners see their practice as a professional occupation that is responsive to political direction. They are more likely to adopt a realist stance on politics and the prospects for change. Still other planners see their work as finding a balance between stakeholders.

A second part of professional style is preferred technique. Planners use many techniques, including advocating, advising, agitating, analyzing, arguing, brainstorming, coordinating, critiquing, developing, designing, educating, facilitating, healing, implementing, inventing, leading, learning, listening, mediating, negotiating, organizing, plan-writing, policy analysis, pressuring, programming, regulating, speaking, strategizing, visioning, and writing. Most planners tend to emphasize a group of techniques, shaped by context, but also as an instinctual first-approach of what to do. A planner's preferred technique may be most noticeable when they are under stress.

A third element of professional style is communication practices. Planners' communication styles range from trusting and inclusive, to informational, strategic, or defensive. While tailoring their approach to context and the particular planning episode, a planner adopts a pattern of communication styles over time. The choice between an open or defensive posture, for example, may rest on a variety of factors – personal experiences, temperament, value commitments, organizational culture, dynamics among colleagues, and professional experiences. Planners can't impose communication practices on their organizations or clients, so they must adapt, but still there are choices to be made.

The personal also includes ethical commitments. As mentioned, AICP members agree to abide by the provisions of the AICP Code of Ethics. The Code does not prescribe particular actions but asserts the factors that an individual planner must consider in arriving at a conclusion. While conflict of interest is clearly prohibited, for example, the Code also forbids the *appearance* of conflict of interest. In this regard, some municipal planners may go beyond the rules of their workplace in not associating or being seen with those doing business with the city in any way, while others might be comfortable attending a consultant-sponsored reception at a conference. The difference in choices while upholding the same ethical code relates to the deeper personal elements previously described.

Table 3.1 includes the term "sedimented experience" to refer to the bundle of professional experiences that shape the planner's professional style. An example of sedimented experiences is lessons learned, good and bad, from previous supervisors, organizations, and community participation. One planner might have ideal experiences in collaborative planning, producing creative and effective plans and programs. Another planner may have a supervisor who scapegoats staff as a way to deal with their own anxiety, or reports to elected officials that seek to influence staff directly without going through the city manager. In the first example, the planner's style is based on personal agency – an ability to make change – and in the second one the planner develops a guarded, defensive style. Sedimented experiences are not just in relation to supervisors, of course, as they develop in political interchanges, interactions with the community, relationships with fellow professionals, experiences with implementation, and so on.

The last element of style discussed here has to do with ambition and career stage. A planner seeking to build their career is likely to have a different style than one approaching retirement. The former is concerned with building their "brand" and expertise, while the latter may be concerned about burnishing their legacy. The mid-level planner may be most risk averse since failure may have the most serious consequences at that career and lifecycle stage.

Ambiguity and Incongruity

The connections between the planner-as-person and the planning episode are not always clear. Many planners experience ambiguity in understanding how their professional role corresponds to their personal commitments, and incongruity between their values or approach and what they are asked to do.

Ambiguity

Ambiguity is not an issue if a planner does not have a clear purpose. But if they do, ambiguity about their purpose and work may arise. A planner with a personal commitment to increasing affordable housing, for example, may feel ambiguity about developing a housing program for market-rate multi-family rental housing. Will the project improve the overall housing situation by increasing supply and reducing pressure in existing housing stock, or will it spur gentrification and displacement? An environmental planner with a public service motivation may feel ambiguity about whether the environmental impact review process is improving the environment or an elaborate exercise in papering over environmental degradation. A transportation planner may work on a suburban rail transit project, knowing it is wasteful compared to bus rapid transit but that the real purpose is gaining middle-class support for a transportation ballot measure. Such a ballot measure would also fund inner-city bus services and indirectly benefit the planner's personal commitment to serve low-income bus riders. Ambiguity is inherent in these complicated situations.

Another sense of ambiguity arises when the planner is charged with solving a problem that they do not have the authority or power to address, as often occurs in large bureaucracies. As Baum (1987) explains, this predicament produces feelings of shame, vulnerability, and anxiety. Similarly, feeling accountable to distant, uninvolved supervisors produces anxiety and anger. In large multinational consulting firms, for example, planning managers are often given business development targets made at distant headquarters without knowledge of local market conditions. Still another example is a planner overseeing cannabis licensing, who may be excited to develop programs in the communities hit hardest by the criminalization of cannabis, but then finds that onerous procedures for licensing harm entrepreneurs from those same communities. Planners work out these ambiguities in conscious and unconscious ways: the point here is that feelings of personal ambiguity are inherent in planning practice.

Incongruity

When ambiguity is not present, planners may still experience incongruity between their purpose as a planner and what they are being asked to do. A progressive planner who is asked to write a staff report to deny an application for a homeless services project on the basis of community "character" must grapple with the coded language employed to oppose facilities. Incongruity is also experienced when a client asks a housing market modeling consultant to change the numbers in an analysis so that an application for external funding will look more attractive.

The AICP Code of Ethics (2019) advises planners to accept the instructions of clients unless they go against a contentiously developed notion of the public good. If that incongruence is too great, responses include *voice* (e.g., seeking to change their assignment, or bureaucratic resistance), *disloyalty* (e.g., leaking information or foot-dragging on an assignment), or *exit* (leaving the organization) (Hirschman 1970, Gerken 2013). The starkness of these choices and the complex moral reasoning required to address them reinforces the idea that ethical choices are personal.

Planners encounter ambiguity and incongruity every day. Some look away, go on autopilot, and forgo their personal mission. Others overreact, demanding a complete realization of their personal purpose. Either response has serious downsides. In other writings, I coined the term *principled adaptability* to explain ways to live in the tension between personal purpose and context (Willson 2018).

And Now to You: Self-Knowledge Is a Lifetime Project

Professional self-knowledge is built using a variety of practices such as professional development, having a mentor, and formal or informal reflection groups, as explored further in Chapter 14. It is supported by personal development that can occur in therapy, religious practice, and community and family life. The various methods are mutually supportive.

My advocacy for reflection on planner–as–person flows from my identity and experiences. To explain that further, and consistent with the idea of reflexivity, Box 3.2 shares my reflection on personal influences in my development as a planner.

Box 3.2 Where I'm Coming From, Personally

Growing up in Windsor, Ontario, Canada, shapes my identity. I was raised in a middle-class household in a working-class neighborhood. Windsor is an automotive industry town that embodies the creativity and destructiveness of capitalism. Residents tend to have a chip on their shoulders, stemming from perceived slights by those who live in the cultural and government centers of Canada. As a child, I peered through the fences of the automobile plants with great excitement to see the superficial styling changes of the new model year cars. There were two paths in high school – into the auto plants for 25 years or leave. I left.

Growing up, the culture schisms in my neighborhood were along these lines: English/French, Protestant/Catholic, Western European/Eastern European ancestry. Windsor played an important role in the Underground Railway – the coded language of escaping slaves was that Detroit was "night," Windsor was "dawn," and the Detroit River was the "Jordan." Growing up, I had little sense of this history; Windsor residents felt removed from the racism and industrial decline in Detroit, separated by a thin strip of blue water.

I am a White male in my 60s. The two identity questions I have faced in my life regard religion and citizenship. I grew up attending the United Church of Canada. My wife is Jewish, and I appreciated the "here and now" and reflective nature of Jewish religious practice. I converted to Judaism in my 40s and actively practice the religion. I view religious texts as divinely-inspired literature rather than journalism or dogma. I confronted the citizenship identity question in choosing to become an American citizen.

Where I'm coming from is influenced by activities beyond work and family. I am a distance runner. Training for races provides a kind of solitude that I find makes room for reflection. New insights and ideas often come to me on the trail. A second hobby is plein air style painting, which puts me outdoors, in nature and city settings, emphasizing observation, attentiveness, and engaging different neural pathways. I'm convinced these practices support my research and planning practice (Willson 2018).

Why all these details? A reflexive approach probes "why" questions, at personal and structural levels. Self-reflection seeks to understand how personal and professional experiences and commitments are enmeshed. Here is one example. I've always had an unreasonable resentment about planning theorists who have not practiced planning. I know it's unreasonable, because over time I've learned a lot from those people. The more I became aware of my resentment, the more I am in dialogue with that knee-jerk reaction, the better I can learn from theory and write from practice-based experience.

I don't imagine a neat, analytic correspondence between experiences and identity, purposes and assumptions, and professional style. It is more like a stew, with many ingredients, simmering. These elements are not fixed or defined either. Reflect on the ecosystem of personal dimensions that affect your aims as a planner and the way you think, feel, and act in planning episodes. If you are starting in the field, the planner-as-person framework prompts are a starting point for reflective practices. If you are an experienced planner, planner-as-person reflection can make visible the background assumptions and habitual ways of acting that are present in everyday practice.

Following the careers of my students, over more than 30 years as a planning educator, convinces me that there are strong relationships between planner-as-person elements and practice choices. Who you are influences the information you notice and ignore, the way you interpret context, the meaning you ascribe to it, and how you decide and act. Rather than proceeding with these dimensions on a tacit, unexamined basis, explicitly consider them to enhance your practical judgments and career effectiveness. That is reflexivity.

Discussion Questions

1. Do you consider talking about emotions an appropriate activity in a professional setting? Is there an appropriate way to do so?
2. What are the consequential elements of you as a person that shape your planning practice approach? How do those elements empower and/or limit you as a planner?
3. Is being a planner changing you as a person? If so, how? If not, are there planning opportunities that could foster your personal growth, such as taking new roles?
4. What theory of change (or theories of change) animate your work? Could other theories of change offer pathways to greater effectiveness?

Note

1 Retrieved from www.themyersbriggs.com/en-US/Products-and-Services/Myers -Briggs.

References

Ahorn, Michael R. 2006. "Spirituality and Planning in a Diverse World." *Planning Theory & Practice*, 7(1): 68–80. doi: 10.10180/14649350500497497.

American Institute of Certified Planners. 2019, September 22. *Code of Ethics and Professional Conduct*. Adopted March 19, 2005; Effective June 1, 2005; Revised

April 1, 2016. Retrieved November 22, 2019 from https://www.planning.org/ethics/ethicscode/.

Banfield, Edward C. 1961. *Political Influence: A New Theory of Urban Politics*. New York: Free Press.

Baum, Howell. 1987. *The Invisible Bureaucracy: The Unconscious in Organizational Problem Solving*. New York: Oxford University Press, Inc.

Baum, Howell. 2015. "Planning with Half a Mind: Why Planners Resist Emotion." *Planning Theory & Practice*, 16(4): 498–516. doi: 10.1080/14649357.2015.1071870.

Beaumont, Justin and Christopher Baker (eds.) 2011. *Postsecular Cities, Space, Theory, and Practice*. New York and London: Continuum.

Berking, Helmuth, Silke Streets, and Jochen Schwenk (eds.) *Religious Pluralism and the City: Inquiries into Postsecular Urbanism*. New York and London: Bloomsbury Academic.

Bolton, Gillie and Russell Delderfield. 2018. *Reflective Practice: Writing and Professional Development*, 5th edition. Thousand Oaks, CA: Sage Publications, Inc.

Catanese, Anthony. 1974. *Planners and Local Politics: Impossible Dreams*. Beverly Hills, CA/London: Sage Publications.

Davidoff, Paul. 1965. "Advocacy and Pluralism in Planning." *Journal of the American Institute of Planners*, 31(4): 331–338. doi: 10.1080/01944366508978187.

Forester, John. 1989. *Planning in the Face of Power*. Berkeley, CA: University of California Press.

Gerken, Heather K. 2013. "Exit, Voice, and Disloyalty." *Duke Law Journal*, 62: 1349–1386.

Golding, William. 1954. *Lord of the Flies*. New York: Perigee.

Habermas, Jurgen. 2005. "Equal Treatment of Cultures and the Limits of Postmodern Liberalism." *Journal of Political Philosophy*, 13(1): 1–28. doi.org/10.1111/j.1467-9760.2005.00211.x

Hirschman, Albert. 1970. *Exit, Voice and Loyalty: Responses to Decline in Firms, Organizations, and States*. Cambridge, MA: Harvard University Press.

Hoch, Charles. 2006. "Emotions and Planning." *Planning Theory and Practice*, 7(4): 367–382.

Jacobs, Allan. 1980. *Making City Planning Work*. Chicago, IL: American Planning Association.

Jung, Carl Gustav. 1980. *The Archetypes and the Collective Unconscious*. Princeton, NJ: Princeton University Press.

Krumholz, Norman and John Forester. 1990. *Making Equity Planning Work*. Philadelphia, PA: Temple University Press.

Lauria, Mickey and Mellone F. Long. 2019. "Ethical Dilemmas in Professional Planning Practice in the Unites States." *Journal of the American Planning Association*, 85(4): 393–404. doi: 10.1080/01944363.2019.1627238.

Levy, John. 2017. *Contemporary Urban Planning*, 11th Edition. Upper Saddle River, NJ: Prentice Hall.

Manouchehrifar, Babek. 2018. "Is Planning 'Secular'? Rethinking Religion, Securalism, and Planning." *Planning Theory and Practice*, 19(5): 653–677. doi: 10.1080/14649357.2018.1540722

Myers, Isabel Briggs. 1962. *The Myers-Briggs Type Indicator: Manual (1962)*. Palo Alta, CA: Consulting Psychologists Press. doi: 10.1037/14404-000.

Patton, Carl, David Sawicki, and Jennifer Clark. 2013. *Basic Methods of Policy Analysis and Planning,* 3rd edition. Englewood Cliffs, NJ: Prentice Hall.

Rawls, John. 1999. *A Theory of Justice.* Cambridge, MA: The Belknap Press of Harvard University.

Sandercock, Leone. 2006. "Spirituality and the Urban Professions: The Paradox at the Heart of Planning." *Planning Theory and Practice,* 7(1): 65–67. doi: 10.10180/14649350500497471.

Schön, Donald. 1983. *The Reflective Practitioner: How Professionals Think in Action.* New York: Basic Books.

Simon, Herbert. 1969, 1996. *The Sciences of the Artificial,* 3rd ed. Cambridge MA: MIT Press.

Shoup, Donald. 2005. *Parking Cash Out.* Planners Advisory Service Report No. 532. Chicago, IL: American Planning Association.

Taylor, Brian. 2017. "The Geography of Urban Transportation Finance." In: *The Geography of Urban Transportation,* 4th edition, edited by Genevieve Giuliano and Susan Hanson. New York: The Guilford Press, 247-272.

Willson, Richard. 2018. *A Guide for the Idealist: How to Launch and Navigate Your Planning Career.* New York: Routledge.

Chapter 4

Context for Planning

Effective planning practice requires an ability to read, understand, and strategically respond to context. By context, I mean elements that frame the planning episode such as social structure, politics, markets, institutions, and history, extending from broad underlying factors to specific circumstances.[1] Compared to professions that apply methods in a relatively straightforward way, context plays a strong role in planning practice choices, and those choices in turn shape context. Context can be seen as a circuitry, with multiple forms of power coursing through it. Understanding context means comprehending and intervening in how the power flows.

The chapter introduces context elements of general setting, planning episode setting, and planner roles. As noted in Chapter 1, the conceptual frame is that the planning episode unfolds in the space between context, addressed here, and the planner-as-person, as discussed in Chapter 3.[2]

Municipal planners with long job tenures have the time to learn about context. But since the setting for planning is incompletely revealed and dynamic, even experienced planners should be alert for changes in formal and informal political and community leadership as well as changing issues and priorities. The broader government policy, economic, and social setting evolves too, and new actors and stakeholders continually emerge. With reflection, previously invisible aspects of context become visible.

Among the sectors of planning, perhaps consultants face the greatest demand to quickly read context across multiple projects in time- and budget-limited assignments. Consultants are attentive to clues in everyday discussions and learn to apply lessons from previous experiences to new assignments. Budget and time pressures can create a tendency to approach problems with a standard toolkit of methods, preexisting plan language, and superficial best practice; this can ignore essential local knowledge. Assessing context in each planning episode can avoid incomplete understandings that lead planners to use flawed theories and strategies, as occurred during the period of slum clearance in the United States.

Over their careers, planners develop a capacity to interpret context and respond to it. Wise planners are attentive to and learn from context; frustrated ones do not understand why an approach that worked in one time or place does not work in a current one. An essential element of a planner's personal agency is to realize that while planners understand and respond to context, their actions also *affect* context. For example, a planner working for a community whose values are different than their own may accept those values or sublimate their own views to them, thereby reproducing them. Or they may seek to change community values through their actions and the planning process.

Evolving Recognition of Context

The planning profession once had a narrow "scientist of the city" approach that saw the planner as a professional who diagnoses and solves problems with detachment and objectivity. That modernist technocratic era carried the notion that technical expertise was the best way to plan, and that certain plans, policies, and programs could be applied under a wide variety of circumstances. The technocratic planner asked "what's the problem?" as if the city was a car that needed repair. This approach required some attention to context, but not enough. Based on limited local knowledge, a planner might consider an issue as one common "type" rather than a unique situation. In this view, context was less important than technical analysis and plan design.

In breaking from this approach, Friedmann (1973) proposed the idea of transactive planning, arguing that analytic expertise must be combined with local knowledge – lived experience – in order to be effective. Lived experience *is* context. Attention to context changes the questions we ask: for example, "what's the story?" is much richer than "what's the problem?" (Forester 1999). A focus on story automatically includes broader context and nuance because we know that planning issues are understood differently based on singular stories held by stakeholders with particular histories. For example, Innes and Booher (2018) provide examples of the importance of local and lay knowledge in environmental planning cases. Since there are multiple stories for every planning episode, we must also ask "whose stories am I hearing?" and "whose stories are untold?" Context also means asking, "where is power?" and "how is it expressing itself?" Understanding power informs strategy by indicating key leverage points in the planning episode.

The maturation of the profession has increased planners' awareness of how practice choices indeed affect context. For example, if planning is carried out in a way that promotes appreciation of interdependency by community members, it may shape stakeholder positions. Community members who understand one another are more likely to support plans to address collective problems. As well, the organization of public participation can encourage communication practices that foster understanding and reconciliation, leading away from demonizing and blame. Within an organization, a planner's refusal to engage in office gossip has an effect on the way in which conflict is addressed. Last, a planner may resist a context that frames planning problems around xenophobia by refusing to reproduce those frames and seeking more inclusive ones.

Deciding how to respond to context requires ethical reasoning because tensions exist within and among personal commitments and professional obligations. In the personal realm, a planner may find that their commitment to participation is at odds with their commitment to evidence-based decision-making. This could occur, for instance, if local community members dispute scientific evidence on climate change. As discussed in Chapter 3, the American Institute of Certified Planners (AICP) Code of Ethics calls for the planner to accept the decisions of employers and clients *unless* they are illegal or out of sync with the planner's reflective conception of the public interest (AICP 2019). And of course, tensions may exist between the personal realm and professional commitments. These tensions are endemic in planning, embedded in a framework that includes context *and* the planner-as-person.

Elements of Context

Table 4.1 summarizes elements of context in three categories: general setting, episode setting, and role(s). These three elements are conceived as existing in a loose, nested hierarchy. For example, state planning law (general setting) guides the approach to specific facts on the ground (episode setting), as does the role and charge given to the planner (role). New planners may find it useful to explore all of the dimensions, while seasoned planners can use the prompts

Table 4.1 Context Reflection Categories

Element	Reflection Categories
General setting	• Society, environment, markets, constitutional law, politics, and institutions • Planning laws and precedent, agency procedures, and professional relationships
Episode setting	• Issue history, affected interests, conflict/collaboration • "Talk" processes; institutional dynamics; implementation options
Role(s)	• Job sector, job function, charge, level of discretion • Professional and interpersonal dynamics

to see if they are missing some elements or whether their interpretation of context needs reexamination. A planner might habitually attend to particular elements of context while ignoring others, and so can use the prompts for a context diagnostic for their practice.

General setting refers to the broad framing elements that shape the opportunities in the planning episode. *Episode setting* addresses the particulars of the planning episode. One issue may have a history of conflict and litigation, while another may have the potential for consensus. The planner's *role* (or roles) frames the set of actions that can be taken. For example, a planning episode may be initiated with a specific charge, as a routine task assignment, or is sometimes vague and open-ended.

The discussion of each context element requires consideration of how power functions, formally and informally. Formal powers are held by a supervisor or an elected official. Informal power relates to professional authority, institutional position, claims of standing, access to powerful interests, economic power, or threat of legal action.

General Setting

General setting refers to society, environment, markets, constitutional law, politics, and institutions, which in turn frame planning laws and precedent, agency procedures and regulations, and professional relationships. While some elements are clearly identifiable, such as planning laws, other elements are fluid, subject to change. Furthermore, the general setting is subject to different interpretations. One planner might perceive local decision-making as a nasty, conflict-filled affair, while another might understand it as exhibiting the normal give-and-take of local government politics.

The social and physical sciences offer frameworks and insights that assist with general setting interpretation. Understanding context with an interdisciplinary perspective makes planning intellectually demanding, but of course that approach is also an invitation to lifelong learning. For example, a planner adopting a neoliberal appreciation of the potential of market mechanisms to solve public problems will have a different understanding than a planner who interprets context through a neo-Marxist framework.

Society

Society refers to the social systems in which the planning effort is occurring and the patterns of relationships between individuals, groups, and institutions. Applying a particular planning approach without reference to societal structure and history leads to failure. Planners have learned, for example, that planning approaches and proposals generated in developed countries cannot necessarily be imposed on emerging economies. Similarly, an aging community has different priorities and approaches than a fast-growing one.

The profession's interpretation of societal context was traditionally based on a modernist notion that there is a single identifiable public interest. That view ignored many people and groups of people, such as those with different experiences and aspirations related to race, ethnicity, age, socioeconomic status, family status, gender identification, religious beliefs, or mental or physical ability. Sandercock's book *Making the Invisible Visible: A Multicultural Planning History* (1998) introduces insurgent planning histories designed to challenge the sufficiency of a simplistic understanding of the public interest. Since that time, awareness of different perceptions, identities, world views, aspirations, and levels of privilege have grown to a point where the concept of a uniform public interest lacks legitimacy for many issues. The society in which planners engage is complex; planners seeking to read context need to learn outside their experience. For most planners, this relativistic approach coexists with global universal interests, such as a physical environment that sustains life and social policies that promote human flourishing.

A planner's interpretations of the social systems within which they operate varies depending on their lived experience and understanding. Planner-as-person elements discussed in Chapter 3 suggest that interpretive lenses vary. A planner in a local planning agency, for example, is positioned between the power domains of society in general, government, markets, community organizations, and individuals. They are part of a network of relationships and actions. But each planner brings their own interpretations.

Even with a conscious attempt to remove forms of bias or blindness in reading context, planners necessarily have a partial view. Many different framings are possible for a single issue. One planner may understand society in a frame of individualist competition while another may see it in a communitarian, cooperative way. These basic assumptions about society shape perceptions of context and forms of planning action.

Environment

Ecological systems form the context for human existence and planning activities. Local systems, such as the functioning of a wetland, indicate constraints and opportunities for local development plans. Global systems, such as the global carbon balance, bear on planning choices related to land use, transportation systems, infrastructure, and energy. Scientific knowledge helps planners understanding how these systems function and interact with human systems as planners translate that knowledge to action. Some planning approaches combine societal and ecological understandings and assumptions. For example, resiliency planning considers the physical and biological capacity of ecological systems as well the ability of socioeconomic systems to absorb stresses and maintain function through adaption mechanisms.

Markets and Constitutional Law

Societies adopt varied economic systems, including traditional and agrarian systems, command systems characterized by central power, market systems, cooperative systems, or mixed-economic systems such as democratic socialism. Planning possibilities are radically different under these systems, as is the locus of planning action, e.g., state agency or a local cooperative. In market systems, planning is traditionally concerned with correcting market failures such as externalities (unpriced effects), remedying underprovision of public goods, resolving prisoner dilemma conditions, and redistribution (Klosterman 1985). In contrast, planners in command systems direct state economic activity. The point of interpreting market structure is to understand it well and figure out how to proceed in working with others who may have different interpretations. Also, two planners may agree that the context for their work is the market system but take different approaches to planning action, as one seeks to reform market systems by pricing externalities and the other sees the market system as the root cause of problems and seeks to replace it.

Further, the ideal version of each economic system and its actual practice may be in sharp contrast. This too requires discernment. Local corruption can undermine market mechanisms by distorting prices and impeding trans-actions, thereby weakening economic growth. Similarly, insufficient under-standing of interdependency, uncertainty, and risk can undermine the aims of command economies.

In U.S. planning systems, market power is recognized in constitutional law regarding property rights, concepts of "highest and best use," and approaches that mitigate the impacts of markets rather than define and implement a com-munity vision or collectively hold land resources. Markets decentralize deci-sions among self-interested individual actors; a bulwark against top-down decision-making that can be inept or corrupt. At the same time, markets value things in dollar terms and discount future values in ways that ignore multi-generational interests and intangibles. In addition, interests seek to colonize or use plans and regulation to achieve market advantage, such as when a devel-oper seeks to restrict competitors' opportunities or uses environmental impact review to transfer mitigation costs to others.

Politics

The national and local political context and legal framework shape the possi-bilities for planning by establishing planning laws, procedures for government action, and the hierarchy of powers from national to local. Planners focus on reading the structure and power dynamics in the political system in which they work. Understanding this context requires knowledge of the structural factors that influence decision-making. For example, a planner cannot under-stand land use patterns in California without understanding Proposition 13, a voter initiative that limits local governments' ability to raise property tax rates. This limitation incentivizes local government to pursue land uses such as retail stores and hotels that generate extra tax revenue, and to avoid land uses that have a less favourable fiscal balance, such as affordable housing.

Elected officials at federal, state, regional, and large city levels have staff to conduct analysis and advise them on planning matters. On the other hand, many municipal planners and planning consultants make their recommenda-tion to laypeople on appointed commissions and part-time elected officials who do not have training or direct staff support. This affects power relations, as elected officials may have limited experience and technical knowledge, increasing the power of the city manager, city attorney, and perhaps the planner. Planners must figure out how to navigate this dynamic network of power.

Understanding local government political context requires comprehending what is important to elected officials. While having an agenda for community change, an elected official's first priority is reelection. They are good at counting – determining where interests and votes lie on a particular issue. That's a different kind of rationality than planners employ, which is why a planner may be mystified when a well-thought-out recommendation is rejected. The rejection may have nothing to do with the recommendation but part of a series of transactions or trades made between members of the elected body, regarding past, present, or expected future issues and political gains.

Interpretations of the successes and failures of democratic representation in government also frame planning action. Just as some planners seek to correct market failure, other planners see their role as correcting failures of representativeness. In local government, for example, pollution harm to low-income residents located next to an industrial facility may be unaddressed because resident groups are excluded, marginalized, or ignored compared to the industrial plant owners. In that case, planners may inform, organize, and empower the community so that its views are represented.

A planner's interpretation of the political clout of real estate developers is another issue to be considered in fairness of representation. Acknowledging developers' profit motive, some planners think that good community development outcomes occur when public sector planners work collaboratively with developers, as occurs in redevelopment activities. Other planners, perhaps in the same planning office, have an antagonistic attitude toward developers, viewing them as corrupt actors using campaign donations and other leverage to acquire excess power that produces community harm. That planner may seek to use bureaucratic tools to reduce the power of the developer.

Institutions

The institutions in which planning occurs provide another element of context that requires interpretation. Mapping and understanding the network of institutional players sheds light on ways to proceed. Institutional players may include government, private, and nonprofit entities with specific roles in plan/policy development and implementation. Organizations, and units within those organizations, have an official mission and informal ways of working. For example, rewriting the zoning code for a city requires the involvement of building and safety officials who will implement and enforce the new code. They have the power of slow-walking, partial, half-hearted, or punative implementation. These officials have different ways of operating, perceptions of risk, and department cultures.

Reading context means understanding how organizations perform, how communities respond, and how decision-making bodies act. Olson (1965) challenges the premise that rational, self-interested individuals can be translated to the behavior of groups, suggesting that groups do not necessarily act in ways that support their interests. Understanding organizational context and group behavior sheds light on the interplay of plans and how each group seeks to represent its interests. Similarly, the decision-making of a city council is not a simple addition of individual elected officials' interests. Reading the context includes anticipating and incorporating these realities into planning strategies.

Institutions have rational aims and methods, but they also exhibit subtle dynamics that lie beyond procedure manuals. Baum (1987) chronicles this "invisible bureaucracy" in which a planner has responsibility for things they do not have the authority to resolve. This may produce anxiety and shame, which is sometimes discharged in rituals, creating outcomes that do not make sense unless one is aware of forces that generate them.

Within the aforementioned broad dimensions, the general setting includes elements regarding planning laws and precedent, regulations, agency procedures, and professional relationships.

Planning Laws and Precedent

Planners understand and interpret planning laws, court cases, and ongoing legislation in shaping their approach. For example, U.S. land use planners must discern the level of regulatory action that is possible without triggering a "taking," which is an excessive, uncompensated reduction in land value by government action. Planning regulations can control density, permitted uses, and development standards consistent with a policy plan, and this may well limit property values, but they cannot deny all economic use of the land. In the U.S., states delegate the authority to local governments to write zoning laws, but they must do so in ways that are consistent with the Constitution and federal and state regulations.

State laws *require* certain planning actions (such as preparing a comprehensive plan) and *define* local powers. Planning action is framed by federal and state laws and regulations addressing issues such as property rights and land use regulation, transportation investments, community development, and environmental requirements. It is also shaped by federal funding programs such as those implemented in community development, affordable housing, or transportation. The actual power in these laws, however, depends on the will to enforce them. State agencies can look the other way when environmental harm occurs; local officials can revise the community plan and zoning every time a developer asks for it.

Agency Procedures

Laws define planning procedures, which are further developed in organizational practices. Procedures give agencies a form of power in tension with politics and markets.

While often characterized as bureaucratic inefficiency, some procedures slow what otherwise might be hasty decisions on matters of consequence. If procedures provide transparency, they are a bulwark against corruption. Planners grapple with corruption because of the profit possible in land development. For example, a developer increases a property's revenue-generating capacity by up-zoning, therefore increasing its value. Planning procedures are a form of resistance against pay-to-play corruption among elected officials.

If procedures are complex, hard to understand, or published only in English, they work against social justice. Many zoning codes are so complex, for example, that only land use attorneys and specialized consultants can comprehend them. This excludes residents from understanding what may happen in their neighbourhood; has a corrosive effect on faith in local government; and prevents small, community-based developers from assessing development feasibility.

Open-meeting laws, which require meetings to be conducted in public and properly noticed, are intended to reduce corruption. Similarly, notification requirements set parameters for informing residents about proposed zoning changes, and other laws set requirements for public participation in plan adoption. These procedures determine a host of factors such as notification, decision processes, contracting, interagency consultation processes, and the like.

In addition to laws and formal procedures, effective planning action depends on understanding informal "how we operate" procedural norms. For example, a planner developing a home improvement assistance program for low-income residents must consider city contracting norms, code enforcement practices, and staff capacity to run a program. Consulting firms and nonprofits also operate within a legal context, and they have their own procedures such as those for making recommendations, for writing proposals, or for engaging donors and foundations.

Professional Relationships

Planners are embedded in a network of individual professional relationships, within their unit and in relation to other divisions and organizations. These relationships include fellow planners and interactions with other professionals such as engineers, lawyers, architects, landscape architects, developers, economists, real estate developers, and finance experts. Early in my professional career, I worked with traffic engineers whose way of understanding traffic congestion led them to advocate for roadway widening, even in dense urban areas. My planning approach, which emphasized regulatory reform, transportation pricing, transit, and mixed land uses, was in conflict with the engineers' framework of prioritizing efficient flow of vehicles.

Episode Setting

Episode setting is context that is specific to the episode including the history of the issue, the interests involved, and the level of conflict. It also includes the "talk" processes that predominate, such as collaboration or negotiation, institutional dynamics, and the range of possibilities for implementation.

Issue History

Planning episodes are preceded by complex demographic, social, and political conditions and histories. Even if the planning episode is a new initiative, antecedents shape perceptions, possibilities for action, and strategy. Understanding the conditions and events that led to the planning episode informs practical judgments about how to proceed. Planners seeking this history adopt mixed methods – data analysis, archival research, and journalism strategies to hear the story from many points of view, using published sources, community engagement, personal information, blogs, media reports, contacts, and mentors. Box 4.1 (next page) provides an example of episode history in which an inadequate understanding of preexisting commitments doomed the effort.

Box 4.1 Project Context and the Poison Pill

Early in my career, I was assigned to develop a peripheral (intercept) parking program for downtown Los Angeles while working for the City of Los Angeles Community Redevelopment Agency (CRA). The program was intended to reduce local street congestion by diverting traffic to parking facilities at the edges of downtown. The concept was to create a mandatory in-lieu fee program for a portion of the parking requirement that would be used to fund shared public parking structures ringing the downtown and public shuttle buses to connect to workplaces.

The idea was developed years before I was hired, and elected officials were frustrated with delays and anxious for action. Rather than start with a broad problem charge to address traffic congestion, my supervisor and I were given the assignment as a predetermined solution. The program had been developed on an intuitive basis without technical analysis. Developers opposed the program, since it would reduce their control over the operations of parking they were funding.

I didn't fully understand this context and history when I started the assignment. I earnestly worked with my supervisor and a consultant to develop a suitable program. When our program was proposed, the development community demanded a "poison pill" that would allow each developer to build their own intercept facility instead of participating in a common parking and shuttle system. In this way, the development community appeared to accept the program, but the poison pill made the system inefficient, since no individual developer could provide a geographic distribution of intercept facilities, and uneconomic because of the high costs of running separate shuttles.

Lacking insight into the history of the issue meant that I didn't realize that for administrators, the program was more of a symbolic gesture toward traffic reduction than a true priority. They wanted to do something to convince the Los Angeles City Council that development could continue. The program was adopted with the poison pill. Unsurprising, it collapsed amid lawsuits and implementation disinterest. A fuller understanding of this history might have enabled me to anticipate the poison pill and a develop a strategic response to it.

Interests

Understanding the interests involved in a planning episode sheds light on the suitability of different planning approaches. Those interests may include developers/ investors/lenders, economic development and advocacy organizations, employers, departments of city planning, public works, finance, economic development, police and fire departments, other government agencies, organized community groups and individuals, homeowners, renters, business owners, nonprofit organizations, social justice advocates, commercial property owners, cultural institutions, universities, regional concerns, and future residents and businesses. In addition to their multiplicity, these groups are not internally monolithic. A typical dynamic in a business district, for instance, is that long-standing retail merchants have different interests than new business owners who are opening bars and restaurants. Similarly, residents concerned about home values have different interests than renters. Minority residents' interests regarding public safety and police behaviour are different than those of majority groups. Discerning well in this landscape of interests creates possibilities for innovative planning.

Interests are not just represented by those who show up at city council meetings or are understood by elected officials. The advocacy planning movement recognized the unequal distribution of representation in communities. Planners are obligated to engage and/or represent those who aren't at the table – residents who do not normally participate or are excluded from traditional public meetings, and the interests of future generations.

The complexity of stakeholder interests is an important element of context. If there are only two interests, such as a city and a developer, a straightforward negotiation approach may be appropriate. If there are multiple parties that have different issue frames, values, and approaches, a more extensive and inclusive engagement and negotiation process is required.

Conflict/Collaboration

Many discourse settings exist. Addressing longstanding disagreements among multiple parties needs a different approach than issues with a track record of collaboration and cooperation. Innes and Booher (2018) describe a situation in which farming, environmental, and water interests were at loggerheads. That setting required a facilitated, collaborative method that built trust before discussing solutions.

Planning episodes also have different levels of turbulence. Some issues unfold in an orderly way and may be amenable to technocratic planning methods because the planning problem "holds still" for analysis. Turbulent planning episodes do not present such conditions: stakeholders come in and out, the problem definition moves around, and the idea of an optimal solution seems silly. These issues often require an incremental approach that tests, adjusts, and attempts to calm the turbulence.

"Talk" Processes

Talk processes shape how the planning episode proceeds. In technocratic settings, talk is limited to communicating evidence about the best solution or plan. For example, analyses for environmental impact documents involve subject experts in assessing impacts and documenting results, compiled in massive reports. Talk in that case is confined to providing a clear project description, accurately reporting results, and identifying mitigation measures. In contrast, in cases where stakeholders have disagreements about values, or the hierarchy of values, talk is the *only* way of resolving the issue. Since power is exercised through talk processes, it is important to assess how dominant groups exclude others in the way in which talk occurs, such as using jargon, making claims not grounded in lived experience, misrepresentation, or bluffing (Forester 1989).

Institutional Dynamics

Institutional dynamics frame the planning episode, within an organization and among organizations (Willson 2018). One distinction is between organizational units with staff and line functions. Staff functions have policy- and advice-giving activities, while line functions involve delivering a service. Planning is generally a staff function in providing advice, plans, and solutions to problems, but planning provides a line function if it delivers programs or implements codes. There is an inherent difference in interests between these functions: those in staff functions tend to be innovative and exploratory while those in line functions tend to be conservative about change because the blame for operational failure falls with them. There is also a power dynamic to be considered. In local governments, for example, police and fire departments often dominate competition for resources because of the claims they make based on their line function.

Another element of organizational dynamics is the structure of the organization in which the planner works. Hierarchical, bureaucratic organizations have organizational charts that look like the roots of a tree. Information and decisions flow up to the top and then back down. Flat organizations have a shallow structure and are more attuned to collaboration between equals. Effective practice requires planners to understand this structure. It helps a planner know, for example, whether to stay within the chain of command or initiate a cross-department approach.

Implementation Possibilities

Traditionally, implementation design comes last, after goals are defined, alternatives are considered, and an approach is selected. But considering implementation possibilities, or options, from the beginning allows them to influence the selection of a plan or strategy.

An example is developing a zoning code to implement a comprehensive plan. Assuming that design quality is the priority of the plan, a key question is whether to achieve that through (i) a detailed and transparent set of regulations that anticipate site circumstances in a way that allows by-right, ministerial approval; or (ii) create design guidelines and require an appointed design review board to make qualitative judgments. Both approaches can work well, but this is where the city's experience with design review boards is relevant. If there is little local capacity and experience with discretionary design review, or corruption, this element of context might suggest a rule-based approach.

Role(s)

Depending on the style of the organization and supervisor, planners possess different levels of personal discretion. Consideration of the role starts with the planner's official job description and the charge a supervisor provides regarding the planning episode. In receiving the charge, the planner seeks clarity on what is expected, in terms of process, products, and outcomes.

Job descriptions and mandates do not communicate unofficial roles. Planners face different levels of personal discretion as the planning episode may also involve unstated expectations that the planner must perceive. Understanding professional and interpersonal dynamics provides valuable guidance, such as those between a planner and an engineer in the public works department. And externally, a planner might be expected to reduce community conflict over an issue that is generating controversy. Planners also need to understand the level of authority granted by their supervisor and position title so they can navigate the space between excessive caution and usurping the supervisor's authority.

Job Sector

Public sector, developer, consultant, and nonprofit organizations have different aims, practices, and cultures. Planners in municipal planning departments are generally assigned current planning (processing development applications), long-range planning (developing community plans, special studies), or both. Public planners at other levels of government often have more specialized roles, such as those in regional, special purpose, joint powers authority, or state or federal organizations. Willson (2018) provides a guide to each sector.

Private-sector consulting planners work for public and private clients in fields as diverse as writing a municipal plan, analysing siting for a retail chain, or developing a real estate project. This sector prioritizes gaining clarity on problem definition and delivering work products on time and within budget.

Consultants generally do not have long-standing relationships in the community. Their work is governed by winning contracts, access to public officials, managing billable hours, and delivering products in a profitable way.

Public planners frequently manage private sector consultants in preparing plans for their jurisdiction, and are then charged with moving recommendations through approval and implementation. They are frustrated if consultant work products are not timely or responsive. Consultants, in turn, are frustrated if public sector project managers do not have the authority to make critical decisions, or change direction for political reasons, mid-project. This separation of duties can be a problematic part of context – the consultant's recommendations may lack realism, and the public sector officials may not feel ownership or a commitment to the consultant's plan. Anticipating this possibility, strategies can be developed in which consultants engage public sector planners more fully in plan creation, and public sector planners involve consultants in implementation from the beginning.

Nonprofit planners work in a context in which funder expectations shape their work, such as those of granting agencies, foundations, or individual supporters. Financial pressures can lead nonprofits to pursue grants that take them out of their core expertise and confuse their mission. Understanding this context element supports strategic decisions about seeking funding because a confused or broad mission does not yield organization effectiveness and undermines fundraising.

Job Function(s)

Most planning job descriptions indicate technical tasks such as reviewing development applications, analysing data, writing reports, and so on. They describe *what* but do not explain *how* the planner is expected to move solutions or plans forward in the organization.

Small organizations tend to have an "anything you can do" approach to work assignments, whereas duties are clearly defined in larger ones. Also, some supervisors want a "do whatever it takes" approach, which may mean completing tasks that are below or above the job classification.

Charge and Level of Discretion

Planning episodes are usually preceded by a charge or mandate. This may be a specific task for each episode that is delivered in a variety of ways, e.g., a formal memo or a quick hallway conversation with a supervisor. The charge may also be part of standard operating practices, such as responding to developer inquiries at the zoning counter. Rather than undertake discrete projects, these planners respond to the work flow as it arrives.

Over time, planners develop understandings of what is required of them, and level of discretion available. Working with supervisors to determine the critical issues that deserve focus and the amount of time that should be spent reduces wasted efforts. A subtler issue is a planning problem that changes over time and is unclear as to problem definition. Conversations about the timing of efforts can help avoid wasted effort if a development project changes in scope too much to complete a study process in a given time frame.

Professional and Interpersonal Dynamics

The professional and interpersonal dynamics of planning episodes are varied because the settings and range of activities is so broad. These relationships unfold in a dynamic way. I assess the conditions and prospects each time I engage in a consulting project. Internal staff dynamics abound. Within a department there are senses of solidarity, collaboration, competitiveness, passive and active aggression, and everything in between.

As discussed in Chapter 3, context includes emotional dimensions. Baum (2015) discusses "practitioners who claim technical roles, emphasizing their ability to analyse problems and find good solutions, but who often complain that decision-makers disregard them and hence wish they had more power" (499). This is the "sour" planner who fears the danger of exercising power and acknowledging the political nature of their work. Positive and negative emotions are a reality for planners, and if a planner ignores them they may not comprehend what is happening.

Insights into how to navigate the planning episode come from explicitly considering professional and interpersonal relationships, and the emotions involved in them. Rather than avoid these factors for fear that they might lead away from technical rationality, planners prosper when they understand and attend to them. For example, a community might need to heal from a traumatic incident before it can engage in planning, or staff in two different city departments may need to honestly address their differences before collaborating.

Ambiguity and Uncertainty

Interpretation of context inevitably involves ambiguity and uncertainty because planning exists in complex social world. Sometimes, context seems unfathomable. Effective practice does not to seek to banish uncertainty and ambiguity, but to manage them.

Ambiguity

Context ambiguity is a situation in which several interpretations can be made of the same statement or action, or where the planner is uncertain of the meaning or intention of others. It might exist in organization structure when a department manager espouses a culture of openness and exploration but the planner finds that new ideas are dismissed. When what is said and what is done do not line up, there is ambiguity regarding how to behave in staff meetings. There may also be ambiguity about a planner's responsibility or authority regarding an issue. Elected officials may espouse support for housing and services for homeless people but find problems with every proposal brought forward, or sanction the planner for taking independent action. Does the elected official mean what they say or are they seeking to mollify or confuse a constituency with no intent to act? The prevalence of ambiguity calls for planners to develop communicative and interpretive abilities and tolerate its inevitable presence.

Uncertainty

Uncertainty complicates the planner's understanding of context. Have all community interests been identified? Are some of them absent? What do unrepresented interests think or desire? Uncertainty also exists concerning communicative distortions. Do stakeholders mean what they say? Are they bluffing? Will a proposal be effective? Moreover, uncertainty is present when the planner is unsure about how individuals and groups (e.g., other departments, external agencies) will react to a proposal. Uncertainty is inevitable: the best a planner can do is be aware of it, seek to lessen it through contingencies, and proceed with knowledge that any understanding is partial and dynamic.

While power is sometimes displayed in brash ways, sophisticated players often disguise their power. They prefer it to be invisible to avoid scrutiny and opposition strategies. In some meetings, the discussants around a meeting table actively engage, but a subtle nod from a powerful person at the side of the room determines the course. Like a watermark, power often does its work and evaporates. All that is left is the mark.

Planners are effective when they understand different forms of power. Certainly, past experience is helpful in understanding the tendencies of planning actors. Given the similar structure of planning in the U.S., lessons learned from cases and past experience can help planners know where to look for the traces of power. The commonsense expression of "follow the money" is an example of a heuristic approach to understanding power relationships. Interpretation of discourse can diagnose coded languages that stakeholders use to transact power.

And Now to You: Savvy Planners Understand Context

A vast array of considerations determines the context for a planning episode – too many to master. You can simplify the process by identifying the ones that are well-known and clear. Then, focus on elements of context that you may have previously ignored, perhaps misinterpreted, or where there is a difference of opinion. Planners starting new positions or new consulting assignments face a daunting task to understand context. The prompts provided here can be used as a checklist to determine which elements warrant the most attention. Then, assess the best way of getting information, whether that be conversations, reading blogs, reviewing documents, or observation. For planners with a longer tenure in a position, context may seem clear. Those planners can use the prompts to ask about less visible aspects of context or whether assumptions about context match the current circumstances.

A simple strategy for context reflection is to focus on elements that are likely to have the largest influence on the particular planning episode. Information comes in many forms, from requesting a city attorney interpretation on a court case, to an informal conversation with a supervisor, to getting to the know the community by participating in local organizations.

After reading the context and interpreting it, you have important choices to make in adapting or seeking to change it. Assume that you are charged with creating participation around a controversial issue over which there are deep differences, anger, and a history of unproductive conflict. One "adapt to structure" approach seeks to avoid worsening the conflict, as planners do when they design workshops that minimize discussions of the whole. A workshop designed to control shared recognition of grievance and escalation of conflict would ask participants to visit information stations according to their interests and record preferences with stickers and other passive devices. It leaves the power of interpretation to the planners and interferes with the development of grassroots political movements. A planner may do this thinking that it will reduce conflict, but it could have the opposite effect of expanding distrust if community members figure out they are being prevented from forming political alliances. Another approach in such as case is to acknowledge the community conflict and design a process to transform context, including commitments to properly facilitate face-to-face dialogues with the goal of healing grievances and reducing conflict.

Time and time again, I have seen wise discernment about context lead to success, and insufficient attention to context lead to failure. You cannot make wise practical judgments in the planning episode without a deep understanding of context. Next, Chapter 5 addresses the planning episode itself, which plays out in the space between planner-as-person and context. Carrying forward context insight and understanding supports wise practical judgments and allows you to design planning processes that are responsive and effective.

Discussion Questions

1. Attention to context may seem automatic or obvious. Most planners are aware of the charge given to them and decision-maker or client preferences. Use Table 4.1 to reflect on elements of context that are *outside* your normal span of attention. If there are elements that you do not normally consider, what are they? Are there consequences for practical judgments? Going forward, how could you assess context in those areas?
2. Some context elements are well known, so much so that they become background assumptions. If there are areas where your knowledge about context comes from assumptions, are there ways that these assumptions help or hamper your understanding of context? In what ways could you achieve a better, more nuanced read of context?
3. Planners on the same team may read context differently. Assemble a group of planners in your organization and ask each person to identify the top five consequential elements of context. Then compare results and discuss.
4. Planners work in interdisciplinary teams whose members may read context differently. Assemble the team and ask each professional in the group to identify the top five consequential elements of context. Then compare results and discuss.
5. Planners often work under tight time and budget constraints that do not allow an extensive context-reading phase in the planning process. What are ways to get a quick read on context on the fly?

Notes

1 Sociologist Anthony Giddens (1984) uses the term *structure* to describe context elements, which refer to "rules and resources" and more specifically to "the structuring properties allowing the 'binding' of time-space in social systems" (17–19).

2 The more theoretical term for planner-as-person is planner as human agent, meaning an individual with a level of agency.

References

American Institute of Certified Planners. 2019, September 22. *Code of Ethics and Professional Conduct*. Adopted March 19, 2005; Effective June 1, 2005; Revised April 1, 2016. Accessed August 23, 2019 at https://www.planning.org/ethics/eth icscode/.

Baum, Howell. 1987. *The Invisible Bureaucracy: The Unconscious in Organizational Problem Solving*. New York: Oxford University Press, Inc.

Baum, Howell. 2015. "Planning with Half a Mind: Why Planners Resist Emotion." *Planning Theory & Practice*, 16(4): 498–516. doi: 10.1080/14649357.2015.1071870.

Forester, John. 1989. *Planning in the Face of Power*. Berkeley, CA: University of California Press.

Forester, John. 1999. *The Deliberative Practitioner: Encouraging Participatory Planning Processes*. Cambridge: The MIT Press.

Friedmann, John. 1973. *Retracking America: A Theory of Transactive Planning*. Garden City, NY: Anchor Press.

Giddens, Anthony. 1984. *The Constitution of Society: Outline of the Theory of Structuration*. Cambridge: Polity Press.

Innes, Judith and David Booher. 2018. *Planning with Complexity: An Introduction to Collaborative Rationality for Public Policy*. New York: Routledge.

Klosterman, Richard E. 1985. "Arguments for and Against Planning." *The Town Planning Review*, 56(1): 5–20.

Olson, Mancur. 1965. *The Logic of Collective Action*. Cambridge: Harvard University Press.

Sandercock, Leonie. 1998. *Making the Invisible Visible: A Multicultural Planning History*. Berkeley, CA: University of California Press.

Willson, Richard. 2018. *A Guide for the Idealist: Launching and Navigating Your Planning Career*. New York: Routledge.

Chapter 5

The Planning Episode

This chapter describes the action that takes place in the planning episode. It examines two pairs of elements that shape a planner's practical judgments: the roles of logic and emotion, and the use of convention and invention. The quality of those judgments builds on a structured, reflexive approach to planner-as-person as discussed in Chapter 3; deliberation about context as discussed in Chapter 4; and the practical judgments and actions during the planning episode, the subject of this chapter. By quality, I mean well-reasoned choices that produce results supporting efficiency, livability, equity, and sustainability.

Planning episodes vary widely and include tasks such as developing a community vision, land use plan, or climate mitigation strategy; creating a regulatory instrument such as a form-based zoning code; or plan implementation in the review of a zoning variance request or the design of a public improvement. Planning episodes also include designing and implementing programs and advocacy work to empower and influence.

Planners make practical judgments in collaboration and interaction with other professionals, decision-makers, and the public, but they reason about their judgments as individuals. The pragmatist conception used here is that effective planners consider the practical implications of choices rather than follow a particular theory roadmap in a doctrinaire way.

Practical judgments are at the core of every planning episode even though the scope of them varies with the degree that planning procedures are defined.

Writing agency comments on environmental review documents might be considered a routine planning task that does not require practical judgments. Yet there are many involved in such as task: interpreting the significance of impacts (content), dealing with delayed comments from another agency (process), considering political pressure (responding to politics), and/or deliberating interagency relationships regarding mitigation measures (responding to organizational structure).

Procedural Understandings of Planning

A traditional way to understand a planning episode is to classify it according to one or more procedural planning theories. While they are not the focus here, major themes of procedural theory are summarized next to set the stage. Whittemore (2015) organizes significant procedural theories as follows:

- Rational-comprehensive – means/ends correspondence with a technocratic, long-range, and systems approach (Faludi 1973).
- Incremental – multiple steps toward problem amelioration (Lindblom 1959, Simon 1972).
- Transactive – knowledge exchange between planners and residents, recognizing everyday experience (Friedmann 1973).
- Communicative – improving discourse and counteracting communication distortions to produce better conditions for democratic deliberation (Forester 1989, Healy 1997, Innes and Booher 2018).
- Advocacy – representing and advocating for the needs of underrepresented groups (Davidoff 1965).
- Equity – expanding choice for those with less power (Krumholz and Forester 1990).
- Radical – addressing injustices of the capital-driven city by asserting social needs (Fainstein and Fainstein 1979).
- Humanist or phenomenological – elevation of context and reflection on unique ways that knowledge is developed and transmitted (Bolan 1980).

Each of these process theories has merit and application. Often, they are used in combination. In my teaching, I suggest that students consider the value of each approach for the particular planning episode and draw freely from all traditions. In a similar classification effort, Brooks (2002) organizes procedural theories according to their assumptions about centralization and rationality. To the process approaches outlined earlier, Brooks adds feedback strategy in which the politically savvy planner tests for agreement.

Each process theory conceptualizes power differently (Moghadam and Rafieian 2019). The rational comprehensive model's framing of a uniform public interest and a regime of regulatory control implies dominant, top-down power. Other models are based on a decentralization of power, through resistance, empowerment, or communicative practices.

No wonder it is hard to explain the profession's method. There are multiple procedural theories, and theorists define them differently. In practice, though, planners freely combine process approaches and change them midcourse based on the evolving context and the problem. As a result, the profession is in a "weak" paradigm condition, meaning that there is not a single unified process theory. To the beginning planner, this may seem disappointing. Other fields, such as civil engineering or architecture, have more clearly defined methods and are more likely to follow standardized practice codes that are memorialized in licensing exams.

In my view, the multiplicity of procedural theories a good thing because it makes planning an innovative and adaptable profession. Planners are not constrained by a particular process theory. In California, for instance, four generations of climate change planning (policy and inventory, mitigation, mitigation/adaption, and integrated) have developed in just two decades. Not tied to a tight professional definition or spending time defending boundaries, planners can innovate. The downside of multiple theories is that the planning profession has a harder time explaining itself and making claims to expertise than professional fields with straightforward methods.

While procedural theory offers useful insight into how to plan, planning process judgments are both explicit, as in following a procedural theory, and implicit, as in habitual ways of doing things. My practice is influenced by many theories from Whittemore's and Brook's lists, depending on context and the nature of the episode. Furthermore, my views have changed as I have gained experience and became more interested in compromise.

Procedural theories help do the work in a planning episode. The use-what-works tactic articulated here is a pragmatic approach. Drawing on this tradition, Hoch (2019) argues that planners should not use theory such as these to *justify* practical professional judgment, as if seeking to prove one's approach correct, but use them as they are *helpful* in making practical judgments and carrying out planning.

The Planning Episode Framework

Figure 5.1 shows the main elements of the planning episode framework. It takes a step back from the individual process theories just reviewed to focus on two

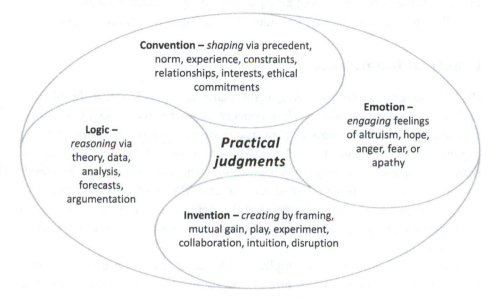

Figure 5.1 Reasoning and Methods in the Planning Episode

pairs of elements. The first pair recognizes that planners use both *logic* (e.g., thinking, discernment, judgment) and *emotion* (e.g., feeling, relations) in reasoning their way through practical judgments. Logic is expressed in various forms of analytic work, data, and theory, but also in ends–means consistency and communicative reasoning. Emotion includes engaging and working with emotions, within the planner themselves and with others. Figure 5.1 includes examples of how planners might use logic and emotion. This conceptualization supports Hoch's (2019) argument about the importance of cognitive objectivity (what I am calling logic) and emotional sensitivity (what I am calling emotion) in planning practice. Together, logic and emotion are considered constitutes of reason.

The second pair of elements considers the basic work that planners do. While planning episodes vary, the interpretive lens used here is *convention* and *invention*. Sometimes planners *shape* plans and proposals so they conform to conventions, whether they be existing policies, plans, laws, community preferences and norms, best practices, development agreements, or design guidelines. They make judgments according to a reference or standard. Other times, planners *invent* something new in collaboration with others, whether that be a community vision, new institutional relationships, new forms of political power, or an innovative program. They engage their imagination and that of those with whom they work. Often, planners do both at the same time.

Figure 5.1 also lists examples of how planners apply convention and use invention. Taken together, they are considered the primary methods of planning.

Practical Judgments

Practical judgments are moments in the planning episode when the planner makes consequential choices. They concern at least three types of decisions: (i) planning process, or how to plan (the design of practice); (ii) responses to organizational, community, and political structures, or how to navigate or maneuver (strategy); and (iii) decisions about the content of plan proposals and recommendations, or what to recommend (the work). As introduced in Chapter 1, practical judgments resolve the complex setting of the planning episode; they are decisions that decipher opportunities and tensions between elements.

A practical judgment, for example, is called for when a consultant responds to a request for proposal (RFP) for the preparation of a community plan. The consultant follows state law and local procedure but has many choices in deciding the type of planning process to propose. Similarly, a practical judgment is made when deciding on the scale of the analysis zone in a traffic impact study, or when a supervisor gives the planner a direction that is at odds with their sense of planning ethics, or when a developer offers a gift in return for favorable treatment. Likewise, a practical judgment is required about how to respond when a consultant client changes the scope and purpose of a project multiple times, sending the project over budget.

Of course, planners can avoid making these judgments by passing them along to someone else, relying on habit, blindly applying procedure, or defaulting to management or political direction. While there are good reasons for following well-tested procedures, planners who do not *own* their practical judgments act as technicians rather than professionals. To be a professional is to possess a level of personal agency appropriate to the position. These practical judgments are particularly important in instances in which routine processes or ways of thinking are not sufficient.

Hoch (2019) focuses on the idea of practical judgment as an alternative to imagining planning in a cookbook-like manner. While procedural and substantive theories offer many insights, *what to do* in a specific instance requires practical judgment. It is more like surfing than an analytic construct. Hoch summarizes three elements of practical judgment, drawing on philosopher Todd Lekan's work (2003). They are (i) drawing on practical know-how rather than strictly following the dictates of a theory; (ii) acknowledging that the planning episode changes as we engage in it; and (iii) understanding that the complexities of the episode cannot be reduced to a set of precepts. The complexity of explaining practical judgments does not undermine the argument that they are central in the planning episode. This is a reason that practitioners often tell planning students that they need something more than theories in their work.

Practical judgments are at the center of Figure 5.1. Ideally, they are made with a reflective interpretation of the past and reflection-in-action based on a clear assessment of the present and anticipation of likely futures.

Examples of practical judgments related to *process* include the following:

- Determining appropriate processes and whether to hybridize procedural models.
- Creating methods of interaction and collaboration with the community, professionals, organization units, and decision-makers.
- Reacting midstream if one procedural approach does not appear to be working well.

Practical judgments about responding to *politics, community, and organizational interests* include:

- Deciding whether to accept an assignment as given, seek to reframe it, or ask to have it reassigned because conflict of interest or value disagreement.
- Choosing ways of interacting with, learning from, and influencing and persuading colleagues, clients, organizational units, professional collaborators, community groups, and political systems.
- Exploring the varied frames for understanding the issue and making interpretive decisions about stakeholder positions and interests, and one's own positions and assumptions.
- Deciding who to listen to and who to ignore. Deciding to take a person's statement at face value or reinterpret it.
- Making choices about whose interests to serve and the reasons why.

Practical judgements about the *content of plans and policies* include aspects such as:

- Determining substantive theories that bear on the recommendation.
- Making choices about the knowledge brought to bear: how much information, the mix of original and secondary (qualitative and quantitative) data, the level of specialized expertise required, methods of analyzing and presenting information, and desired results.

- Deciding how to synthesize findings and stakeholder views to support a decision.
- Evaluating the merits of alternative courses of action and deciding what to recommend.

The case studies focus on consequential practical judgments in each planning episode. While theory is relevant to these judgments, planners also use tacit intuition that combines thought and feeling. Among the planner's abilities engaged in practical judgments are moral sensitivity, social craft (engaging with others), technical skill, and political savvy. We cannot know how different judgments would have changed the outcome, but the choices do have effects. Rather than seek an unassailable argument from theory, practical judgments seek better ways forward. By avoiding a doctrinaire approach, practical judgment allows for innovation.

A career based on reflective practices and reflexivity leads to responsible, innovative, and ethical practice. As Bolton (2009, 7) describes, "Effective reflective practice and reflexivity are transgressive of stable and controlling orders; they lead cogs to decide to change shape, change place, and even reconfigure whole systems." The next section explores each of the elements in those practical judgments.

Logic and Emotion

The Figure 5.1 framework prompts planners to consider how logic and emotion are experienced and employed, and how they shape the planning episode. A planner strongly adhering to logic alone, for example, may miss emotional dimensions that shape perceptions and decision-making, or miss opportunities for generating change. That planner may develop plans that are not adopted, symbolic, or not implemented. Similarly, a planner who only engages and works with emotions may underestimate technical and process issues, leading to the adoption of ineffective or harmful plans. A planner employing both logic and emotion can approach the broad goal of reason. The paragraphs that follow discuss each element.

Logic

Planners add value to decision-making by bringing more logic than would occur without planning. This doesn't mean they *impose* their logic on others, but that they are advocates for it. Logic has specific, highly debated meanings in philosophy. For our purposes, logic is defined as a way of thinking guided by supportable principles or axioms, and achieved by making valid inferences. Logic is one of the planning profession's claims to legitimacy, one in which planners dispassionately analyze problems in a quasi-scientific manner (Hoch 2006). Early planners promised to bring varied forms of logic to decision-making in chaotic market and political conditions, as evidenced in the development of zoning regulations in the early 1900s. Since those origins, the view of planning logic has become more inclusive, including a wide variety of technical, process, communicative, and ethical conceptions.

A planner's logic encounters stakeholders and elected officials who may start with conclusions about what they want rather than engage in the kind of logical ends-to-means processes core to the profession. In my planning practice, for instance, I often work backward from what stakeholders say they want: I ask them *why* they want it, explore whether their idea is likely to achieve the desired ends, and then consider those ends from a broader standpoint of efficiency, equity, and sustainability. We could say that planners have a fiduciary responsibility to add logic to decision-making processes, as it counters wishful thinking, self-interest, corruption, demonization, and ignorance. The public and decision-makers expect this of us. Table 5.1 provides examples of how planners employ logic.

Logic applies to deliberations, as described in the first row of Table 5.1. Planners acting with this kind of logic push back against distorted or untrue claims, and/or elicit and push forward the views of unrepresented or underrepresented groups (Forester 1989). In one episode setting, discussants may represent all stakeholder groups, speak in understandable manners, offer evidence for claims, express views in a sincere manner, and consider the legitimacy of the claims they make. In another setting, it may be the opposite: stakeholders are excluded, and participants use jargon, make unsupported claims, exaggerate and bluff, and speak beyond their lived experience. In the second case, the planner seeks to bring the logic of communicative rationality to bear by reducing communicative distortions, increasing representation, and enhancing the quality of deliberation.

The second row of Table 5.1 discusses logic in the planning process, such as ends–means coherence. *Ends* concern the ultimate result or outcome of planning efforts, often expressed in vision and mission statements, goals, objectives, standards, or metrics. They are statements of sought outcomes built on values and vision, and negotiated through politics. A city council, for instance, may adopt goals related to efficiency, equity, sustainability, livability, and so on. Logic can help decision-makers reason about these goals, especially in making

Table 5.1 Logic in the Planning Episode

Dimension	Examples
Deliberation, argumentation, and dialogue	• Convene discourse in ways that improve the quality of claims made and reduce communicative distortions. • Seek to the improve accuracy, comprehensibility, and logic of community dialogue; challenge distortions.
Planning process	• Explain the meaning and consequences of goals (ends) and the relationships between them. • Clarify ends–means coherence. • Broaden the inclusion of interests so that decision-making is better informed.
Existing and future conditions	• Improve understanding of existing conditions using data, models, and substantive theories. • Predict future conditions, develop scenarios, manage uncertainty, and provide a long-term, systems-based perspective.
Causal relationships and unanticipated consequences	• Use causal relationships to identify consequences of action, intended and unintended. • Identify interrelationships and interdependencies between plans. • Distinguish between risks associated with theory and implementation failure.
Social justice	• Link principles of justice to planning outcomes. • Show decision-makers the consequences of exclusion and inequality.

determinations about their relative priority, and what do to when different values point toward different strategies. Planners also use logic in evaluating whether means will accomplish desired ends. *Means* are ways of accomplishing ends – the policies, regulations, programs, capital works projects, and other tools that effectuate change. Planners seek means that are well-suited to achieving those ends from the standpoint of effectiveness, costs, equity, sustainability, and so on.

Substantive theories are employed in the logic types discussed in rows three and four of Table 5.1 – existing and forecast conditions and causal relationships. These theories include ideas and models about how cities and regions function spatially, environmentally, economically, and socially, drawing on natural and social sciences. They help planners make predictions and test the efficacy of planning interventions. Psychological and sociological theories are also relevant regarding issues such as emotion, loss, meaning, and change (Marris 1974). Social sciences for planning include economics, sociology, political science, geography, anthropology, psychology, organizational behavior, and the like. Natural sciences inform planners about aspects such as biological systems, climate, engineering feasibility, physiology, and human health. Lastly, planners use policy sciences and financial analyses to bring logic to decision-making.

Economic theory is one way to understand existing conditions and forecast future ones. Yet the range of knowledge that should be applied in a logical analysis is far more than that. For example, Talvitie (1997) illustrates the psychological dimensions of travel behavior in showing how apparently value-neutral transportation planning models use economic utility maximization principles that only partially recognize the motivations of human behavior. Driving a 6,000-pound sport utility vehicle to a corner store to buy a quart of milk can hardly be explained by the vehicle's cargo capacity – other, noneconomic factors surely are a play. Using a Freudian perspective, Talvitie reveals how the dark side of human behavior is often ignored, leading to unrealistic plans. Planners who recognize psychological dimensions have a better understanding of human responses to plans.

Lastly, logic applies to considering the social justice outcomes of planning. Planners use logic, in part, to develop a theory of justice and connect it to progressive planning outcomes. This doesn't ensure that decision-makers agree, but draws connections between principles and the impacts of plans and policies. For example, regional transportation plans comply with federal requirements for environmental justice by assessing how plan alternatives address environmental and public health concerns in vulnerable communities.

Emotion

Planners work in an emotional encounter with the world whether they acknowledge it or not.

> The desires and preferences we hold direct our attention, motivate our interests, compel our assent and alert us to risks. Yet, despite the ubiquity of emotions and feelings, planning practitioners and analysts rarely focus on them as a resource for comprehending future oriented, purposeful action.
>
> *(Hoch 2006, 367)*

Personally, planners experience or encounter emotions such as anger, sadness, fear, shame, disgust, or guilt. Equally, they may experience or encounter joy, pride, hope, or altruism. These emotional experiences are internal (within the subject) and external (engaging with politicians, community members, and developers).

Plan-making and planning activity generate strong emotional responses in communities because they affect issues that are core to a community's sense of identity and changing conditions on the ground. But who is the community? In many cases, the idea of community is contested across race, ethnicity, class, gender identity, immigration status, and other dimensions, so the concept of community itself seems coercive and exclusionary to some. For example, exclusionary sentiments to prevent affordable housing construction are often couched in terms of not being compatible with "community character." Community is a contested, emotional subject.

Planning also involves emotion because planners are passionate about their work, as it concerns both process and normative ideas of what should be done. I am elated when my efforts achieve results and feel despair when they fail. Rather than consider emotions as risking bias, emotional sensitivity is a prerequisite for effective practice.

Emotion is prominent in the planning episode itself, among the groups with whom planners plan. When community groups such as homeowners or merchants feel threatened by infill development, they show up angry at city hall. When they distrust real estate developers or local elected officials, they experience fear and rage that the system is rigged. Emotion points to meanings. In my consulting practice, I often propose reforms to parking standards, changes that are often unwelcomed by local stakeholders who wish to continue the status quo. It wasn't until I was involved in a land use dispute in my own neighborhood that I fully understood these emotions. In that case, my side of the dispute was in the right, legally and technically, but the other side won with the help of a well-connected lobbyist who, aided by a city attorney who didn't follow the law, convinced a planning commission to ignore environmental review requirements. I then understood the anger residents feel when it seems that the game is not fair.

Planners benefit when they develop sensitivity to the emotional dimensions of their practice. One way to use this sensitivity is to anticipate, counteract, or tame emotions, taking the view that a planning process dominated by emotions may not be well thought out, or may systematically favor the angriest group or a group that dominates others.

Another perspective on emotions is that they are a powerful companion to rational thought by directing our attention to things that matter. Positive emotions such as caring can bring about reconciliation and healing, while anger

Table 5.2 Emotions in th[e]

Dimension

Emotional dim
understand
histories

can be an impetus for change. Hoch (2([obscured]
that "the careful discernment of emoti [obscured]
ments we make and actions we take" ([obscured]

Baum (2015) argues that we should [obscured]
about emotions in planning. Everyday l [obscured]
or things that *happen* to us and others. [obscured]
mind. Drawing on Shafer (1976), he e [obscured]
are expressed in actions and ways of acti [obscured]
linguistically by verbs and adverbs" (Bau [obscured]
more active way encourages planners a [obscured]
part in emotional action. When planners better understand their own emotions, and those of others, they can more fully engage, making emotions an explicit part of planning rather than a danger to be avoided.

Table 5.2 summarizes roles of emotions in planning. The first row shows the role of emotions in understanding place and community histories. Over the last few decades, planners have developed techniques to open planning to emotional expression. The second row discusses the roles of anger in motivating productive action. Rather than see anger as something to be quelled, it is a form of energy that can motivate action.

Planners can address conflict directly, seeking healing, dialogue, and negotiation processes, as noted in the third row in Table 5.2. For example, mutual gain negotiation seeks to move conflict from win-lose conceptions to trading innovative solutions to produce an overall win–win. Emotions of love, hope, faith, encouragement, and empowerment, as discussed in the fourth and fifth rows of Table 5.2, are equally important. These emotional states can underpin new initiatives and plans. Well-designed and implemented processes for resolving conflict often generate positive emotions that fuel implementation commitment. Working from conflict and grievance to resolution and action is among the most inspiring planning experiences. It engenders hope and empowerment, as discussed in the sixth row of the table.

Self-care is required when a planner is blamed or scapegoated for something beyond their control, or simply feel the pain of injustice or ignorance, as noted on the sixth row of Table 5.2. When decision-makers have a political disagreement that they cannot resolve, for example, they sometimes put the burden on the planner(s), sending them back for "more study" rather than seeking a direct resolution of the political conflict. Additional study will not resolve the political conflict, and so the blame is doubled down because the planner's work on further study does not solve the issue. Another example is directing a planner

	Examples
...ensions of ...ng place and	• Create planning processes that provide emotional availability to others. • Open discourse to stories, qualitative dimensions, feelings, and learning. • Engage in play, storytelling, placemaking, arts interpretation.
Anger and frustration	• Provide tools for translating community anger into action. • Create activities that reduce isolation of groups and increase communication across shared experiences.
Conflict	• Recognize grievance, empower with process, encourage parties' acknowledgement of responsibility and reconciliation. • Organize and facilitate mutual gain negotiation.
Mutual caring, mentorship, and love	• Develop processes that allow expression of altruism and caring for others. • Interrupt cynicism and blaming.
Hope and empowerment	• Create conditions that allow and build on expressions of hope. • Generate conditions that result in group and individual agency.
Planner's personal self-care	• Develop mindful practices to recover from disappointment and scapegoating, avoid cynicism and burnout; recognize long-wave change processes; and generate meaning.

to write a plan that bridges a disparate set of contradictory goals. The only way to do this is to write a vague plan. Then, the plan is criticized for its vagueness. In response to being unfairly blamed, some planners suppress their emotions and adopt an affect of a cool professional who is under control and impervious to others. The better alternative is to engage in acts of self-care that attend to the emotional well-being.

Including emotions in the framework places them in an appropriately central role. Box 5.1 (next page) provides a commentary from a seasoned practitioner who warns about letting emotions dominate practical judgments. An interplay between emotions and logic is essential to clear thinking. Without logic, emotion is partial, susceptible to prejudice, and can lead to impulsive action that undermines effectiveness.

Box 5.1 A Cautionary Note About Emotion
Tad Widby, Retired Planner, formerly with WSP
and Parsons Brinkerhoff

Emotion is an important element of the Chapter 5 framework. Having practiced planning in various ways over nearly 50 years, I have two responses: (i) feeling emotion about one's work is unavoidable, and (ii) emotions can get in the way of doing a professional job.

Being engaged in planning work requires investment of one's self. You cannot help but feel something about the nature of the work, the character of the people you are working with, the process being used, and/or the import of the topic. Planners do not enter the field as uncaring beings. Most want to make the world a better place, and that entails judgments about why they want to and how it can be made better. Unavoidably, that means emotions are at play.

Consider the planner as a public servant who informs decision-makers about key information so that a good, workable decision can be made. In that circumstance, the planner works within the policy and process framework of the decision-makers or helps shape that framework. Conflict is inevitable between a planner's recommendation and the decision-makers' preferences, so the planner needs to determine whether resolving this conflict can be done ethically. A key to this is keeping one's focus on the overall objective.

When facing a conflict, the planner can follow the decision-makers' preferences, step aside, or recommend a different approach. Poor decisions result when one's emotions about the subject override reasoning about what to do. I am not alone in having faced that circumstance a number of times. Sometimes, the best course of action is making your recommendation and accommodating the decision-makers' decision to go a different way. Sometimes it is not.

If emotions overtake your practice, you run the risk of becoming the issue for the decision-makers to confront. This tends to occur when the planner operates as an advocate. Unless the decision-makers are looking for the planner to be an advocate, this is a danger zone. Emotion can lead to the planner becoming part of the problem. The planner needs to work within the client's system or make recommendations for improvements. It is not helpful to operate from the frustration that can build up if emotions run high.

A former boss told me to "listen to that voice in the back of your head." He meant that if it feels like something is going wrong it is time to pay attention, get a better understanding, and take corrective action. Ultimately, that corrective action may be to step away from the role being played. I have done that more than once.

Recognizing and accepting emotions in my practice came slowly to me, as early on I had negative associations with strongly held emotions. Without emotion, though, logic is ungrounded, incomplete, and detached. When planners proceed *only* on the basis of logic, "planners end up thinking with only part of their mind about part of what matters to people, part of why they act as they do, and part of what would move them to act consistently with plans" (Baum 2015, 513).

Convention and Invention

The second pair of framework elements refers to the work that is done in the planning episode – applying convention and/or generating invention. Convention and invention usually coexist in the same planning episode.

Convention

Planning activities often cause outcomes to conform to norms. When a planner interprets the zoning code in reviewing a development application, they are applying community convention in the form of development regulations. The planner might indicate a need for project redesign because the proposal exceeds the permitted height. The project is altered, or shaped, to meet community design conventions.

The idea of convention lies at the heart of land use regulations. Zoning, for example, was developed to manage land use compatibility issues more efficiently than relying on privately adjudicated processes in which property owners sue one another to obtain compensation for externality impacts such as pollution or blocking access to light. The argument for zoning is that governments can efficiently resolve land use conflicts with a standardized, district-based approach. Zoning manages externalities by imposing conventions on building use, height, setbacks, and other development standards. This is thought to improve the conditions for investment and property upkeep since property owners have an expectation of neighborhood stability. In this way, planners avoid prisoner dilemma conditions, a circumstance in which everyone underinvests in their properties because there is no tool to control externality impacts.

Conventions are sometimes based on precedent in which past actions are used to guide current decisions in similar situations. Seeking consistency with past action is partly done to avoid charges that a planning decision is arbitrary and capricious. Decision-makers also consider the precedents they *create* in current decisions, knowing that they may affect future choices.

Conventions are also applied in planning processes, as occurs when agencies define thresholds of significance for environmental impacts. In a particular environmental review, a planner compares predicted impacts to those thresholds to determine if impacts are significant and must be mitigated. Planners also apply *process* convention when they apply a standard analysis and decision protocol, as when local planners follow a city template in completing staff reports for variance requests. In addition, planners apply a convention, that of recognizing and validating existing community stakeholder interests, when they seek a solution that "balances" those interests.

Practice habits are a form of convention, in the ways that a planner responds to conditions that shape attention, thought, and actions. They might describe this as "rules of thumb" or good professional practice. These habits are created over time and may be largely invisible to the planner, only to be realized when they move to a different institution, encounter a difficult problem, or engage in dialogue with a fellow planner or new supervisor. For example, a designer colleague of mine describes a "rope-a-dope" response strategy in response to criticism of design proposals in public meetings. "Rope-a-dope" refers to a boxer's practice of accepting blows along the ropes while minimizing their damage, inviting the adversary to wear themselves out punching, and then initiating the action at the end of the fight. My colleague describes absorbing a series of criticisms, avoiding "punching back" in a defensive manner by defending the design, and then turning the sentiment at the end of the meeting to accept the design proposal.

Table 5.3 provides examples of how planners apply convention. The first three rows discuss convention in process while the remaining ones address convention in planning outcomes. Planner habits are personal "ways of doing" developed with experience. Protocol applies convention by applying systematic steps as found in agency practices, state planning laws, and implicit or explicit models of the planning process; the planner does not start with a clean sheet but rather a prescribed process (Hoch 2019, Hopkins 2001). Coherence and coordination, noted in the third row, apply conventions in seeking coordination between plans and intentions of government, private entities, nonprofit organizations, and individuals. Of course, the risk of these uses of convention is that there is insufficient attention to the unique dimensions of context and/ or a lack of innovation.

The fourth row of Table 5.3 addresses precedent, including the realm of best practice in which planners justify recommendations based on what peer

Table 5.3 Convention in the Planning Episode

Dimension	Examples
Habits	• Act according to local standards of civility, dialogue, collaborative processes, professional deference. • Engage in "check-ins" with management and elected officials.
Protocols	• Apply standard investigation, problem-solving, and reporting mechanisms. • Apply standards to cases, e.g., threshold determinations in environmental document, park supply per capita standard.
Coherence and coordination between plans	• Coordinate among the multiple plans of public agencies, private entities, nonprofit organizations, community groups, and individuals.
Precedent/best practices	• Draw on effective plans and strategies used elsewhere, translated to local context.
Management of change, pace, and impact	• Manage the pace and characteristics of change so that they do not exceed the capacity of existing residents, businesses, and stakeholders. • Use regulatory tools to reduce externality impacts from one property to another, supporting neighborhood stability. • Align growth with infrastructure and natural system capacity.
Land use and design norms	• Link community design standards to community identities. • Create fair, transparent, and predictable processes in development regulation and design review.
Fiscal stewardship, economic vitality, sustainability, and legal conformity	• Shape outcomes toward positive fiscal impact and economic vitality. • Moderate environmental impacts, increase resiliency, restore ecological systems. • Seek consistency with planning law, court interpretation. • Promote due process, fair treatment, notification, enforceable agreements.

organizations have done. Precedent has clout because risk-adverse planners and decision-makers want assurance that an approach has been proven elsewhere.

Box 5.2 (next page) provides campus planner David Salazar's comments on how wise application of best practice is at the heart of his planning practice. He also discusses the importance of honest assessment of plan success to keep the application of best practice relevant.

Box 5.2 Notes on Best Practice and Feedback Loops
David Salazar, FAICP, Campus Planner

Planning theory is just the beginning. For me, practicing planning is an expression and expansion of that knowledge. As I began practicing campus planning, the planning theories I learned in school moved to the background. They provided a useful orientation and foundation, but my practice focused more on accumulated experience and best practice. I looked outward, finding out what other planners were doing and what was successful. I asked myself, Can concepts, approaches, ideas be replicated in the work that I want to accomplish?

With time and experience, I became more refined and strategic about how I approached planning tasks and problems. I developed a framework or formula for approaching a project or planning problem, much like an alchemist. Although every planning situation is different, there are many similarities. I use my intuition, knowledge base, and best practice understanding to create innovative concepts and models for project development and implementation.

Once a plan is complete and implementation is underway, further reflective assessment is needed. It may turn out that elements of the plan cannot be realized or that a different approach is required. Planners need to be honest and open to this change, even to the extent of abandoning an approach, rather than defend the plan because they think it is only way. Countless plans stagnate and calcify because the authors/leaders of the plan become defenders of the status quo and are not open to new ideas and options. Having an ongoing feedback loop from implementation to plan approach is essential to keep best practice ideas relevant.

Sometimes planners do not recognize the extent of their ego involvement in a particular plan. When you are the principal author and leader of an initiative or plan, it is inevitable that there is a measure of ego involved. A pitfall of this is that you get wrapped up in yourself, your own ideas, and your ownership of the plan. That is why it is important to step back on a regular basis and reflect. Reflecting while practicing means that I build in milestones so I can assess how things have turned out at their various stages and allow for modifications and adjustments.

As noted in Box 5.2, identifying and applying best practice is a core element of many planner's practice. I am continually on the lookout for best practice in parking management to support my consulting practice. Planners attend conferences to harvest best practice ideas from presentations and borrow from award-winning projects. There are, however, downsides to uncritical application of best practice. Box 5.3 (next page) provides a review of those downsides and some ways of addressing them.

Box 5.3 Best Practice: Mindless Repetition or Effective Strategy?

Best practice plays a role when planners and decision-makers ask, "Where has this been done before?" Planning awards programs elevate certain planning efforts as examples to be emulated. Rather than rely on a theory or theories to guide planning, practitioners scan for applicable, and successful, plans or programs. This box discusses criticisms of this approach and suggests ways of making best practice justifications work well.

At its worst, best practice is the blind leading the blind. For examples, cities commonly copy the parking requirements of neighboring cities in setting their own requirements. This reduces the risk that their requirements are more stringent than their neighbors, which might reduce their ability to attract development. The problem is that if the other cities' requirements are excessive, then cities follow one another in collectively overrequiring parking. This lowers density, undermines sustainability, and promotes solo driving. Copying parking requirements also replicates the power relationships in those cities, where drivers' rights are elevated over those who use transit, walk, or bicycle.

Searching for best practices lessens the demand for original thought and innovation. It reduces experimentation, as planners cannot convince decision-makers to try an approach without providing an example of where it has been done. City managers often won't attempt an approach that has not been implemented in a comparable city. But a best practice approach can go astray if insufficient attention is placed on the applicability of an approach from one place to another. What works in one economic, social, and political context does not necessarily work in another.

There are, however, justifications for best practice, as noted by Salazar in Box 5.2. The reason why practitioners seek best practice is that they need to see the idea in action and with its full context. Studying best practice reveals unanticipated consequences that may emerge in implementation, known as theory failure (the idea was wrong) or program failure (poor implementation resulted in failure), or a combination of the two. Best practice shows how all the systems in place react to the intervention, which can reveal unanticipated consequences. For example, a well-meaning attempt to improve design standards for granny flats may lead to more unpermitted construction, and health and safety harms associated with those practices.

Best practice works when practitioners know that the prospects of an idea depend heavily on the implementation context. They are attentive to whether similar conditions exist in the best practice comparison city and are adept a judging whether an approach will work in a different context. For example, a business improvement district will fare differently in a district with owner-occupied businesses versus absentee property owners.

Best practice consideration is engrained in planning practice for some good reasons. The key to making it work is to critically examine the effects of best practices and to attend to the role of context in discerning whether an approach used in one place is appropriate for another.

The fifth and sixth rows of Table 5.3 describe traditional planning justifications: managing the pace of change and impacts so that they do not exceed a community's capacity to absorb them, and regulating development so it meets land use and design norms. While some places are declining rather than growing, a core role for planning in growing communities is moderating growth and making it compatible with existing built form. This occurs by applying land use and design norms to new development proposals such as building setback, height limits, or street frontage treatments. Zoning, subdivision regulations, and design review provide these functions. The last row in Table 5.3 addresses fiscal stewardship, economic vitality, sustainability, and legal conformity – realms in which planners seek to shape decisions for the long-term health of the community and in ways that sustain legal conformity.

Convention helps society navigate the dynamic and disruptive processes of urbanization by moderating the pace and extent of change so that it can be accommodated. Of course, applying convention can be entirely the wrong approach. The type of convention required by traditional zoning, for example, has produced bland suburban environments in which place is hard to discern. Similarly, applying a convention that "everybody drives" results in cities that disadvantage those who cannot, choose not to, or cannot afford to drive, and it makes transit service uneconomic.

Convention's dark side is evident when claims about community character are used to exclude low-income renters, minorities, and immigrants; to round up homeless people; to deny services in multiple languages; and a host of other actions that are opposite to planning ideals. For example, minimum parking requirements for apartments prohibit developers from building units without parking for those seeking lower housing costs. Or, a planner could have a habit of ignoring a particular group in the community because of a negative interaction, stereotypes, racism, or barriers to interaction. Convention can be a lazy practice, reflecting blindness to issues and perspectives, and it can be code language for discrimination and exclusion based on class, race, or other personal characteristics. Planners benefit from a self-aware, self-reflective approach to their role in applying convention.

Invention

Invention is a hallmark of planning; Table 5.4 provides examples. One aspect of invention is new forms of planning processes, such as negotiation, community reconciliation, or problem-solving. Such invention is often called for when planners are stuck, stymied, and have reached a roadblock. Invention is

Table 5.4 Invention in the Planning Episode

Dimension	Examples
Community engagement	• Illuminate limiting narratives, disrupt hegemonic stories. • Reframe issues to identify new approaches. • Foster new community stories and visions through planning and art processes.
Innovative planning methods	• Employ design charettes and participatory workshops. • Brainstorm and conduct iterative process. • Organize mutual gain negotiations. • Recover community memory and process issues through creative writing, council process.
Institutional arrangements	• Collaborate in problem-solving within and among organizations. • Organize public–private partnerships. • Arrange cross-disciplinary teams.
Forms of power and influence	• Engage in community organizing to produce new community and political leaders. • Create forums for the representation of community groups such as youth in planning.
New analytical methods	• Harness big data to understand planning issues. • Advance statistical techniques to recognize simultaneity in causal relationships.
Experiments	• Develop pilot projects, reversible initiatives. • Create kit-of-parts programs to allow grassroots, community-based initiation of improvements such as parklets.
Plans, policies, and programs	• Broaden the range of approaches considered, e.g., capital investment, pricing/taxing, regulation, and education/marketing. • Enhance comprehensiveness by integrating plans and policies.

also required in methods and planning ideas when existing solutions are insufficient or there are no precedents. In those cases, planners invent by developing new methodologies, fresh visions, innovative plans and regulations, novel development programs, and create new tools for implementation.

The first row of Table 5.4 addresses invention in community engagement. Planners create new forms of community engagement such as grassroots efforts that meet community members where they are. The second row highlights innovative planning process methods that reframe issues and foster community stories about the future through urban design charette, which generates design ideas with a brainstorming approach that emphasizes new ideas. The third row describes institutional or working arrangements such as new forms of interdisciplinary teams. The fourth row describes community organizing as a way to generate new forms of power and influence for underrepresented members of the community and new community leaders and elected officials. The fifth row recognizes invention in analytic methods such as scenario development models or the use of activity-based transportation models to understand multimodal transportation demand.

Invention is sometimes provisional; the sixth row of Table 5.4 discusses the use of experiments in process and strategy. These are pilot projects that can be assessed, and revised or reversed if they do not work as intended. This frees up creativity because greater risk can be taken if the project is reversible. Bike corrals, parklets, and road diet projects are examples of these. The seventh row discusses innovation in new types of plans, policies, or programs. In the realm of programs, for instance, transportation planners invent when they use travel demand management instead of a traditional predict-and-provide approach. Recently, planners have advocated pricing consumption of scarce resources as an alternative to regulating it, such as found in carbon taxes and carbon trading mechanisms.

Interactions Within and Outside the Framework

Figure 5.2 provides a detailed representation of the framework that was introduced in Figure 1.1 (see Chapter 1), showing all terms and prompts. Two new features are included. The first feature is the clouds shown above and below the planning episode, separating it from planner-as-person and context. This symbolizes the inevitably imperfect understanding of how the planning episode is connected to these realms, obscured by many forms of uncertainty, ambiguity, and incongruency. Yet a successful planning episode depends on a good assessment of context, and a successful planning career requires congruity between the planner-as-person and the planning work. In the case accounts, the authors discuss instances when they were unsure if they were reading the context accurately and the level of congruence they experienced between planner-as-person and the roles they played.

Figure 5.2 also adds multiple, miniature versions of the planning episode graphic, shown on the right-hand side of the diagram as *interactions, dialogues, and learning with others.* Planners work in webs of interactions and networks with people, organizations, and informal groups, all of whom bring their own frameworks of understanding to interactions and collaboration. This includes other planners within and outside their department, other professionals, elected and appointed officials, community members, stakeholder groups, developers,

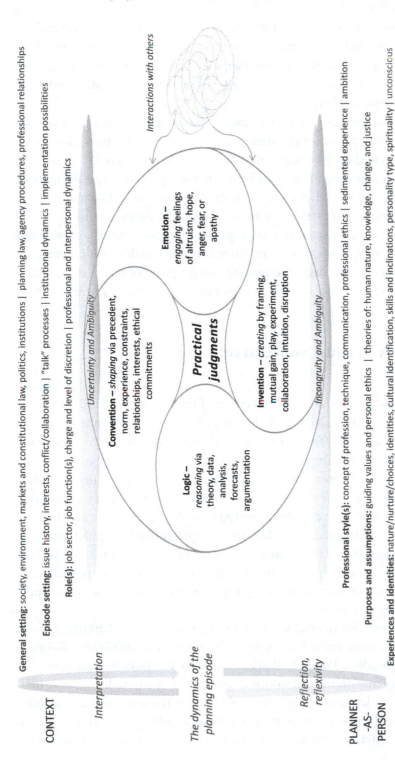

Figure 5.2 Reflection Framework With Prompts

individual constituents, and many others. Each other party has its own framework of interpretation; planners speak, listen, collaborate, learn, and negotiate with individuals bringing varied frameworks of meaning and action.

This interaction is fruitful if based on self-awareness of a planner's own framework and a curiosity about the frameworks of others. Planners cannot impose their mental model of the episode on others, nor can they expect others to see things as they do. Acknowledging that complexity and interdependence, there are some ways to make this communication less daunting.

The first step is to recognize that frameworks, whether explicit or implicit, are used to make meaning by the parties with whom the planner interacts. Second, a planner can become more self-aware of their own assumptions, perceptions, and ways of acting by reflecting on their own framework, whether it be similar to Figure 5.2 or something different. Last, through experience and dialogue, a planner can learn about the frameworks of other planners. They can also learn about frameworks of architects (e.g., design), engineers (e.g., design and problem-solve), developers (e.g., return on investment), elected officials (e.g., reelection), residents (e.g., neighborhood quality), homeowners (e.g., property values), environmental activists (e.g., scientific evidence), social activists (e.g., justice), community organizers (e.g., power and mutual learning), or lawyers (e.g., agreement clarity and risk minimization).

The Dynamic Nature of Practice

The case authors use the Figure 5.2 framework to interpret planning episodes and explain the practical judgments they made. Across the cases, there are different planner-as-person identities, contexts, and approaches to logic/emotion and convention/invention. Even so, most of the cases touch on all elements in the framework. Planners proceed in a dynamic way through the planning episode, which calls for attentive practice, attuned to context, and strategic action in the moment.

Figure 5.3 arrays the logic/emotion, convention/invention elements. Let's consider a hypothetical case in which a resident is seeking a permit to build an accessory dwelling unit in their backyard. In reviewing the resident's proposal, the planner applies convention in the form of interpreting the zoning code and finds that the project does not meet the sideyard setback. The episode, therefore, starts in the logic/convention quadrant. The applicant becomes angry upon hearing this, disparages government "bureaucrats," and threatens to call elected officials with complaints about unresponsive planners. The planning episode moves to the emotional dimension. Despite the

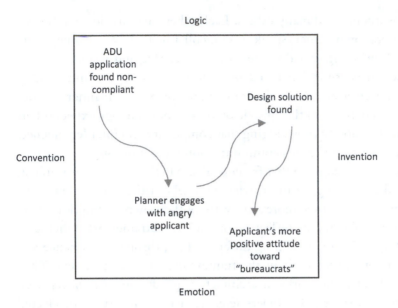

Figure 5.3 Interplay of Reason and Methods

slight and threat, the planner stays engaged, acknowledges the applicant's anger, and asks if the applicant would like to brainstorm design solutions. The applicant is skeptical that the planner really intends to help but is willing to listen because the alternative is to give up on the project. The planner acknowledges the frustration of missing the standard by a small amount, explains the reasons for the sideyard setback, and gives some examples of how that regulation has benefited the community. After a pause, the applicant agrees to explore solutions to the problem. The episode moves to the invention side of the diagram. The planner sees an opportunity for a small, low-cost design change that would meet the code. The applicant agrees to the change and the issue is successfully resolved.

This ultimately happy scenario could have broken down at many points. The planner could have stuck to the noncompliance determination with the rationale that designing the project is the job of the applicant and their architect. The applicant could have insulted the planner to the point where the planner was unwilling to continue the conversation. And the small design change might have created an expensive redesign, added to construction cost, or created another issue that causes a neighbor to object to the project. The point is that a seemingly technical planning job at the zoning counter, normally thought of as in the logic/convention mode, involves significant emotional work and invention. The payoff for the planner is facilitating the production of an additional housing unit, having a positive interaction with a constituent, and, more generally, increasing faith in government. Using field observation, Hoch provides a rich account of a planner engaging with constituents on a sideyard fence location issue that reveals similar dynamics (Hoch 2019, 27–28)

And Now to You: Making Practical Judgments on the Fly

This idea that planners engage logic, emotion, convention, and invention is not comforting to those who expect planning to be clear-cut. Moving between logic and emotion may lead you to ask, "What I am doing here? What is my job, a scientist or a psychologist?" Similarly, switching back and forth between regulatory work (convention) and design innovation and problem-solving (invention) might seem like two different jobs for two different types of professionals. But that is planning. The ability to engage all four dimensions appropriate to a planning episode makes planning intellectually engaging, keeps you growing, and allows you to be a versatile and effective actor in private, public, and nonprofit settings. The lack of stable ground may feel like vertigo if you are unprepared for it, or feel like the exhilaration of surfing if you accept it.

Previously, I mentioned ambiguity in the realm between the planning episode and context, and between the planning episode and the planner-as-person. Planning episodes are replete with ambiguity. Effective planning, therefore, requires ambiguity tolerance – being comfortable in a shifting process that requires full engagement, does not offer certainty and may involve cognitive dissonance. This may be innate for some, but it can be cultivated over time. At its core, it reflects curiosity and a love of learning.

The case studies in the chapters that follow provide first-person accounts of what really happened in seven planning episodes. They show how planners think, feel, and act in the shifting landscape of the planning episode. None of them provided an opportunity for the planner to set up shop, so to speak, with one planning theory or another, but rather required them to move through the planning episode with their eyes and hearts open. We hope you will read our accounts with the same sentiment.

Discussion Questions

1. What is your reaction to the claim that professional planning requires practical judgments? Do you agree? If so, does that understanding make

you excited about your practice career or concerned about the responsibility of making practical judgments?

2. Which comes to you more naturally, logic or emotional work? How can you increase your capacity in the realm that does not come naturally to you?

3. Which comes to you more naturally, convention or invention? How can you increase your capacity in the realm that does not come naturally to you?

4. Take a practical judgment you have made at some point in your work career. Retrace your steps and understand how you made it. Do the logic/emotion or convention/invention pairs have relevance?

References

Baum, Howell. 2015. "Planning with Half a Mind: Why Planners Resist Emotion." *Planning Theory & Practice*, 16(4): 498–516. doi: 10.1080/14649357.2015.1071870.

Bolan, Richard. 1980. "The Practitioner as Theorist: The Phenomenology of the Professional Episode." *Journal of the American Planning Association*, 46(3): 261–274. doi: 10.1080/01944368008977042.

Bolton, Gillie. 2009. *Writing and Professional Development*, 3rd edition. London: Sage Publications Inc.

Brooks, David. 2002. *Planning Theory for Practitioners*. Chicago, IL: American Planning Association.

Davidoff, Paul. 1965. "Advocacy and Pluralism in Planning." *Journal of the American Institute of Planners*, 31(4): 331–338. doi: 10.1080/01944366508978187.

Fainstein, Norman and Susan Fainstein. 1979. "New Debates in Urban Planning: The Impact of Marxist Theory Within the United States." *International Journal of Urban & Regional Research*, 3(1:4): 381–403. doi: 10.1111/j.1468-2427.1979.tb00796.x.

Faludi, Andrei. 1973. *Planning Theory*. Elmsford: Pergamon Press.

Forester, John. 1989. *Planning in the Face of Power*. Berkeley, CA: University of California Press.

Friedmann, John. 1973. *Retracking America: A Theory of Transactive Planning*. Garden City, NY: Anchor Press.

Healey, Patsy. 1997. *Collaborative Planning: Shaping Places in Fragmented Societies*. London: Macmillan Press Ltd.

Hoch, Charles. 2006. "Emotions and Planning." *Planning Theory & Practice*, 7(4): 367–382. doi: 10.1080.14649350600984436.

Hoch, Charles. 2019. *Pragmatic Spatial Planning*. New York: Routledge.

Hopkins, Lewis D. 2001. *Urban Development: The Logic of Making Plans*. Washington, DC: Island Press.

Innes, Judith and David Booher. 2018. *Planning with Complexity: An Introduction to Collaborative Rationality for Public Policy*. New York: Routledge.

Krumholz, Norman and John Forester. 1990. *Making Equity Planning Work*. Philadelphia, PA: Temple University Press.

Lekan, Todd. 2003. *Making Morality: Pragmatist Reconstruction in Ethical Theory*. Nashville, TN: Vanderbilt University Press.

Lindblom, Charles. 1959. "The Science of 'Muddling Through'." *Public Administration Review*, 19(2): 79–88.

Marris, Peter. 1974. *Loss and Change*. London: Routledge and Kegan Paul.

Moghadam, Seyed Navid Mashhadi and Mojtaba Rafieian. 2019. "If Foucault Were an Urban Planner: An Epistemology of Power in Planning Theories." *Cogent Arts & Humanities*, 6(1): 1–17. doi: 10.1080/23311983.2019.1592065.

Shafer, Roy. 1976. *A New Language for Psychoanalysis*. New Haven, CT: Yale University Press.

Simon, Herbert. 1972. "Theories of Bounded Rationality." In: *Decisions and Organization*, edited by C. McGuire and R. Radner, pp. 161–176. Amsterdam: North-Holland.

Talvitie, Antti. 1997. "Things Planners Believe in, and Things They Deny." *Transportation*, 24(1): 1–31. doi: 10.1023/A:1017957016112.

Whittemore, Andrew H. 2015. "Practitioners Theorize, Too: Reaffirming Planning Theory in a Survey of Practitioners' Theories." *Journal of Planning Education & Research*, 35(1): 76–85. doi: 10.1177%2F0739456X14563144.

Chapter 6

Creating a Climate Action Plan at Cal Poly Pomona

The California State Polytechnic University, Pomona (Cal Poly Pomona, also CPP) *Climate Action Plan: Pathway to Climate Neutrality* (CAP) is a case study of developing an environmental plan. It examines how the CAP was created to support a goal of a carbon-neutral campus. The discussion traces the author's role as a consultant to CPP, on a special assignment from serving as a professor in the Department of Urban and Regional Planning. It highlights three practical judgments: (i) proceeding under conditions of technical uncertainty, (ii) using cost-effectiveness analysis to select measures, and (iii) determining the scope of the plan. Since the CAP was adopted in 2009, notes on how the plan fared over time are also included.

Campus planning is an important field of planning in itself and has application to other large-scale activity centers that have a mix of land uses, activities, and user groups, such as workplaces and hospitals. The case also relates to planning opportunities where land and resources are under the control of a single entity such as a port complex or master-planned community. Lastly, the case shows the dynamics of planning decision-making under an executive management structure similar to a consulting agency or private company.

The CAP was a new initiative for CPP that had no precedent and few constraints on its development. The planning team had autonomy and flexibility to design the planning process and content, following a top-down mandate from the CPP president. As "blank sheet" planning, the case is differentiated from settings where legal requirements, precedents, and protocols shape process, form, and content. Opportunities like the CAP arise when there is a new subject for which legal requirements do not yet exist and/or where innovation is required.

The CAP mandate was to develop a climate action plan to guide CPP toward carbon neutrality by 2030. Carbon neutrality means that the CPP's direct and indirect greenhouse gas (GHG) emissions are zero, accomplished by reductions in campus emissions and/or reductions that take place elsewhere to offset campus emissions.

Increasing GHG emissions associated with human activity has led to rising global average land and sea temperatures, sea level rise, extreme weather patterns, and threats to ecosystems (IPCC] n.d.). Box 6.1 (next page) provides background on climate change and key terms. At the time of the project, CPP's sources of emissions, in order of magnitude, were transportation to and from campus; electricity consumption purchased from a utility; on–campus energy consumption, e.g., burning natural gas; and amounts from solid waste, agricultural operations, and refrigerants. As a commuter-oriented campus, carbon neutrality was and is an audacious goal since commuting trips are counted as campus emissions, yet CPP does not have influence over surrounding land use or transportation systems.

Description of the Planning Episode

The intended outcome of the CAP was selecting and programming GHG reduction measures to reach carbon neutrality by 2030, effectuated through an adopted plan that specifies benchmarks and implementation procedures.[1] The CAP's quantitative target of zero net emissions offered a direct measure of implementation progress. This chapter reviews the one-year CAP development process in the 2008–2009 period (Willson and Brown 2008, Willson 2011). I was hired on a consulting summer appointment to participate on the team.

Institutional Setting

Cal Poly Pomona is a large organization and midsized university, with a current student body of about 26,000 students, and about 1,200 faculty and 1,200 staff (Cal Poly Pomona 2019). The campus is located about 30 miles east of

Box 6.1 Glossary of Climate Change Concepts and Terms

Concepts

Global climate change refers to climate and natural system responses to anthropogenic (human-caused) greenhouse gases being added to the atmosphere in the industrial period. The primary greenhouse gases (GHG) are carbon dioxide, methane, nitrous oxide, and fluorinated gases. Fossil fuel consumption accounts for roughly three-quarters of carbon dioxide emissions in the U.S. Increased concentration of these gases in the atmosphere has caused raised global air and sea temperatures since the 1950s, decreased snow and ice, and increased extreme weather events with widespread effects on human and natural systems. Global carbon dioxide concentrations continue to increase despite attempts to reduce emissions. The state of knowledge in climate change science and policy responses can be found in the resources of the Intergovernmental Panel on Climate Change (IPCC). This UN-sponsored group produces summaries of research about climate change and responses to it (www.ipcc.ch).

Terms

CAP – climate action plan.

carbon neutral – a condition of zero net GHG emissions accomplished by reducing or eliminating emissions from each source, generating renewable energy on campus, sequestering carbon through tree planting or carbon capture, and/or causing emissions to be reduced elsewhere, such as purchasing carbon offsets.

climate action planning – efforts drawing on science, social science, and design fields to (i) reduce emissions and (ii) develop ways to adapt to changes underway.

eCO_2 – a calculation of the carbon dioxide equivalent of all GHG, summed to determine a measure in CO_2 units. The calculation considers the potency of each gas and its length of life in the atmosphere.

GHG – greenhouse gases, including the following:

  CO_2 – carbon dioxide (82% of U.S. emissions)
  CH_4 – methane (10% of U.S. emission)
  N_2O – nitrous oxides (6% of U.S. emissions)
  Fluorinated gases, e.g., HFC, PFC, SF_6, NF_3 – gases associated with refrigerants, propellants solvents, etc. (3% of U.S. emissions)

downtown Los Angeles in Pomona, California. It is 1,400 acres in size with a suburban campus design and has sizable agricultural activities. While there are some campus dorms, most students commute. These features lead to a high dependence on single-occupancy (driving alone) commuting: 83% for faculty, 71% for staff, and 79% for students (Kim and Willson 2016). Figure 6.1 shows the campus as located at the eastern edge of Los Angeles County in the larger Southern California region. An image of a portion of the campus built-form and layout is shown in Figure 6.2.

CPP is notable for a learn-by-doing motto and professional schools in engineering, business, environmental design, and hospitality management, along with liberal arts, social sciences, and education. The student composition is diverse, with about 45% of students identifying as Hispanic/Latino (any race), 21% identifying as Asian Only, 16% identifying as White Only, and 3% identifying as Black/African American Only (Cal Poly Pomona 2019). Tuition is affordable. Many students are the first in their family to attend college, and the campus is nationally recognized for its role in advancing social mobility.

The CPP president is advised by a cabinet comprised of vice presidents of divisions and the Cal Poly Pomona Foundation Inc. (CPP Foundation), which operates certain campus services and develops resources for the institution. CPP is part of the 23-campus California State University system that enrolls almost half a million students. There is significant system-level oversight of member campuses, with ultimate accountability to the state legislature.

Figure 6.1 Cal Poly Pomona Regional Context. Image source: Google, Landsat/Copernicus

Figure 6.2 Cal Poly Pomona Campus. Image source: Author

CPP has a track record of environmentalism as an early adopter of reclaimed water and host to the John T. Lyle Center for Regenerative Studies (LCRS) established in 1994. The LCRS program is an interdisciplinary approach to sustainability that seeks renewal of natural processes, community action, and human behavior. Prior to the CAP, various campus stakeholders, staff, and students worked on green initiatives independently.

While CPP's environmental record is a source of pride to campus stakeholders, CPP operations generate substantial emissions. Because of the campus's relatively new buildings, combined with state energy efficiency requirements, campus buildings are energy efficient. As well, the sources of purchased electricity are greener than those in most other states. However, CPP is located in a suburban setting and developed with an assumption that the private automobile was the primary travel mode. The campus has separated uses, abundant surface parking, and commuting levels that generate substantial pollution and GHG emissions. CPP agricultural operations also produce GHG emissions.

Overview of Planning Process

The CAP was an initiative taken as part of the American College & University Presidents' Climate Commitment, now a program of Second Nature, a nonprofit organization devoted to accelerating climate action in, and through, higher education. The planning process responded to the charge to develop a CAP in response to the Climate Commitment program. The program was intended to generate university leadership support for climate action and establish accountability through public posting of commitments and implementation progress.

The Climate Commitment specified elements of the planning process that included (i) conducting a GHG inventory; (ii) setting a target date and interim milestones for climate neutrality; (iii) taking immediate action by selecting from a list of short-term measures; (iv) integrating sustainability into the curriculum; and (v) making the action plan, inventory, and progress reports publicly available.

The faculty–student team that developed the CAP included two faculty members: Kyle Brown (then-director of LCRS) and me (professor of Urban and Regional Planning). The team also included LCRS master's students Cristina Halstead, Michelle McFadden, and Anne Pandey. The plan was developed in the 2008–2009 period. The team's expertise included urban and regional planning, landscape architecture, and regenerative studies. The effort was guided by a cross-divisional Sustainability Task Force co-chaired by Ed Barnes, vice president of Administrative Affairs, and Brown. Box 6.2 (next page) provides a summary of key individuals and groups involved in the effort.

The team selected and operationalized a GHG emissions forecasting model, made GHG predictions for a base-case 2030 scenario, and developed an annual GHG reduction target toward the 2030 zero emissions target. Then we evaluated candidate GHG reduction measures and wrote a plan specifying benchmarks and implementation measures.

A Sustainability Task Force of 20-plus internal stakeholders met regularly. Members included vice presidents of campus divisions, implementing staff and managers, leader of the CPP Foundation, faculty, students, and other campus stakeholders. Campus workshops were held concerning the draft plan. Work products were reviewed by the Sustainability Task Force, composed of campus stakeholders, and the plan was adopted by the CPP President's Cabinet.

Completing the CAP in-house rather than by outside consultants was consistent with the CPP's learn-by-doing commitment. The initiative required cooperation across organizational units because strategies affected elements such as energy purchases, transportation access, facility operations, class scheduling, environmental education, campus life, and the operations of the CPP Foundation. There were no California university CAP examples to draw upon, as climate planning at that time was primarily carried

---

Box 6.2 CAP Participants and Groups

Participants

Dr. Michael J. Ortiz, President (2003–2014), retired

Dr. Edwin Barnes, Vice President, Division of Administrative Affairs, Co-Chair, Sustainable Task Force (2006–2013), retired

Dr. Kyle Brown, Director, John T. Lyle Center for Regenerative Studies and Co-Chair, Sustainable Task Force (2004–2017), CAP co-author, current Professor, Department of Landscape Architecture

Dr. Richard Willson, Professor, Department of Urban and Regional Planning, CAP co-author

Key CPP Individuals and Groups Mentioned in the Case

Current University President: Dr. Soraya Coley, President (2015 to present)

Academic Senate – recommends curriculum matters to the President

Associated Students, Inc. (ASI) – student government and operations of student facilities

Cal Poly Pomona Foundation Inc. – fiduciary responsibility for business and facility operations and resource development

President's Cabinet – decision-making body composed of division Vice Presidents

Sustainability Task Force – advisory group for climate change planning, including faculty, staff, Cal Poly Pomona Foundation, and students

---

out through state agencies, such as the California Environmental Protection Agency and California Air Resources Board, and by local governments. Common local government practices included adopting GHG policy statements, conducting GHG inventories, and prioritizing GHG mitigation measures.[2]

The Core Problem

The core problem was achieving carbon neutrality to fulfill the Climate Commitment. Top-down leadership support was met by bottom–up enthusiasm from faculty, students, and some staff. Disagreements were largely confined to technical concerns about the type of measures, speed of implementation, and/or cost.

Intended and Actual Outcomes

In seeking carbon neutrality by 2030, the CAP addressed Scope 1 (direct emissions controlled by CPP), Scope 2 (indirect emissions as the result of CPP operations, such as purchased electricity), and Scope 3 (indirect emissions from CPP activities outside the direct influence of the campus, such as students commuting to campus). The CAP included nine benchmarks for each emission category. Figure 6.3 shows the CAP's proposed trajectory from over 60,000 metric tonnes per year in 2009 to 20,000 metric tonnes in 2030. Carbon offsets were proposed to reduce the last 20,000 metric tonnes to zero.

The plan was adopted by the President's Cabinet in 2009. It called for climate change educational initiatives and the consideration of alternative class scheduling and online learning to reduce commuting. These matters are within the purview of the campus Academic Senate, but it did not formally consider or adopt the CAP. Similarly, the Associated Students, Inc. (the student senate) and the CPP Foundation did not consider or adopt the CAP. Those groups were represented on the Sustainability Task Force, so their input was received, but formal approvals were not sought. Monitoring and implementation activities followed plan adoption, supported by the Sustainability Task Force and staff in operational departments.

As mentioned, the only way to reach carbon neutrality was to purchase carbon offsets for about one-third of the emissions. In buying offsets, CPP would pay others to reduce emissions elsewhere on the CPP's behalf. This can efficiently reduce carbon emissions, as an industrial-scale solar energy

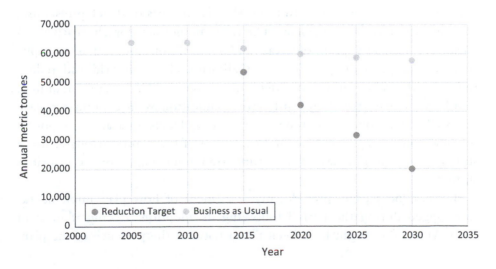

Figure 6.3 Greenhouse Gas Reduction Time Frame

facility in a prime solar insolation zone is less expensive than installing individual rooftop solar panels on campus buildings. Buying carbon offsets takes money away from other campus objectives, however, but this element was accepted because neutrality with solely on-campus actions was deemed infeasible.

The CAP can be better understood using Hopkins's (2001, 36–37) identification of five ways that plans do their work. This helps clarify the frequently multiple functions of plans. According to Hopkins, plans provide:

- Agenda – lists of things to do.
- Policy – if-then rules.
- Vision – images of what could be.
- Design – targets, outcomes.
- Strategy – contingent actions.

The CAP document has all of these functions, not through a deliberate decision but as emerged in the process of plan-writing. The plan articulates the *vision* of carbon neutrality, compelling for many stakeholders, although not as amenable to expression as a traditional physical plan. A lack of emissions cannot be imagined as can a land use or design proposal. Regarding *policy*, the CAP mandates cost-effectiveness analysis in selecting emission-reduction measures. *Agenda* and *design* functions of plans are found in quantified targets, benchmarks and implementation measures.

The *strategy* function of the CAP is limited, as it did not include a SWOT (strengths, weaknesses, opportunities, threats) analysis or develop responses to implementation contingencies. The team did not develop alternative scenarios for academic, technological, and societal conditions. For example, statewide progress in greening the California electrical grid and reducing vehicular GHG emissions affects the extent of CAP action required. Similarly, societal trends toward online education reduce building space required and the amount of student commuting. Devising strategic responses to these contingencies was beyond the scope of the team's mandate. More strategy work might have better supported implementation as priorities shifted.

Box 6.3 (next page) provides my assessment of how plan implementation lagged during the period following its adoption. Asking if most of the CAP actions might have been taken without the presence of the plan,

Box 6.4 (next page) summarizes a separate CAP evaluation study (Alexander 2014). That research concludes that the plan produced social, political, and intellectual capital that would not have been realized without the CAP effort.

Box 6.3 Plan Implementation Under Changing Leadership

Unconstrained plan-making opportunities carry a risk that they lack long-term, institutionalized implementation support. In this case, the CAP implementation commitment declined in the decade after its 2009 adoption. One factor in that decline is that the champions of the effort retired or followed new priorities. The campus president who signed the Climate Commitment retired in 2014 (Ortiz). The Sustainability Task Force stopped meeting in 2014, after the divisional vice president co-chair retired in 2013 (Barnes) and the faculty co-chair (Brown) moved on to new projects. Core responsibilities shifted to discrete tasks assigned to staff members.

Current CPP President Dr. Soraya Coley arrived in 2015, and members of the cabinet of Division Vice Presidents changed, save one person. This transition occurred just after the Cal State University (CSU) Board of Trustees adopted a Sustainability Policy in 2014, including systemwide GHG reduction targets. CSU commissioned a 2017 assessment showing that 11 of 23 campuses had published a climate action plan (Cal State University 2017). These reports may have indirectly lessened campus-level impetus to implement because they indicated that the CSU would prepare a Systemwide Climate Action and Implementation Plan in 2018. It was conceivable that state actions building efficiency, renewable energy, and sustainable transportation could preclude the need for local campus action.

As mentioned, the President's Cabinet adopted the plan, but since campus constituencies such as the Academic Senate, Associated Students, Inc., and the CPP Foundation did not they had less "ownership" of implementation. The impacts of the Great Recession on budgets and staffing also lessened implementation efforts as the institution focused on its core task of educating students.

The shift of implementation responsibility from an administrator/faculty pair to staff members reduced the visibility of the effort, severed the link with faculty and academic governance, and likely reduced implementation resources. Inventory updates were completed, but no comprehensive, documented inventory has been completed since 2009. The 2018 emissions update shows approximately 44,803 metric tonnes of emissions, but there was no independent faculty expert review of the methodology. A 2019 Climate Action Plan update on the Second Nature site restates the original plan's target and benchmarks but does not offer specifics on implementation.[3]

Box 6.4 Assessment of Plan Legacies

Serena E. Alexander, Assistant Professor, Department of Urban & Regional Planning, San Jose State University

My evaluation of the CAP focused on two major questions: (i) Could CPP achieve similar GHG emissions reduction without a CAP? (ii) What factors contributed to slow or stalled progress toward meeting CAP goals?

The results of the evaluation indicated that GHG emissions reduction actions could have been taken in the absence of the CAP, but the planning process yielded social, political, and intellectual capital that are essential for long-term success. The CAP development process led to enhanced intellectual capital by helping the CPP community to (i) better define the problem; (ii) develop an agreed-upon fact base; (iii) engage faculty, staff, and students in a productive collective learning process; (iv) raise public awareness about climate action on campus and beyond; (v) develop innovative strategies; and (vi) establish partnerships with external entities and individuals committed to sustainability. Additionally, the CAP provided a framework for effective communication, collaboration, and coordination among various CPP divisions, departments, and offices, thereby contributing to social and political capital.

In areas where progress was slow or stalled, there was a lack of effective collaboration, a mismatch between plan strategies and organizational norms, or a perceived or real lack of efficacy. Although the CAP process created new collaborations among different departments and divisions, CPP's climate action planning network was not evenly distributed among the entire campus community. As a result, although individual faculty members added climate education materials to their syllabi, incorporation of climate awareness into the curriculum was not formalized in the entire university. Another major hurdle was the outcome of a mismatch between priorities and strategies of a CAP with that of the university's. For example, CPP values face-to-face interactions and hands-on learning in a traditional classroom environment, whereas the CAP encourages online classes that reduce transportation emissions. Lastly, slow or stalled progress was evident in areas where CPP community members expressed concerns about a lack of efficacy for GHG reduction, especially where outcomes were seen as beyond CPP's control. For example, CPP had little control over transportation emissions because of the mobility requirements of its diverse population and the insufficiency of viable public transportation options.

No matter how successful the implementation of a CAP is, the planning process leaves legacies – even if the plan itself gradually fades away. Not all of those legacies are direct or tangible, and it is essential for evaluators to assess both the tangible and intangible impacts. There is a tendency to only measure the direct effects of a climate action plan (e.g., the reduced amount of GHG emissions) and ignore the outcomes that might be difficult to measure. This might lead, for example, to underestimating the value of the intellectual capital that accrues to the organization or the society as a whole.

Examination of the Planning Episode Using Framework Elements

This section addresses planner-as-person elements, context, and the ways in which reasoning and methods were employed.

Planner-as-Person Elements That Shaped the Approach

The CAP was an opportunity to work on a project in my field at my own institution, bringing together my academic and consulting identities. I have taught in CPP's practice-oriented planning program since 1986 and was team-teaching a LCRS climate change planning course with Brown in 2009.

Personal Framework Elements

My planning practice during this period was transportation planning in the rational/analytic style. I wasn't an environmental planner but my transportation work sought to reduce environmental impacts. Sharing views with researchers who use an economics approach to public policy, I was motivated to seek policies that are efficient, sustainable, and equitable.

My transportation expertise was relevant to the CAP transportation initiatives, but aspects such as green building technology or integrated landscape management were outside of it. In those instances, I applied research, policy analysis, and plan-making skills to these new topic areas.

The underlying assumption of my approach was that decision-makers seek and respond to good evidence, leading to an analytical concept of expertise – providing research-based information on effective GHG reduction strategies. I hoped that evidence would lead to selection of cost-effective GHG mitigation measures and the rejection of boondoggles, symbolic but ineffective projects, and executives' pet projects.

Despite my commitment to evidence, progress depends on people changing their minds, a complicated human and communicative affair. At the time, I was exploring communicative approaches to transportation planning and academic governance (Willson 2001, 2003). Although my "turn" toward communicative planning was in process during this time, the clear-cut technical nature of the assignment displaced a communicative action approach.

Personal Incongruity and Ambiguity

The assignment supported my desire to create local action to reduce GHG emissions, providing congruity between my personal commitments and the

CAP. Many aspects of the work were outside my core expertise, but I accepted a steep learning curve. Unlike other consulting assignments in which my values might be at odds with goals of clients' and other stakeholders, I agreed with the goal; furthermore, the team had the freedom to devise an optimal plan within time and budget constraints.

Interpretation of Context

The context for the planning episode has similarities to municipal planning in that there were many functional departments and a wide variety of stakeholders. The difference is that managers made the decisions, not elected officials. The President's Cabinet met, deliberated, and decided; its process of receiving recommendations was less formal than in a typical city. As mentioned, other campus units had significant authority (see Box 6.2). Lastly, all actions were required to comply with the Cal State University system rules, in response to a Board of Trustees and, ultimately, the state legislature.

Context Framework Elements

My previous CPP work as a department chair and a campus strategic planner provided insight into institutional goals and processes, but I had little information on the positions and backgrounds of stakeholders regarding climate change, or cabinet-level policy processes. President Ortiz signed the Climate Commitment at an out-of-town conference without consulting campus stakeholders or his cabinet. I lacked information on why he signed the commitment and how operational departments would respond to specific mitigation proposals.

Unlike situations in which planners must make a case for an initiative, this one was handed to the team, supporting work we were already doing. There was enthusiasm among the team and many stakeholders. Other administrators may have seen the effort as a diversion from the CPP's core purpose – delivering education – but the strong leadership commitment may have discouraged dissenting stakeholders from speaking openly against it. Because no opposition was expressed, possible arguments against the effort were not known to the project team.

I was accustomed to encountering resistance to change, so the openness of the assignment, and the support for action, was stirring and somewhat disorienting.

My assessment of context included a sensitivity to a potential cultural split that can exist between faculty and administrators. In previous experiences as department chair, interim dean, and academic strategic planner, I found that some administrators viewed faculty as theoretical and ineffective in the "real world." Some faculty members, in turn, viewed administrators as "make-work" bureaucrats who do not contribute directly to students' educations. In this case, the CAP process mixed faculty and administrators together in ways that appeared to reduce such characterizations.

Overall, the CAP effort had a positive effect on organizational culture. While organizational conflicts were present in dialogues, the usual divide between managers/staff and faculty was bridged through the activities of the Sustainability Task Force because it was co-chaired by an administrator (Barnes) and a faculty member (Brown). In addition, the faculty members on the committee were practical-minded, reducing stereotypes of faculty as thinkers who don't know how to do anything. The initiative and enthusiasm of staff reduced faculty stereotypes of staff as bureaucrats who are unwilling to innovate. The experience of working together provided a positive example of administration–academic cooperation. It was inspiring and seemed to make participants feel good about their institution.

Context Uncertainty and Ambiguity

This initiative challenged assumptions about the identity of CPP, particularly for administrators who viewed the campus as a suburban activity center. Years before this effort, a proposal to build a golf course on environmentally sensitive land revealed a cleavage between campus constituents who had a suburban development vision and those who favored sustainability and compact development. While green buildings and green infrastructure were widely approved of, measures that changed the suburban campus identity were more controversial. Reducing emissions from the transportation sector, for example, requires measures to increase transit use and decrease solo driving. I was unsure of support for these changes across different divisions and among staff in different departments.

An example of an ambiguity was the CPP's ongoing conflict with the local transit operator, Foothill Transit, at the time the CAP was developed. A previous dispute about campus pavement damage by bus operations led CPP to move an on-campus transit center to a less convenient off-campus location. Funds were procured for campus road improvements to allow it to return, but in 2004, in response to inquiries about why the buses were not back on campus, a CPP spokesperson said, "No one has barred Foothill from campus. We have never said they are banned from campus. But where (we want them) on campus still has to be determined" (Roemer 2004). Transportation was the biggest source of campus GHG emissions, but in 2009, buses were still pushed to the edges of the campus. The "happy talk" about a GHG-neutral institution existed in parallel to actions that undermined transit access. I attributed this to attitudes that buses were damaging to pavement, dangerous, and loud; and that "nobody rides the bus," classism, and that buses bring undesirable "outsiders" to campus. The CAP was unable to bring these views to light or subject them to rational analysis. Box 6.5 (next page) provides an account of continued resistance to transit development until President Coley changed direction.

An additional ambiguity about support for the plan is that the 2030 target year for climate neutrality put the CAP's success or failure outside the tenure of CPP's leaders. The benefit of supporting the plan – demonstrating leadership in public policy – was delivered when the plan was adopted. CPP gained positive ratings on sustainability rankings. The costs of implementation, considering money and political capital in advancing institutional change, occur over the lifetime of the plan. As well, we did not consider the challenge of convincing a future-year president to spend scarce campus resources for carbon offsets. Sometimes leaders endorse bold plans knowing the political risk is low and that ex-post (after-the-fact) evaluations are infrequent. Caught up in the excitement of creating the plan, this dynamic did not occur to me at the time or affect how the plan was written. A response to this possibility would have been proposing a fund to bank annual CPP contributions to pay for future emissions offsets.

The Planning Episode: Reasoning and Methods

My role on the CAP focused on designing transportation strategies, developing cost-effectiveness evaluations for prospective measures, and contributing to plan preparation. This section refers to the way in which the elements at the center of Figure 5.2 (see Chapter 5) – logic, emotion, convention, and invention – shaped practical judgments. All four were instrumental in the case.

The ease with which the team's proposed measures were accepted, without argument or extensive scrutiny, was unprecedented for me. On one hand, this motivated the team and made the planning process efficient, but those

Box 6.5 Lagging Progress in Transportation Measures

Progress on GHG emissions associated with campus transportation has lagged since 2009. While continuing to offer rideshare and transit incentives, a de facto policy of prioritizing commuting by car has continued. In 2016, the university opened a new 1,800-space parking garage. The structure increased GHG emissions from transportation by allowing growth in campus population to primarily commute by private vehicle.

After the Sustainability Task Force stopped meeting in 2014, I was not involved in campus climate issues. In 2019, however, President Soraya Coley asked me to advise the campus on parking and transportation. CPP had grown and campus stakeholders were complaining about insufficient parking. CPP was the only university in the subregion without a free student bus-pass program, and prime freeway bus service passed by the campus without stopping. It seemed as if the aggressive transportation goals of the CAP had been forgotten.

As I reengaged in the issue, I encountered mixed attitudes about transit and alternative transportation among campus administrators. Transportation programs were managed by the Police Department, which seemed to prioritize auto drivers and public safety. In 2019, a new CPP express shuttle bus was added to serve remote parking lots, but it passed by the regional bus stop at the edge of campus without stopping. Administrators were either blind to the opportunity to serve transit riders or resisted serving the bus stop. A renewed effort to create a partnership with Foothill Transit, the transit agency serving the campus, was launched in 2019. Progress on transportation measures is proceeding after a 10-year pause.

President Coley is supporting initiatives that will lead to free transit passes for students, expanded bus service and a new transit center, and joint transit marketing. This reengagement was helped along by changes in management personnel. Two people recently appointed to administrative positions formerly worked in Boston, and used transit while there, and an Executive Director of Transportation and Planning has been appointed. The tide has shifted regarding public transit connections.

The delayed action on transportation show that planners cannot rely on the existence of a plan to compel implementation. Administrators and decision-makers continually assess priorities, and plan implementation must compete with other priorities. Plans do so by being relevant, actionable, and, in this case, waiting for the moment when transportation moved near the top of the priority list. Planners should be ready to seize opportunities for advancing implementation.

who were not in favor of climate action may have been hanging back, hoping this initiative would blow over. Staff with line responsibilities had power over implementation; they were on the job full-time while Brown and I were on a temporary assignment. Some were enthusiastic, but if someone was opposed to a certain measure, they could wait out the dissolution of the task-oriented team.

Logic

There was no difficulty identifying candidate GHG reduction ideas in team discussions and committee meetings. Proponents of certain measures argued for them individually without a systematic comparison of their cost and effectiveness. Sometimes, ideas would be popular because they had co-benefits, such as building student dorms, which also promised improved campus life. Other measures had appeal for ribbon-cutting or campus promotion. I prioritized the logic of cost-effective calculations so that potential measures could be ranked and compared with the option of purchasing carbon offsets from off-campus providers, which were available for about $20 per tonne per year at that time.

I advocated for this simple "bang for the buck" metric of cost-effectiveness in evaluating GHG mitigation strategies. The metric is based on the estimated capital costs of a measure, if any, amortized over its life to yield an annualized capital cost. That value is combined with estimates of the measure's annual operating costs and revenues to yield an annualized cost (or revenue) estimate. The effectiveness part of the equation, reduction in annual tons of eCO_2 (defined in Box 6.1), is determined by estimating responses to programs and actions, and entering those forecasts as inputs to the Clean Air–Cool Planet GHG model. The model produces an estimate of eCO_2 with the measure in place, which is compared to a baseline estimate to determine the level of GHG reduction. Then, the cost-effectiveness of candidate measures can be compared. Since some of the reduction strategies were interrelated; they had to be evaluated as packages of measures. For example, increasing the green energy mix reduces the impact of a plug-load reduction program since those consumption reductions are applied to a lower level of GHG emissions per kilowatt hour associated with green electricity.

The logic of cost-effectiveness countered proposals for GHG reduction measures that were inefficient. For example, some stakeholders wanted to build a commuter rail station near campus to reduce GHG. This strategy had emotional appeal – a ribbon-cutting opportunity, putting CPP on the transit system map, and the attractiveness of rail transit as compared to bus. It also served to keep buses out of the core of the campus, as some desired. The problem was that the rail station project was expensive to build and the commuter rail line it served had limited service and reliability problems. Further, the station would require a shuttle bus connection to the campus, which would add a transfer, increase travel time, and be costly to operate. Without cost-effectiveness analysis, the new station might have been included in the plan. When cost-effectiveness was estimated, the proposal had the highest cost per ton of GHG reduced, and, as a result, was not included in the CAP.

Although this work made claims based on logic, there was an issue with false precision. While the process for estimating cost was straightforward and the Clean Air–Cool Planet model accurately translated inputs such as electricity consumption and vehicle miles traveled into eCO_2, there was uncertainty about the impacts of interventions. For example, it is difficult to accurately predict behavioral responses to programs designed to reduce solo driving to campus by faculty, students, and staff. Compared to a traditional journey-to-work trip, student travel involves a fluctuating schedule and linked trips for work and family obligations. Also, previous elasticity studies were based on environments that were more urban in characteristic than CPP.[4] While the team did not overstate confidence in the predictions, the precise nature of the GHG model outputs disguised that uncertainty.

Scenario forecasting techniques could have addressed this uncertainty by generating a range of possible responses to candidate strategies, but I did not think of generating scenarios at the time. Scenarios could have also been created to represent different future contexts for implementation, such as high campus support, low campus support, the CSU supplanting campus efforts, or changing state and federal mandates. In hindsight, I realize that my desire to complete a plan with a clear set of recommendations obscured that opportunity. In a decision-making environment that was saying *yes*, qualifying the recommendations with alternative scenarios did not appeal to me.

Emotion

The opportunity to plan for GHG reduction at the institution I had worked at for decades was inspiring. I experienced positive emotions: delight (and surprise) that the CPP was taking this action and pride in the president for making the commitment. This emotion coexisted, however, with a general sense of dismay about the lack of national and global progress in recognizing and acting to limit climate change.

The advisory committee members were positive, collaborative, and curious to learn about the range of climate actions. The team had an egalitarian spirit. The experience demonstrated elements of Habermasian undistorted communication in its commitment to dialogic process, discovery, and its lack of hierarchy (Forester 1989). At a personal level, I was anxious about being exposed as dabbling in areas in which I did not have sufficient expertise, but the positive vibe associated with the effort made that relatively unimportant.

The technocratic nature of the assignment meant that the team did not engage with the emotions of stakeholders to either resolve disputes or as a tool for supporting action. The top-down initial charge placed the effort in a more traditional, instrumental setting. The lack of controversy in the planning process and the collaborative spirit at meetings meant that the discourse did not involve emotions such as anger or fear. Rather, the general emotional tenor was interest, anticipation, and fulfillment. Of course, I may have been naïve about the unstated emotions of some participants.

Convention

Convention played a small role since the plan was brand new. There was no legislative mandate to complete it and no required elements. The Climate Commitment, however, defined required elements of the effort such as inventorying emissions, taking early actions, making a plan, etc., but there was flexibility in the form and content of the plan. I brought no process or outcome conventions in the form of past practice, and the expectations of clients or constituents did not explicitly shape my role or point of view. While there were some campus climate action plans on the website for the Climate Commitment, many were from East Coast universities that have a different energy and emission profiles. Other Cal State universities had sustainability initiatives at that time, but there was no adopted climate action plan in the CSU. Since there was little precedent, the directive from the university president and cabinet was to develop the best plan we could.

Another form of convention applied, however, in expectations I developed over years working with stakeholder responses to plans and tracking their implementation. Having been involved in plans that overreached and were not fully implemented, I believed that the CAP should stick to core measurable aims and demonstrate cost-effectiveness.

A second form of convention was organizational knowledge about the segmentation of roles across campus divisions. Strategies that required cross-division collaboration or decision-making, such as changing class scheduling, were harder to accomplish than those controlled by a single unit. I had learned about organizational culture tensions in a previous assignment on an Academic Affairs Strategic Plan. In that case, varied views of the nature of the organization were in tension and interfered with the development of a consensus vision and strategy (Willson 2006).

Invention

The team invented the CAP's form and content as we went along. Invention occurred in all aspects of the plan – developing GHG reduction strategies, estimating their impact, selecting measures, writing the plan, and proposing implementation measures. Many procedural planning theories include developing and evaluating plan alternatives, but the CAP process did not present alterative plans for consideration by decision-makers. Instead, we evaluated measures individually and then proposed a package of reduction measures to a create single plan proposal.

The team used its collective understanding of the literature, combined with a brainstorming approach, to generate GHG reduction ideas and screen them for feasibility in terms of GHG reduction, cost, implementation ease, education potential, and other measures. Ideas came from each member's disciplinary background. Starting with the CAP outcome of carbon neutrality, we tested packages of measures to see how close we could get to zero. We missed the target by 20,000 metric tonnes because CPP is a commuter campus that does not control outside land use patterns and transportation emissions. As mentioned, the final one-third of reduction required the purchase of offsets, carbon reductions implemented elsewhere. This was an unfamiliar approach to an institution used to managing its work within campus boundaries.

The invention element emphasized the development of the plan, rather than its implementation. The team assumed that the Sustainability Committee would oversee implementation, but the missing aspect of invention was designing institutional mechanisms to support ongoing implementation, monitoring, and evaluation. Those might have included securing endorsement by different units in the organization, revising mission statements of units, assigning tasks, changing job descriptions, dedicating budget, and establishing oversight mechanisms.

Discoveries

Reflection on the case is presented in two commentaries: (i) the practical judgments made during the planning episode and (ii) takeaways that might apply in other planning situations.

Practical Judgments

Three practical judgments shaped my actions during the planning episode. They are (i) planning with incomplete information, (ii) adopting a rational/analytic role, and (iii) resisting mission creep.

Practical Judgment 1: Proceeding with Insufficient Technical Information and Analytic Uncertainty

As mentioned, the inputs to the Clean Air–Cool Planet model were somewhat speculative, such as the travel characteristics of faculty, staff, and students (distance, mode, frequency), the amount of natural gas consumed, fertilizer use, and so on. Yet no one challenged the estimates since the breadth of knowledge required to assess all categories was beyond any individual stakeholder or expert. Another example of potential imprecision is the "do-nothing" scenario for the 2030 baseline, which is used to assess the impact of the plan progress. Because California was moving fast in mandates for renewable energy, it was uncertain how much improvement would occur if CPP did nothing.

I proceeded, as did the team, despite the uncertainty of our forecasts. We could have slowed the effort, commissioned a series of technical studies, and sought the advice of subject matter experts through outreach or Delphi panels. This would have added years to the effort and required more funding.

The team decided to proceed quickly. We applied expert judgment in estimating the impacts of proposed programs, yet many judgments were outside our direct expertise. Team members talked through evidence and estimates and proceeded until someone said wrong or stop. The analysis of the path to 2030 carbon neutrality was a scenario as much as it was a forecast, yet we presented it as a forecast.

My estimates of the impact of candidate programs were made with the best empirical evidence at hand, but since examples of plan interventions were few, that evidence was partial or required translating results from another setting. I relied on theory about economic and human behavior, my past experience, and the views of other team members. I considered precedent, if available, and used a holistic approach to apply understandings of how systems work to the CPP setting. For example, I used price elasticity of demand estimates for parking derived from traditional workplaces since none existed for university campuses. Drawing on program development experiences from my consulting practice in transportation planning, I considered possible unanticipated consequences and issues affecting implementation.

This faster, less rigorous study process emerged in an organic fashion as the team responded to a unique opportunity within time and budget limits. The harm of this approach is if inaccurate forecasts led to the selection of ineffective measures. But the risk of error seemed justified because the Climate Commitment called for regular reporting. Careful monitoring, if completed, would identify and correct off-target measures over time. It was better to take advantage of the political opening that existed, even if imperfect, rather than wait. The assumption of close monitoring of strategies, however, did not prove accurate.

Practical Judgment 2: Adopting a Rational/Analytic Role in Undertaking Cost-Effectiveness Evaluation

A politically attuned approach would make a "happy" plan that includes strategies pleasing each stakeholder interest. Such an approach is helpful in building a coalition to support plan adoption and implementation, but taken too far, results in plans that are bloated, ineffective, and expensive. Since climate change measures are linked to other benefits, e.g., new campus dorms reduce student commuting and support other campus life objectives, I might have taken such an "assembly of interests" approach if there was less support for the initiative.

The president's personal pledge to achieve carbon neutrality provided an opportunity to seek a more economically disciplined approach. Testing the cost–effectiveness of candidate measures affected the selection of those included in the plan. At a subconscious level, I sought to counter administrators' possible perceptions that faculty are theoretical and impractical, thinking that the "bottom line" focus would appeal to them.

Practical Judgment 3: Resisting "Mission Creep" and Seeking a Narrow Definition of Plan Purpose

My collaborator Brown and I had a friendly difference of opinion on the issue of mission creep. I opposed it, seeking to keep the plan focused on the most cost-effective measures so that positive quantifiable results would be obtained. Broad, ambitious plans are politically vulnerable to criticism that they exceed their mandate, overstep, micromanage individual choice, and represent unstated agendas.

Brown was more welcoming of measures that didn't offer large GHG reduction, such as composting, because they supported a broader sustainability agenda and engaged the commitment of a wider set of stakeholders. An exaggerated way of illustrating this is the following: if all of CPP's emissions could be offset by funding a large solar installation in an off-campus desert location for the lowest cost per ton of GHG removed, my view would support that approach. On the other hand, Brown might object that such an approach leaves many other relevant aspects on the table – broader sustainability gains, building a campus constituency for climate change implementation, educating students, generating research opportunities, and/or demonstrating leadership. All these other benefits might be worth a higher cost. My approach focused on directly solving the GHG emissions problem. Brown's approach added a concern for building a broader movement around campus sustainability.

We found a middle ground on this issue. In hindsight, the weakness of my position is that it assumed implementation support would continue in the future. That turned out not to be the case, so the benefits of Brown's approach of building a broader constituency might have led to more sustained action. Of course, even a broader movement can flounder if it is not institutionalized in procedures, job descriptions, and annual work programs and budgets.

Takeaways for Practice

This case suggests three takeaways for practice. They draw from the planning episode and the insights into how the plan fared in implementation as discussed in Boxes 6.3 through 6.6. The planning takeaways concern (i) seizing windows of opportunity; (ii) recognizing the importance of grassroots support, co-benefits, institutional buy-in, and supportive organizational culture for long-term implementation; and (iii) recognizing the planner's role in bringing evidence to planning processes.

Takeaway 1: Seize Windows of Opportunity, as Change-Making Is an Opportunistic Endeavor; Act, Even Though Your Effort Is Insufficient to Solve the Entire Problem

For years prior to the CAP, students, faculty, and staff had been working on reducing CPP's GHG emissions, with modest impact. Since the institution's mission is education, it was difficult to attract policy attention, political capital, and resources to the climate change issue. The State of California was taking many initiatives at this time through AB 32, The Global Warming Solutions Act of 2006, in areas such as renewable energy and vehicle efficiency standards, so one could argue that these initiatives would address the problem on a broader and more systemic basis than CPP actions. Why should CPP act if the state was going to take care of the problem?

President Ortiz's signature on the Climate Commitment changed this dynamic by raising the priority for climate change planning among vice presidents of campus divisions and other leaders. It was the time-limited window of opportunity that would have been missed if there had not been readiness and willingness to respond in the form of prior work on the part of faculty, staff, and students. Similarly, if there had not been internal capacity to do the plan, it may have been assigned to an outside consultant with less institutional knowledge and limited implementation capability, or it may have been dropped.

Responding to a window of opportunity required extra work and a willingness to reprioritize plans and tasks. That was an easy call, but in cases where planners are burdened with many other responsibilities, the ability to work on a new initiative requires negotiating staff additions or work reductions, or developing process improvements for existing work so that the time is available.

In 2009, there was a possibility that concerted global action could keep global average temperature increases below two degrees centigrade. My experience with the pace of political and institutional change made me skeptical about that possibility, and the continued increase in global CO_2 concentrations since then proves my assumption correct. I moved forward on this initiative anyway, knowing that the effort is insufficient on a bigger scale. Planners do not give up, even when it is clear that their efforts are insufficient. Planning is an act of faith, made without a guarantee of outcome. We start where we are with the tools and support at hand. We hope that small changes build a broader movement, as proof of concept is established and stakeholders understand the problem.

Box 6.6 (next page) describes how the climate planning activities are being renewed more than ten years after the plan's adoption, echoing some of Alexander's observations about plan legacies in Box 6.4.

Takeaway 2: Create Grassroots Support, Co-Benefits, and Institutional Change to Support Durable, Long-Term Reform

Leadership support for long-term objectives only goes so far. Strong support from President Ortiz did not provide the broad and stable constituency to support ongoing implementation of an effort with a 2030 target year. While plans

---

Box 6.6 Seeds of Renewal

Box 6.3 describes some ways that CAP implementation commitment declined. While no action has been taken to suspend or terminate the CAP, it is an infrequent element of current campus discussions and decisions. Implementation activity continues where initiatives have become standard practices or where there are staff-level champions.

In 2018, the campus adopted a new University Strategic Plan, the broadest policy guidance document for CPP. The Strategic Plan includes sustainability as a goal, but only in relation to facility operations. This is a logical consequence of the primary implementation voice for the CAP being in the Facility Management Department. The CAP commitment to carbon neutrality is not mentioned in the plan itself.

The CAP still has influence, however, as noted in Box 6.4 and as demonstrated by other plans incorporating CAP ideas. A consultant-developed Campus Master Plan proposal (akin to a community plan) references the CAP and includes many elements that will lower GHG emissions such as multimodal transportation and green buildings, yet it does not include a commitment to carbon-neutral operations. In addition, a new sustainability plan is under development as an implementing document under the University Strategic Plan. This plan will take a broad approach to sustainability, including measures anticipated in the CAP, campus growth capacity, and issues of financial sustainability. It is not clear whether this plan will include a commitment to carbon neutrality.

The answer to what happened to the CAP is complex. It spurred many actions, but over time the implementation commitment faded. It was not directly endorsed by the current University Strategic Plan effort, but many elements are taken up in the Campus Master Plan and may be in the new sustainability plan. It is neither a complete success nor a complete failure. Rather, the CAP is a chapter in the ongoing development of vision and implementation commitments at the university. Hoch (2019) offers a perspective that plans shape intention rather than direct action, that they "offer provisional support for a judgment about what to do for the future" (72). That view of the role of plans particularly fits this case of a plan that did not have mandated implementation powers.

---

with regulatory mandates are sustained over time, policy plans born of individual initiative are susceptible to being forgotten as priorities or leaders change. President Ortiz retired in 2014, the same year as the last meeting of the Sustainability Task Force. Discussions were held about reconstituting the group around a broader sustainability issue, but that did not come to pass.

The speed at which the plan moved meant less effort occurred in a slower process of engaging implementing departments at the grassroots level, seeking their approval, and building a broad constituency. For some stakeholders, climate change was the "issue of hour" sure to be replaced by another one in the cycle of policy concerns. In hindsight, I and the planning team should have thought more about future implementation contingencies as we developed the plan. Doing so would not eliminate contingencies, of course, but would have led us to generate strategies anticipating changing CPP leadership, the press of competing issues, and the increased State of California and CSU roles in GHG reduction.

Co-benefits continue to drive GHG mitigation actions, as progress continues on initiatives that save money or serve other objectives. For example, recent actions to improve transit address campus access and parking problems also reduce GHG emissions. But the CAP is not playing a role in ensuring that the most effective measures are being pursued. The mixed record of implementation indicates that the GHG mitigation mission did not become a widespread, powerful element of campus policy or organizational culture. The implementation activities that advanced the most are explained by them having co-benefits, by individuals' initiatives (champions) in departments, and the momentum created by the CAP.

Universities have complex organizational cultures, and the characteristics and experiences of leaders and managers shape evolving organization culture. Embedding implementation commitments in statements of organizational mission, annual work programs and budgets, job descriptions, and ongoing reporting of results can support institutional change.

Takeaway 3: Advocate for Technical Rationality as Resistance to "Something for Everyone" Plans

Interest group advocacy and political maneuvering can easily overwhelm the planning process. As planners appropriately move away from top-down, technocratic approaches, it is possible to focus so much on gathering stakeholder input that important questions about plan effectiveness and cost are ignored. There are simply too many plan proposals for the resources available, and those proposals are often in contradiction with one another. The method of assessing which elements are included should rely on more than heeding the loudest or most powerful voices. Planners have a responsibility to bring technical evidence and logical thought to the table, and if the evidence or reason contradicts a plan idea, push back. This case focused on cost–effectiveness evidence, but in other instances planners have a responsibility to assert findings from physical and social sciences. In the case of climate change denial, for example, a planner must know the scientific evidence, explain it in ways that a lay audience can understand, and endure the uncomfortable experience of disagreeing with a constituent or elected official.

And Now to You: Playing the Short and Long Games

Hopefully, your career will include planning assignments as unconstrained as this one. These projects draw on all your resources, since there are no precedents – sometimes called "go-bys" – and few initial mandates from decision-makers. They are instances when you most need planning theories, since you will design planning processes, conceive of and choose plan components, and develop implementation tools from scratch. I found my way through this episode, in collaboration with the team, using the tools at hand – substantive theories, process theories, and experiences – in a synthetic, intuitive way. Box 6.7 (next page) is written by Linda Dalton, a planning professor and seasoned academic administrator. It provides further insights on the institutional context for planning, plan implementation, and the need to consider social justice as an element of sustainability.

The CAP is in the general class of long-range plans that set out vision, goals and objectives, evaluate alternatives, and recommend implementation strategies. While the CAP was not required by a regulation, many policy plans are, such as the land use or community revitalization plans adopted by cities, or Regional Transportation Plans (RTPs) adopted by metropolitan transportation agencies. Laws and regulations often prescribe the process and content elements of these plans, and may well require approval by another level of government. Laws and regulations also govern plan implementation, such as a requirement that zoning conform with its corresponding comprehensive land use plan and mandates that these plans be renewed and adopted at regular intervals. The entities adopting those plans cannot ignore them, as was possible in the CAP case.

Despite the formal requirements of many types of plans, those preparing them sometime wonder about the extent of their effect. The comprehensive plan can be modified by the city council, as shown in the Chapter 12 Hawthorne, California, case, and the RTP is redone every four years, as mandated by federal law. If you are doing this type of planning, then, you may wonder if your plans have teeth and whether you working

---

Box 6.7 Considerations in University Climate Action Plans
Linda C. Dalton, PhD, FAICP, Professor Emerita, City and Regional Planning Cal Poly, San Luis Obispo

This case suggests three topics for further reflection: institutional context, plan implementation, and social justice as an element of sustainability.

Universities are corporate rather than democratic governmental institutions, although they value collegiality and involve faculty, staff, and students in policy-making. This case highlights the role of presidential leadership and senior administrative staff in initially providing the opportunity to develop a climate action plan, and later, directing attention to other priorities under a new president. How can planners sustain attention to a critical value such as sustainability in such a shifting context? One way is institutionalization by assigning responsibility to an administrative department or adding it to an individual job description.

While the California State University expects its campuses to become more environmentally sustainable, the system did not require CPP to develop a CAP leading to carbon neutrality. Willson stresses that this allowed the planning team to create an innovative CAP that met CPP's perceived needs. However, the lack of a mandate made follow-through challenging when university leadership changed. The research on plan and policy implementation can provide some guidance. It stresses the importance of building commitment as well as the institutional structure to implement plans during the policy-making process. (See, for example, Dalton and Burby 1994, Goggin et al. 1990, Mazmanian and Sabatier 1989, Sandfort and Moulton 2015.)

Despite a lack of explicit follow-through, Willson finds that the sustainability values and goals embodied in CAP carry forward in the new campus master plan and emerging sustainability plan. In addition, the CAP process could have taken advantage of an opportunity to demonstrate how social justice (and economic or fiscal health) are integral aspects of environmental sustainability (Campbell 1996). For example, CPP's dependence on single-occupant vehicles for commuting is not only a challenge in reaching carbon neutrality, but also an economically inefficient form of transportation that limits access for students without their own cars. CPP could still incorporate this holistic view into the University's Strategic Plan and Campus Master Plan.

---

in a revolving door of plan preparation and policy. Is, in fact, the real work of planning being done by the current planners who apply the zoning code to development projects, create private–public partnerships, and facilitate decision-making? That answer is that while implementation work has tangible results in decisions and leads to concrete outcomes, long-range plans *do* have significant impacts. You need to be attuned to the subtle ways they work – through the multiple functions of agenda, policy, vision, design, and strategy noted by Hopkins (2001).

In the case of the CAP, it was the merits of individual strategies included in the plan, more than the plan itself, that explain which proceeded and which languished. The plan didn't direct implementation as much as organize attention to a goal, carbon neutrality, and a set of strategies for possible implementation. Changing conditions, though, can give new life to programs that do not initially make progress. For example, as noted in Box 6.6, campus growth pushed parking issues to the fore independent of the CAP, and student attitudes embrace car-free lifestyles more than before. That pressure gave new life to CAP tactics to improve transit and other modes of access. Similarly, concerns about water supply have spurred activity between CPP and surrounding cities to use water more efficiently.

The short game in plans can produce big wins such as the adoption of the CAP, but the long game of implementation requires attention to the interplay between the plan, evolving social and economic conditions, and implementation capacity. Find ways to test the feasibility of measures during plan development, as might occur through pilot projects or detailed examination of implementation requirements. This will provide robustness for the plan's measures and allow you to develop contingencies that specify "Plan B" if a major element encounters resistance or is found to be flawed. Such a process might have indicated the challenges to transit improvement in the CAP case.

Plans are usually not implemented in predictable, regular ways, as their meaning, authority, and effect exist in a shifting landscape of issues, leaders, and mandates. That doesn't mean they don't make change, though because they influence understandings, intentions, and relationships. Making plans with a recognition of the realities of implementation makes them more likely to make change rather than collect dust.

Discussion Questions

1. What should planners do about technical uncertainty? How should they manage the space between honest disclosure and maintaining professional authority?
2. How can implementation commitments be built into planning processes so that plans do not end up sitting on the shelf?

3. A longer, more scientific approach to creating the CAP may have led to a different result. How do you suspect that it would it be different, and what are the likely effects?
4. Planner's knowledge about problems means that planners know that many of them, like climate change, are intractable. How do you deal with feelings of despair about the future? How do you stay inspired to act?

Notes

1 The plan is available at www.cpp.edu/~sustainability/pdf/CPP_CAP_091109.pdf. Online reporting on plans and monitoring is provided at http://reporting.secondna ture.org/institution/detail!270#/%23270#270.
2 Since then, California climate planning has evolved rapidly through many stages, include full integration of mitigation and adaptation planning in comprehensive plans. At the time of the CAP, adaptation planning (strategies to adapt to impacts on temperature, water supply, air quality, etc.) had not yet been integrated into climate change planning.
3 Available at http://reporting.secondnature.org/cap/cap-public!1378.
4 Elasticity refers to the relationship of amount consumed to price. More specifically it is defined as the percentage change in consumption divided by the percentage change in price.

References

Alexander, Serena. 2014. "Campus Climate Action Plan Legacies and Implementation Dynamics." *Planning for Higher Education*, 42(3): 42–57. doi.org/10.1111/hea.12065_32.

Cal Poly Pomona. 2019. *University Enrollment, Fall 2018.* Accessed October 25, 2019 at https://www.cpp.edu/~arar/just-the-facts/university-enrollment.shtml#GenderEthn.

Cal State University. 2017. *Sustainability in the California State University. The First Assessment of the 2014 Sustainability Policy, 2014–2017.* Accessed December 4, 2019 at https://www2.calstate.edu/impact-of-the-csu/sustainability/Documents/2014-17 -Sustainability.pdf.

Campbell, Scott. 1996. "Green Cities, Growing Cities, Just Cities?: Urban Planning and the Contradictions of Sustainable Development." *Journal of the American Planning Association*, 62(3): 296–312. doi.org/10.1080/01944369608975696.

Dalton, Linda C. and Ray J. Burby. 1994. "Mandates, Plans, and Planners: Building Local Commitment to Development Management." *Journal of the American Planning Association*, 60(4): 444–461. doi.org/10.1080/01944369408975604.

Forester, John. 1989. *Planning in the Face of Power.* Berkeley, CA: University of California Press.

Goggin, Malcom L., Ann Bowman, Lames Lester, and Lawrence O'Toole. 1990. *Implementation Theory and Practice: Toward a Third Generation.* Glenview, IL: Pearson Scott Foresman.

Hoch, Charles. 2019. *Pragmatic Spatial Planning.* New York: Routledge.

Hopkins, Lewis. 2001. *Urban Development: The Logic of Making Plans.* Washington, DC: Island Press.

Intergovernmental Panel on Climate Change. n.d. "The Intergovernmental Panel on Climate Change." Accessed March 12, 2020 at https://www.ipcc.ch.

Kim, Dohyung and Richard Willson. 2016. *The Foothill Gold Line and Cal Poly Pomona: Travel Patterns, Millennials' Preferences, and Transit Advocacy.* Monrovia, CA: Foothill Gold Line Construction Authority.

Mazmanian, Daniel A. and Paul A. Sabatier. 1989. *Implementation and Public Policy, with a New Postscript.* Lanham, MD: University Press of America.

Roemer, Diana L. 2004. "Cal Poly, Bus Firm Clash; Transit Stop No Longer on Campus." *San Gabriel Valley Tribune,* March 5, 2004.

Sandfort, Jodi and Stephanie Moulton. 2015. *Effective Implementation in Practice: Integrating Public Policy and Management.* San Francisco, CA: Jossey-Bass.

Willson, Richard. 2001. "Assessing Communicative Rationality as a Transportation Planning Paradigm." *Transportation,* 28(1): 1–31. doi.org/10.1023/A:1005247430522.

Willson, Richard. 2003. "Planning Theory in Our Own Backyard: Communicative Action in Academic Governance." *Journal of Planning Education and Research,* 22(3): 297–307. doi.org/10.1177/0739456X02250318.

Willson, Richard. 2006. "The Dynamics of Organizational Culture and Academic Planning." *Planning for Higher Education,* 34(3): 5–17.

Willson, Richard and Kyle Brown. 2008. "Carbon Neutrality at the Local Level: Achievable Goal or Fantasy?" *Journal of the American Planning Association,* 74(4): 497–504. doi.org/10.1080/01944360802380431.

Willson, Richard. 2011. "Beyond the Inventory: Planning for Campus Greenhouse Gas Reduction." *Planning for Higher Education,* 39: Planning Volume 2: 49–55.

Chapter 7

Planning for Resilience

Preparing Resilient Planners in Mamallapuram, India

Laxmi Ramasubramanian

Both planning scholars and practitioners recognize that planning is simultaneously visionary and pragmatic (Ramasubramanian and Albrecht 2018). Planning projects are rendered complex precisely because visionary ideals and innovative practices are embedded within pragmatic actions. In the case study that follows, I reflect on my experiences as a planning educator leading a group of American planning students to work on a planning project in Mamallapuram, near Chennai, India. The project was completed by students at Hunter College in New York, in collaboration with Anna University in Chennai. The case study is relevant for professional planners working in diverse cultural and institutional contexts in the United States and abroad. Three practical judgments are highlighted: (i) facilitating rather than managing the emergence of a plan, (ii) creating an engagement in cultural competence, and (iii) allowing the experience of disappointment. For those who champion the cause of one-world planning education, this case serves as a cautionary reminder about the need to prepare planners who are culturally competent to work in different country contexts.

interesting

Description of the Planning Episode

In most academic planning programs in the United States, the planning studio serves as a required capstone experience. A studio simulates a real-world planning experience (albeit with some built-in safeguards) to prepare students to make the transition from student to practitioner. Planning studios strive to weave together the information and knowledge gathered from different types of courses, preparing students to make practical judgments and take action – a preview of their lives as planning practitioners. The planning studio provides a setting that calls for students to reflect on their aims and methods.

Institutional Setting

The Hunter College planning program, where I worked, is rooted in a long tradition of community-oriented advocacy planning. Graduate students enter the program championing social justice ideals and are well-versed in community organizing and engagement (Angotti et al. 2011). Studios are organized to allow students to utilize the skills and knowledge they have accumulated in the program by addressing planning problems within particular sociopolitical and institutional contexts. At the time I taught, the studio was organized as two courses of three credits each, extending over the fall 2009 to spring 2010 academic year. Responding in part to students' desires to have international planning experiences, I proposed a studio project set near the city of Chennai (formerly Madras). Following the norms established at Hunter College, I arranged for my graduate students to work in small teams to investigate planning issues at the request of a project sponsor. The studio project sponsor usually commissions the planning study and agrees to receive the recommendations proposed by the students. Project sponsors are generally nonprofit community organizations, coalitions, or government agencies.

Similar to the time constraints encountered by planning consultants, one of the main challenges of any studio experience lies in defining a feasible and robust scope of work that can be performed during the academic year. The work must first and foremost serve the needs of the project sponsor and advance the state of knowledge in the field, thus providing a new contribution to the practice literature in the form of professional reports and presentations. Project reports typically include at least three sections: background/context, analysis of planning issues, and recommendations. As a planning educator, I want my students to learn how to

- Situate planning activities within the larger sociopolitical context for planning.
- Develop a scope of work for a protracted project that involves multiple actors and activities.
- Research complex problems, issues, and potential solutions using quantitative and qualitative methods.
- Work as a professional team, as if part of a planning agency or consulting firm.
- Interact in a respectful and ethical manner with the project sponsor, community members, and other stakeholders.
- Develop high-quality plans and recommendations for the project sponsors.
- Produce a professional-quality written report and graphically engaging visual presentation.
- Communicate work-in-progress and final results to different audiences through formal and informal presentations.

Overview of the Planning Process

Working in partnership with my counterpart at Anna University, I proposed a studio project that would develop a comprehensive plan for the coastal town of Mamallapuram (also known as Mahabalipuram), near Chennai in South India. Mamallapuram (pronounced Mah-malla-puram) is situated about 60 kilometers (about 40 miles) south of Chennai, on the Bay of Bengal. Chennai is the capital of the state of Tamil Nadu. The chairperson, council members, and the Executive Office of the Mamallapuram Town Panchayat (Council) were the sponsors of the project. Figure 7.1 shows the town's location in southern India.

Mamallapuram is a historic site of special cultural significance to the people of Tamil Nadu. The town was a flourishing seaport of the Pallava dynasty that ruled the region between 600 and 750 AD. The town draws its name from King Narasimhavarman, who was also called Mah-Mallan (the great warrior). Mamallapuram is listed among UNESCO's World Heritage sites, one of thirteen such sites situated in India (UNESCO 2020). It is a popular tourist destination for sites such as that shown in the Figure 7.2 image of Shore Temple.

In the early 2000s, the population of the town was around 12,000, although regional trends suggested rapid urbanization and population growth. In Mamallapuram, the seasonal population shifts are also significant. During the winter months, between November and February, the number of visitors increases dramatically, associated with a state-sponsored dance festival that

Figure 7.1 Mamallapuram (Mahabalipuram) Regional Context. Image source: Google, TerraMetrics

Figure 7.2 Tourism Site in Mamallapuram. Image source: Laxmi Ramasubramanian

takes place for a week in mid–January. The dominant employment activities in Mamallapuram include fishing, stone carving, service activities associated with tourism, and some farming. Everyday life for the seafaring members of the community was negatively affected by the tsunami that hit the region in 2004. The development and management of Mamallapuram is influenced and impacted by the growth of the nearby state capitals Chennai and Pondicherry. Figure 7.3 shows Mamallapuram's location and regional context.

Figure 7.3 Mamallapuram and Surrounding Areas. Image source: Laxmi Ramasubramanian

The overarching goal for the studio was to propose a comprehensive plan for the town of Mamallapuram. During the fall semester, students were required to (i) develop a vision statement to anchor their work, (ii) conduct background research on the issues described earlier, and (iii) identify best practices for adaption to climate change in other coastal cities. Students were expected to share the knowledge gained during the semester through formal presentations to the group, instructors, and guests. The presentations were collectively intended to prepare the group for a field trip in January 2010.

The objectives of the field trip included (i) learning more about the town through conversations with stakeholders, (ii) assessing the feasibility of the student's proposals, and (iii) negotiating with Anna University students to formulate a combined work plan for the spring semester. During the spring semester, students were to synthesize the knowledge and information from the previous semester and the field trip in order to create the planning document agreed upon in Mamallapuram. This document was to include recommendations and a plan for implementation. The students were expected to make a final presentation to students, faculty, and guests at Anna University through video link. These expectations were articulated in the syllabus. I invited a professor who is an expert in sustainability and climate change with international experience working in Asia to serve as a co-instructor.

The Core Problem

Students were charged with developing a strategic long-term vision for the spatial, social, and economic development of the town *fostering resilience to climate change*. The definition of resilience was purposefully broad, including the need to develop resilient infrastructure systems, response programs, and preparedness as well as strengthening the capacity of formal and informal governance systems. Once the vision statement was finalized, the students were to work individually or in small teams to develop proposals that address housing, historic preservation, economic development, environmental management, infrastructure, and transportation. For each of the proposals, students were expected to identify medium-term (3–5 years) goals, threats, and opportunities; and propose an implementation plan. In other words, the students were asked to develop the framework for a comprehensive plan.

Intended and Actual Outcomes

Typically, the scope of studio projects is determined before students enroll in the class. The Mamallapuram studio was no exception. As the lead instructor,

I initiated conversations with my counterparts at an established architecture school in Anna University immediately before I pitched the studio idea to my department. The selection of Mamallapuram as the study location was determined, in part, by the fact that Anna University was planning a spring 2010 Master in Planning studio class at the same location. The program head of the planning department (Professor S, as we will refer to him) became my ally and partner in this collaborative endeavor. In our conversations, Professor S and I agreed that a common studio location was a good way to bring two groups of students who could work together and learn from each other. In this case, U.S. and Indian students would exchange ideas and collaborate to address local planning problems, i.e., learning by doing.

As the lead instructor and the champion of this "experimental" international studio experience, I invested personal time, resources, and social capital to jumpstart the collaboration. My academic colleagues at Anna University expressed some skepticism about the technical competencies of the American students based on previous experiences with international students, a concern that I initially brushed aside. However, Professor S and I planned ahead to manage these anticipated differences – we agreed that we would deliver two planning reports to the project sponsor; one developed and written by the Indian team and another by the American team. The students would collaborate during fieldwork. In our discussions, Professor S and I assumed that the students would hang out together, talking about planning issues and sharing knowledge and experiences about how planning is done in different cultural contexts.

Professor S developed his own studio syllabus; it emphasized the creation of a master plan (similar to the vision of a comprehensive plan that I articulated in my syllabus). The two syllabi differed in one key aspect. The Indian studio students were expected to conduct a rigorous land use study that resulted in a map of future land use. Most planning practitioners in the U.S. will not be surprised by this requirement – it is the bread and butter of planning work, the world over.

The Indian planning program curriculum used a studio-based approach. The students who enrolled in the Mamallapuram studio had several advantages compared with their U.S. counterparts. The Indian students were accustomed to working intensively in groups on a studio project, were full-time students, and did not encounter language barriers while working in the field. The American students did not know each other prior to the start of the studio. Most of them incorrectly assumed that a studio was similar to a regular graduate course and did not anticipate and prepare for the complexities of undertaking a real project.

The plan was for the U.S. students to spend the fall semester of 2009 learning about planning for resilience and about the Indian geographical, historical, and sociopolitical context. The three-week field experience in India was built into the syllabus. Three students from the Hunter College studio class decided to stay on in India during the spring semester. The class then agreed that those students would help support the follow-up data gathering. The studio pushed the technological boundaries of the time (2009–2010) using free online communication tools to anticipate and plan for the complex communication challenges ahead.

As in planning practice, part of any studio project is problem framing. Problem framing requires the students (with the instructor's guidance) to understand and articulate the planning issues in a way that they can be meaningfully addressed during the academic year. Initially, I had framed the problem as the need to manage rapid growth/expansion and urbanization of Mamallapuram. In emphasizing the need to create resilience to climate change and protect archeologically significant sites, I hoped that the students would think holistically about the development/redevelopment of the area, addressing housing, transportation, and environmental considerations. I expected them to make practical judgments in creating a future land use map that reflected their research and analyses. I anticipated that the students would make both short- and long-term recommendations that would allow the local decision-makers to gradually shape the land use patterns towards environmental/cultural protection, resilience, and planned urban development.

In reflecting upon the experience some ten years later, I now realize that the students never signed on to the way the problem was framed for them. In part, they did not seem to understand the value of long-term planning that anticipates the needs of future generations in a resource and land-starved setting like Mamallapuram. As articulated in the syllabus, the students had two major sets of tasks to undertake – one, to understand the impacts of climate change, specifically sea-level rise and its impacts on coastal communities; and two, to understand the histories, geographies, economic, cultural, and institutional contexts of the place (Mamallapuram) and to a larger extent, India. The students seemed to be unable to take on either of these two tasks, much to the chagrin of my co-instructor and myself. As we peppered the students with information (presentations by guest lecturers, short films, and videos, and assignments), I observed several instances where students avidly looked for short cuts to circumvent the tedious due diligence that all planners have to do in order to produce a comprehensive plan. The students often appeared frustrated that spatial data and information was not easily available or accessible. I got a small research grant to buy high-resolution aerial imagery of the area to alleviate these concerns. By the time the dates for the January field trip rolled around, I had the feeling that the students were more interested in going on a holiday trip rather than using the time to gather data and evidence. After 15 weeks together, the American studio group did not work as a cohesive group; strategies that I devised to share workloads and responsibilities were only partially successful.

The students arrived in India and spent two days getting settled. The American group was received warmly by the university leaders and introduced to their Indian counterparts. The joint field trip began with a conventional land use survey organized and directed by my Indian counterpart. We paired Indian students with the American students so that the visitors would not feel disoriented or unsafe as they walked around the town conducting the land use survey. The survey included gathering demographic data through household surveys to update and verify "official" statistics that were collected from visits to government offices. The language barriers faced by the visitors meant that they were no longer in the proverbial driver's seat when undertaking these household surveys.

During one of our debriefings, the American students claimed that the Indian students were "making up" their numbers; that they were not rigorous in collecting the data; that they were only talking to the men (not women); and that they were accepting the data provided by the head of household without verification. As their instructor, I listened to their concerns with trepidation and anxiety. I advised them to discuss the issues directly with the Indian students (all the Indian students were fluent in English). I reminded my students that they were encountering cultural and linguistic differences in communication and that the informal data gathering approach deployed by the Indian students was not necessarily without rigor. I failed to reassure them. About one-third of the American students decided that they would not use any of the demographic data gathered from the household surveys; that decision impacted the work of all the students.

The students who were doing the building and land use survey encountered a different challenge – they found the work tedious and difficult. Walking around, counting structures and assessing the building conditions, they felt, was not a good use of their time. They expressed shock that the land use data was not easily available for download like it was "back home" in New York. About a third of the class engaged and made friends with the Indian students and made a diligent effort to work with them, learning about how the locals went about doing their studio projects, while the others kept to themselves and became "tourists" rather than working on studio projects.

Returning to the United States, I engaged the class about the development of a future land use map, which in my view was critical to the development of a comprehensive plan. Planners have to make practical judgments, supported with data and evidence. They correctly discussed their ambivalence about making these judgments in the absence of "good data." The students made some progress on this work and by the time spring break rolled around, I felt that they had a viable framework of how to complete the project even with obvious data gaps and incomplete research. They were supported by the three students who stayed in India and attended classes at the local university, keeping us informed about the work progress in the other studio. We learned that the Indian studio team had moved into production mode – preparing the various existing and future land use maps. The American students in New York felt that the Indian students were behaving like technocratic planners – merely "following the rules" and not being reflective about what they had seen and heard in the field.

After spring break, three weeks before the report was due, the students informed me that they reframed the focus of the project to be about sustainable economic development – sustainable tourism – and advised me that they were developing a sustainable tourism plan for Mamallapuram. I felt that the effort that my co-instructor and I had put into shaping and guiding the project had been rejected. We reluctantly and somewhat resentfully accepted the students' decision to reshape and redefine the scope of the project. I vetoed some of their more impractical and paternalistic recommendations, for example, that the town panchayat (equivalent of the county government) undertake structural land reform, taking land away from the wealthy and redistributing it to the poor and needy. Such a recommendation was out of the scope of the studio project and definitely not within the scope of a sustainable tourism plan. We had an uncomfortable and unproductive discussion about the politics around land/real estate in NYC. The students could not understand why I declared their structural land reform proposals infeasible and I was flabbergasted that they were so naïve.

The students' 19 recommendations were interesting and useful but not necessarily supported with data and evidence. Furthermore, there were some proposals – like advocacy for regional rail, the development of a multimodal transportation center, and the development of a new tourist center, each of them good recommendations – that were not linked explicitly with the future land use map. The comprehensive plan was less of a plan and more of wish list.

By the time the semester ended, it appeared that the students had lost energy and interest in the project. They wanted a grade, preferably an A, and they sought to move on with their lives. Several students were graduating at the end of the semester and they shifted their focus away from wrapping up the studio project. In the meantime, the Indian students presented their final report to the sponsor. The American students who were based in India presented a brief update about the work of the New York studio.

As the instructor of record, I had an obligation to submit a final report to the sponsor. The students submitted a final draft report to me and my co-instructor. In the summer, assisted by two students (interestingly both students of color), a faculty colleague, and a graduate student volunteer, the final report was laid out and formatted. On a subsequent private trip to India, the report was handed over to the sponsor. The client received the report and appreciated the unique "student perspectives," and expressed his enthusiasm for some of the easy-to-implement suggestions presented in the report.

So, why did a group of relatively talented, tech savvy, and progressive New Yorkers have so much difficulty working in a non–New York context? This is the question that has bothered me over the last decade.

Examination of the Planning Episode Using Framework Elements

Drawing on the Figure 5.2 framework (see Chapter 5), this section provides reflection on my thoughts, feelings, and actions during the case. It organizes the observations in three elements: (i) planner-as-person, (ii) interpretation of context, and (iii) reasoning and methods in the planning episode itself.

Planner-as-Person Elements That Shaped the Approach

I am formally trained as an architect in my home country, India. I was admitted to a prestigious engineering college to begin my architecture studies. Without even realizing it, I had broken a barrier of sorts – I was one of only three women who were admitted as the first cohort of women to join this premier, all-male college for undergraduate engineering education. Although I struggled, I prevailed, graduating at the top of my class in architecture. As I began to establish myself in private practice, I quickly realized that I did not want to spend my life designing beautiful homes for wealthy clients. Having taken an elective urban planning class and learning the basic principles of planning, I determined that I could link my passion for creating functional and aesthetically pleasing public spaces with my deep commitment to equity and social justice by becoming an urban planner. I moved to the United States to pursue graduate studies in planning and a PhD in architecture, focused on environment-behavior studies and research.

Personal Framework Elements

My teaching philosophy is shaped by my own academic and professional training in architecture and planning, and my commitment to participatory planning. I believe that practicing planners should have strong quantitative and technical skills and a commitment to social justice. Serving marginalized communities, including communities of color, requires more than goodwill. Planners need to have the skills to challenge spurious technical analyses and question token forms of community engagement in order to facilitate better outcomes and policies for vulnerable populations. In keeping with this philosophy, I always use project-based learning in real-world settings. I want my students to walk the walk, in other words demonstrate their capacity to really understand the complexities of community-based planning. Linking scientific and rigorous data analysis with an awareness of the political and social complexities of doing planning prepares them to become effective advocates to create a more just and livable society.

In preparing to write this case, I reflected about my own motivations for undertaking an international planning studio. As a recently tenured associate professor, I felt fairly secure taking on an ambitious project. I was egged on to undertake it by students who asked me to teach an international studio. In selecting Mamallapuram as the case study site and by partnering with the local university, I felt confident about navigating institutional, cultural, and language issues that may arise. Reflecting on my motivations now, I believe I was unconsciously very proud of the opportunity to take students from my academic home to the country/region of my birth. I hoped that the students would develop an appreciation of rich and complex history of a country and her peoples. In planning the field trip, I included opportunities to introduce the students to an array of cultural experiences.

Personal Incongruity and Ambiguity

I strive to treat everyone with respect. I anticipated and expected that my students would do the same – therefore, it never occurred to me that students could treat their Indian counterparts disrespectfully or that they would not be self-aware to recognize their own situational privilege.

I assumed that the graduate students would have prepared themselves for the field trip in India. During the fall semester, we watched documentaries and received guest lectures from experts about the geography, history, and politics. I was surprised that competent students suddenly became helpless as they coped with everyday situations, for example, avoiding the use of public transport or being in crowded public places. Suddenly, it appeared that the majority of the students stopped behaving like savvy New Yorkers. One of the students who remained calm and unfazed had previously worked as a Peace Corps volunteer and had lived/worked abroad. A couple of the students acclimatized by hanging out with the local students and immersed themselves in "seeing" and "doing" alongside their Indian counterparts. In a few days, these students seemed to be more settled and got into the groove of doing fieldwork. Yet, at least two-thirds of the student group did not acclimatize well. When some of these students complained about "horrendous" air quality, the heat, the dust, the humidity, and other environmental variables, I began to take it personally – that I, as a person of Indian origin, had to somehow "fix" these problems and make my students comfortable. The role shift, from professor to caretaker, was one that I was not prepared for or considered.

As an established educator, I already knew that race and gender influence student–teacher interactions. However, my interactions at Hunter College until that point had been largely positive: I had received good teacher evaluations, my classes were full, and I often found myself advising many students. I had co-taught a studio with another colleague in 2007, a couple of years prior, and things had gone well. Thus, at the time, I was unprepared for the disrespect and discourteousness: students did not follow my guidelines and recommendations; they challenged my judgment and approaches to undertaking field work; they were tardy; and in a variety of ways communicated a resistance to being "managed" in any way. Many of the students (not all) were not patient or accepting of local cultures and norms, and expressed resentment and frustration about how day-to-day life matters and planning issues were approached by the locals. Gradually, I also began to notice that the interactions between White students and students of color in the studio were also discourteous: students of color were labelled as slackers, their opinions were silenced or ridiculed during class discussions, and sidebar conversations (among subgroups) became the norm.

Interpretation of Context

The previous section on intended and actual outcomes addressed significant elements of context. This section adds further comments on how I interpreted context at two levels: (i) context for the project itself with the client; and (ii) context for managing the studio class, analogous to managing a planning team.

Context Framework Elements

Planning in India is a complex endeavor, shaped by the legacy of colonialism and the vestiges of British town planning that created multiple layers of bureaucracy. The students struggled to accept the reality that a technocratic spatial planning ethos was the norm. The New York–based advocacy planner students trained in the Davidoff school struggled to connect with the marginalized and vulnerable populations they wanted to advocate for: the students did not speak the local language; did not really understand the lifestyles, culture, and occupations of the disenfranchised (the fisher folk, the farmers, the stone carvers); and did not grasp how networks of wealth and power operate in the Indian context. Some of this could have been understood by reading the literature or accepting the descriptions provided by their Indian counterparts.

I did not select the students who participated in the India studio – students self-selected into the project based on a brief project description provided to all students. The program coordinator allowed some students with good grades but who had not taken a land use class to sign up for the studio; I found out about this right before the field trip. Financial variables were a factor in the decision-making; some students did not participate in the studio because they could not afford the additional costs of the required India field trip.

Context Uncertainty and Ambiguity

When the studio was in the planning stages, several Hunter College colleagues expressed interest in traveling to India along with the studio. Being a newly tenured associate professor, and with the intent of being collegial, I accepted the overtures of a faculty member who wanted to "tag along." Subsequently, a student (not part of the studio class) signed up for an independent study with that faculty member and organized her trip along with the studio class. Another faculty member loosely affiliated with the department also decided to join. The American colleagues did not directly contribute to the studio project, although they offered practical logistical support. They also engaged with the students on a day-to-day basis during the field trip and provided advice and support. In retrospect, their participation may have diluted my authority as an instructor/leader in managing the studio team while we were in India.

On the other side, my Indian counterpart (the Anna University professor leading the planning studio) established the contact with the executive officer of the local government body (the Mamallapuram Special Grade Town Panchayat). The executive officer served as the client for both projects. He provided an overview of the area's planning challenges and opportunities, described planned improvements, provided access to data and information, and received the presentations and the final reports. Gender played a role in the interactions with these elected officials – my male Indian counterpart took the lead in the communications and managed the site visits. I felt anxious that we (my students and I) did not connect with nongovernmental organizations or other activist groups in the area, and relied too much on the "official" government view of the situational context. However, since my students were not prepared to or able to undertake this research, I had to abandon my interest in getting a robust and complex understanding of the local context.

The Planning Episode: Reasoning and Methods

My role in this planning episode involved initiating, designing, and teaching the studio class. This section addresses the elements at the center of Figure 5.2: logic, emotion, convention, and invention. All were instrumental in my approach.

Logic

The studio required that the students develop a strategic long-term vision for the spatial, social, and economic development of the town fostering resilience to climate change. As mentioned, the studio had two instructors. My co-instructor (the climate change/sustainability expert) suggested that the end product be a series of alternative visions (for example, a pro-growth plan, a pro-environmental conservation plan), allowing decision-makers and elected officials to have the final say. I argued that the students could develop alternatives, but could also advocate for their preferred vision. Both of us emphasized the need for a set of spatially anchored recommendations. To some extent, given the students' limited understanding of local context, the "sustainable tourism" approach was a compromise of discussing social and economic development and fostering resilience, albeit neglecting the spatial analysis that was required to formulate a strong plan.

Friedmann (1987) postulates "planning as social learning" as one of the traditions of planning. In this approach, practice and theory building are joined together where social values inform social actions and are mediated by political strategy. In other words, planners figure out "what works" by trying things out in particular situational contexts. My approach to studio teaching was very much in this vein – where individuals work together on a common task/goal and resolve their different understandings of the planning issues as they work. In the studio context, this means being a facilitator and a coach, providing prompts and guidance, rather than being a boss telling the students what to do. In hindsight, it appears that when faced with the unfamiliar, students sought "a boss" and were frustrated when they didn't receive clear marching orders.

Emotion

I worked very hard during the fall semester to prepare the students to be thoughtful planners. To my surprise and puzzlement, the students were voyeurs and exhibited the very traits of "orientalism" and "romanticism" that I was hoping they would avoid. I was frustrated, annoyed, and disgusted during the field trip, and I found myself losing respect for them. I was disappointed with the performance of the teams, their reluctance to undertake serious research and analyses, and avoidance of making meaningful recommendations. They did attempt the task at the very end, but they struggled because they did not have useful and relevant best practices to back them up.

What I remember during the last weeks of the studio was profound feelings of disappointment, sadness, and betrayal. As mentioned, some class members made a decision to refocus and realign the product to propose a sustainable tourism plan rather than a comprehensive plan to make the town resilient to climate change. I was shocked that this shift was orchestrated through a consultation with a recent graduate of the program who was working as a staff person in the department at the time. I was told, "M came over and worked with us; she said …" I expressed my surprise but allowed the students to reframe the project as they preferred and helped them accomplish their goals. I persuaded them to provide reflective feedback to their peers (anonymously). I held individual exit interviews with them and it was during these conversations that I learned how deeply some American students distrusted their Indian counterparts. I also learned that they felt negatively about their own peers in the class, some of which were targeted toward specific individuals. Some students were angry with me because I did not act like a "boss" telling people what to do, how to do it, and firing people they deemed incompetent.

I was further surprised that the students did not wrap up the project and produce a professional quality report. The draft they submitted (as final) was incomplete. This had never happened before in other project-based classes.

I must thank the two students, Tanya Rodriguez and José Pillich, who worked (without compensation) in the summer to wrap up the report, one of whom includes reflections on the studio in Box 7.1 that follows.

Convention

I planned ahead and prepared seriously to undertake the studio. I was cognizant that students in a public university like Hunter College did not often get exposure and international site visit opportunities that come to students from more affluent universities. Thus, I worked hard to tailor an affordable learning experience. I demonstrated proof of concept drawing on best practice conventions in international studios. However, the department decided that Hunter College should not attempt international studio projects after this project – this decision was political, not pedagogical. The international studio option became an experiment that was not repeated.

I tried to uphold the conventions of professionalism, including expectations that students would engage seriously with the issues of climate change, sea level rise, impacts of coastal communities, and planning for resilience. I was not successful in encouraging our planning students to take spatial analysis seriously – ultimately they shied away from rigorous spatial planning.

Invention

At the time, I did not realize the level of invention in this international planning studio – including having two studio classes work together and separately on the same project. The opportunity to work across cultures is the kind of invention that planning needs. For me as an Indian academic working in the U.S., it was a opportunity to work with my Indian counterpart and learn with and from him about how he approached studio teaching.

The nature of planning continues to change and adapt (as it should) to societal needs, expectations, and political imperatives. In 2020, climate change is front and center in planning conversations, and perhaps a studio about resilience was ahead of its time ten years ago. Similar in timing to the Cal Poly Pomona Climate Action Plan (Chapter 6), the invention in this studio has continued in the climate planning field to produce new methods and types of plans.

Pushing boundaries – expanding ideas, challenging students' skills and capabilities, and the expanding the visions of the project sponsor, are all desirable goals for any studio project and required for continued invention in the field.

After all, if a studio just delivers a consultant's report, done cheaply using student labor, it limits the potential of planning education to create transformational change through the students' greater freedom to push the envelope.

Before the field trip, I invited scholars of Indian origin based in New York City to discuss the complex sociopolitical issues affecting the region. In retrospect, the disconnect between the students and those guest instructors should have provided a clue about what was to come. Yet, it is important that planning students become comfortable learning with/from "local experts," be they academics or practitioners. Likewise, planners need to embrace the reality that they will inevitably be "outsiders" in many situations. Developing authentic ways of connecting with the locals and developing strategies and tactics to connect with them is an important skill. The studio did help prepare students for inventing new forms of planning in the globalizing and hyperdiverse world of work.

Discoveries

The combined educator/planner role played in this planning episode speaks to other situations where planners are conveners of planning efforts by community members and interest groups. It leads to observations about (i) practical judgments made during the planning episode and (ii) broader takeaways for planning.

Practical Judgments

Reflecting on the evolution of the studio, I identify three points where I made practical judgments: (i) deciding to facilitate rather than tightly managing, (ii) seeking to combine an engagement in cultural competence and studio planning (Angotti et al. 2011), and (iii) allowing myself to experience disappointment.

Practical Judgment 1: Facilitating the Emergence of the Plan Rather Than Manage Plan Tasks Toward a Predetermined Product

Studio teaching, as described by Donald Schön (1983, 1987), is an art form – the instructor does not "teach" per se, nor does he or she actually "know" the answer to the question that they pose to the student. When studio teaching works well, there are series of dialogues – experimenting, questioning, and challenging students to solve a particular problem. In an architecture studio, the problems are anchored on a site and aligned with a design program, and the experience is similar in a planning studio. I had a breakthrough with my class soon after we came back from our field trip. I had created three teams to develop three future land use map scenarios, including a scenario that favored development and one that favored land conservation. The small teams worked intensively on anchoring their analyses to the spatial context, and at the end of the session, those who participated felt an intense breakthrough. Although the group chose not to continue these efforts, this process of working through a problem and taking on the difficult questions is undoubtedly the best experience to prepare a planning student for professional life. My joy when I observed the students "doing planning" is a feeling that I still cherish. This approach is risky in an academic environment where negative student evaluations could tarnish a professor's career; however, with the risk comes great reward. Planning managers face similar choices in deciding whether to focus on managing the quality of product or allow their planning team to struggle and learn for the purpose of building team capacity.

Practical Judgment 2: Creating an Engagement in Cultural Competence at the Same Time as One Devoted to Producing a Planning Project

Cultural competency should be required in all planning curricula. As we know, unconscious bias is a complex challenge to overcome. Well-intentioned individuals and groups can think and act in harmful ways even if they are not aware of the reasons for doing it. As individuals, we carry many prejudices and they manifest more visibly when we are in a vulnerable state. We need to invest energy and time thinking about how to manage unconscious bias when planning with diverse populations.

Bringing students from two different cultural frames together required invention at every turn. For example, even as I introduced the American students to a wide range of cultural experiences, I realized that they were not able to absorb and appreciate its value, in part, because they had not prepared themselves to be open to new experiences.

Box 7.1 provides a commentary from one of the students in the class, looking back at the studio in hindsight. Planners and educators rarely get to know what studio participants' really thought of the experience. This account provides valuable insights.

Box 7.1 A View From a Studio Participant
José Pillich, Geospatial Consultant

The Mamallapuram studio provided me with an opportunity to do something unique to finish my master's degree. Failures and successes were abundant, both from a personal and team perspective. Nevertheless, the experience truly shaped my personal and professional paths in a positive manner.

After finishing the studio, Professor Laxmi encouraged me to pursue a doctoral degree, much to my bewilderment. I dismissed her advice due to my challenging experiences during the studio. One year later, Professor Laxmi wrote my recommendation to the City University of New York (CUNY) Graduate Center. Ten years later, I completed my doctoral degree, a postdoc, and I am currently working in the private sector as a consultant. I provide this personal narrative because without the studio experience, I believe that my success would have been harder to achieve.

I am a military brat, a seasoned traveler, and am technically competent. As a result of this background, I thought I was highly prepared to participate in an international studio. The studio's objectives were ambitious, but I believed my fellow graduate students would be competent and able to produce a polished deliverable. Professor Laxmi's reflection about the studio align with my views, but I can add a few other insights.

The lack of team cohesion created a domino effect that impacted every aspect of the studio. Due to the inability of students to entertain new ideas from their peers and a lack of collaboration, group brainstorming was unrealized. I also suspect that certain biased undertones contributed to hostility. At the same time, I must take some responsibility for this failure within the group. I now realize my strong technocratic views and inability to pitch ideas in a manner that was welcomed affected my ability to be an effective team member. Unfortunately, our highly competent Anna University counterparts were treated in the same manner, which further impacted the final deliverables.

In spite of these difficulties, there were successes. Being an international studio, challenges necessitated that the team try new techniques and technologies. For example, the team communicated using Google Wave, which, while challenging, provided us a glimpse into the future of enterprise software that is now commonly used for team projects. At times, this mentality of technological dependence forced us to confront other challenges such as the Mamallapuram town council's lack of data for our analysis. A few of us created methodologies that allowed us to produce new datasets and then documented the process to justify it.

Toward the end of my trip in India, I decided to go by myself to the poorest parts of Chennai. Due to the poverty that I witnessed, I realized that planning is a powerful tool to positively change society. Ten years later, I can say the Mamallapuram studio helped me learn these lessons in an expedited way. I also hope it impacted my studio members in a similar fashion.

Practical Judgment 3: Allowing the Experience of Disappointment

My disappointment in the direction the class took and their failure to realize my expected level of cultural competence could have been avoided by more strongly structuring class assignments, and by limiting and managing interaction between the Indian and American planning students. On the other hand, running the studio more like a tourist expedition would have resulted in happier students. While I cannot assert that the experience had longer-term effects that students might realize when they have more experience and maturity, neither can I say that it did not. The possibility of that growth, even outside the studio was enough for me to proceed in the manner I did.

Takeaways for Practice

Planning education and many forms of planning practice have similar aims and techniques regarding learning, empowerment, and client self-management. This case offers three takeaways for planning educators and planners working on grassroots planning efforts.

Takeaway 1: Respect and Develop the Capacities Required in Order for Planning Participants to Engage in Good Faith and With Open Minds and Hearts

Introducing U.S.-based students to international planning, including opportunities to get involved in a planning project, is a valuable experience. However, student selection is critical. The selection criteria should have included an assessment of emotional readiness as well as technical competence. I relied on self-selection, which did not work when the students moved out of their U.S. comfort zone. It is important to invest time in preparing and working with students before traveling to an international context, such as creating role-play situations and other interactive exercises to show what is and is not accepted in different cultural and institutional contexts. Instructors should prepare for the worst so they have ready responses when issues arise.

Takeaway 2: Engage in Collaboration That Is Sensitive to the Capacity of Community Hosts, and Avoid Harm Before Other Objectives

When academics plan international study abroad experiences, we should consider if we are able to offer the same opportunities for our collaborators in those countries. It appeared that the connections worked for some American students – they shared information, ideas, and knowledge as co-equals – during and after the field trip. I feel a twinge of guilt that I was never able to give the Indian students the same exposure to the U.S. context. Perhaps, if the American students had hosted the Indian students in New York, a franker and complete exchange of ideas would have taken place. I now feel like I burdened the Indian university by setting up the visit and that the Indian students did not really benefit from the exchange.

Takeaway 3: Develop Capabilities for "Ground-Truthing" and Simple Analytic Methods, Because Advanced Data and Methodological Tools Are Not Always Available

U.S. planners have an abundance of data, and much of it is freely available. Many students and planners are unprepared to work in a data-poor environment. They do not have the tools to use proxy measures and approaches to gather information through unconventional ways. For example, U.S. planners know how to identify "quasi-legal" sublet arrangements, or how to do a homeless count, but these skills have to be tweaked to be applicable in countries of the global south.

And Now to You: Planning From the Heart

The case study reveals that planners have to seriously engage with "hidden" programs that we all carry in our minds and hearts, and directly confront internalized attitudes about the value of expertise, technical knowledge, and decision-making approaches. If you are a practicing planner who does not work internationally, I believe that the lessons about cultural competency apply in all settings, including diverse U.S. communities.

For planning educators, studio teaching should be at the heart of planning education for all the reasons discussed earlier and its potential to generate reflection. In addition, we should place cultural competency at the heart of the planning studio, regardless of where it is set. According to Agyeman and Erickson (2012), this requires addressing attributes of awareness, knowledge, skills, and behaviors including professional practice in designing the curriculum. This reflective exercise has been cathartic and educational, allowing me to remember both the highlights and lowlights of the experience. The lasting friendships that I formed with Professor S and Dr. José Pillich are some of the positive outcomes that I will cherish. Another outcome is my commitment to go back to work on an international planning studio with another group of students in the future.

Discussion Questions

1. In the current geopolitical moment, is it feasible or even wise to explore the idea of international planning collaborations, especially in resource-poor countries?
2. Should planning students be required to be proficient in a language other than English?
3. Do you think American students should accept the cultural norms and power structures in the country they visit, or actively challenge those norms and traditions?
4. In this age of big data, in what ways can we prepare students and practitioners to plan in data-poor environments?

References

Agyeman, Julian and Jennifer Sien Erickson. 2012. "Culture, Recognition, and the Negotiation of Difference Some Thoughts on Cultural Competency in Planning Education." *Journal of Planning Education and Research*, 32(3): 358–366. doi: 10.1177/0739456X12441213.

Angotti, Tom, Marly Pierre-Louis, Laxmi Ramasubramanian, Sigmund Shipp, and Angela Tovar. 2011. *Cultural Competence in Urban Affairs and Planning: Engaging New York City's Puerto Rican and Latino Communities*. Report Prepared by Center for Community Planning and Development (CCPD) and Centro de Estudios Puertorriquenos at Hunter College. City University of New York.

Department of Urban Affairs and Planning, Hunter College. 2010. *Mamallapuram Sustainable Tourism Plan 2030. Mamallapuram Studio Final Report*. New York: Hunter College. Available from the author of this chapter.

Friedmann, John. 1987. *Planning in the Public Domain: From Knowledge to Action*. Princeton, NJ: Princeton University Press.

Ramasubramanian, Laxmi and Jochen Albrecht. 2018. *Essential Methods for Planning Practitioners: Skills and Techniques for Data Analysis, Visualization, and Communication*. Cham, Switzerland: Springer.

Schön, Donald. 1983. *The Reflective Practitioner: How Professionals Think in Action*. New York: Basic Books.

Schön, Donald. 1987. *Educating the Reflective Practitioner: Toward a New Design for Teaching and Learning in the Professions*. San Francisco, CA: Jossey-Bass.

UNESCO. 2020. *Group of Monuments at Mahabalipuram, World Heritage List, United Nations Educational, Scientific, and Cultural Organization*. Retrieved February 24, 2020 from https://whc.unesco.org/en/list/249/.

Chapter 8

Equity Planning When the Rubber Meets the Road

Adopting Inclusionary Housing Policies in Portland, Oregon

Lisa K. Bates

Decades ago, Norm Krumholz urged planners to address social and economic disparities by planning with a simple rule: take actions that benefit the least well off in the community (Krumholz et al. 1975; Krumholz 1982; Krumholz and Forester 1990; Krumholz and Clavel 1994). This guideline for equity planning has persisted since the Cleveland Policy Plan of 1974 and is often repeated in courses on planning theory, but it is rare that we break down how, exactly, to follow Krumholz's rule (City of Cleveland 1974). Equity planning is both a technical and a political exercise. It requires analytic tools to assess the benefits and costs of policy and investment options for different groups, and political skills to navigate bureaucracies and elected bodies to change resource allocations in favor of those who have not historically had power in the planning process.

This case of the development of a plan leading to adoption of an inclusionary housing zoning (IZ) policy in Portland, Oregon, addresses the roles and choices of planners in both of these realms. IZ ordinances require the provision of affordable housing units in new developments, in which buildings of a defined size provide a percentage of units at rents affordable to defined income levels. My roles in this process were multiple: a member of a Technical Advisory Group in Equity (TAG) and a paid consultant to the City of Portland. The case highlights three practical judgments: (i) getting political, (ii) advancing knowledge and analytic frameworks in an advocacy context, and (iii) rebuilding relationships to move forward.

Description of the Planning Episode

Portland, Oregon, made an explicit commitment to equity planning in 2012 as part of The Portland Plan, a strategic plan to realize a vision of "a prosperous, educated, healthy, and equitable Portland into the future" (City of Portland 2012). The Portland Plan defined equity, and specifically an imperative to address racial disparities, through a two-year process of community engagement with staff in the Bureau of Planning and Sustainability (BPS). Figure 8.1 illustrates The Portland Plan's equity concept map, revealing the interconnections of equity with economic prosperity and access, a healthy connected city, and thriving educated youth.

The equity goal from The Portland Plan and the goals of the city's climate action plan were to be carried into the city's 2035 Comprehensive Plan (Comp Plan) by BPS to address land use, zoning, and public facilities. Throughout the Comp Plan process, a community-based coalition, Anti-Displacement Portland (ADPDX), pushed planners to embed equity goals and policies into the Comp Plan, especially in the housing chapter (see Bates 2018 for a description of this planning process which called for an IZ ordinance).

Institutional Setting

Portland, Oregon, is a city of 633,115 residents. Figure 8.2 shows the regional context of Portland, located on the Willamette River as it approaches its confluence with the Columbia River. Regarding demographics, Portland is differentiated from the U.S. population in the following ways. Portland data is listed first; the U.S. data is in brackets (U.S. Census 2020):

- Fewer young people: persons under 18 years, 18.1% (22.4%).
- Less diverse: Black or African American alone, 5.8% (13.4%); Hispanic or Latino, 9.7% (18.3%); Asian 7.8% (5.4%). Portland has the fewest people of color of any large city in the U.S.

Figure 8.1 Portland Plan Representation of the Equity Lens. Image source: City of Portland www.portlandonline.com/portlandplan

- Lower home ownership rate: owner-occupied housing rate 53.1% (63.8%), with substantial racial gaps in homeownership for Black, Latino, Asian, and Native American people (the overall communities of color homeownership rate is 45%).
- Lower risk to social well-being: persons without health insurance 7.8% (10.0%).
- Somewhat higher income: 2014–2018 median household income in 2017 dollars, $65,740 ($60,293), but growing economic inequality.

Portland has a national reputation among urban planners for its *urban growth boundary*, sustainability initiatives, and commitment to transit and bicycle planning. The city has attracted young and college-educated residents with its

Figure 8.2 Portland Regional Context. Image Source: Google, Landsat/Copernicus

"hipster" reputation, and it has been named one of the most gentrifying cities in the country. In 2012, the Coalition of Communities of Color, representing multiple local nonprofits, published a series of reports titled "An Unsettling Profile" that revealed deep racial inequality in the Portland area along every metric for health, well-being, and economic self-sufficiency. These reports' findings startled many decision-makers in the city and became important to The Portland Plan, a multisector strategic plan.

The Portland Plan culminated with the city committing to equity and racial justice outcomes after a multiyear community engagement process. The TAG that developed the equity principles included city staffers and representatives from a diverse set of communities, learning and strategizing together. The group's work was intensely collaborative, and forged new relationships and cooperation between communities and the city. However, the inside-outside advisory process did not continue in the same form into the more focused Comp Plan. BPS, Portland's long-range planning agency, is innovative and change-oriented; as indicated by its name, it went through a process of integrating city sustainability efforts into its work, and it houses the climate action plan. The hope was that BPS would adopt equity as a guiding principle in the same way it had created a sustainability lens for its work. However, by the

Comp Plan process, BPS had not yet fully incorporated "equity" as a decision metric, only a stated value. The other major city player in the case is the Portland Housing Bureau (PHB).

Overview of the Planning Process

As mentioned, the limited role for equity-oriented stakeholders in the Comp Plan led to the formation of ADPDX and its advocacy campaign to push more specific planning and land use policies to achieve equity goals. For the communities experiencing the affordable housing crisis, the experience with Portland's planning system does not align with its international reputation. As the city has grown and become more popular and "cool," lower-income renters and people of color have voiced their belief that plans are not "for" them or their communities. For many advocates, the Comp Plan would gentrify neighborhoods. The idea of using plans to make equitable policies and resource allocations opened a new arena for advocacy. As ADPDX received technical assistance and education, the coalition continually articulated the expectation that it would co-create goals, policies, and programs, claiming the expertise in community needs and equity policies. This insistence on engaging with the specifics of land use analytics and regulation development was at odds with the BPS's self-perception and belief in planners as experts, a vision in which very strong technical teams produce sophisticated analyses and models.

While community advocates were becoming increasingly vociferous about a crisis of affordable housing, leaders in BPS were expressing frustration at being asked to solve a problem that they saw as outside their purview, and were directing attention toward their counterparts at PHB as being responsible for meeting housing goals. Portland leaders decided to convene an "expert panel" to formulate an IZ policy as soon as a state preemption on IZ was lifted. The IZ expert panel was created in this context of continued engagement but simmering discontent. Figure 8.3 is an image from community activists protesting at city hall.

The Core Problem

The Comp Plan development process was an opportunity to use public planning powers to address the provision of goods to less advantaged renters who were increasingly squeezed in the housing market, despite a huge development boom. As in the equity planning literature, this process included both stakeholder

Figure 8.3 Anti-Displacement Protest at Portland City Hall. Image source: Pamela Phan

engagement and technical analysis in a larger political contest about development and gentrification. Any planner wading into this problem would need to consider technical issues in modeling short- and long-term policy effects for individual developers and the aggregate impacts on the location, type, and amount of housing development in the city and region; at the same time, they must be prepared to navigate the politics of any proposal. With specific details emerging about what the new commitments to equity would mean in terms of changed conditions for developers, interest groups of private real estate actors were preparing to advocate from their typically powerful position, while the ADPDX stakeholders, who had recently won several policy victories, were flexing new muscles.

Intended and Actual Outcomes

The IZ expert panel had representation from private developers, housing finance institutions, community-based organizations, and housing policy experts or researchers. I was selected for the final seat as a member of the faculty at Portland State's planning school who studies housing. Resources on inclusionary zoning included Schwartz et al. (2012), Sturtevant (2016), and Thaden and Wang (2017).

The expert panel was to work with city staff and external consultants to advise on the specific regulation for inclusionary housing, taking into account the local development context by analyzing development pro formas under different policies. In Portland, the staff were from two bureaus: BPS, whose purview is development regulation for the private market; and PHB, which funds and oversees subsidized, regulated affordable housing. PHB was in the lead; BPS staff were also involved with analysis; and there were multiple advocacy groups seeking to influence the expert panel as well as the Planning & Sustainability Commission and City Council, both of which would have to approve the policy.

The resulting Comp Plan includes racial justice and anti-displacement as not only aspirational values but as required dimensions of analysis for rezoning/up-zoning, significant development sites, and public investments in infrastructure or economic development. The concept of pairing new development with anti-displacement and equity-promoting strategies was adopted in principle. However, the planning process did not result in a detailed implementation program for what an equity analysis should entail, let alone what mitigating actions by a developer or offsetting public investments would be required in response to findings. While ADPDX was pressing to be part of the development of these concepts, an early opportunity arose to test the housing equity policies.

One of the policies adopted in the Comp Plan, through intense advocacy by ADPDX, was that the city would pursue a mandatory IZ ordinance as soon as the state of Oregon dropped its preemption of this kind of regulation. IZ ordinances are used in many jurisdictions to ensure that new private housing development creates some income-restricted units. Typically, an IZ ordinance sets an "inclusion rate" or percentage of units that must be set aside for low-to moderate-income renters, and creates incentives for the developer to offset those costs —often higher density allowances or expedited permitting processes.

At the time the Comp Plan was being developed, Oregon did not allow cities to use mandatory IZ as an affordable housing production tool. The provision that Portland would pursue IZ at a time when it was not allowed by Oregon statute was a contentious issue with multiple land use attorneys weighing in for BPS and ADPDX. On both sides, there was a palpable fatigue with the struggle to define and embed equity planning as a practice.

As the Comp Plan neared passage, a coalition of housing advocates successfully lobbied the state legislature to lift this preemption, so the inclusion of this provision became relevant more quickly than expected. The new state law allowed cities to adopt mandatory inclusionary housing programs within a set of sideboards: IZ could apply only to buildings of at least 20 units, the units could be affordable at a minimum income level of 80% of area median incomes, there was a maximum 20% inclusion rate, and the state provided a list of specific developer incentives to offset costs. In the end, the inclusionary housing proposal from PHB passed at City Council.

Examination of the Planning Episode Using Framework Elements

Drawing on the Figure 5.2 framework (see Chapter 5), this section provides reflection on the case. It organizes the observations in the three main framework elements: (i) planner-as-person, (ii) interpretation of context, and (iii) reasoning and methods in the planning episode itself.

Planner-as-Person Elements That Shaped the Approach

I come to urban planning with a strong social justice mission and a desire to transform structural conditions. In college, I thought of becoming a social worker and spent a couple of years volunteering and interning in social service settings. I was struck by the repetitive nature of the work when it came to housing problems – calling the evictions court, printing form letters about rates, and clients perpetually short on rent and worrying about the creep of renovations and gourmet grocers that signaled the neighborhood was about to change. I shifted my focus to policy and planning in hopes of addressing the deep segregation, inequity between rich and poor neighborhoods, and poor housing conditions I saw around me in Washington, DC.

Personal Framework Elements

As a Black American with family in a disinvested city, I was already aware that cities had been places of both great opportunity and great oppression for

Black folks and people of color. I was also deeply unimpressed by the analysis of poor Black neighborhoods that was ascendant in the 1990s – the depiction of a "culture of poverty" that needed to be interrupted by removing the social safety net as an incentive to work. As I entered planning school, I was more interested in the ways that policy-makers and planners had disrupted Black and Brown communities' social and economic structures with urban renewal while supporting White wealth creation with discriminatory development and real estate practices. I believe that planning has made its worst mistakes by insisting on its expertise and "scientific" knowledge, which has reinforced disadvantage. When we don't acknowledge how our institutions, infrastructures, and policies were built on racism and classism, we can't actively pursue equity. Without knowing our history we won't be able to correct our analyses or rebuild democratic relationships with disenfranchised communities.

My work is deeply rooted in these values, but my focus on housing policy means I have a grounding in economics and quantitative analysis. Much of my research, from my dissertation on, is about how planners model housing markets and use analysis to support their strategies for housing and neighborhood change. Often, this work focuses on how planning is not well served by its analytics due to the limitations of available data and flawed models that are based on an oversimplified view of economic theory. My pet peeve is hearing something say "it's just Econ 101!" about a housing policy – there is nothing "101" about how housing markets work!

Personal Incongruity and Ambiguity

Developing an inclusionary housing zoning regulation for Portland was one facet of the implementation program for the agreed upon concept of "anti-displacement." It was a first attempt at developing a technical analysis and regulatory structure for this somewhat nebulous concept. As I've described, there was high conflict among external stakeholders and disagreement among city staff from different professional orientations. My assigned role as the researcher on the expert panel was an evolution of my ongoing relationship with both BPS and PHB.

I had been involved with the work of the city to develop both its overall equity planning practice and its response to gentrification and housing displacement. Often, my engagement has been as part of an advisory body. I was a co-chair for the Technical Advisory Group on Equity that first developed the racial justice "lens" for city policy-making (see Figure 8.1). As the Comp Plan process started, I was appointed to a Policy Expert Group focused on development in higher-density corridors. In these settings, my role was not defined by the BPS and I could offer my own thoughts based on my own knowledge and opinions about good planning. Because I was often aligned with representatives from the community-based organizations that would ultimately form ADPDX, I found that I played the part of an interlocutor between planners and community. I thought of myself as being like a language interpreter – translating community concerns about affordability and displacement into "planner speak" and helping folks understand what the planners meant in turn. I developed relationships with the staff, but also pushed them hard to take on more responsibility for fulfilling the equity planning goal – making sure always to ask for the analysis of benefits and costs differentiated by race and income, and to insist on looping back to representatives from historically underrepresented communities. In these roles I had a high level of discretion – in fact, the Equity TAG had completely reframed the discussion of The Portland Plan and even successfully advocated for the city to create a new Office of Equity and embed new practices by creating equity manager positions in all city bureaus, an outcome not at all imagined at the Comp Plan's outset.

In part because of the trust between these groups and myself, but also because of my recognized policy expertise, I also became a paid consultant to BPS, creating an analysis of gentrification in the city and a strategy for countering its effects with long- and short-term planning policies (Bates 2013). As a consultant, my work looked different from a volunteer adviser. I worked closely with staff to address their desired scope of work, and while I suggested ways to expand the role of planning beyond BPS practices at that time, the strategy was not "radical." BPS staff enlisted my help to present the work to their commission and elected officials, cementing my status as a certified "expert" in these venues.

In the meantime, I was also maintaining a relationship as an advice-giver and technical assistant to the groups forming the ADPDX. As several community organization staff were my former students, we worked to educate folks in the community about what the land use plan is and could do, and share potential tools for achieving anti-displacement goals. I also helped enlist legal support from 1000 Friends of Oregon, a land use and environmental advisory organization on whose board of directors I served. These relationships were all known to the planning staff, and represented a bit of a double-edged sword: on the one hand, I could be useful in bridging the two groups' preferences, but on the other hand, I didn't have a clear organizational allegiance and didn't maintain deference to client wishes as a sometime-consultant to the city.

These overlapping roles in the planning processes that led up to the inclusionary housing policy development, and my role as a professor at Portland State, were complicated to say the least! I was involved in many ways and with multiple stakeholders in the topics of equity, housing, and gentrification, and had to be clear about which hat I was wearing at any time. There were city staff and community organizers who had either been my students, which created a certain relationship and power dynamic; others are alums of Portland State's program or are potentially hiring our students; therefore, maintaining positive relationships was important. In general, I was learning that the Portland planning community just isn't that big!

Knowing that I'd be working with the same folks – not only city staff but also the professional planning consultants, community advocates, and developer representatives – I needed to think about the long-term implications of my own choices. I clearly wanted to keep pushing the city to do better and more on its equity planning, and to more directly address anti-displacement issues. I also wanted to maintain good relations with planning and housing staff, hoping to support the difficult challenge of taking on equity analysis and policy-making, knowing that institutional change would not succeed overnight.

Interpretation of Context

Developing the implementing regulations for the Comp Plan's anti-displacement policies meant working in a space of considerable uncertainty. Over several years, a BPS accustomed to accolades for its expertise was challenged by outsiders on the grounds of data and analysis. ADPDX demanded that policy analyses be disaggregated to look at impacts for communities of color, low-income residents, and renters. These tasks were not technically difficult, and learning to think about equity impacts was part of the evolution of the institution toward its own goals. More conflict emerged about analysis and policy choices that related to housing supply and its role in preventing displacement – and the inclusionary zoning proposal was central to this debate.

Context Framework Elements

Housing supply is a challenging issue for any planner. Real estate development isn't in the span of control of the land use plan – we set the conditions for development, but planners don't directly supply housing, affordable or not. Everyone – from BPS and PHB staff to the community-based organizations – agreed that planning is not solely responsible for either causing or preventing displacement.

Inclusionary zoning policy development would be shared between two bureaus operating in a new area of work. As noted, BPS focuses on land supply and zoning for market development, with its analysis focused on getting more units built in the city. PHB determines how and where affordable housing dollars will be spent, attending to subsidized units, and while it does make policy about housing, PHB has engaged only infrequently with the land use aspects of housing. Even though the inclusionary zoning tool has been in use for 40 years in other jurisdictions, after 15 years of state preemption, there were very few Portland staffers who had any experience with the mechanisms of IZ and how to balance its incentive structure to get the private sector to produce more rent-restricted units.

Context Uncertainty and Ambiguity

The IZ advisory body was labeled as an "expert" group, but clearly the knowledge basis of each member would be understood as having different value to the process by the various stakeholders. There was no agreement about the fact basis from which to develop the policy, despite what looked like sufficient guidance and expertise. PHB had hired two consultants: a local firm with extensive ties to the Portland development industry and a national economic analysis firm whose staff had little interest in local political squabbles.

The PHB and BPS staff created models independently and would or could not reconcile their analyses, with housing staff at PHB supporting a more expansive program requirement to address increasing economic segregation, and planners from BPS insistent it would slow down the housing market at a critical time for high-density production. Real estate industry groups created their own independent analysis of substantial impacts on all housing development, but without transparency about their data. Anti-displacement advocates argued that the focus on analyzing developer decisions obscured the assessment of impacts for low-income people and communities of color, failing to consider how the policy could create more affordable units even if it reduced some market-rate supply. These questions emerged during the policy development and adoption continued into the evaluation of its early implementation. Some of the actions and choices around the IZ policy have had ramifications for relationships, institutional evolution, and the continued efforts to adopt the equity planning model.

The Planning Episode: Reasoning and Methods

Norm Krumholz taught planners to "just do" equity. But how do we know what that is, and what role is there for the community in defining the implementation plans for doing it? Equity planning is technical, analyzing alternative regulations; and it is political, requiring advocacy for polices that go against the status quo. In the development of IZ in Portland, both of these dimensions became part of my planner role.

Logic

In the work to build a planning equity framework in Portland, I had previously co-chaired a committee with a mix of city staff and community advocates, where we built a community of learning and knowledge. Members worked to understand one another's values, professional commitments, and to create a shared analysis of the opportunities and constraints for city government to shift its work toward more equitable outcomes. I wondered if the IZ panel could and would operate similarly, given that its members all articulated a concern for affordable housing.

The IZ advisory panel included development professionals and community-based anti-displacement advocates. In sitting on the panel, it was clear that for some members, the voice of community was useful in advocating for the policy to exist, but its representatives were seen as having insufficient knowledge of real estate finance and development to debate the terms of the regulation. I met numerous times with these advocates, in the kind of technical translator role I had played through the Comp Plan process. We reviewed the data and models before meetings, and I shared research on inclusionary housing policies.

On the other hand, development professionals had an obvious self-interest in creating a lenient policy with maximum financial incentives, or even in scuttling the entire proposal. While I was understood to be "pro-IZ" I was still able to meet with some development industry representatives to learn more about how they viewed the policy as a change in their business model. Because I was able to speak the language of policy and economics analysis, I found they were willing to engage in discussions about market data and model assumptions with me, often trying to convince me of their position.

As the panel reviewed and debated the market models under different policy analyses, the idea of building a common set of assumptions became untenable. The two consultant teams and the local real estate industry actors each brought their own numbers to the table. No matter whose data was being used, the analysis itself was a complicated assessment of residual land value that was conceptually difficult – essentially, the goal was to design an inclusionary policy that would have requirements for affordable housing and offsetting financial incentives that would create an equilibrium with respect to land prices.

At the public hearing on the policy, BPS staff, who are considered more technically sophisticated than the PHB staff, called the proposal into question. I solicited the assistance of a nationally known economist, Dr. George Galster, introducing him to the PHB staff as a resource for countering their arguments (Galster 2016). Galster's appearance at the hearing was very strong, reviewing research in detail and arguing that Portland was behind the times in not adopting IZ as a tool. Galster provided evidence that debunked four myths about inclusionary housing:

- Myth 1 – Inclusionary housing will slow the production of housing.
- Myth 2 – Inclusionary housing will slow the filtering down of housing to moderate-income households and thus hurt them.
- Myth 3 – Inclusionary housing will raise housing prices overall.
- Myth 4 – Inclusionary housing will generate few affordable units.

Where the real estate developers had dominated the expert panel with their knowledge and disparaged the community viewpoint as naïve, at City Council, the pro-IZ side clearly had the weight of "certified smart people" with the testimony of PhD-holding scholars backing the housing proposal.

All the stakeholders, the IZ panel members, staff leadership, and elected officials claimed they were working for equity, but with different conclusions, it was clear that underpinning the debate there were fundamental questions about knowledge, expertise, and the use of technical analysis in a politicized situation. As we worked together, I realized that the values misalignment was too great to continue to work for a common set of data and analyses. While the policy development seemed like "objective" technical work, it was actually based on competing and highly value-laden visions of the future of the city. Instead of articulating trade-offs – between density and affordability, and between developers and renters – each stakeholder group was simply presenting its preferred option as "the equity choice" and using the panel as a space to win supporters, not to consider alternatives. With this recognition, I turned to a second strategy that was much more political and confrontational, taking sides in the debate between BPS and PHB staff.

Emotion

An element of emotion in the planning episode relates to relationships between staff planners and advocates. In order to ensure their priorities were achieved in the comp plan, ADPDX was assertive in going past staff planners to speak directly to planning commissioners and City Council. This political strategy had been taken poorly by some of the planning staff. Some staff felt their collaborative efforts to add equity to the draft plan were sincere and struggled with the implication that they weren't doing enough; others were pushing back on the community coalition's land use legal analysis and wanted to assert and maintain the leadership role of BPS.

The inclusionary housing proposal from PHB passed at City Council. Along with my colleagues in community-based organizations, I was pleased about its potential. I was also aware that the BPS staff might be unhappy with how I had joined in advocacy and criticized their work. In a small professional community, I want to have positive working relationships with staff across the city and also remain free to be critical when efforts to move the equity agenda fall short. As we emerged from the IZ policy process, I worked to reassert my role as a critical friend and colleague, rather than a consultant who only responds to the client's preferences.

Beyond my personal relationship to BPS and its staff was the issue of how planners will relate to community anti-displacement advocates in future policy development and implementation work as outlined in the Comp Plan. The IZ ordinance process made clear that some planners felt the community's role in the Comp Plan – setting goals and broad directions for policy – was acceptable, but that when it comes to the specifics of land use, *only* the planners have the technical knowledge to create regulations. Community advocates had seen how the planning staff regarded market rate development as the highest goal, and had not provided an equity analysis. Coming up on the policy docket was the proposed Residential Infill Project, which would dramatically reshape single-family zoning; new housing design codes; and a light rail extension project, all of which had opportunities for community participation. The ADPDX coalition was prepared to engage in all of these discussions.

Convention

In this planning episode, my effort was to change the status quo – to disrupt the convention of developing policies that were blind to racial justice and had unanticipated consequences. However, an element of convention was bringing "best practice" research to the policy discussion, as I attempted to use empirical research literature on inclusionary zoning to support the panel having a good knowledge basis for discussing what for Portland was a new policy. In this new arena for Portland planning, with conflict all around, bringing data and evidence to a policy question was highly politicized rather than merely conventional.

The most relevant instance of convention – acting in accord with practice norms – was my rebuilding of relationships with planners after this episode to continue collaboration on the shared goals of creating a more equitable city. I am mindful that while consultants may fly home after their reports are filed, our local public sector planners have long-term relationships with stakeholders and the publics they serve. As part of the Portland planning ecosystem, I also try to maintain relationships with my colleague planners as well as community advocates.

Invention

As previously described, invention was at the core of this planning episode: moving racial justice from broad plan language to implementation commitments. Most of the invention was determining my role as an advocate and technical expert. Portland values collaborative processes and weighing many voices in its policy-making. Advisory groups, panels, and committees abound in the bureaus, and are often collegial spaces for discussions. But for those of us trying to push the city away from its status quo policies to ones that clearly address the needs of the least advantaged, the compromises emerging from these processes are often not good enough. I recognized that whatever good work came from the technical expert panel, the real decisions would be political. The final decision body was City Council – the elected officials who would hear testimony for a few sessions, not sit and puzzle through months of analytic, legal, and scenario wrangling. To change the policy would require the invention of an advocacy strategy outside of the norms of practice in Portland.

Discoveries

The combined advocacy/technical expert role I played in this planning episode speaks to other situations where planners have more than one professional identity. It leads to observations about (i) practical judgments made during the planning episode and (ii) broader takeaways for planning.

Practical Judgments

Reflecting on the evolution of the panel and policy process, there are three turning points where I chose to operate as a professional planner in distinct modes: (i) deciding to get political to push equity, (ii) advancing knowledge and analytic frameworks in an advocacy context, and (iii) rebuilding relationships to move equity forward.

Practical Judgment 1: Getting Political to Push Equity

The expert panel process moved forward with all sides presenting new data and analysis at each meeting, never agreeing to each other's fundamental assumptions or methods. Stakeholders were beginning to go public with blogs, media interviews, and communicating directly with City Council members.

I believed that the policy as proposed by PHB was sound; the dire warnings of market collapse in the face of an affordability requirement were overstated and that the lack of experience with IZ was scaring decision-makers more than necessary given its record of success. I sought to reframe the issue of analysis, pointing out that the entire policy development process had been dominated by development interests and did not take into sufficient consideration housing needs or the equity policy. I was also able to go into detail about the analytic assumptions in a way that other community advocates could not.

The question of whether IZ would become Portland policy was about trade-offs between developer profits and community housing needs. There were and are genuine costs and benefits for all parties in the policy; equity planning requires that we prioritize the impacts to the least advantaged members of the community. I took a political stance to call attention to the ways that the planning staff and developers were failing to address the questions raised by the adopted equity goals. I raised questions about the use of the industry's alternative models and pointed out that developers had been pleased by the policy process and consultant analysis plan until it became clear that the results were not as they expected.

I agreed to be available to the City Council at its work sessions on the policy, where some members of the expert panel were questioned about our work. In these sessions, I leaned heavily on my visibility as a partner of the city and a planner with a PhD who is an "expert" beyond just being named to a panel. City Council members are generally respectful of planning staff, but they are also very interested in the opinions of faculty in my department.

Practical Judgment 2: Advancing Knowledge and Analytic Frameworks in an Advocacy Context

The previous section on the application of logic in the planning episode explains this practical judgment. In my role as a member of the expert panel, I had to make choices about how to operate on the panel and how to engage with both agency staff and community partners. My role on the panel was defined as a policy research expert, which implied a status of knowledge about inclusionary zoning. I was also a visible partner of ADPDX and not considered "neutral" on the issue of housing affordability. I used my knowledge and analytic frameworks to advance advocacy positions.

Practical Judgment 3: Rebuilding Relationships to Move Equity Forward

I committed to working with the coalition and the BPS staff to build on the comprehensive plan anti-displacement platform. The debate in the political realm over IZ was the first of many highly contentious issues playing out with many stakeholders and communities weighing in. If BPS and PHB staff didn't further develop the equity lens on their analysis, they would be developing policies with unintended consequences for those vulnerable to housing market changes. This new work to actively shape the housing market toward inclusion and affordability needed collaboration, which in my opinion meant the recognition that staff didn't hold the monopoly on expertise. Despite some tensions, I've joined the new iteration of a joint community–city working group whose members are committed to learning together, focusing on finding new practices in other cities facing gentrification. At the same time, it is clear that there will be more episodes of political tension as community members push the planners to address inequity and institutionalized racism. The transformation toward equity planning will not happen overnight, and it felt important to be part of that work as a partner, while being clear that equity work can include political opposition as well as collaboration.

Takeaways for Practice

As we try to implement equity planning as a model for the city, I recognize that Norm Krumholz's decision rule – implement the option that best supports those who are least well off – is difficult work!

Takeaway 1: Generate Disaggregated Analyses and Modeling Reform to Support Equity Planning

As planners, we don't always have the analytical tools to answer the question. In the area of housing in a gentrifying city, planners' work is highly consequential, but we often don't have certainty about the outcomes of our proposals. Predicting future housing supply and price in response to regulations isn't a perfect science, and there are differing opinions even among "experts" about how markets work under different conditions. We have disputes over data and analysis that are rooted in worldviews and assumptions. It can be difficult for planners to let go of their role as experts to incorporate alternative assessments and to recognize when their technical work is reinforcing the status quo. Yet it is essential to disaggregate modeling analyses to reveal equity implications.

Takeaway 2: Focus Analysis on Trade-Offs, and Differential Benefits and Burdens, to Bring Equity Issues to the Forefront

Equity planning means acknowledging trade-offs and different benefits and burdens across the community; understanding how underrepresented communities experience those outcomes requires their knowledge. Making space for community advocates to participate in equity planning work means truly treating those advocates as experts in developing policy and evaluating its implementation. I was effective in a role translating information and language between technical planners and community-based planners, and holding space for knowledge from multiple points of view to be incorporated into deliberation. As a planner who studies the long history of our profession's intervention into low-income neighborhoods and communities of color, I am particularly attuned to the negative consequences of planners' interventions. When planners insisted on their unique expertise and downplayed uncertainty, we damaged communities with urban renewal and, more recently, gentrification.

Takeaway 3: Recognize That Change Is Iterative, Political Work

Institutional change toward equity takes multiple strategies. Learning together is important, and we can create new structures for deliberating on policies. There is still resistance to many equity-oriented policies. Equity work is political work; it attempts to make change to resource and power distribution. Stakeholders for whom the status quo operates well, who may have to give up some benefits, will work politically to defeat new approaches.

Equity planners and their community-based partners have to be ready to communicate with media and elected officials, making their case for change. In our professional community, it's still a challenge to navigate personal and organizational relationships that include both collaboration and conflict, especially when parties use available platforms to speak directly to elected officials instead of just debating inside the bureau conference room. In the relationship among planning staff, ADPDX advocates, and me in advisory and consultant roles, there are times when stepping outside of the technical work for political communications work creates friction. Staff planners are more constrained in how they can operate politically and can feel that their work is being disparaged. With the resumption of an ongoing work group, I hope having regular communications will at least make those moments unsurprising and understandable as part of the strategy to turn Portland into an equity planning city.

And Now to You: Advocacy Planners Are Technical Planners Too

Most planners today recognize that our professional forbearers made mistakes. Urban renewal, highway expansion, and sprawl have all contributed to segregation and inequality by race and class. We know that planners of the past didn't include all community voices in their processes. While these results may have been unintentional, we can criticize the top-down planners who made these choices. Much of our work today is addressing the negative consequences of old policy paradigms. We have a harder time recognizing how our actions today – even as we embrace participation and sustainability – may continue to reinforce the status quo when it comes to inequity.

Choosing to practice in an equity planning model means you'll be questioning every step of planning – from the framing of a problem, to the data gathering and analysis, to the policy options presented, to the engagement with communities. The questions you will raise could create a stir: How are we affecting those least privileged, those most disenfranchised, and those most burdened by the negative externalities of planning? Are we choosing to reduce those burdens and to direct benefits to these communities, even when those options are not favored by those who are politically and economically more powerful? You will need to develop new analytic skills, possibly beyond what you learn in the university or on the job – and you'll need to not only project the future trajectory we're on, but imagine a different path for your community.

Bringing the people who have been most harmed by planning into the lead is a significant change; asking those communities to be part of policy development, implementation, and evaluation is not yet the norm in practice. You will be letting go of some of your professional mantle as an expert and acknowledging uncertainty about how conventional plans may unfold in communities that are wary of planning intervention.

Many equity planners work outside of government, in community-based organizations with the support of colleagues and constituents. That work requires strategizing and organizing to advocate for your vision both in bureaucratic and political decision-making bodies. Norm Krumholz urged those of us who want to seek social justice to work *in* government as agents of transformation. If you ask equity questions as a public sector planner, you will be asking your planning colleagues to rethink assumptions and restart processes; that may mean pushing back against bosses and going up against powerful interest groups and political figures. You will need strategies for change inside of institutions, assessing how quickly you can move and developing communication skills to persuade others to join your work. There are challenges on the path to making change!

Discussion Questions

1. How should planners use the information and analysis of stakeholder groups in making policy? Should all participants be considered "experts"?
2. What kind of process would you create as a planner faced with a new policy option that was hotly contested?
3. As you reflect on your own commitments and personal style, would you take a more collegial or a more confrontational stance in trying to move a new idea forward?

References

Bates, Lisa K. 2013. *Gentrification and Displacement Study: Implementing an Equitable Inclusive Development Strategy in the Context of Gentrification.* Report prepared for the City of Portland Bureau of Planning and Sustainability. Portland, OR: City of Portland. doi: 10.15760/report-01.

Bates, Lisa K. 2018. "Growth Without Displacement: A Test for Equity Planning in Portland." In: *Advancing Equity Planning Now*, edited by Norman Krumholz and Kathryn Wertheim Hexter. Ithica, NY and London: Cornell University Press, pp. 21–43.

City of Cleveland. 1974. *Cleveland Policy Plan.* Cleveland, OH: City of Cleveland.

City of Portland. 2012. *The Portland Plan.* Accessed February 25, 2020 at https://www.portlandonline.com/portlandplan/index.cfm?c=58776&a=405753.

Galster, George. 2016. Testimony Before the Portland City Council Re: Proposed Inclusionary Housing Ordinance. *Official Minutes, City of Portland.* Special meeting held December 13, 2016: 21–22.

Krumholz, Norman, J.M. Cogger, and J.H. Linner. 1975. The Cleveland Policy Planning Report. *Journal of the American Institute of Planners*, 41(5): 37–41.

Krumholz, Norman. 1982. A Retrospective View of Equity Planning: Cleveland, 1969–1979. *Journal of the American Planning Association*, 48(2): 163–174. doi.org/10.1080/01944368208976535.

Krumholz, Norman and John Forester. 1990. *Making Equity Planning Work: Leadership in the Public Sector.* Philadelphia, PA: Temple University Press.

Krumholz, Norman and Pierre Clavel. 1994. *Reinventing Cities: Equity Planners Tell Their Stories.* Philadelphia, PA: Temple University Press.

Schwartz, Heather L., Liisa Ecola, Kristen J. Leuscher, and Aaron Kofner. 2012. "Is Inclusionary Zoning Inclusionary?: A Guide for Practitioners." *Research and Report.* Accessed March 11, 2020 at http://www.rand.org/pubs/technical_reports/TR1231.html.

Sturtevant, Lisa. 2016. "Separating Fact from Fiction to Design Effective Inclusionary Housing Programs." National Housing Conference Report. Accessed March 11, 2020 at https://www.nhc.org/publication/separating-fact-from-fiction-to-design-effective-inclusionary-housing-programs/.

Thaden, Emily and Ruoniu Wang. 2017. "What Do We Know About Inclusionary Housing? A National Survey of Programs." *Grounded Solutions Network.* Accessed March 10, 2020 at https://groundedsolutions.org/tools-for-success/resource-library/inclusionary-housing-prevalence-impact-and-practices.

U.S. Census. Accessed March 9, 2020 at https://www.census.gov/quickfacts/fact/table/portlandcityoregon,US/PST045219.

Chapter 9

Miami 21 Form-Based Code, Miami, Florida

Ana Gelabert-Sánchez

The Miami 21 form-based code moved the City of Miami, Florida, from a traditional Euclidean zoning approach to one based on principles of new urbanism and smart growth. It received first reading 2009, with final approval occurring in 2010 after a five-year development period. This case provides my perspective on the process as planning director for the City of Miami during code development, adoption, and early implementation.

The Miami 21 effort was a comprehensive approach to planning and code development comprised of six elements: zoning regulation, economic development, historic preservation, parks and open spaces, arts and culture, and transportation. The focus here is on form-based zoning regulation and the community plan revisions necessary to support it. The case reveals three practical judgments: (i) addressing vision and implementation simultaneously; (ii) using a bottom-up, community-based process that directly addressed disagreement and distrust; and (iii) being responsive to political support for action.

Description of the Planning Episode

The planning episode describes my role in supervising the preparation and adoption of the Miami 21 form-based code (Code). A form-based code is an approach to zoning that focuses on predictable regulation of physical form in relation to the public realm. It differs in purpose from the traditional Euclidian approach of separating land uses. My role was to oversee the process to develop and adopt the new Code along with the vision and goal-setting process to support it. I supervised the lead consultant team, Duany Plater-Zyberk & Company; communicated with elected officials, city departments, and the community; and brought in other consultants as needed.

Mayor Manny Diaz was the igniting spark and the primary driver for the Code, which he set in motion at a small meeting discussing a wide-range of planning issues – considering what was not working in Miami and how we could change it. We reviewed images of places and neighborhoods and examined everything we understood not to be working well. We spoke about walkability, improving the public and private realms, the need for transit, the need for open space and parks, and the opportunity for economic development – in short, the qualities of a livable city. Mayor Diaz resolved to support a new approach to zoning and this became the defining moment to implement my dream, the opportunity to plan for and improve the quality of life in Miami.

Institutional Setting

Located in Miami–Dade County, Florida, the City of Miami had a population of 470,914 in 2018. Figure 9.1 shows the city in its regional context. Miami is a fast-growing South Florida center of cultural, economic, and financial activity, set in a metropolitan area of 6.1 million people. The city has an international flavor, both in terms of residents and businesses. The following provides demographic information; Miami data is listed first; the U.S. data is in brackets (U.S. Census 2020):

- Fewer young people: persons under 18 years, 17.9% (22.4%).
- Very diverse: Black or African American, 17.9% (13.4%); Hispanic or Latino, 69.1% (18.3%).
- Lower share of owner-occupied housing: owner-occupied housing rate 52.2% (63.8%).

- More risk to social well-being: persons without health insurance 20.0% (10.2%).
- Somewhat lower income: 2013–2017 median household income in 2017 dollars, $47,636 ($57,652).

The largest economic sectors in Miami–Dade County are trade, transportation and utilities, government, professional and business services, and education and health services. The city is host to many company headquarters, particularly those with connections to Latin America.

Miami has a city manager form of government. Department heads report to the city manager who in turn reports to the mayor and five city commissioners. The commissioners represent the different neighborhoods in the city.

As noted, the lead consultant was Duany Plater-Zyberk & Company, a firm known for innovations in new urbanism and based in Miami. Together with a small core group of staff planners, I took a hands-on approach to managing the consulting team. Separately, we hired economic and transportation consultants to advise us. We also hired an outside land use attorney who worked directly with the planning department in coordination with the City Attorney's Office. The involvement of an experienced land use attorney was a valuable element

Figure 9.1 Miami Regional Context. Image source: Google, Maxar Technologies

in the process. We held frequent meetings with the consultant team through-out code development and into implementation – biweekly meetings at first and then weekly meetings. Mayor Diaz was very involved in this hands-on approach to managing the consultant.

Overview of Planning Process

The new approach emphasized form rather than use; the goal was to encourage and promote sustainable economic urban development, and protect and promote the character of Miami neighborhoods. The Code created new development entitlement processes that addressed issues of design compatibility, affordable housing, historic preservation, and parks and open spaces. In a city of almost a half-million people, the challenge was to develop and implement a new code while continuing to manage the unprecedented level of development that was occurring.

The Miami 21 effort involved extensive public meetings, 500 in all. A key strategy was to create stakeholder and focus groups at the beginning of the process. These group meetings mixed residents with specialized constituencies such as architects, developers, business organizations, and housing advocates. We created a series of forums to get stakeholders talking and understanding one another's issues and concerns. The project developed outreach methods suitable to each community and stakeholder group.

Participation and public awareness were critical to the Miami 21 process. Because of Miami's unique composition and diverse neighborhoods, we adopted a multipronged strategy for the outreach. It included print media coverage, television, radio, printed and promotional materials, e-marketing, a Miami 21 website, a Miami 21 hotline, and advertising. In addition, there was a strong public outreach program run by City of Miami Neighborhood Enhancement Team (NET) offices that reached out to neighborhood associations, community/business organizations, faith-based organizations, and community centers.

The Core Problem

There were two core problems, one relating to urban form and one related to process. Regarding form, the intention was to move Miami away from a suburban sprawl, bedroom-community model with high levels of automobile commuting to a mixed-use, sustainable development model. This shifted the focus from preventing crowding and separating uses, in the old code, to creating mixed-use districts. Miami, like all U.S. cities at the time, had Euclidean zoning that separated land uses to prevent negative externalities, such as occurs when a factory is located next to a residential area.

Regarding development and planning approval processes, the code had been revised many times throughout the years, making it difficult to read and understand. Community groups and residents faced uncertainty about interpreting code, and so could not readily understand permissible levels of development that could affect their neighborhoods.

The city had a design review process in place but the review was based on existing regulations that didn't necessarily address community vision. Based on a project review, the Planning Department made recommendations, not a final decision. The recommendation was part of an application that would go before the governing body where the final decision was made.

Miami has always encouraged development, but the 11000 Ordinance – the previous zoning ordinance – provided entitlements without regard to planned growth and the quality of life. For example, to meet parking requirements, developers were allowed to rezone abutting residential properties, creating an adverse condition on those properties. Another provision was the ability of a developer to increase project density by sometimes 25% or more for a one-time fee rather than provide a comprehensive mitigation program. Impacts on adjacent properties and the neighborhood were not fully anticipated in the 11000 Ordinance, resulting in negative and adverse effects.

Miami 21 moved development regulations from a reactive mode to a more proactive stance of identifying prescriptive standards that could be clearly understood by all while at the same time promoting appropriate character and scale for each neighborhood. Miami was the first major city to adopt such a code, but now many other cities are developing their own form-based codes to increase transparency; Box 9.1 (next page) provides an account from a current effort in the City of Los Angeles.

Intended and Actual Outcomes

The intended outcome of the effort was the adoption of a code that supports and implements good urban planning principles and smart growth goals. This regulatory approach uses a transect system of classifying neighborhoods, encouraging mixed-use development, anticipating changes of use over the life of a building, attending to the public realm, and promoting transit. The intention

---

Box 9.1 Regulatory Transparency Makes Planning Possible
Tom Rothmann, Principal City Planner, City of Los Angeles

Zoning regulations should provide development parameters in a clear and work-able way to foster growth in a manner consistent with a city's long-range goals. Property owners, planners, developers, and community groups need access to unambiguous zoning requirements so that they can all understand what is the legal development potential of a piece of property.

Some local governments have straightforward rules that require little back-ground to comprehend. However, as cities evolve and their zoning regulations become more complex and layered, zoning regulations become more out of reach to the nonprofessional.

The Los Angeles Zoning Code has maintained a structure created in 1946 that has accommodated 70 years of policy changes, state laws, and legal interpreta-tions. This has culminated in a code that is more of a patchwork of exceptions and relief than a succinct document. In 2013, the City of Los Angeles embarked on creating a new modular system of zoning to replace the outdated Euclidian model that made land use consulting a necessary go-to profession for those interested in developing property in Los Angeles.

The new Zoning Code, expected to be released in 2020, will be a game changer. With skilled consultants, the Department of City Planning worked with a zoning oversight committee to offer a new, responsive zoning system. Planners went to great lengths to ensure that the project maintained existing policies while over-hauling the basic zoning structure for the city. Blunt and inflexible zones are being replaced with a five-component modular system, erasing the need for additional zoning tools such as overlays and site-specific ordinances.

The new system will allow planners to provide the zoning that responds to the community's needs. The planning policy function remains with Community Plans, but the new code makes it easier for stakeholders to envisage what new plans and policies mean in concrete terms. And the modular system can be easily updated if a new zoning solution is discovered, allowing implementation tools to support the new vision. Like Miami, Los Angeles is seeking regulatory transparency that will build trust in planning systems.

---

was to create a code that is easy to understand and proactively asserts design and land use features. Miami 21 had eight transects, representing the transition from "nature" to the most urban districts. Each transect zone is accompanied by a diagram indicating the general pattern of land use and transportation net-works in that zone.

The Code espouses two goals: conservation and development. Its requirements manage and encourage growth while preserving Miami's unique neighborhoods.

Seeking to improve citizens' quality of life through managed growth, the Code does not dictate design, rather it emphasizes form and the transition between land uses. We knew that at times we may lose some quality in design in moving away from discretionary review, but that was a cost we were willing to accept in order to preserve and maintain character in the neighborhoods.

The Code was adopted in 2010 – the first adoption of a form-based code in a major U.S. city. The major obstacle was overcoming years of lax development regulations that allowed for haphazard growth. This required the city and the consulting team to gain the community's trust and provide the understanding that these new regulations would ensure the preservation and character of neighborhoods. As well, the development community wanted to be reassured that the new Code would not unduly reduce development rights but provide more prescriptive rules to manage intensity, density, and scale within the city's distinct neighborhoods and districts.

Key features of the Code and examples of its provisions are as follows:

- Comprehensibility – use a transect system of form types.
- Predictability – adopt a development capacity ratio that includes parking and mechanical areas and a redefinition of lot area so that residents can determine what is permitted; limited rezonings to one transect change.
- Form compatibility – set height limits on commercial areas in relation to context and bulk setbacks.
- Walkability – codify design features that contribute to use of the street as public space such as setbacks, edge treatments, etc.
- Sustainability and preservation – remove barriers and provide incentives for green buildings, open space provision, and historic preservation.

The Code allowed the city to provide more flexibility regarding permitted land uses. For example, the previous code defined only one Industrial category, while Miami 21 created three: Industrial (no residential allowed), Waterfront Industrial (promote and encourage waterfront uses), and Light-Industrial (allow a certain percentage of residential uses within the Industrial category). This greater flexibility in permitted uses helps promote work–live units in emerging neighborhoods such as the Wynwood Art District, Allapattah, and Little Haiti. Residential use in that case was limited and secondary to the main industrial use. The evolution of industrial zoning to permit other uses is also reviewed in the Hawthorne entitlement case discussed in Chapter 12.

The Code has been amended and revised since adoption, with the last amendment in January 2018. Resources on the development process and the

Code text are available at www.Miami21.org/finalcode.asp. To help set the context, Box 9.2 provides a summary of academic research on the general concept of form–based codes and research evaluations of the Code. As the first of its type, Miami 21 won numerous national awards and recognitions.[1] It also brought personal recognition to me.[2] Since its adoption, many cities in the U.S. have embraced form–based codes and hybrid form–based/conventional codes.

Box 9.2 Academic Research and Perspectives on Miami 21

Talen (2013) outlines the criticisms of conventional Euclidian zoning in five categories: (i) micromanaging land use patterns without a rationale, (ii) requiring large dimensions (lots and buildings), (iii) requiring homogeneity in design, (iv) separating land uses, and (v) limiting possibilities for spatially defined open space (e.g., providing a sense of enclosure). The result of these effects is sprawl. In contrast, form-based codes foster compact urban form, diversity of land uses, connectivity between uses, a high-quality public realm, and reduced environmental impact, among other attributes. Talen sees good prospects for form-based codes fulfilling these goals, with over 200 adopted in U.S. jurisdictions by 2013.

Garde et al. (2015) compare Miami 21 with the previous Ordinance 11000 with respect to the criteria of the Leadership in Energy and Environmental Design for Neighborhood Development (LEED-ND) certification. The evaluation is organized into three LEED-ND themes: (i) smart location and linkage, (ii) neighborhood pattern and design, and (iii) green infrastructure and buildings. Comparing the Miami 21 transect zones with the traditional Ordinance 11000 zones reveals that Miami 21 provided stronger support for LEED-ND criteria. The authors suggest more attention should be given to mixed-income diverse communities and certified green building in future codes.

Hananouchi and Nurworsoo (2010) examine parking requirements in Miami 21 and Ordinance 11000. Excessive minimum requirements are complicit in sprawl and present difficulties in building compact development. Form-based codes allow alignment of parking requirements, if provided, with transect types rather than individual uses. Hananouchi and Nurworsoo concluded that parking requirements were relatively consistent between Miami 21 and Ordinance 11000, and that the expected decrease in parking requirements from the Suburban transect to Urban Core transect was not significant as one might expect.

There is a parking requirement reform movement in the U.S., parallel to the form-based code movement, but it started later than the Miami 21 effort. Also, the political capital required to both reform codes and parking requirements can be too much for one effort. Further parking reform may be considered in the future evolution of Miami 21.

Examination of the Planning Episode Using Framework Elements

This section reflects on the case drawing on the Figure 5.2 framework (see Chapter 5) and organizes my observations in the three elements: (i) planner-as-person, (ii) interpretation of context, and (iii) reasoning and methods in the planning episode itself.

Planner-as-Person Elements That Shaped the Approach

I have over 25 years of experience in the planning field, and served as planning director for the City of Miami from 1998 to 2010 while I led the Miami 21 initiative. Originally engaged by the Planning Department in 1985 as a consultant for the Downtown Master Plan, I was then hired as a junior planner and worked my way up to senior planner, neighborhood enhancement administrator, and planning director.

I hold bachelor's degrees in fine arts and architecture from the Rhode Island School of Design, have a master's in landscape architecture from Harvard's Graduate School of Design, and am American Institute of Certified Planners (AICP) certified. In recent years I have also worked as an urban planning and design critic at the Harvard Graduate School of Design. This combination of education attuned me to the design of the public and private realms. My on-the-job training as a planner helped me see the way in which design vision can be made to happen through plans and entitlement management.

Currently, I am principal of Gelabert-Sanchez LLC, a planning and design consulting firm based in Miami. In 2010, I was awarded a Loeb Fellowship at the Harvard University Graduate School of Design.

Personal Framework Elements

My planning career is motivated by a desire to contribute to building great cities and communities, and to make quality of life attainable for everyone. I believe that public service is an opportunity to become an agent of change, and to be an urban planner is to know that we can make a difference in our communities and our cities. I was fortunate to have found that path through the design profession.

I was born in Havana, Cuba, have lived in Puerto Rico and Venezuela, and currently reside in the U.S. This background gave me perspective on the views and needs of different communities. While each city is different, I developed insight into common elements of urban planning – aspects such as scale, sense of community, needs for and roles of open space, and the importance of walkability.

My values emphasize empowering planning staff and communities. These values have been influenced by the good fortune of having supervisors who gave me opportunities, trusted me, and always backed me up. And when I did not succeed, they helped me and encouraged me to not give up but perhaps reposition my strengths and weaknesses. I seek to do the same when I manage staff.

Personal Incongruity and Ambiguity

I did not experience incongruity or ambiguity regarding my role on this project. It never took a direction that was out of sync with my values or purposes as a planner. City leadership was keenly aware of the problems the needed to be addressed. As a manager, I was able to place my personal and professional values at the forefront of my decision-making, allowing me the opportunity to improve the quality of life in Miami.

Land use regulations can have positive or negative physical impacts in neighborhoods, from a land use or zoning decision on an individual block to a citywide plan. I was able to make decisions and recommendations to improve the character of Miami's neighborhoods and tailor the Code so that land use decisions would promote walkability and maintain the character of neighborhoods. My work reflected a deep respect for particular neighborhood characteristics: a given intensity and density can promote character and walkability in one neighborhood, while negatively impacting it in a different one. Overall, I felt comfortable that I was implementing my commitment to the values and needs of the community.

Early in my career in Miami, I remember attending a community meeting in an affluent neighborhood where the neighbors asked for basic things such as safe streets, sidewalks, trees, more recreational opportunities, and improved neighborhood services. When the meeting was over, a gentleman who was standing in the back of the room, not a resident of this community but a less affluent neighborhood, approached me and said: "Everything they are asking for, we also want in our community. We all want a safe place for our families and our children."

Interpretation of Context

Interpreting context required good lines of communication with elected officials, the city manager and other department heads, the development community, and the residents. My extended tenure in multiple roles in Miami gave me insight on neighborhood characteristics, issues the development community faced, and the interests of elected officials. The primary element of context was correctly interpreting the range of stakeholder viewpoints.

Context Framework Elements

The city manager provided me with the direct communication with the mayor's office in this effort. This was a change from normal practices and was instrumental in allowing fluid and direct communication. The mayor took a direct and personal interest in the project and was a champion for it. He reviewed the proposed Code, page by page, and made his mark on it. As a result, the Code reflected the mayor's political leadership.

The City of Miami has a weak-mayor form of government. While the mayor's political leadership was crucial, we also needed the support of the five elected city commissioners. Understanding this element of context led me to have extensive one-on-one briefings with the commissioners and their respective staffs. Some were in favor and quickly gave their support. Others considered the project a waste of time.

The context was an ever-changing landscape. Mayor Diaz completed an eight-year term in 2009. Then, Miami elected a new mayor, who had not previously been supportive of Miami 21, and three new commissioners (out of five). These political shifts changed the context for adoption, necessitating a new process to understand and educate the political leadership. Nonetheless, the Code was adopted and took effect in May 2010.

My experience in Miami provided an opportunity to learn about context in multiple ways over an extended period. After working as a consultant to the city, and then a staff planner, I was promoted to Neighborhood Enhancement Team (NET) administrator in 1993. Miami had created a new concept of "mini-city halls" within the neighborhoods called NET offices. The 12 NET offices were intended to be the face of local government. An administrator was designated for each office; representing the city manager, we administrators worked with the police and fire departments, responded to neighborhood issues, and ensured delivery of city services. I served as NET administrator for two offices: Upper Eastside neighborhood and Downtown. Since NET administrators were not provided independent budgets, I learned to get things done with limited resources and established working relationships with other city departments.

This NET experience provided two important elements of context. First, I gained a deep understanding and knowledge about Miami's neighborhoods.

Second, it involved me in all aspects of the city's administration and provided the opportunity to establish a track record of solving problems. I worked with all city departments and understood the impact of their work in the community. These two context elements made my work on the Code more effective since I was not coming in as an outsider.

Regarding administrative context, the Planning Department had about 35 planners at the time of the project, organized into departments of community planning, urban design, land development, and historic preservation. When I became director, the Planning Department was somewhat fragmented and staff had varying levels of motivation. My interpretation of this context led me to seek to understand the core expertise of different staff members and effectively delegate responsibility. In seeking a better alignment of staff expertise and responsibilities, I provided backup and support. Some staff members excelled being in the limelight, while others thrived when using their technical skills.

Understanding context meant attending to department culture. In addition to meeting with division managers, I held department-wide meetings to achieve understanding and cooperation regarding goals and to build a strong sense of team. This helped me deploy staff resources effectively. By the time Miami 21 began, the department had the capacity to add the Miami 21 assignment to its work program.

Context Uncertainty and Ambiguity

In seeking to understand community preferences and concerns, I found that the use of terms had a bearing on public reactions to our proposals. For example, we used the term *new urbanism* to describe our broad aims because it defined the qualities we were seeking. But sometimes that label was a problem. New urbanism likely meant different things to different people. Many times, I found myself defending the label more than the ideals behind the movement. If I were to do it again, I would call what we were seeking "good urban planning principles," which are not new or old, just good.

The Planning Episode: Reasoning and Methods

The development of Miami 21 involved an interplay of logic, unfolding within an emotional dynamic on the part of residents, other stakeholders, elective officials, and the planning team. The effort relied on convention in the form of certain universals about urban from, and invention in the development of a new regulatory approach.

Logic

Logic helped us understand and respond to our audience. How do we ask the right questions in the right format so we can translate them into vision and planning goals? As an example, an effective method was to ask stakeholders to identify elements or features of their favorite cities that they found most attractive or desirable. This enabled us to take their needs and translate them, using logic, into the planning and regulatory language.

Another application of logic was my emphasis on having outside legal counsel advise on the Code, in coordination with city attorneys. Outside counsel was essential in keeping proposals on strong legal ground, such as avoiding claims against Miami should the Code overstep a level of regulation supported by court interpretations of constitutional law.

Emotion

Some community participation revealed public distrust of the effort – the suspicion that the Miami 21 process was selling out to developers. Certain residents wanted all regulations changed in a way that lowered density and the intensity of use. Even when features that protect neighborhood characteristics were introduced, for some residents "we were not doing enough." At the same time, some in the development community thought we were doing too much, restricting and limiting their ability to develop, which they viewed as a "taking" of their property rights. Both parties felt strongly about their positions. Our response to this was to seek to keep residents and development interests in the same room to avoid having each group develop positions in isolation from the priorities and perspectives of the other group. This also allowed the planning team to work with more transparency. We asked residents and development groups to discuss their issues directly. Also, the staff and consultants were community-oriented, and so they acted according to an idea of reaching agreement rather than imposing a template.

The planning team and I could make appeals for reasonableness because there was widespread agreement that the existing code did not serve either party very well. Community members had a hard time discerning what it permitted and developers faced a lengthy, byzantine permit and approval process. The desire for all parties to better understand what is permitted and the prospect of predictable implementation of processes had appeal for both parties. Support for the new Code did not eliminate, however, the desire of some community members to preserve design review by the Planning staff – an additional step in the planning process – as a further safeguard for review and raising concerns.

A last element of emotion was the emotional disposition of the Planning Department staff. When I became director, I sought to bring together the department team. My approach was to recognize the expertise and approach of each planner so that I could align their work efforts with their strengths and professional interests. I provided staff members the opportunity to have a meaningful role (responsibility and recognition), gave credit where due, and was there for backup if they needed it. I believe that we attained our goal, as the department worked as a team, not as individuals. An important element of creating a sense of team was holding regular meetings with the entire staff, not just division managers.

Convention

The effort appealed to residents' conventions about good neighborhoods and places by asking them about what they valued in their communities. I could then use my training, experience, and education to connect their vision with the language of community design, and also provide my own perspective on urban planning based on my experiences in other communities. In that way, the effort sought to apply universal notions of urban planning – which certainly show up differently across places – to Miami. My global experiences gave me perspective on how planning ideas work elsewhere, but the challenge was to translate those universals to the particulars of Miami's communities.

While the Miami 21 process invented a new way to develop a code based on transects, the type of land use and design features reflected the conventions of good urban planning.

Community feelings about convention are a consideration in the pace of change. When change exceeds the capacity of the community to absorb or understand it, it brings a reaction that often opposes all development indiscriminately or tightens controls on plan changes, such as requiring voter approval for minor changes to plans, as occurred in Dana Point, California, as reported in Chapter 10. This demand to keep things as they are can have negative impacts on housing production, economic development, and investment in infrastructure. The Code recognized the need for convention in the sense of a reasonable pace of change by changing the rules as to how zoning changes could be requested. Three elements offered predictability and assurance: zone changes could only be done twice a year, a zone change could only go up to the next transect classification (not two or three), and the entire block had to be considered rather than just the developer's proposal.

Invention

As the first form-based code in the U.S., invention was at the core of Miami 21. While the ideas of new urbanism and transect planning were already in existence, the element of invention was finding forms of those ideas appropriate to Miami. There was no comparable large city zoning code that could be used as best practice precedent.

An example of an ordinance innovation is the new T-4 zoning category. This zone provides for a transition block between higher-density neighborhoods and low-density neighborhoods to ensure appropriate transition in scale. The Code also includes R (Residential), L (Limited), and O (Open) zones. The Residential zone preserves neighborhoods that needed to remain strictly residential; the Limited zone calibrates the percentage of commercial/office uses within a neighborhood, as appropriate; and the Open zone allows mixed uses without limitations.

An element of invention in the process was inventing a creative, legally supportable way of addressing community concerns. Often, the invention involved finding a different way than residents proposed to solve a problem, but nonetheless addressing their issue. We sought to understand the roots of the problem and then sought an implementable way to address it. For example, some community members said, "We want Miami 21 to prohibit chain stores in our community." Once we learned more about the reasons for this position, the primary concern was not the chain store as a business type; rather, the concern was the size and scale of the business. The solution was to set a standard regarding maximum floor plate and establishing frontage requirements. This prevents large store footprints from disturbing a fine-grained district scale. This form of regulation was an invention that responded to a community concern.

Discoveries

This section discusses three practical judgments I made that shaped the team approach. Then, I provide broader takeaways that flow from the case.

Practical Judgments

Three practical judgments were consequential to the success of the Miami 21 effort, relating to simultaneously addressing vision and implementation, using a bottom-up process, and being responsive to political support for action.

Practical Judgment 1: Addressing Vision and Implementation Simultaneously

Miami embarked on a complete revision of the planning and zoning code. This decision was made with encouragement from the mayor and was carried to success based on his strong support throughout. Miami was a pro-development city, so it was possible to frame the discussion about the type of development, not whether development should occur.

The comprehensive approach provided the opportunity to start with a clean slate: to address in clear language and intent the vision, goals, and objectives for Miami, and to have a coherent organizational structure. A new code – with clear language making it easier to understand the impact of zoning and land use regulations – was supported by the community as a whole. This process led to revisions to the city's comprehensive plan; community engagement about the code provided tangible information about broader policy and planning concerns.

Practical Judgment 2: Using a Bottom-Up, Community-Based Process That Directly Addressed Disagreement and Mistrust

Without extensive community participation, Miami 21 would not have been adopted or implemented. Public outreach was critical to gaining input and support for the Code, including print media, television, and radio, e-marketing, the Miami 21 website and hotline, and strong public neighborhood outreach. While the transect idea and new urbanism goals involved broad ideas, the application of standards to communities required knowledge of neighborhood-level context. This cannot be accomplished in a top-down process.

The commitment to participation meant engaging a wide variety of stakeholder issues and addressing perspectives that were not amenable to a technical or design solution. As mentioned, some residents felt that the Miami 21 process was selling out to developers while developers thought we were restricting development rights too much. These conversations were difficult and required a healthy compromise between stakeholders, where all were in the same room.

Practical Judgment 3: Being Responsive to Political Support for Action

I decided to take advantage of windows of opportunity presented by political leadership. I was willing to revise the department's work programs to respond and had the knowledge and trust that staff would see this as an opportunity. As mentioned, Mayor Manny Diaz provided leadership and political impetus from concept to implementation. He believed in creating a livable city, understood that change needed to happen, and recognized the importance of his leadership for the political effort. Since Miami does not have a strong mayor system, this change also required a broad base of political support. A key feature was finding a champion for the effort on the five-member elected commission.

The political support provided what was perhaps a one-time opportunity to develop a form-based code for Miami. It took effort and true dedication to reach out to political and private stakeholders and develop the vision for Miami. Mayor Diaz was involved in the everyday decision-making throughout the project. The mayor that followed him was initially an opponent of Miami 21, so it was critical to bring the effort to a decision in a timely manner. Three of the incumbent commissioners were replaced immediately after the adoption of Miami 21, and we started over with elected official education. It was touch and go for a while but the new Code stood. Miami 21 was approved.

Takeaways for Practice

I suggest three takeaways for professional practice: ground participation on community members experience of form and place, use the tangible nature of zoning to engage questions about vision, and create a structure for success.

Takeaway 1: Ground Participation in Community Members' Experience of Form and Place

Participation works well when planners start public dialogue about place characteristics, not plans, policies, drawings, or regulations. This approach takes longer because it engages feelings, history, and identity, but is ultimately more robust. Also, focusing on place avoids silos in which different stakeholder groups speak to planners and the consulting team individually. Instead, mix residents with all stakeholder groups so they have direct dialogue about place.

Stakeholders understand and can describe features of their city, or other cities, that they like and that they feel make a city great. We translated the language of zoning (i.e., setback or street wall) into language that describes the desired characteristics for the community and city. This approach facilitated community understanding of the desired outcome and enhanced engagement.

This process also reached out to the community before code drafting began. The goals for conservation and development were broad, so the outreach focused on calibrating a unique balance between the goals for *each* community, but discussion occurred within established parameters because the broad goals had agreement. Not all stakeholders agreed on the calibration between goals, but there was a shared view that they were the correct general parameters and encompassed a shared vision for our city.

Takeaway 2: Use the Tangible Nature of Implementation Tools Like Zoning to Engage Questions About Vision

Thinking about implementation and vision together throughout meant considering the level of local political support, the prospects for state regulators approving the comprehensive plan that guides the Code, and the response of building and planning officials who would implement it. The outside legal team's analysis of legal issues was also critical for the successful implementation of the Code. Zoning's specificity makes it easier to engage vision questions.

As part of the initial meetings, the planning group met with the Building and Zoning Department, Code Enforcement Department, Community Development, NET offices – everyone who was going to be part of the permit process. The goals and the understanding of *why* we were embarking in this effort were key in gaining their support.

We regularly briefed state regulators because their approval of the General Plan–Comprehensive Plan that guides the Code was required. The Comprehensive Plan establishes the long-range goals and objectives for a community and is the framework on which the zoning regulations are created. Then zoning regulations could be approved by local government. This effort included educating Tallahassee lawmakers (the state capital) about Miami's characteristics, as our goals, values, and character are unique to the State of Florida.

Takeaway 3: Build a Multifaceted Base of Political, Administrative, and Community Support for Reform

I sought to create a base that would support the project over time and through ups and downs: to foster political support; create a team of staff and consultants; and build on deep community knowledge and connections. The project started with the mayor's commitment and continued with extensive briefings for other Miami district commissioners. Through numerous briefings with the five commissioners, I was able to explain how the draft Code provisions would deliver outcomes their constituents wanted and needed.

Regarding the administrative team, I empowered Planning Department staff to take roles that fit their skills and inclinations and delegated responsibilities.

The staff took a proactive stance to being involved with the consulting work. My takeaway is that planning leaders should listen but should not be beholden to a consensus. We are responsible to make a recommendation based on our professional training.

Since city staff would use the Code long after the consultant was gone, it was important that it not be a "study" that would land on someone's desk without consideration of how it would be implemented. Outside consultants reporting directly to the Planning Department provided an extra measure of objectivity. Planning staff should drive the consultants' efforts, otherwise a plan will go off course and not achieve implementation.

And Now to You: Think Big

Miami 21 gave us a unique opportunity to *reimagine* our city and plan for its future.

As Mayor Diaz said about the Miami 21 planning effort, it was a "defining moment, a moment that will shape the lives of Miami's people."

I trust that as planners you will have the opportunity to effect change, and shape and guide the growth of your cities and communities. You will have the unique responsibility to lead and engage others in this effort. Sometimes everyone will be on board with your idea from the start, other times they may not be, which will require time and possible reevaluation of your thoughts and methods. I believe that it is in this process that we become better planners and better advocates for our community.

Miami 21 was a process that started with a big idea, a vision for our future. I frame the process and provide advice in three important steps: visioning, communication and engagement, and implementation.

Vision – Vision is your guiding tool. It is broad because it must encompass the present and allow for the future to evolve. The Big Idea, the issue, is the aspirational goal. As Daniel Burnham was quoted "Make no little plans; they have no magic to stir men's blood." All plans need to have room to evolve in order for them to be successful. The Big Idea – expressed as the vision – is the framework used to implement the present and guide the future.

Communication and engagement – Effective communication is required to express clearly, as well as to listen carefully, in order to understand, effectively reflect, and communicate the overall goals of the community. Understanding the community – stakeholders and decision-makers in the process allows you to not only address issues and concerns within your plan but to effectively develop a path toward implementation.

Implementation – As planners, we don't want our work to end up on a shelf. From the start, understand what you need in order to implement your ideas, anticipate obstacles, and consider the departments and agencies that will be affected and involved in implementation. Taking all the players into account, develop a strategy that will allow you to fully implement your plan.

Lastly, we come to understanding the role of the planner. Although the process is collaborative and political, do not forgo your technical knowledge and a broader understanding of the issues as you lead the process.

Discussion Questions

1. Defining the vision and goals for a community and effectively communicating are instrumental in the successful implementation of any plan. What methods would you use to define the vision and goals for your community? How would you communicate the vision and goals for your community?
2. Participation and public awareness were critical in the Miami 21 effort. Key to the successful implementation was the understanding of who were the stakeholders. Based on your reading of the case, did the Miami 21 effort miss any stakeholders? What would you do differently, if anything, to engage decision-makers and stakeholders?
3. The Miami 21 effort was lengthy due to the need and desire for an extensive public engagement process. Inevitably, public engagement brings conflicting ideas and recommendations from different stakeholders. How would you reconcile these differences? How would you present a final recommendation based on good planning principles?

Notes

1 Project awards for Miami 21 include the American Planning Association, National Planning Excellence Award for Best Practice 2011; the American Planning Association, Florida Award of Excellence, Best Practices 2010; the Driehaus Form-Based Code Award with the Paul Crawford Distinction Award for a groundbreaking code 2010; and the American Architecture Award, Chicago Athenaeum.
2 Ana Gelabert-Sánchez receive the following awards: Top Public Official of the Year 2010, *Governing* magazine; CNU Groves Award on Leadership and Vision 2011; Outstanding Service Award, Community Partnership for the Homeless; Distinguished Service Award, Greater Biscayne Boulevard Chamber of Commerce; Outstanding Service Award, Federation of the Upper East Side; Outstanding Service Award, Belle Meade Homeowners Association; Certificate of Appreciation, Bayside Residents Association; Certificate of Appreciation, Shorecrest Homeowners Association; Waterfront Development Master Plan, City

of Miami, American Planning Association; European Honors Program, Rhode Island School of Design; and Architectural Thesis Honors, Rhode Island School of Design.

References

Garde, Ajay, Cecilia Kim, and Oscar Tsai. 2015. "Differences Between Miami's Form-Based Code and Traditional Zoning Code in Integrating Planning Principles." *Journal of the American Planning Association*, 81(1): 46–66. doi: 10.1080/01944363.2015.1043137.

Hananouchi, Rob and Cornelius Nurworsoo. 2010. "Comparison of Parking Requirements in Zoning and Form-Based Codes." Transportation Research Record: Journal of the Transportation Research Board 2187 (1):138-145 doi: 10.3141/2187-18

Talen, Emily. 2013. "Zoning for and Against Sprawl: The Case for Form-Based Codes." *Journal of Urban Design*, 18(2): 175–200. doi: 10.1080/13574809.2013.772883.

U.S. Census. 2020. Accessed March 12, 2020 at https://www.census.gov/quickfacts/fact/table/miamidadecountyflorida/POP060210.

Chapter 10

Parking Management Deliberation and Strategy in Dana Point, California

Some planning episodes are primarily based on stakeholder dialogue and public participation. This chapter addresses such a case – the development of parking management strategies for the Dana Point, California. At first glance, parking may seem to be a technical topic appropriate for quantitative study, but parking issues evoke a broad range of community visions and concerns. In Dana Point, a tension existed between a suburban vision of free and plentiful parking and an urban vision of multimodal transportation. Addressing this tension required engagement and communication. The case shows the process used to achieve this engagement and find incremental ways forward.

The case provides my perspective as a consultant to the City of Dana Point in 2017 and 2018. The reflection yields insights on three practical judgments: (i) deciding that "talk" was more important than technical studies, (ii) deliberation and "nudging" rather than arguing, and (iii) understanding complaints about parking inconveniences as an avenue to addressing substantive planning issues.

The case is of direct application to those interested in multimodal transportation planning, parking management, neighborhood planning, and local economic development. In addressing a community controversy, however, it has insights for a wide variety of situations where planning processes based on technical studies and formal hearings are not enough to make progress.

Description of the Planning Episode

The project involved listening sessions and deliberations with decision-makers, a public workshop, and preparation of a report recommending process-oriented actions. That report summarized the input received; recommended a policy framework; reviewed candidate parking management measures; and proposed that an advisory committee be formed to select, prioritize, and monitor actions. The report was presented to the Planning Commission in June 2017; City Council received and filed it in August 2017. Implementation activities were then carried out by a newly created Parking and Circulation Oversight Task Force.

The planning episode was preceded by many efforts: the 2008 Town Center Parking Study, a 2013 consultant presentation on a Town Center Parking Plan to City Council (revisiting the 2008 study), and the 2014 Town Center Lantern District Parking Plan. The latter plan addressed parking supply and management issues to support the Dana Point Town Center Plan (referred to as the Lantern District).[1] Independent of this effort, a specific plan was prepared for Doheny Village, a potential mixed-used area located next to the Lantern District. The Doheny Village Form-Based Code Specific Plan proposed a land use and design approach that reflected new urbanist ideas, including lower parking requirements. That effort started in 2010, was renewed in 2015, and a draft code was circulated in 2016.[2]

The 2014 Town Center Lantern District Parking Plan was approved by City Council in a 3–2 vote, but it spurred responses by those who opposed it, which led to a citizen's initiative. Measure H: 2016, Dana Point Town Center Plan and Parking Citizen Initiative was approved by voters, prohibiting deviations from building heights and existing parking requirements, and it revoked the parking management actions approved by City Council in 2015.[3]

Measure H restrictions on plan changes affected Dana Point's economic development by limiting the financial feasibility of development projects. Economic development is a priority for California cities, as Proposition 13 limits property tax rates. In response, cities often promote commercial development to obtain sales and hotel bed taxes. Simultaneously, they often limit new homes in order to limit the number of residents able to share those tax revenues. A city's ability to consider plan changes and variances can facilitate private investment and aid economic development, but Dana Point officials faced a loss of flexibility in negotiating with developers under Measure H. The initiative upheld a building height limit of 40 feet and other building restrictions, prior parking requirements, and introduced the requirement that voters approve *any* changes to the adopted Town Center Plan. The last feature represents ballot-box zoning.

I became involved in 2017 when the city sought to restart deliberations on parking policy. I wrote a scope of work and was hired as a sole-source consultant.

Institutional Setting

Dana Point is a coastal city of 33,730 residents located in Orange County, one of five counties in Southern California. Figure 10.1 shows the project's location in the general vicinity of Orange County. Dana Point is differentiated from demographic features of the U.S. population in the ways listed next. Dana Point data is shown first; the U.S. data is shown in brackets (U.S. Census 2020):

- Fewer young people: persons under 18 years, 16.7% (22.4%).
- Less diverse: Black or African American alone, 1.5% (13.4%); Hispanic or Latino, 16.4% (18.3%).
- Similar level of home ownership: owner-occupied housing rate 60.3% (63.8%).
- Somewhat lower risk to social well-being: persons without health insurance 8.8% (10.2%).
- High income: 2013–2017 median household income in 2017 dollars, $90,310 ($61,015).

Compared to rest of Orange County, Dana Point is less diverse, older, and more affluent. The subregion in which Dana Point is located has significant employment shares in professions such as health care, biotech, and finance. The city has a five-member City Council, elected at-large.

The project was my first in Dana Point. I reviewed previous parking plans and found that I agreed with most of their suggestions, but my task was to listen to stakeholders, engage in deliverations, and find a way forward in a process that had been halted. I did not emphasize the former plans in my dialogues since city officials sought a fresh start.

Figure 10.1 Dana Point Regional Context. Image source: Google, Maxar Technologies

The city was doing a good job of organizing shared public parking in private developments, implementing the previous consultant's recommendations. However, most residents were not accustomed to on-street parking management using parking meters or residential parking permits. Residents and visitors were used to parking in the most convenient and visible spaces. This often led to motorists filling up the on-street parking, sometimes in residential neighborhoods, even when ample (but less visible and harder to access) underground parking existed at their destination. Until the 1980s, parking for private development in Dana Point was provided at grade, with suburban-style building design. Thereafter, high land values, limited parcel availability, and minimum parking regulations meant that some new projects began to rely on other solutions, such as supplying parking in expensive, below-grade facilities.

Overview of Planning Process

The planning process involved a series of briefings/listening/deliberation sessions with members of City Council and the Planning Commission, city staff, and key stakeholders, and analysis of a city parking survey. I also wrote summaries of good practices in parking management. Supporting city staff, I advised on and participated in a community-wide public meeting on parking issues. As noted, I proposed a list of candidate parking management measures, developed implementation process recommendations, made presentations to the Planning Commission and City Council, and attended the first Parking and Circulation Oversight Committee meeting.

City staff organized and facilitated the public meeting held at the local high school on May 15, 2017.[4] Figure 10.2 provides an image from that event; in addition to varied engagement methods I presented my report to planning commissioners, City Council, and the public. Additional stakeholders in attendance included the Chamber of Commerce, property developers, residents, business representatives, and neighborhood groups.

The Core Problem

The core problem articulated by city officials and residents was dissatisfaction with parking supply and/or convenience. Many residents thought that parking was hard to find in the commercial district, that it impacts adjacent neighborhoods, and that high levels of vehicles per household creates crowding in

Figure 10.2 Public Meeting Regarding Parking Management. Image source: Author

residential neighborhoods. The following anonymous resident comment from a city survey summarizes this view:

> The lack of parking in the lantern district is unbelievable, with the restaurant employees and customers parking in the residential neighborhoods. Family and friends of mine have nowhere to park. It is ruining our neighborhood. Why would the city planners not put in a parking structure. It is a no brainer!!!!!!!![5]

This narrow framing supports an argument for more parking. Not all stakeholders agreed with this view, though, as some were in favor of parking reform. They saw the core problem as a need to transition from an auto-first approach to a multimodal transportation system that supports economic development and sustainability. Some residents supported a "park-then-walk" model that includes bikes, shuttles, and walking. There was also a perception that onerous parking requirements made new development infeasible, and indeed there were many undeveloped lots in the downtown Lantern District.

Like many other suburban cities, Dana Point is transitioning from a development era in which parking was free and easy to find to one in which on-street parking was not necessarily available in front of the destination. Intensification of land uses, beginning in the 1980s, meant that commercial parking spillover had been impacting neighborhoods for years. Many residents converted their garages into storage or living space, and instead park their own vehicles on the street, creating additional competition for curb parking spaces. Coastal cities throughout Southern California particularly face this situation as growth occurs and coastal access is sought by the regional population.

Previous parking plans showed there was no aggregate parking deficiency (meaning that total parking supply exceeded the highest level of demand) and proposed a series of parking management programs. This frustrated those who strongly believed that there was a parking shortage. Box 10.1 (next page) provides the perspective of Patrick Siegman, who wrote the prior parking study. That study took a similar approach as the effort described here, and Siegman reflects on how that process unfolded. His perspective was only known to me when I invited him to comment on this chapter. It is typical in consulting assignments to have limited information on what came before, especially if there was controversy. Siegman's commentary shows the value and necessity of learning about context, and that the landscape of stakeholder interests changes even over a short period of time.

Box 10.1 Stand-Alone Parking Reform Versus Serving a Larger Vision

Patrick Siegman, Siegman and Associates

My memories of what happened and why during the years before you began your work in Dana Point are *very* different from those reported in this chapter. Our impressions probably differ for several reasons: (i) we worked independently of each other; (ii) we were both part-time consultants, with less detailed knowledge than full-time staff or residents; and (iii) there was significant turnover among staff and elected officials.

Like you, I quickly concluded that *talk was more important than technical analysis*. I performed no new technical analysis. I also set out to listen to stakeholders and then engage with them.

Our studies had different goals. My study sought to craft a parking plan that would help achieve the vision set forth in the Dana Point Town Center Plan, that is, "the creation of a compact, lively and walkable town center with a critical mass and mix of shops, offices, housing and bicycle and pedestrian amenities." By contrast, the core problem you were asked to solve was "dissatisfaction with parking supply and/or convenience."

I did not observe, as you did, a tension between a suburban vision of free and plentiful parking and an urban vision of multimodal transportation and priced parking. It was apparent to me that there was virtually no appetite for implementing priced parking. While you encountered some stakeholders who saw the core problem as "a need to transition to a multimodal transportation system," I don't remember that coming up.

Instead, I observed that on the one hand, many stakeholders believed that development of the type envisioned in the Town Center Plan was generally not financially feasible given existing regulations, notably onerous minimum parking requirements and height limits. They also supported allowing new apartments to support projects' economic feasibility. Homeowners with the opposing view believed that developers would profit from developing new multistory buildings, even with the existing parking requirements and the plan's height limit. Those homeowners were also generally opposed to allowing more housing. The city did not engage an outside economist to provide an analysis of which view was most likely right.

These differences converged in the controversy over the City Council's 2014 decision to approve the Majestic mixed-use development, with 30,000 ft.² of ground-floor retail and 109 for-sale apartments on two to three levels above. This was the first project to turn the 2008 Town Center Plan into something real. To approve it, the council had to, and did, grant a slight variance from the height limit, a variance to allow payment of in lieu of parking fees (instead of building all required spaces on-site), and a conditional use permit to allow roof decks. Granting the variances – a decision based in part on my draft parking plan – aroused fears among some homeowners that existing spillover parking problems would worsen

Box 10.1 (continued)

and a feeling that the project had been allowed to "ignore the rules." Many opponents also objected to the buildings' height and mass.

In my experience, the best way to develop a parking plan for a compact, walkable, mixed-use town center is to do it while the overall plan for the town center is being developed, working hand-in-hand as an integral part of the overall planning team. The parking planner should be part of an interdisciplinary group of professionals – urban designers, transportation engineers, land use economists, landscape architects, and other professionals. Ideally, the overall plan should include the parking policies needed to make it financially feasible for people to build the desired vision under normal regulations, without requiring variances. Those policies then become just one element of the plan. When decision-makers vote, they vote on the overall plan as a package deal.

When such an integrated approach is taken, the focus and public attention is on the larger goals of the plan – achieving design excellence, economic growth, a high quality of life, and environmental sustainability. Managing curb parking to prevent spillover parking complaints, off-street parking requirements, and height limits become means of achieving the plan's goals, instead of as an end in themselves. Parking planning done in this way often receives little attention and does not arouse controversy. Even when it does lead to debate, changes to parking requirements and parking management are often accepted as a worthwhile price to pay for achieving the big picture goal.

Unfortunately, I was hired to do a standalone parking plan as a follow-up to the Town Center Plan that had been completed five years earlier. Many homeowners who were drawn to meetings focused on parking convenience, not on broader goals. People who care about other issues (such as housing affordability), who likely would have turned out for a town center planning effort, stayed away. That's understandable. Managing curb parking makes it possible to remove off-street parking requirements, which in turn makes housing more affordable. But connections like that are hard to perceive, unless someone – like a skilled analyst who knows how parking regulations affect housing affordability – points them out.

Intended and Actual Outcomes

The intended outcomes of the effort were to address parking concerns and return to normal development decision-making procedures. The voter initiative had made planning and implementation for individual projects in the Lantern District difficult and halted progress on adopting the Doheny Village Specific Plan. Specific parking concerns included addressing neighborhood parking issues, managing impact of new development in the Lantern District, and reaching agreement on parking requirements for the Doheny Village Specific Plan.

The direct project outcomes were "listening" meetings and dialogues, the public workshop, and the report. In August 2017, as mentioned, the City Council created the Parking and Circulation Oversight Task Force (Task Force), which then met regularly and developed a plan of action items.[6] The Task Force issued its report on March 19, 2019. Supported by staff, the Task Force's Citywide Parking Implementation Plan contained short-, mid-, and long-term goals and action items. Examples of proposed short-term measures included marketing public parking, residential garage clean-out programs, updating parking permit programs, updating zoning code parking requirements, trolley improvements, parking enforcement, restriping spaces for greater supply, and reconsidering parking requirements in the Doheny Village Specific Plan. Even so, the development limitations imposed by Measure H are still in effect.

Examination of the Planning Episode Using Framework Elements

This section organizes observations in three elements: (i) planner-as-person, (ii) interpretation of context, and (iii) reasoning and methods in the planning episode.

Planner-as-Person Elements That Shaped the Approach

This project was part of my consulting practice in parking and transit-oriented development. This work is a sideline to my primary job as a professor of urban and regional planning at California State Polytechnic University, Pomona, where I have taught since 1986. I have operated this consulting practice since 1989, serving as a subconsultant to larger firms or working directly for public, private, or nonprofit clients. My expertise in parking analysis began early in my practice career, where I worked on parking reform in downtown Los Angeles. Later, it extended through my PhD dissertation that studied commuter travel mode responses to parking pricing.

Personal Framework Elements

Most of my outside consulting work is technical in nature, as described in Chapter 12, yet this case relied on communicative and deliberative methods.

My contributions were process design, issue framing, listening, dialogue, and interpretation. While in support of an evidence-based transportation planning agenda, this communicative role emerged later in my career, best described as being a parking "whisperer."

Process and deliberation facilitation was not an explicit part of my planning education. I learned it in practice by observing and working with participation and facilitation professionals, and by teaching it in my courses. My first experience with this type of work was facilitating board workshops at the Bay Area Rapid Transit District (Willson et al. 2003). This mode of planning action grew with the progression of my career and in response to the needs of clients.

Mutual adjustment of positions enables the incremental development of programs and projects to address community concerns. While the planning profession is committed to advancing the broad public interest, stakeholders often seek to advance narrower interests, often presenting them as claims to the public interest to increase their legitimacy. For example, if it is difficult to find a parking space, a stakeholder may seek to have more parking created and paid for by developers or the city. In situations in which values of tolerance and mutual respect are not widely shared, stakeholders engage in bluffing, bullying, and aggression, seeing the setting for planning as a win-lose battlefield.

My inclination is to bring reconciliation to community conflict. Over my career, I have often found that change is blocked until people are willing to hear and understand those with whom they disagree, consider their axioms and evidence, and become open to modifying their positions. In these instances, I seek to improve the conditions of discourse, placing attention on the dialogue qualities of accuracy, comprehensibility, sincerity, and legitimacy (Forester 1989). Changing one's mind is a complex, human, and communicative affair, not achieved with analytic evidence alone, and elusive if a party feels that they, or their views, are threatened.

Personal Incongruity and Ambiguity

Planners sometimes experience incongruity when working for a community that has a different economic profile and political culture than their personal experience and commitments. Dana Point is an affluent community compared to U.S. averages. I live in an urban community with people from a broader range of incomes, diverse backgrounds, races and ethnicities, and different political affiliations. Reflecting this last difference, the Democrat/Republican voter registration percentage point difference is +40.2% in my home city of Los Angeles versus −20.8% in Dana Point.[7] I usually work for communities that are more diverse, politically progressive, and mixed-income than Dana Point.

Waiting in a coffee shop for a meeting to start, I overheard a Dana Point resident expressing political views that I oppose. After expressing negative statements about people with views like me to his friends, he got up to leave and caught my eye. I was surprised when he gave a nod and generous smile and said hi as he walked away. He may have assumed, because of my age, gender, and dress that I shared his views. I was out of my normal context.

The type of problems encountered in parking work – such as inconvenience in finding a parking space – seem trivial compared with homelessness, structural racism, or global climate change. Compared to the climate change planning case discussed in Chapter 6, this project scope was narrow. Consequently, I experienced ambiguity about whether I am putting my efforts in the best place. I chose to live with the ambiguity, rather than turning down parking work, by recognizing that reform supports broader goals of reducing automobile dependency; supporting multimodal transportation; generating demand for transit that supports those without cars; and improving housing affordability, economic development, sustainability, and equity. Having a specific niche of developed expertise makes me able to contribute to that broader planning agenda.

Many consulting firms do not apply a social relevance litmus test when deciding whether to compete for an assignment, especially those under financial pressure.[8] But I could have done so in this case since this was not my main employment. At the time, I didn't think about turning down the job because I wanted to help and sought yet another learning experience in working through parking conflict. Also, the project's goal of reconciliation and incremental progress was a close fit with planning purposes that have become important to me as my career has progressed.

Interpretation of Context

Discussions about parking are usually pitched at a high emotional level. They are often divisive, with many voices demanding action to make parking easier. Common lines of argument are territoriality ("the on-street space in front of my store or housing is 'my' parking space"), victimization ("I have been denied my favorite parking spot and suffer inconvenience"), and bluffing ("I won't shop there anymore if I have to pay for parking"). Loud voices drown out or intimidate interest groups such as service workers, bus riders, cyclists, pedestrians, renters, or newer businesses that lack clout. As with any planning exercise, careful discernment of claims is necessary.

Context Framework Elements

An early staff briefing and site tour provided me with a general understanding of the city and the controversy, but I had no experiential knowledge. I had recently worked on parking issues for another Orange County beach community and drew from that experience. As with most consulting assignments, there was no budget for me to get to know the community – I was reliant on staff interpretations and my interactions with stakeholders. I read between the lines to comprehend the broader story.

Parking is an issue where positions don't neatly line up with party affiliation. Normally, one might expect a Republican-leaning community would favor deregulation of parking requirements and support market parking prices. In this way, the market could determine supply and price outcomes. Municipal parking requirements, on the other hand, interfere with private-sector decisions about parking supply. As well, pricing a scarce commodity such as on-street parking at zero goes against economic principles. Yet local government often reflects a small "c" conservative view that the past was a better time and that things should be kept as they were, which underpins arguments to keep parking plentiful and free.

Regarding institutional context, parking management requires collaboration among city departments and with other agencies. Different visions and ways of working between departments of planning (policy function) and public works (staff function) can impede change. Planning departments focus on broad goals and plans, and advocate for change. Public works departments deliver and manage infrastructure and are more reluctant to deviate from existing practices. In municipal parking, these tensions can also be found between the planning and departments of police, finance, or engineering. In this case, all city departments seemed on board for the effort, but a critical issue was that police services were contracted with the County Sheriff, so enforcement actions would require their participation.

Dialogues with city commissioners and council members revealed a diversity of views about parking. One group favored higher minimum parking requirements and public investment in parking structures, and another group favored parking management and pricing.

Usually, local government has full autonomy regarding parking requirements and on-street parking management. In this case, however, the state-appointed California Coastal Commission ensures that local government and property owners do not exclude people from beach access within a defined coastal access zone, and has interpreted access to include parking availability.

Cities in these coastal zones must receive state approval for plans and policies regarding parking in coastal access zones. This limitation of local authority is often a point of resentment.

Moving forward with a partial understanding of context is common for planners, especially consultants. As I completed the listening sessions and the public workshop, however, the shape of the arguments and the controversy became clearer. In the past, I have worked in situations in which no City Council members were in favor of parking management. Rather than encountering a uniformly skeptical attitude, some council members were familiar with the research on parking management. I had the impression that some stakeholders hoped I would provide a compelling conclusion for assertive parking management, like a referee settling a dispute, but I avoided such a role to avoid alienating any one group.

Context Uncertainty and Ambiguity

Unlike many consulting assignments, this project included small group discussion time with staff, commissioners, and council members, as well as a major public workshop. These activities provided a good basis for crafting ideas. Nonetheless, opportunities to get to know the community were limited, so I used past experience from listening to stakeholders in other comparable cities. Given my lack of experience in Dana Point, I operated with ambiguity regarding political structure and what came before, but was able to piece together a view based on the activities and my experience. I felt my way through, knowing that translating from past experience can be useful but can lead me astray if those experiences are not sufficiently comparable. As Seigman notes in Box 10.1, his "read" of the community in the previous effort was different than mine.

The Planning Episode: Reasoning and Methods

Given the emphasis on communication and dialogue, emotion and invention were important elements of the episode, but this section shows that all four elements (logic, emotion, convention, invention) were consequential.

Logic

The level of controversy in this case meant that appeals to logic, while essential, could not be relied on as the sole form of reason. I used logic in a "soft" way in small group meetings and the public workshop, not to win arguments but to clarify what was at stake in the argument and the choices available. This involved making logical connections between ends such as goals and objectives, and means such as policies and programs (e.g., if you want *x* [an end], *y* [a means] is a good way of getting there). I didn't argue against strong claims for ends with which I disagreed, such as views that parking should be plentiful and free. Instead, I encouraged consideration of implementation realities: Who would pay for such as strategy? What would be the impact on walkability? How would economic vitality be affected? Illustrating problems with pursuing particular ends worked better than arguing that the end in itself was wrong. And agreeing to disagree kept the conversation going.

Workshop participants explained the problems that they saw and argued for the solutions they wanted. I introduced new ideas about means that could accomplish their desired ends. For example, a desire for more commercial on-street parking availability can be addressed by requiring more off-street parking, but that does not guarantee easy on-street parking because parkers prefer parking on-street than in a structure (Willson 2013). That strategy could lead to many seldom-used off-street spaces and a continued perception of restricted on-street availability. Logically, only dynamic on-street parking pricing can deliver the desired on-street parking availability and convenience.

Stakeholders often treat parking supply and policy issues as if there should be a logical right answer. In fact, parking policy depends on the goals being pursued as well as the starting point for implementation. To illustrate this last point, I developed a chart that showed various levels of parking management – beginning, intermediate, advanced, next generation, etc. This was helpful in directing attention to where the community is now and asking for logical next steps, rather than discussing why the most advanced methods were not being recommended, such as dynamic pricing.

I held back from claiming that there was no parking shortage, as had an earlier report, and focused on the perceived shortage. I wanted to keep those opposed to parking reform engaged in the process and avoided staking out a position that would give them a reason to dismiss the whole effort.

Emotion

My core effort was emotionally validating listening and deliberation. The public workshop that city staff designed and facilitated sought the same approach. There was *room* for a communicative approach because the assignment came on the heels of controversy, and a *need* for it for the same reason. Since parking issues evoke strong emotions, usually negative, I prepare for those expressions, tone down my reactiveness, and seek to be an engaged, empathetic communicator. That way I could hear common stakeholder frustrations such as finding parking, mourning previous conditions (e.g., "in the old days, parking was easy"), dislike of the impacts of "outsiders" visiting the beach, and resentment about parking impacts from residents who live in rental housing.

An example of emotional openness concerns the question of peak parking occupancy in the Lantern District. Consultant data showed that there was plenty of available parking, even at peak times – on the aggregate. Of course, total parking availability disguises the reality that not all of the inventory is available as public parking, and ignores the individual's experience of searching for a parking space. When residents can't find the parking spaces in the place they want, at the time they want, they conclude that there is a parking shortage. Framing the problem as a shortage naturally leads to proposals for parking construction. Outside consultants are unpopular when they tell such a person that their problem really isn't a problem. Knowing that individuals' experiences were different than the aggregate situation helped me understand the claims of these residents. With that emotional sensitivity, I made suggestions with a light touch. This "reasonable" role drew on my academic credentials as well; I sought to portray myself as objective rather than a planner with a reform agenda.

The dark side of coastal parking attitudes is exclusion. In working in other coastal cities, stakeholders have "othered" beach visitors of lower economic status and different ethnic and racial identities. In the geography of Southern California, telephone area codes are used to make such designations. In this region, 909 is the area code for the Inland Empire, a subregion that has a lower-income and more diverse demographic profile than Dana Point. I watched out for claims about community character that may have been coded language about keeping those from the "909" out.

Convention

Desire for convention was evident in residents' desire for easy parking, a hallmark of post-WWII suburban land use and transportation practices. Many residents wanted those norms to continue.

I used a different form of convention in sharing information on best practice in parking management. Cities frequently decide what to do by norming their approach to that of comparable cities. Decision-makers seek precedent for change in comparable cities, i.e., "Where has this been done before?" This application of convention is useful, but if taken too far does not align strategies with local context. If all of a city's neighboring municipalities have an ineffective strategy, then following their convention replicates bad practice (see Boxes 5.2 and 5.3 in Chapter 5).

I also considered the way that convention holds sway in city departments that operate and manage parking. While existing practices may need reform, the people who implement those practices may be reluctant to change them. I pondered conventions and perceptions of risks when I suggested policies and regulations, new technology, and approaches. Helping staff manage the risk of adopting new practices supports agreement. This includes perceptions of risk and actual risk since implementing departments are often blamed if things go wrong, not the planning department or a long-gone consultant.

A third way that convention shaped my approach was appreciating how deeply parking management proposals are tied to community identity. Changes in parking conditions and policies often symbolize other dimensions of change. What was at stake for some was the way Dana Point had been, with a laid-back, small beach-town vibe. Parking management is often a symbol of undesired urban intensification. One parking project can't change these feelings, but I listened for the emotional elements behind the story.

Invention

Invention took a different form than commonly expected, where it might mean creating a new policy, plan, or program that did not exist before. The invention in this case was process – finding a way out of an impasse and developing processes that lead to incremental improvement.

Planners are sometimes criticized for being process-oriented rather than outcome-oriented, as found in the stereotype of bureaucrats who go to meetings but don't *do* anything. Regardless, my primary recommendation was to create a stakeholder process to move from a long list of potential measures to early implementation steps.

When I presented this process idea to the City Council, I apologized for suggesting yet another committee but explained why it was necessary to keep attention on the issue and needed implementation steps. None of the individual measures were particularly innovative in themselves but moving forward was an innovation, and the council approved the process.

Discoveries

The centrality of engagement in this planning assignment leads to observations about (i) practical judgments made during the planning episode and (ii) broader takeaways for planning.

Practical Judgments

Three practical judgments were pivotal in this planning episode: an emphasis on talk; deliberation, "nudging," and framing rather than arguing; and finding relevance and impact in a narrow planning issue.

Practical Judgment 1: Prioritizing Talk Over Technical Analysis

The Town Center Parking Plan and draft consulting study recommended a comprehensive set of strategies for parking. The city wasn't interested in doing another such study nor was it necessary because that document provided solid information and recommendations. Controversy was holding up planning decisions, not a lack of ideas. The process needed to become "unstuck." Rather than do my own independent study, I agreed that the key issue was engaging stakeholders in an incremental process.

I previously studied how theories of communicative action are applicable to transportation planning (Willson et al. 2003) and had good experiences with facilitated processes. Of course, the talk approach carries risk. It can be expensive, time-consuming, and it doesn't guarantee results. More talk, poorly facilitated, can make things worse by expanding conflict or being dominated by powerful, narrow interests. If those at the table have more economic and political power than those not present, talk processes reinforce that structure.

The talk approach in this case sought to place attention where it was needed – on differing experiences, understandings, and prescriptions – and focused on finding ways forward. When technical studies are used to paper over value conflicts, it wastes time, money, and obfuscates the issues. While technical studies can be efficiently produced, they cannot resolve value differences.

Practical Judgment 2: Focusing Efforts on Deliberation, "Nudging" and Framing

Participating in group meetings required careful navigation and deliberate efforts to stay engaged with all stakeholders. I tried not to offend those who opposed parking management so they wouldn't reject me as too radical, too urban, too intellectual, or too impractical. Having a PhD increased my legitimacy for some, but others may have dismissed me as not sufficiently "real world." Avoiding sounding like an academic and taking a light touch meant holding my tongue sometimes.

In one meeting, a constituent presented a government vehicle ownership forecast for Orange County. The forecast was used to make the claim that much more parking was needed in the future. In my view, the forecast exaggerated future levels of vehicle ownership but the participant referred to it as "data." The data claim implied that the case for more parking was clear. I did not challenge that view even though I disagreed with it. Playing such a role meant deciding between roles as technical expert and an even-handed facilitator. I modulated between these roles during the planning episode. This approach comes with potential public confusion about what I was doing – Was I consultant who answered when asked, an advocate for change, or a facilitator concerned with good process and open to any outcome? In Box 10.2 (next page), Martin Wachs explores considerations planners face in selecting planning roles.

Practical Judgment 3: Working on a Narrow "First World" Problem Instead of Pressing Social and Environmental Issues

Not finding a parking space, when and where you want it, is a minor problem in the larger scheme of social and environmental issues. Yet this issue was driving planning and politics in Dana Point. I was interested in this work as yet another window into the dynamics of local parking and gladly accepted the assignment. I could have spent the same amount of time doing pro bono work for low-income neighborhoods with parking problems. Such an effort could have benefited neighborhoods in the Hawthorne case study, as discussed in Chapter 12, in which residents experienced on-street parking problems. At the time I accepted the work, I did not think this through. On reflection, my view is that reforming parking in affluent communities benefits all by supporting multimodal transportation modes, which reduce environmental impacts and provide more options for those who do not drive. But the reflection has made me realize that I can contribute to housing solutions more effectively by working on parking management that do not have the resources of Dana Point.

Takeaways for Practice

This case shows the important role of communication and deliberation in planning, far beyond speaking clearly and listening carefully. To fulfill its potential, communication is best seen as a form of action that addresses points of view, explanation, contingent exploration of options, and forming the will to take action. Three takeaways for professional practice are suggested.

Box 10.2 Role Conflicts Always Challenge Planners
Martin Wachs, Distinguished Professor Emeritus of Urban Planning, University of California, Los Angeles

Parking is central to planning in every community. It largely is a technical matter, governed by formal codes and addressed by standard procedures. But parking affects every resident, employee, shopper, and business. It directly influences the cost of new development. The Dana Point parking episode is typical of many planning assignments. Though the issue at first appears to be mundane, competing interests and bureaucratic complexities soon raise their heads and apparently simple questions lead to bitter disagreements.

What is the role of the professional planner? This case demonstrates that the answer to this simple question is, like parking, far more complicated than it first appears. A planning firm fulfilled one role – that of the technical expert who had prepared a plan in compliance with local regulations and customs and according to standard methods. Other planners, including Siegman (Boxes 10.1 and 10.3) and Willson, were called upon to fill quite a different role – to facilitate a conversation or mediate a dispute between parties whose views differed. A third possible role might have been to represent the interests of particular community groups or land developers in the planning process. In principle, the role of mediator or moderator calls on a planner to be independent and unbiased – to hear all sides and to facilitate their capacity to listen to one another and to work toward a compromise.

But planners, trained to be technical specialists, are far more familiar with the data, regulations, and technical processes that produced the first report than are those who came to the meeting pursuing their interests. It is difficult to leave our technical knowledge at the door. Should we try to? Professor Willson, for example, tried hard to listen fairly to all participants, but he also "nudged" them. Is it a planner's responsibility to educate and inform lay people at a meeting so they can make wiser choices? If so, when does a nudge become a shove? Is it his or her responsibility to facilitate discussion while avoiding trying to influence the outcome? It appears to be the planner's responsibility to do both at the same time, but that is not usually possible. Making a choice about what to say in a split second in front of a crowd can easily heighten hostilities that lie just below the surface. Listening to people make statements that are factually wrong makes us want to play the expert. Doing so just a bit too aggressively leads people at the meeting to distrust and discount us.

Like Goldilocks, planners try to find a balance between competing roles that is "just right." Every situation is unique and no textbook can prepare us in advance to arrive at the right approach. Recognizing the challenges hiding in what appears to be a straightforward assignment, however, enables us to benefit from each such experience by increasing both our skill as facilitators and our confidence as planners.

Takeaway 1: Understand the Dynamics of Consultant–Agency Interactions in the Process of Change

The consultant/adviser is an "intruder" with partial knowledge of context, who inserts themselves into a client's organizational culture for a short period of time. As mentioned, this requires a quick study of organizational cultural and power dynamics. But the dynamics themselves deserve further note. Baum (1987), using a psychological approach, explains this dynamic. The ostensible reason for hiring consultants is to solve a problem that the organization cannot address. A source of non-instrumental organizational behavior is that the client feels shame that they are responsible for problems but lack the resources, authority, or will to solve them. A consulting process widens knowledge of their failures and can make them feel vulnerable. This includes an inability to resolve a political conflict or difference. The anxiety of being "stuck" can be discharged in the relationship with the consultant – through a variety of activities such as scapegoating, flattery, discrediting the consultant's competence, withholding information, or sabotaging solutions.

Consultants should be aware of the ritualistic dimensions of their work. It is not just solving a problem but attending to evolving organizational and political dimensions. In hindsight, I realized how limited my understanding was of what had come before. The staff told me what they thought I needed to know; consultants usually don't have time for more research than that. As a result, consultants are always flying partially "blind," not fully knowing what came before. Whatever we can do to get the full story, we should do. And our planning strategies will be more robust if we the plan with the understanding that what we know is partial.

Recommending an advisory committee provided a way of processing community and organizational issues, an opportunity for incremental progress, and a sense of ownership of the strategies. As consultant, I provided ideas but did not offer a specific set of recommendations. In this way, I sought to manage the reality of being an intruder and lower the risk that I had missed something by emphasizing local process.

Takeaway 2: Discern the Opportunities and Limits of Technical Rationality, and Use Talk Processes for "Wicked" Problems

Analytic, expert-driven plans do not resolve controversy – rather, pragmatic, dialogue-based mutual adjustment is required. The Town Center Lantern District Parking Plan provided a comprehensive and logical set of proposals, won approval, and had moved to implementation, but it also produced a backlash. It may have contained more advocacy for values and approaches than city officials and stakeholders could accept at that moment. Planning cannot proceed independently of context. Process is how context is revealed and negotiated.

Workshop processes address stakeholder conflict more effectively than adversarial, nondialogical public comment at meetings.[9] The 2017 Dana Point workshop designed by city staff employed appropriate elements of engagement – short presentations, information stations where attendees could address topics of interest, marks on maps to identify problems, and city staff availability to answer questions at each station. The city also used effective community outreach methods, including an online survey to gain a wider range of stakeholder views. Good process doesn't eliminate stakeholder conflicts but improves understanding and lays the groundwork for compromise, reconciliation, and innovation. A good faith effort builds community trust in planning. And a process of framing problems through dialogue – understanding them in different perspectives – can lead to the discovery of mutual gain, win-win strategies.

Of course, planning solely based on process can replicate dominant community views that are impossible to meet or are inequitable. Planners encounter many questions of how much to push back in the process instead of simply searching for an accommodation of stakeholder interests. Process to the exclusion of evidence can lead to wasteful projects (e.g., ineffective or bloated by including something for every interest) or inequitable ones (e.g., a "balance" among empowered groups leaves out community stakeholders who aren't at the table).

Not all cities have the capacity to engage in such participatory processes. Cities that experience continuing political upheaval, shortages or high turnover in staffing, or financial crises are too busy putting out fires to do so (Irish 2016). In this way, Dana Point's institutional capability, combined with the willingness of stakeholders to participate, enabled it to succeed in this process. Professional organizations should assist communities that don't have the necessary resources for talk processes.

Takeaway 3: Attend to Localized Problems as a Way of Helping Communities Solve Bigger Issues

Local concerns and problems frequently drive broader policy – solve them and movement is possible on those broader issues. As shown here, parking problems are highly localized yet they drive broad concerns about transportation, growth and real estate development. If there isn't a process for identifying and responding to neighborhood-level concerns, broader disenchantment occurs. In Dana Point, a residential street is impacted by the Lantern District as employees of bars and restaurants park on that street and return to their cars late at night, after work. That activity bothers residents, some of whom are community leaders, which may have been part of the impetus for the parking controversy.

The public workshop made it clear that neighbors had specific concerns about issues on their block that they felt were not being addressed. Creating a quick-response city team to address these issues can lay the groundwork for broader policy initiatives. Residents want to know that progress is possible. Small wins can support broader changes.

City planners often work in an institutional structure that separates planning and implementation tasks. Partnerships between planners and departments such as public works can reduce conflict and complaints, and produce confidence in government. That can create a basis for engaging controversial issues and supporting innovative planning efforts.

Box 10.3 provides a narrative that expands on how the dynamics of parking spillover into neighborhoods drove broader planning issues.

Box 10.3 Small Problems Drive Broad Policy
Patrick Siegman, Patrick Siegman and Associates

I completed the 2014 Town Center Lantern District Parking Plan prior to the effort described in this chapter. During my work, I heard a handful of residents complain about parking overflow from restaurants and other businesses into adjacent residential streets. However, many other residents on those blocks felt that it was a minor issue, if one at all. It didn't appear that most residents wanted to proceed with spillover prevention measures like residential parking permit districts. Therefore, I described the situation as "a large overall [parking] surplus, with spot shortages in a few popular blocks and many underutilized parking lots elsewhere."

At the request of staff, my report described spillover issues in overall terms ("spot shortages on a few popular blocks") and offered solutions in general terms (residential parking permits, etc.). This avoided singling out individual business owners as "the problem" and individual residents as "the complainers." The disadvantage to this approach was that we didn't provide an immediate, detailed, and fine-grained solution to each spillover parking problem. This may have made it appear that I was insensitive to the individual problems that they were experiencing.

Box 10.3 (continued)

In January 2014, I presented that parking plan to the City Council. I recall it being positively received by the members of the public in attendance, but with a few complaints. The council voted to move ahead on the plan and to draft implementing ordinances to address spillover parking problems and change parking requirements. We submitted them to the council for approval in July 2015.

In each of the cases where residents observed a spillover parking problem, I had a good idea of which businesses (or residences) were causing the complaints and what measures would fix the problem. In one case, customers preferred to park in easily accessed on-street spots in front of people's homes rather than in the underground garage at their actual destination: the restaurant next door. It seemed obvious that building a new parking structure wouldn't solve the problem because existing underused spaces were literally beneath the diners' feet. Managing the curb spaces in front of the adjacent residents' homes in a way that would deter employees and customers from parking there seemed like the only viable solution.

We moved forward with some short-term actions, such as converting underused private lots into shared public parking, while working through a lengthy public outreach process. The disadvantage to this approach was that the world did not stop and wait while we worked on public engagement. By October 2014, the City Council had approved a major mixed-use development (Majestic), including approving variances. Our proposed measures (e.g., residential parking permits) to solve existing spillover parking problems and prevent future ones were not yet in place. As described in Box 10.1, that exacerbated fears that existing spillover parking problems would intensify.

The Measure H initiative discussed in this case study reversed the new parking requirements that I had recommended and the council had adopted. It couldn't, however, reverse the Majestic project. Those new shops, restaurants, and 109 homes are nearing completion.[10]

It won't ever be clear to what extent the initiative was sparked by a dislike of the Majestic project, versus anger over existing spillover parking, versus dislike of my recommended parking strategy, or a simple dislike of the entire vision contained within the Town Center Plan. My sense is that all of these contributed, with the Majestic development and my recommendations being the prime factors. This is a case that illustrates the difficulty of predicting, in advance of an election, whether an approach has majority support from both the people's elected representatives *and* a majority of the city's electorate. We had listened to hundreds of people over more than a dozen meetings, but that turned out not to be a representative sample of the electorate. While a majority of elected representatives preferred the proposed approach, the next election revealed it didn't have majority support. It then became the task of the next council, new city staff, and the next consultant to see if they could solve these long-standing issues.

And Now to You: The Communicative Planner

This case shows that insightful analytic work is not enough to move planning forward. The process of understanding, reframing, acquiring knowledge, compromising, and deciding is an essentially human, communicative one. It takes time. And an apparently unsuccessful effort can be the seed for a later successful one because community dynamics are in constant flux.

Communicative and deliberative planning processes were central to this case. This may seem obvious to you, and if so, seek knowledge from this case study and other accounts of practice, obtain training in participation and negotiation techniques, acquire mentors and coaches, and develop your portfolio of experience. If, on the other hand, you are drawn to analytic techniques such as modeling and impact analysis, it may be a stretch to think of communication as tool for planning. As a transportation planner, it took me a while to learn this. Once I learned it, however, I was a more adaptable and effective professional.

Communicative approaches *do not* mean you forsake evidence but rather finding productive ways to use it in dialogues. It can feel disorienting to move toward a communicative planning model because it may seem that the loudest voice will win. But that can be addressed as planners seek to reduce distortions to communication that happen in the rough and tumble of political conflict.

Parking requirements are just one example of technical requirements embedded in zoning codes that profoundly influence outcomes in sustainability, social and economic equity, and efficiency. Those requirements, along with parking management rules, are often "set it and forget it" approaches implemented by public works departments (Willson 2015). It is tempting to consider these issues as mundane aspects that are not consequential. The lesson from this case is that seemingly mundane topics have large impacts on outcomes. Unmanaged public parking and excess minimum requirements affect housing, multimodal transportation, economic development, historic preservation, livability, and human health. Working on these issues, as a "bottom-feeder" of the policy world, as my colleague Donald Shoup says, can yield change as great or greater than lofty visions and goals.

Discussion Questions

1. Are there ethical issues associated with a planner not saying what they think in order to maintain dialogue with those with whom they disagree? In this case, I chose not to argue back when a stakeholder made a claim that had weak analytic support. Was that the correct path? If yes, should

a planner set limits to such a practice, and if so, how? You might consider this from the standpoint of the American Institute of Certified Planners (AICP) Code of Ethics or in a more general way.

2. An extensive public engagement process can make things worse as well as better. What are the factors that lead to an engagement process worsening stakeholder conflict? How can processes be designed to avoid that?

3. Should a planner expect to find alignment between their values and the organization or client for which they work? How can a planner discern when the lack of alignment is so great that they need to change jobs?

4. How should a planner know how much to compromise in order to keep stakeholders engaged? Does the AICP Code of Ethics provide guidance in this area? If so, how do you interpret it?

Notes

1 A presentation on the study can be viewed at www.danapoint.org/home/showdoc ument?id=12749.

2 Information about the Doheny Village Specific Plan effort is available at www.d anapoint.org/businesses/doheny-village.

3 Analysis of the initiative is available at https://ballotpedia.org/Dana_Point,_Cali fornia,_Town_Center_Plan_and_Parking_Citizen_Initiative,_Measure_H_(Ju ne_2016).

4 Video of the workshop is available at https://youtu.be/HTTejpuQIV8.

5 Accessed November 12, 2019, at https://docs.google.com/forms/d/e/1FAIpQ LSfYvnOLAlrH_OgRqf2SmgR3Egxnc-bkouUJV3fVXmqSUAH-5A/view analytics.

6 Link to Citywide Parking Implementation Plan www.danapoint.org/residents/ city-news/parking. Link to Willson report www.danapoint.org/home/showdoc ument?id=23241.

7 Data source: https://en.wikipedia.org/wiki/California_locations_by_voter_regis tration#Cities.

8 Patrick Siegman provides this note on my statement: "At Nelson/Nygaard, I and many of my colleagues did apply a social relevance litmus test. We were privately owned, not publicly traded, so we could afford to take a long-term approach to being profitable. As my friend Alan Loomis says, 'you get the work you take.' By first volunteering my time at design charrettes led by New Urbanists, while refusing auto-oriented projects, I lost some work and income. But in the long-term, Nelson/Nygaard became known for particular expertise in sustainable transportation. We developed depth of experience in transit, transit-oriented development, bicycle and pedestrian planning, and traffic calming. That helped us win work in these growing fields, and it helped us recruit talented young people who care about sustainability, even though we often couldn't offer the best pay and benefit packages in our industry."

9 Resources at the Harvard Law School Program on Negotiation are useful for planners: www.pon.harvard.edu.
10 An article about the controversy can be viewed at www.danapointtimes.com/city -council-approves-majestic-project/.

References

Baum, Howell. 1987. *The Invisible Bureaucracy: The Unconscious in Organizational Problem Solving.* New York: Oxford University Press.

Forester, John. 1989. *Planning in the Face of Power.* Berkeley, CA: University of California Press.

Irish, Aiden. 2016. "Assessing Local Government Capacity for Implementing Sustainable Transportation: The Role of Political Culture." *International Journal of Public Administration,* 40(5): 1–10. doi: 1080/01900692.2015.1122037.

U.S. Census. 2020. Accessed March 11, 2020 at https://www.census.gov/quickfacts/f act/table/danapointcitycalifornia/INC110218.

Willson, Richard, Marianne Payne, and Ellen Smith. 2003. "Does Discussion Enhance Rationality? Communicative Rationality in Transportation Planning." *Journal of the American Planning Association,* 69(4): 354–367. doi.org/10.1080/019443603089 76324.

Willson, Richard. 2013. *Parking Reform Made Easy.* Washington, DC: Island Press.

Willson, Richard. 2015. *Parking Management for Smart Growth.* Washington, DC: Island Press.

Chapter 11

Bringing Fresh Produce to Inner-City Corner Stores in Detroit, Michigan

Kameshwari Pothukuchi

This chapter discusses a campus–community collaborative effort to assess the availability of fresh produce in corner stores in underserved Detroit neighborhoods and to increase fresh produce offerings by those corner stores. The effort was a project of SEED Wayne, a campus–community food system program I led, with a goal of increasing access to fresh and healthy food for Detroit residents.

Implemented over the five years as Detroit FRESH, the project spanned a series of activities to assess and recruit corner stores, provide participating stores with equipment and technical assistance, link them to produce wholesalers, and implement social marketing campaigns to engage residents and enhance their connections to corner stores. The project employed students of Wayne State University and local organizations in documentation, social marketing, neighborhood outreach, and special events.

The discussion traces my role as a professor and director of a food system program, highlighting three practical judgments: (i) navigating the planning episode, step by step; (ii) choosing to address a part of the overall problem in a focused and limited way; and (iii) extending the familiar to develop innovations.

Description of the Planning Episode

The Healthy Corner Store Project, later renamed Detroit FRESH, started in 2008 as a partnership with the Capuchin Soup Kitchen's (CSK) Earthworks Urban Farm (EWUF) on Detroit's Lower Eastside. Conversations with the CSK guests, convened by EWUF staff, highlighted the challenges neighborhood residents faced to obtain healthy and fresh foods given the paucity of supermarkets in the area. They also revealed past experiences with neighborhood-based food access and possible avenues to increase access to fresh and healthy foods. The idea of assessing nearby corner stores for their fresh and healthy food inventory emerged as a next step, which led to a group of students and CSK staff and guests fanning out into the surrounding neighborhood with a collaboratively developed survey instrument.

Two projects emerged from these initial steps: one led by a group of residents who decided to offer a small-scale neighborhood mobile market – operated out of a car – with produce purchased from Eastern Market's wholesale market. The other, Detroit FRESH, was coordinated by me with support from an external grant and is the focus of this case. These activities occurred at a time when neighborhoods were starting to feel the impacts of the Great Recession, and to which corner stores, as we discovered, were scarcely immune. These and other details are reported in Pothukuchi (2005, 2015, 2016).

My approach to Detroit FRESH was prompted by four interrelated findings:

1. A growing literature on the food environment in inner-city neighborhoods and its impact on dietary health, particularly in impoverished communities of color.
2. Research – including mine – on abandonment by grocery supermarkets in Detroit, particularly the 2007 closure of several Farmer Jack stores, which prompted the Detroit Economic Growth Corporation to convene stakeholders to identify solutions (DEGC 2008). The process, however, excluded corner stores, which are ubiquitous in Detroit's neighborhoods.
3. Prevalent narratives of the African American community's experience of corner stores as representing an extractive economy that caters primarily to addictions (alcohol, tobacco, junk food, and lottery), treats African American shoppers with disrespect, and returns little of real value to the

community. The corner store industry in Detroit is dominated by Chaldean Americans, a group that traces its ancestry to Iraq.

4. The aforementioned dialogues within the CSK, which identified needs and assets for healthy food access. The conversations uncovered a history of mom-and-pop stores run by neighborhood residents and seasonal truck-based vending of fresh produce in the neighborhood.

Institutional Setting

The institutional setting for this project is characterized by a history of neighborhood isolation from the city's redevelopment efforts, fragmented regulatory frameworks that allow businesses to derive lucrative profit while returning little in real community value, and a weak food market despite the availability of public spending in the form of SNAP and WIC nutrition programs.[1] Larger market and policy structures thus thwart neighborhood-based efforts to develop viable solutions.

Over the last seven decades, Detroit has experienced significant disinvestment and depopulation, with Eastside neighborhoods particularly hard hit. Figure 11.1 shows Detroit's location in its regional context as a border city

Figure 11.1 Detroit Regional Context. Image source: Google, TerraMetrics

separated from Canada by the Detroit River. Detroit's 1950 population of 1.8 million shrank to a mere 713,777 by 2010 and further to an estimated 680,281 in 2014 when the study ended (see also Figure 11.2 showing population change 2000–2010 and Table 11.1 with 2010 socioeconomic data for the CSK neighborhood). These neighborhoods were also experiencing a high rate of home foreclosures as the project started.

The presence of corner stores in these neighborhoods offered a starting point for planning for many reasons. First, corner stores represent a ubiquitous neighborhood infrastructure for year-round food sales, with the ability to do business in the poorest of neighborhoods. Second, a big part of their food sales is enabled by the availability of federal nutrition dollars (SNAP and WIC), which are expressly intended to foster food security for low-income households. Figure 11.3 shows the Corners Party Store, which was among the first stores that agreed to participate in the Detroit FRESH program. Third, local and state government permits also allow the sale of alcohol and lottery tickets in corner stores, which are highly lucrative. However, the permits make no reciprocal demands to directly benefit the health of residents from whom

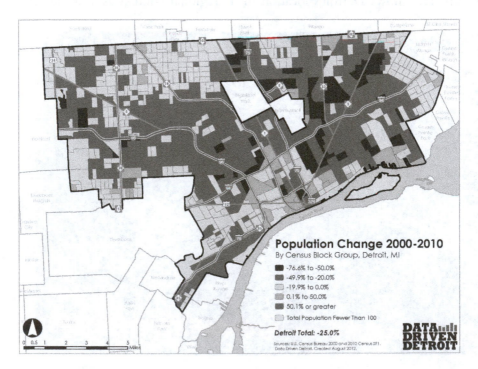

Figure 11.2 Population Change between 2000 and 2010, Detroit. Image source: Data Driven Detroit

Table 11.1 Socioeconomic Characteristics of Neighborhood Residents Around the Capuchin Soup Kitchen, Compared to Detroit and the USA

	Census Tracts in the Capuchin Soup Kitchen Neighborhood							City of Detroit	USA
	5163	5164	5152	5153	5166	5167	5168		
% Persons age 19 and under	22	22.4	24.5	17.8	31.3	24.4	22.7	30.5	26.9
% Persons age 60 and over	22.7	17.8	27.9	29.9	19.3	23.3	19.1	16.6	18.5
% Black or African American	92.4	88.9	92.1	90.6	95.9	96.1	92.5	82.7	12.6
% Vacant housing units	31.3	36.5	32.8	18.3	6.8	6.5	23.9	22.8	11.4
% Owner-occupied housing units	49.3	46	56.4	13.1	17.7	15.9	49.1	51.1	65.1
Median household income, past 12 months*	$37,955	$31,181	$27,621	$19,597	$16,025	$25,321	$13,958	$28,357	$51,914
% Families below poverty level	20.9	20	20.1	26.4	49.6	31.5	62.7	29.4	10.1

Sources: 2010 U.S. Census; 2006–2010 American Community Survey 5-Year Estimates.

* In 2010 inflation-adjusted dollars.

Figure 11.3 Corner's Party Store. Image source: Kameshwari Pothukuchi

the businesses derive extensive profits. Thus, these subsidies and permitting frameworks suggest an opening for investigating and pursuing broader public interest possibilities. Fourth, when economic development initiatives around larger corner stores started to emerge in Detroit, they tended to focus on only a handful of businesses and on such physical categories as façade improvements, interior refurbishments, and equipment upgrades rather than a deeper appraisal and reconfiguring of supply chain capacities for fresh and healthy foods, which, as this project documents, is vastly more complex to achieve. Finally, given the relative isolation of neighborhoods in the history of the city's redevelopment planning efforts, there is a rich history of community-based actions to resolve problems with local resources.

I initiated the project as an extension of my community involvement over the previous decade in assisting, among other things, the development of community food projects and the city's food security policy, and in research on healthy food access and urban agriculture. In these efforts I seek, wherever possible, to leverage my university role and resources. Since 2008, these efforts coalesced under the umbrella of SEED Wayne, a sustainable food system program I led, with several engaged-learning components located on campus and in the community. The program's four goals are (i) improving access to fresh

and healthy foods in underserved communities; (ii) building closer connections between the city's residents and local food producers, including Detroit-
based growers; (iii) increasing capacity of individuals and organizations to
participate effectively in the food system; and (iv) linking food system goals
to broader community goals related to social and economic justice, ecological
sustainability, neighborhood improvement, and public health.

SEED Wayne kicked off with a $100,000 grant from the Ford Motor
Company Fund, with CSK–EWUF named as one of many community partners. Following Phase I, SEED Wayne raised an additional $90,000 with
EWUF as a partner for several entrepreneurial activities including Detroit
FRESH. As the corner store project unfolded, I shared details informally
and in formal presentations with stakeholder groups. For a variety of reasons,
despite a positive initial conversation with the deputy director of the city's
public health agency, Bill Ridella,[2] building an ongoing relationship for the
corner store project with the city's health department proved to be a challenge.

Overview of Planning Process

The planning process had four phases, with each subsequent step emerging
from reflection on previous ones:

1. Neighborhood participatory assessment.
2. Proof-of-concept pilot of store–produce distributor–community relation-
    ship and fund-raising based on initial lessons.
3. Project implementation and modification over two iterations.
4. Overall project evaluation and dissemination of findings.

Lacking a blueprint for such a process, I formulated the steps in conversation
with food system and community leaders. More generally, the approach is
consistent with planners' use of consensual group processes. Such processes
are needed to invent solutions to problems that lack well-defined publics,
precedents, or support for top-down actions; contain multiple competing and
sometimes conflicting interests; and elicit strong emotions. Solutions to such
problems also require coordination among different groups and are often characterized by sequential interdependence, such that the input of one is the out-
put of another (Innes 1996, Innes and Booher 2010). The problems taken up
here exemplify these characteristics.

The approach is also informed by community development frameworks
asserting that problems experienced by impoverished communities have

their roots in society, and that communities also have assets to meet needs and resolve problems. Collective action creates both shared knowledge as well as greater solidarity. Through collective action, individuals and organizations potentially build capacity to challenge larger structures of power and inequity (Kretzmann and McKnight 1993, Checkoway 1995, Fung 2003, Bobo et al. 2001).

Finally, the project embraces participatory action research (PAR) frameworks. PAR researchers work intentionally and in partnership with practitioners and intended beneficiaries. Unlike traditional social science research, its purpose is not primarily or solely intended to understand social arrangements but rather to effect desired change as a path to generating knowledge, empowering stakeholders, and enriching democratic possibilities (Bradbury-Huang 2010, Gergen 2003, Mies 1983, Reason and Bradbury 2001). In short, PAR seeks to understand the world by trying to change it, emphasizing principles of collective action, experimentation, and reflection. PAR scholars eschew viewing practice simply as a specialized set of methods, but rather see it as emerging in the act of doing. This is also consistent with the pragmatic approach favored by theorists such as Schön (1983) and Forester (1999), in which practitioners are urged to engage with the messy reality of context and contingency, and trial and error, to generate knowledge as well as the Chapter 3–5 framework.

In Phase I, EWUF staff and guests, along with students of my Cities and Food course assessed stores within a one-mile radius of CSK and interviewed storekeepers. The assessment recorded the availability of fruits and vegetables in the stores, prices, and the store keepers' current and past experiences with selling produce. We also recruited stores to participate in a pilot, which started with three corner stores. These stores were connected to a produce wholesaler who agreed to free and discounted delivery of orders. We set up the stores with supplies such as baskets and scales as needed, and information on produce merchandising and management. Stores received discount coupons to make initial produce orders with two wholesalers who agreed to participate in the project. We regularly checked in with the stores and the distributors to document their experiences, gather data, and troubleshoot.

Based on this pilot, I secured a grant to launch a larger project. A team of student employees enlarged the geography of store assessment and recruitment in Phase II, which led to a total of 26 participating stores (see Figure 11.4). Dialogues now involved a larger group of stakeholders including store owners, produce wholesalers, and community partners in the neighborhoods of participating stores. As before, we offered supplies (including a small refrigerator to one store), technical assistance to participating stores, and connected them to

Detroit FRESH Stores

By Census Tract, Detroit, MI

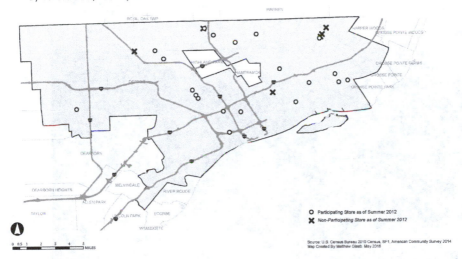

Figure 11.4 Stores that Agreed to Participation in Detroit FRESH, 2009–12. Image source: Kameshwari Pothukuchi

suppliers. A couple of operators sourced produce from outlets more conveni-ent to them, such as larger superstores located in the suburbs where they lived.

We conducted outreach to residents in the store's immediate neighborhood and checked in at regular intervals with stores and distributors to document their experiences and collect data. As more stores came on line, the project expe-rienced challenges regarding the reliability with which stores carried produce and shared sales data. Several were also experiencing lower sales overall due to neighborhood depopulation, leading six to drop out of the project prematurely. At this point, store assessment and recruitment ceased as I considered next steps.

Based on dialogues with a few store operators, in Phase III we intensified outreach to residents in the form of Healthy Food Fairs (HFFs) offered in partnership with select stores. HFFs included cooking demos of healthy meals using store products, "motivational interviews" with participants related to diets, participant surveys to understand how corner stores could best meet needs for fresh produce, and greater social marketing of fresh snacks to replace the processed snacks typically purchased with SNAP funds. Figure 11.5 shows a community workshop in action.

Nineteen out of the 26 stores that participated in the project remained in summer 2013 when the project wrapped up. We analyzed the project's find-ings and shared lessons with local community development and broader food planning and policy audiences.

Figure 11.5 Participants at a Healthy Food Fair. Image source: Kameshwari Pothukuchi

The Core Problem

Detroit FRESH focused exclusively on corner stores as a source of fresh produce, with other sources such as farmers markets, grocery stores, and community gardens addressed elsewhere in SEED Wayne. As a planner interested in community infrastructure, I decided to emphasize increasing stores' capacity to carry fresh produce rather than residents' consumption or even purchases of produce. The scope of the project was also defined by the limited resources at hand – a small budget supplemented with student labor – and constrained by what participating store owners were willing to do in the context of declining overall sales.

The problem had many components, including:

1. Lack of fresh produce in neighborhood corner stores; general lack of store operator interest to offer fresh produce (as it turned out, only 26 out of 214 stores assessed agreed to participate in the project).
2. Lack of store capacity for produce marketing and merchandising, absence of an existing produce distribution system, and residents' negative perceptions of corner stores.

3. In the absence of baseline sales data in stores, uncertainty about types, amounts, and frequency of produce orders. Given the likelihood of high produce unit prices and limited choice, uncertainty about amounts residents might reasonably spend on produce.
4. (Later on) Given relatively consistent levels of SNAP spending in stores for snacks, the possibility of shifting such spending on healthier snacks such as fruit.

Only a small fraction (12%) of the assessed stores agreed to participate, which was disappointing even if unsurprising. The initial plan was to assess corner stores in the entire city! Early on in the assessment, some stores clearly indicated that produce was not part of their business model, while others had tried it and given up or greatly cut back in terms of quantities, varieties, and year-round supply – with summer months bringing more demand for certain varieties. Those who agreed to participate in Detroit FRESH were willing to give produce a shot or, if they were returning to carrying it, another shot.

Conversations with wholesalers led me to imagine efficient distribution logistics as suppliers delivered to multiple stores in the same neighborhood on any given day. Given the trickle of interest, however, we had to cope with a much sparser geography for developing a distribution system and had to integrate some storekeepers' desire to procure from ultra big-box stores in the exurbs as a way to control costs and timing of merchandising (to meet the food-stamp-supported sales early in the month).

Thus, while we were interested in developing a proof of concept for a corner store system (consisting of distributor–store–customer linkages), as the assessment expanded following the pilot, the project focused more on keeping *individual* stores going and bolstering their capacity, and became less about developing and testing a multistore distribution system incorporating wholesalers. Larger questions arose during the project's implementation about possible ways to leverage positive store practices. Furthermore, given the public interest objectives of healthy diets, another question related to whose responsibility it was to ensure that an adequate public and private infrastructure for fresh produce exists within neighborhoods, especially impoverished ones.

Intended and Actual Outcomes

I hoped to accomplish the following when the project was completed:

1. Consistent supply of fresh produce in participating corner stores – with produce sourced from distributors identified by us or by the stores themselves – and enabled by increased sales.

2. Stores that accept WIC benefits would consistently adhere to requirements related to produce availability.
3. Shoppers would divert a portion of their SNAP spending overall in corner stores to healthier snacks (such as an apple or banana or a bag of baby carrots).

Nine stores performed as intended; another ten stores performed inconsistently. Seven dropped out of the project or shut down operations during the project's timeline. Thus, the project was successful in kick-starting the chain of relationships and flow of products needed for sustainability for the first set of stores. Stores that dropped out did so due to contextual challenges or inability to keep up with project demands. At a broader level, however, reliable produce stocking is stymied by lack of economies of scale in supply and distribution, perishability of the product, lack of adequate refrigeration/management capacity in stores, and, of course, anemic sales. Corner stores are unwilling or unable to provide the subsidy for produce that larger supermarkets do. We noted a small increase in SNAP spending on fresh produce following outreach events, but it was too little and rarely consistent.[3]

As a first study of its kind that investigated corner stores in the context of their relationships with neighborhoods and possible supply chain networks, the study delivered other outcomes, including awareness, knowledge, and relationships on a range of issues within neighborhoods that hosted participating stores, local food security and community development groups, and the food planning and academic world. Given the instability experienced by many stores and their neighborhoods during the study, however, it is unclear to what extent these lessons and relationships have endured.

Examination of the Planning Episode Using Framework Elements

This section organizes reflection in three elements: (i) planner-as-person, (ii) interpretation of context, and (iii) reasoning and methods in the planning episode.

Planner-as-Person Elements That Shaped the Approach

I have worked in Detroit since taking up my university position in 1998. With degrees in architecture and urban planning, I am interested in design thinking in general – physical, program, and institutional – with emphasis on

collaborative and participatory methods. By design thinking, I mean the application of creativity – what Innes and Booher (2010) might term *bricolage* – to
realizing a community's solutions to needs and wants with available technologies and resources, in particular contexts. When I arrived in the United States
as a student, from India, I was struck immediately by inequities in American
cities related to transportation and housing; planning coursework educated me
about broader social and structural inequalities. I became involved in community food systems planning in 1996 following an invitation by the late
Professor Jerry Kaufman to co-teach the capstone planning seminar in winter
1997 at the University of Wisconsin–Madison, where I taught for a couple of
years as a visiting assistant professor. I have continued this work for more than
two decades in Detroit.

Personal Framework Elements

I approach planning by facilitating bottom-up solutions and try to ensure that
the voices of those who are served or impacted are included. My involvement tends to be hands-on, up close, and experimental, with a stance that
is constantly reviewing relationships and processes toward goals. My theory
of change was that the program's actions would result in a new or enhanced
flow of products from wholesaler to store to customer, and of information
and money in the other direction in ways that would become self-sustaining
over multiple iterations. Thus, my hope was that the project would become
redundant.

Although not a member of the American Institute of Certified Planners
(AICP), I am inspired by the exhortation by the AICP Code of Ethics to
expand choice and opportunity with special attention to the needs of the disadvantaged. As an outsider to the aforementioned communities many times
over, I frequently confront questions of identity, communication, legitimacy,
belonging, and security in my community engagement.

For example, my interactions while recruiting store operators were sometimes colored by our shared immigrant status. One operator, upon learning of
my Asian Indian background, wanted to talk about Bollywood movies familiar
from his youth! Another readily shared his prejudice of African Americans as
a way to elicit solidarity from a fellow immigrant ("We come here and work
hard and succeed; why can't they work hard too?"). While neither of these
operators signed up to participate in the project, such interactions required balancing polite and open communications to advance project goals with setting
boundaries and refusing to reciprocate expressions of prejudice. I was more

open to sharing about myself and my background with a Chaldean storeowner couple and others who participated in the project whose interactions with community members I witnessed to be more respectful and warmer.

My role in this project drew on prior relationships within the community; the grant's budget supported partners' involvement. Although the project emerged out of conversations with residents on the Eastside, and proceeded to engage other stakeholders and students, I was familiar with related projects that were being developed in other cities (notably Oakland, California, Philadelphia, Pennsylvania; Baltimore, Maryland). My participation in the national Community Food Security Coalition's board also put me in national networks with leaders of these initiatives. Thus, I was able to draw from and share these efforts as much as possible in our deliberations.

Personal Ambiguity and Incongruity

As a faculty member with extensive volunteering in the community, participating in collaborations to identify and resolve food access problems presented little ambiguity or incongruity for me, personally. However, as described next, the specifics of the project did involve certain ambiguities and incongruities.

Corner stores typically have a bad reputation in the community and among advocates as constituting an extractive economy, as purveyors of addictions, and managed by outsiders to the neighborhoods in which they operate. Their physical environments reinforce these negative images with garish signage outside advertising liquor and lottery, the organization of merchandise inside, and the bulletproof barrier between staff and shoppers. There is also anecdotal evidence of tensions between stores and neighborhoods (Sengstock n.d., Meredith 1999). Thus, framing corner stores as potential solutions to food access problems was not without internal ambiguity – that is, within the project team – and external incongruity, especially in communications with some neighborhood leaders who are familiar with particular stores and their histories.

My conviction was – and continues to be – that neighborhoods ought to support daily lives in the businesses and services that exist there, and conversations about healthy corner stores in national food security networks helped me resolve any personal ambiguity (and ambivalence). The interest expressed by store operators who came on board early in the life of the project was also helpful, even though I was under little illusion that the project would alter their business model or main inventory. As it turned out, conversations with residents suggested that they, for the most part, understood and supported our efforts more than did neighborhood leaders.

The incongruity of fresh fruit and vegetables pushing against chips and candy was inescapable. We organized our first Healthy Food Fair in the vacant lot next door to a corner store whose operators were especially enthusiastic participants. As we set up the food image cutouts and other props for the motivational conversations (Miller and Rose 2009) and cooking demos, the store owner came out with bags of candy, cookies, and chips to distribute to fair participants. It was an enthusiastic gesture of goodwill born out of years of support for social events in the neighborhood. I countered the offer with as much diplomacy I could muster by explaining the purpose and objectives of the *Healthy* Food Fairs. We proposed and accepted with profuse gratitude replacement bags of zucchini and onions which could be incorporated in the quesadillas that were being made in the food demonstrations, and which we presented to the store owners to taste afterward. Thus, even with enthusiastic participants who were persuaded by our arguments and approach, we faced an uphill battle related to healthy food access given the habits, expectations, and messages in the broader social context.

Interpretation of Context

I envisioned a system for produce distribution that mimicked the one that currently exists for soda, beer, and potato chips, with suppliers delivering and replenishing inventory on a regular basis. Developing an efficient logistics of produce distribution, however, was challenged by the geographic distance between participating stores and by a distribution system that was patched together with existing resources and tailored to store preferences. Thus, the rare cases when store and community cooperation fell into place quickly and supply chains smoothly seamlessly coordinated with social marketing campaigns marked points of celebration among partners.

Context Framework Elements

The pilot phase of the project suggested an approach that involved three major elements: (i) work with and in the store (assessing space, infrastructure, and operations; setting up the store with basic supplies; offering technical support in merchandising and social marketing; etc.); (ii) linking the store with a distributor; and (iii) canvassing in the surrounding neighborhood, distributing flyers, and, whenever possible, conversations with residents. Much of the work with stores that came on board following this phase involved discovering additional contextual elements and responding to them.

For example, despite several sequential two-way communications between project staff, store operator and the distributor, one store delayed placing an order for several weeks. This store was close to the route undertaken by the mobile market (and store) run by a neighborhood nonprofit called Peaches and Greens. I requested that the mobile market stop at the store to help matters along. The store agreed to purchase from them after negotiating price and quantity of a specific inventory. Peaches and Greens's willingness to charge wholesale prices for smaller quantities led us to add the mobile market to our distributor options for stores. While this addition increased choice for some stores, it also complicated project operations when a store dropped a wholesale distributor who had previously supplied the store. Thus, a basic approach to program implementation developed from the experience in Phase I became a more or less tailored approach with stores as particular constraints and resources were identified.

Achieving a consistent high-level of participation by store owners was a challenge due to their constrained schedules – most are family operations in which members spend long hours at the cash register – and the difficulties associated with stocking and managing fresh produce at a small scale relative to total sales. I also encountered skepticism from some leaders of community-based organizations, such as churches and neighborhood groups, who did not trust corner stores to serve the community's interests. Partly, this attitude was a product of the stores' main inventory of liquor and cigarettes, but also because of the racial and ethnic separation of residents and store owners.

There exists examples of successful implementation of corner store programs in other cities. Their contexts, however, differ from project neighborhoods in Detroit, and they also tend to be larger in their scope of interventions and the amount of subsidy. While we were generally aware of the recession's impacts on Detroit's neighborhoods, we did not appreciate the extent to which stores were impacted in the worst off areas until after the project unfolded.

Finally, an important element of context was understanding the dominant response from corner store operators – both those who participated in the project as well as those merely responding to assessments – is that residents simply will not buy produce. This claim is accurate as far as it goes, especially as it relates to corner stores. However, neither diets nor corner store purchasing decisions are shaped in a vacuum. They are a product of many forces, of which availability and affordability are just two. Small-scale projects such as the one described here are scarcely adequate to transform practices of businesses that are themselves marginal in the retail ecosystem and to affect change in neighborhoods that cope with many disadvantages layered over several decades.

As mentioned, the Eastern Market had been involved in food programs before this one. Box 11.1 provides the broad context for the case in an account from Dan Carmody.

Box 11.1 Context for Supply- and Demand-Side Healthy Food Strategies
Dan Carmody, Eastern Market

Over the last decade and a half, Eastern Market has collaborated with Detroit organizations to increase the consumption of healthy diets with plenty of fruits and vegetables. In 2006, Eastern Market developed the Farm Stand Program to bring fresh produce to neighborhoods with limited access to supermarkets. The Farm Stand set up seasonal pop-ups to make Michigan-grown crops available to nearby residents. In addition, we worked with many partners to create a network of neighborhood-scaled farmer's markets called Detroit Community Markets, which set up seasonally at 14–16 sites throughout Detroit. Such markets typically feature Detroit-based farms and businesses that sell prepared foods.

We also offer incentives to low- and moderate-income households to support purchases of nutritious food. In 2009, a project called Mo-Bucks – later renamed the Double Up Food Bucks – was first piloted at Eastern Market and two community markets, including the Wayne State Farmers Market. Sponsored by the Fair Food Network, Mo-Bucks matched SNAP spending up to $20 per household on Michigan-grown fresh produce. Another innovation, Fresh Prescriptions, provides financial support to "fill" food prescriptions doctors issue to support produce purchases at participating markets. Lastly, we have increased the number and type of food education offerings to help households gain knowledge and confidence to prepare healthier meals, including cooking with unfamiliar crops.

Despite much progress made by Eastern Market over the last 15 years, we have a long way to go in increasing affordable access to fresh and healthy food in Detroit. For one, changing eating habits is difficult – only three out of ten Americans' diets meet the U.S. Department of Agriculture's Healthy Eating Index criteria – and for another, decades of disinvestment have hollowed out many of the city's neighborhoods and left them bereft of healthy food outlets. To be successful in low-density, urban environments is as much about addressing weak demand as it is about increasing weak supply.

During a recent sabbatical, I observed programs in Belo Horizonte, Brazil – the city that adopted the policy that access to good food is a basic human right – that combined a cultural preference for meals with fresh fruits and vegetables with increased supply by creating a modest subsidy to sustain access to affordable healthy food. The city purchased nearly 30 small grocery spaces and conducts auctions every five years to award leases to operators for those stores. Winning bidders must sell a core group of 11 different fruits and vegetables at prices

Box 11.1 (continued)

determined by the municipal authority, while selling the rest of their inventory at market rates.

The system, over 30 years, has remained robust. Single-store sales are high and prices for commonly consumed vegetables remain low, providing a healthy food incentive at a relatively low cost to the local government. High densities and local diets high in fruits and veggies are underlying conditions that enable this program to flourish.

Thus, while local efforts to increase the supply of fresh and healthy food in Detroit's neighborhoods are promising, they need to be accompanied by a range of initiatives that support the uptake of these foods. These initiatives include encouraging the consumption of healthy food, reducing poverty, repopulating the city's neighborhoods, and improving overall neighborhood quality of life.

Context Uncertainty and Ambiguity

An ambiguity emerged related to the following substantive issue: fresh produce tends to be a smaller portion of grocery spending by low-income households due to its higher costs per calorie (Drewnowski 2004). Thus, even as we were attempting to increase stores' inventory of fresh produce, it was clear that buying produce here in large quantities made little economic sense from a shopper's perspective given the lower volumes, fewer varieties, and higher costs of products. We reviewed the objectives of the project, first by asking what produce items might be most likely to be purchased, and then if corner stores were even a reasonable target for increasing the consumption of fruits and vegetables in several neighborhoods. The last question was especially pertinent in the context of the recession, when stores were experiencing declining sales.

Surveys of Healthy Food Fair participants confirmed that residents did the bulk of their "stock up" grocery shopping in more distant supermarkets. Addressing this ambiguity led to a shift in our social marketing campaign – to get corner store customers to redirect a portion of their SNAP spending in stores to healthier, fresh snacks such as fruits. Customers spent SNAP funds within these stores, mostly on processed snacks and occasional staples such as bread, milk, and potatoes.

Given the high cost per calorie of fresh produce, prices need to be lower than corner stores are able to sustain without a high level of outside subsidy, which the project could not provide. Thus, it is unrealistic to expect neighborhood stores to consistently deliver fresh produce in sufficient variety and affordability. While the increased availability of SNAP incentive programs – such as the Double Up Food Bucks in Michigan – is encouraging, few prospects exist for widespread and year-round availability of fresh produce at highly subsidized rates in many Detroit neighborhoods.

The project's communications helped build a degree of understanding across divides between the store and neighborhood residents. However, even as participating store owners bought into the overall goals of the project, several chafed at the periodic check-ins and record-keeping, and the seeming trespass these activities made into their business domains. Debriefing meetings with students following community canvassing raised other incongruities as they recounted the harsh realities of the recession in 2008–2013. These meetings sometimes raised broader questions related to the meaning and impact of our work with corner stores in some neighborhoods. Were we playing violins on a sinking Titanic?

The Planning Episode: Reasoning and Methods

This project began with conversations about the problems residents faced with access to fresh produce and a participatory assessment of stores in an underserved neighborhood. Even with the Detroit FRESH grant, it was an extremely low-budget initiative. Thus, it was important that solutions be designed to use resources that already existed nearby and be developed to the extent possible to be self-sustaining as business relationships.

I facilitated the community processes, including dialogues at CSK, and led the development of the assessment and its analysis. If an assessment-recruitment encounter elicited a positive response from the operator, I met with them and developed related agreements. I also engaged stakeholders such as wholesalers and leaders of community development organizations and churches; oversaw the development of communication materials in training and social marketing; oversaw check-ins and evaluations, including troubleshooting; supervised students and project staff and volunteers; and liaised with university structures for project implementation. Some stakeholders came in or exited at different stages of the project; I developed the logistics of the participation of each group.

Logic

Given SEED Wayne's proposed goals of increasing access to fresh and healthy food in Detroit, learning more about residents' lived experiences with and needs for the food environments in their neighborhoods was a logical first step as the program got off the ground. Logic played a role in my assessment of corner stores as a potential solution for Detroit neighborhoods' problems from two other perspectives, one top-down and the other, bottom-up. First, owners of corner stores know how to make money in the poorest neighborhoods, tend to persist in the face of economic downturns, and a few already carry elements of the requisite inventory. Second, the community conversations in Phase I invoked a more positive historic image of corner stores as run by and for community members. Absent a large body of experience when I first conducted a food assessment in Detroit (1998–1999), I was attracted to corner stores as a potential source of healthy foods. By 2008, when the project started, more literature existed about urban food access issues and some experiences.

The project's substantive questions were guided by my knowledge of the city's historical context of retail grocery and the literature on social determinants of health. The literature argues that many factors, including economic and environmental ones, influence diets (Morland et al. 2002, Drewnowski 2004, Gallagher 2007). If unhealthy diets are the result of coping strategies due to lack of availability/access, then a first step to changing diets should be to increase availability/access in neighborhoods that are underserved by supermarkets and other outlets for fresh, healthy foods. Implicit in the understanding of these relationships was also a social justice argument – residents in transportation-challenged neighborhoods especially should have a density of basic needs fulfilled nearby.

As mentioned, diets with minimally processed foods and fresh fruits and vegetables are more expensive. From a supply perspective, although fresh produce is a loss leader in retail grocery, supermarkets pile fresh fruits and vegetables in attractive assemblies close to entryways to draw customers in who then can be persuaded to buy high-margin items. Fresh produce is a particularly challenging category; a store that succeeds in managing fresh produce can easily offer other categories of healthy foods. Rather than track shoppers' diets or even purchases, I decided to track the stores' produce inventories with the assumption that stores would stop carrying particular varieties that did not sell.

Emotion

Corner stores evoke strong emotions in Detroit's neighborhoods for a variety of reasons: as perceived economic predators and ethnic outsiders who project fear of the community in the bulletproof glass behind which operators conduct business. Although these themes tend to dominate community conversations, I am also aware of the structural context in which immigrants and ethnic minorities come to populate particular business niches (Koreans in retail grocery in Los Angeles, for example, or South Asians in the motel industry). Even though I am critical of businesses that operate in neighborhoods with few healthy options whose revenues rely predominantly on sales of tobacco and alcohol, I am also sympathetic to immigrants' strategies to cope with racism and exclusion and their efforts to succeed in their adopted country.

I used the positive emotional language of moral economy in my interactions with store owners – that is, concepts of interdependence, empathy, and reciprocity. I was also careful not to threaten to report noncompliant WIC-authorized stores. With neighborhood leaders, I asked for assistance to make stores more accountable to the community and for greater store–neighborhood dialogue to make relationships more sustainable following the project's completion.

As the project unfolded, team members – myself included – expressed many emotions in meetings: disheartenment at ongoing neighborhood abandonment; disgust with the business model of most corner stores; and frustration with the challenges with getting the parts of our store–wholesaler–community "system" to work smoothly. The project had many moving parts, and they worked optimally for only a handful of stores. We also experienced positive emotions when store operators broke stereotypical expectations, when community partners went above and beyond in mobilizing participation in Healthy Food Fairs, and as unexpected opportunities emerged, such as when a community arts group painted a mural on the wall of a participating "good neighbor" store. These positive experiences provided vindication for the project and its aims, momentum to our activities, and shaped what later became "model" practices.

Convention

I drew examples from history, my urban food advocacy networks, my knowledge of corner stores' business practices in Detroit, and the then-scarce national literature on corner stores. As previously mentioned, historical models exist – generally and specifically for Detroit – of greater availability of fresh produce within urban neighborhoods. These have taken the form of peddlers selling produce out of trucks, mom-and-pop stores run by residents in neighborhoods, and farmers markets (such as the Russell Street market) nearby. Conversations with neighbors uncovered these models and posed the implicit question: Can something similar be created once again to benefit the community? I was also part of national conversations about the possibility of targeting corner stores as a resource for healthy food access within underserved urban neighborhoods. Finally, budget and other resource constraints also shaped the particulars of the project as did nearby assets in the form of wholesale distributors in Eastern Market and community organizations in project neighborhoods.

Invention

Project elements were constructed in dialogue with residents of the CSK neighborhood and with stakeholders whose involvement was necessary for the project. It took several trial-and-error attempts to link existing resources to needs and add new resources – such as the Peaches and Greens mobile market – to the mix as they became applicable. As project initiator, I had free rein to propose steps but typically proceeded to implement them only after checking with at least one or two key partners who were most knowledgeable about or closely connected with that step.

For example, proposed project interactions with produce wholesalers involved the Eastern Market Corporation, which anchors the district and hosts a variety of markets. Introductions to wholesale operators by Eastern Market's Dan Carmody (see Box 11.1) helped build new relationships and incorporate them into the project. Nuanced information about context also resulted in the development of new strategies. For example, community canvassing to advertise the availability of fresh produce in one neighborhood led to the discovery that some residents had never patronized the store believing that it had few healthy options. Thus, we realized that we needed to do more to "reintroduce" the stores to their neighborhoods, beyond canvassing and distributing flyers. In discussing this finding with a couple of store owners and neighborhood leaders, the idea of the Healthy Food Fair was born, which demonstrated affordable, conveniently assembled recipes using ingredients available in the nearby participating store. The fairs also offered important opportunities for interactive dialogues with residents on healthy diets and surveys on related grocery shopping. Healthy Food Fairs also invariably involved outreach to and partnerships with nearby community organizations, including churches. Proceeding in this manner, learning and responding, meant that invention was a continual element of the process.

Discoveries

Reflection on the case resulted in two types of commentaries: (i) making explicit the practical judgments during the planning episode, and (ii) identifying takeaways from the case that have broader application.

Practical Judgments

Three practical judgments shaped the process: (i) navigating the planning episode step by step rather than seeking to implement a defined work plan, (ii) choosing to address a part of the overall problem in focused and limited ways, and (iii) extending the familiar to develop innovations.

Practical Judgment 1: Navigating the Planning Episode Step by Step Rather Than Seeking to Implement a Predefined Work Plan

We did not have a roadmap for our goals – each step was informed by the previous one, in conversation with stakeholders and by our knowledge of and discoveries about context. Even the strategy of first assessing corner stores for their inventory and possibly recruiting them to offer more fresh produce emerged from an initial set of conversations with Eastside residents. Later, following the pilot phase, operational approaches were tweaked based on responses of shoppers in surveys and of store owners in monthly check-in visits.

For example, our approach to tracking produce sales – after setting a store up with equipment, wholesale–supplier connection, merchandising/handling tips, and neighborhood canvassing – was adjusted several times. We started out with a sample survey of shoppers exiting the store but found that they exaggerated or falsely claimed produce purchases. Neither were store receipts a reliable source of information, as many stores' cash machines did not specify produce among grocery items. We ultimately settled upon produce orders as obtained from the wholesale distributor (or the store itself) minus the amount of product that was discarded, along with price-per-unit for each produce item. Many stores failed to track waste on a consistent basis; in some cases, the instructions proved to be too burdensome. Many simply could not be bothered with the data-gathering efforts given the relatively low value of produce to their sales. In the end, produce orders turned out to be a key proxy for the store's volume of business in produce. We reasoned that if a store had a lot of waste in a particular category, it would modify its orders accordingly – an assumption that was borne out in practice.

Similarly, stores varied in their motivations for participating in the program. Some were sincerely interested in serving their customers better; others desired the positive publicity from the association with the university; yet others were concerned about being "reported" to the state for their only partial compliance with WIC produce requirements. Knowing this helped us to hone our technical assistance as well as messaging, stressing one or another aspect of the service we would provide to the store. Thus, in our attempts to secure store cooperation, we tailored aspects of the project to the specific contexts of store and neighborhood conditions. Had we adopted a single approach across all stores, fewer stores would have participated as consistently as they did.

Practical Judgment 2: Choosing to Address a Part of the Overall Problem in Focused and Limited Ways

The conversations that led to the projects themselves were proposed in the grant for, and part of, the larger project, SEED Wayne. In SEED Wayne, I envisioned addressing issues of sustainable food systems through several discrete activities, each incorporating the defining values of sustainable food to a greater or lesser extent depending on the activity, its setting, constituencies affected or targeted, other factors, and what and how much program staff – myself and student leaders – could influence.

For example, the campus garden incorporated all of SEED Wayne's values/goals: increasing access to fresh and healthy food; strengthening linkages between local producers and consumers; supporting sustainable agriculture; and augmenting community capacity related to food systems including growing and preparing healthy food and related policy awareness. On the other hand, the campus farmers market focused on increasing access to fresh and healthy food, and linkages with local producers with consumers. A demand for organically grown produce was less important with this activity. With "policy-making at the CSK table" as the Detroit FRESH project started out, the initial aim was simply to learn about residents' experiences with access to healthy food in neighborhoods, with the goal of building local policy and planning capacity.

The corner store project was born as CSK conversations highlighted the need to assess nearby corner stores, and assessments identified a handful of interested stores. This path-dependence from and relationship to SEED Wayne's goals led to this interest in corner stores as a possible solution for healthy food access within underserved neighborhoods.

The concept represented continuity as well as innovation. Continuity took the form of preexisting relationships with Eastern, the CSK's Earthworks Urban Farm, and other Eastside organizations. The innovations are the activities and relationships that followed the CSK conversations. To avoid overextending the program's resources, we focused initially on corner store capacity, with attempts to build a distribution network and incorporating the Healthy Food Fairs coming later as new resources were mobilized. Conceived of as a programmatic response to develop food infrastructure rather than a research project, Detroit FRESH could not feasibly also delve into residents' purchase of products or their consumption. Thus, at every stage, we chose to address emerging issues in focused and limited ways rather than more expansive or comprehensive ones so as to stay within the bounds of our resources and knowledge.

Practical Judgment 3: Extending the Familiar to Develop Innovations

Attempting to support corner stores' sales of fresh produce involved activities that were entirely novel for me, constituting new relationships with store operators, produce wholesalers, and neighborhood organizations; and new understandings of neighborhood social and business contexts. At the same time, I never ventured into deeply unfamiliar territory in any single activity. As previously discussed, the project took off by initiating a new set of activities albeit with already networked actors.

Similarly, with positive feedback from the Healthy Food Fairs, a strategy idea took off to connect to neighborhoods *without* participating stores. These "new" neighborhoods contained a neighborhood organization familiar to me or a leader who was part of a citywide network related to urban agriculture, food policy, or another planning issue. At this time, SEED Wayne was also attracting students with interests in volunteering in the community. Thus, we started to offer Healthy Food Fairs in more neighborhoods, and it became yet another discrete project of SEED Wayne, for which I was able to raise funds separately the following year.

At the same time, as word spread about our activities in the community, the project also attracted new resources, which expanded participating stores' neighborhood visibility. For example, when I was contacted by an arts organization about ideas for developing murals by working with neighborhood youth, I immediately directed them to an Eastside store whose operators were respected by neighborhood residents. Thus, even though the mural project was a leap to an entirely new concept, its constituent parts were familiar to me or existed within extended networks.

Takeaways for Practice

Key takeaways from this planning episode, for me, are that planners should decipher context, develop deliberative group processes, and incorporate reflective processes in the midst of planning episodes. In initiating this project, I did not expect to resolve the larger problems of neighborhood disinvestment and abandonment, and retail grocery concentration. The project's experiences nevertheless offered a collective learning experience on an aspect of neighborhood economy in Detroit that previously was shrouded in a less than wholesome reputation. The project discovered corner store operators who cared about their community while also confirming the many challenges to healthy diets in impoverished neighborhoods. It also brought together members of the business community (corner store operators and wholesalers), neighborhood residents and leaders, and students and myself in novel networks, and successfully changed the practices of a few stores, some in enduring ways.

Planning Takeaway 1: Decipher Context and Develop Responsive Planning Processes

Toggling between local conversations and broader literature, I educated myself about Detroit's history of neighborhood abandonment and disinvestment, local supermarket closures, and changes in the broader food retail industry. Relevant facets of these contexts were reinforced and illustrated in dialogues with community residents, who also contributed experiences of shopping at mom-and-pop stores of their youth and, in more recent times, at corner stores run by members of outsider groups. The history of neighborhoods' isolation in the city's redevelopment efforts and of planning leadership offered by community organizations were additional contextual elements – constituting convention – as were the regulatory frameworks, which both enabled business operation and constrained operators.

These contextual investigations also surfaced the assets and resources that were available or potentially available to resolve the identified problems. While leadership by staff of community organizations and residents is not extraordinary in Detroit's neighborhoods, seeing corner stores and produce wholesalers as assets and, more important, as solutions was an invention in this project. Planners should weave together convention and invention in context-responsive processes.

Planning Takeaway 2: Develop Deliberative Group Processes

The rich, experientially based knowledge of guests and staff of CSK, together with their participatory assessment of neighborhood corner stores alongside students, set the stage for formative dialogues on dimensions of food access and incorporated individuals whose paths otherwise would seldom, if ever, cross. Representatives of corner stores and wholesale businesses could rarely join these meetings with residents and community leaders. Thus, the particular constraints of each stakeholder group required interactions governed by their turf, attention, and time. Regardless of location, the sharing of personal stories, literature reviews, research design and implementation, research presentations, what-if speculations, and what-now questions cumulatively offered opportunities for collective knowledge and analysis, judgment, and creative visions and strategies. They were also opportunities for each party to better understand and grapple with others' needs, motivations, professional and business interests, hopes, and possibilities for extra effort, and to build trust and human connection. These deliberative processes lie at the heart of innovative planning.

Planning Takeaway 3: Incorporate Reflective Practice in the Midst of Planning Efforts

It was only as implementation began that some aspects of context that the project sought to influence – store operation and resident purchases – became clear. For example, seeing WIC program signage on a store led me to delve into official WIC basket requirements, especially as they related to fresh produce. WIC stores were required to carry at least two types each of fresh fruit and vegetables, not including potatoes. Thus simply posing a question about fresh produce in a WIC store, where produce was nowhere to be seen, by someone who did not appear to be from the neighborhood, had a loaded quality without my ever mentioning the official requirement. We used this finding of a gap between the WIC rules and their compliance to coax a handful of owners to participate in the program, all the while asserting our university identity and roles. Some ambiguities and uncertainties dissolved while others appeared or intensified. Therefore, we could not keep repeating previous actions; the realities that were being uncovered needed reflection, tweaking of strategy, and at a couple key points, reassessment of the strategy altogether. Thus, entirely new directions such as the Healthy Food Fairs emerged. This lesson shows the importance of feedback and learning during the planning process.

And Now to You: Planning as Program Development and Implementation

Planning's core rationale is to ameliorate the effects of and to prevent market failure and to promote equity. Furthermore, planners agree that the profession exists, among others, to meet the basic needs of communities and to attend to the interconnections between systems (ACSP 1997). This case shows the value of program development in achieving such direct and indirect outcomes.

Stepping back, this experience poses questions for planners who work in disadvantaged communities: What is planning's role in environments marked by poverty and deprivation, where the market structure to meet basic needs for health is thin? What tools can planners wield to support, incentivize, or subsidize desired private or community sector actions? Can planners use regulatory frameworks to shape, guide, and prod businesses into serving low-income communities without the need for subsidy? For example, Belo Horizonte, Brazil, licenses produce kiosks to locate in better-off neighborhoods on condition that they also operate in poorer neighborhoods (Rocha 2001). Better-off communities usually negotiate with developers to contribute a pocket park or plaza during the application approval process. Might regulators similarly leverage permits to sell liquor, tobacco, food, and lottery in urban neighborhoods? Alternatively, city planners might direct public investments in neighborhood or business improvement to "good neighbor" stores and their neighborhoods.

Planners see their roles as offering a framework for private sector investment and decision-making; seldom do they concern themselves with whether the results work for communities that are less mobile, why, and what to do about it. If that is your mission, how will you rate proposals for neighborhood-based businesses, implement social and health impact analyses, and enforce performance standards related to healthy food access? How will you design them in communities with lower capacity to attract investments to distressed neighborhoods where businesses also face specific challenges? How can you build on efforts that already exist to meet needs in such neighborhoods to offer a starting point or inspiration for planning approaches? These are the questions I ponder in my practice; I invite you to join me in this hopeful endeavor.

Discussion Questions

1. Community economic development policy-makers often debate whether place-based or people-based approaches are more appropriate to meet the varied needs of impoverished households. What are your thoughts about either approach to meet the need for healthy food? Are there other approaches?
2. What role(s) should the city planning agency play in neighborhoods marked by widespread, chronic poverty and decline? What are the strengths and limitations of the roles?

3. Urban redevelopment often includes public–private partnerships and deal-making with corporations, developers, and other large-scale private-sector entities. What roles might the business sector play, beyond particular projects or deals? How might planners engage with businesses to benefit urban neighborhoods experiencing decline?
4. Urban communities of color are particularly vulnerable to food insecurity. Discuss. What are some impacts of food insecurity? What solutions exist in your community to resolve the problem?

Notes

1 Formerly called the Food Stamp Program, SNAP, or Supplemental Nutrition Assistance Program, is a means-tested federal cash assistance to households with incomes at or below 130% of poverty to support grocery purchases. WIC, the Women, Infants, and Children Special Supplemental Nutrition Program, supports the purchase of a basket of food and other needs of pregnant and breastfeeding moms and children 5 years and younger.
2 The program's development and implementation also coincided with the Great Recession of 2008–2009 and the foreclosure crisis, which hit Detroit especially hard. In 2013, the city declared bankruptcy. A few years prior, the city's public health agency also underwent significant transformation, plagued as it was by scandal following a federal investigation of fiscal mismanagement. This resulted in closure of the department, with key services subcontracted to a private nonprofit called Institute for Population Health. Early in the life of SEED Wayne, I met with Deputy Public Health Director Bill Ridella to apprise him of projects and seek his support, but the chaos associated with the agency's transition during the spinoff stymied follow-up or an ongoing relationship with the health agency.
3 www.clas.wayne.edu/detroitfresh/. Several SEEDLING newsletter issues also offer real-time updates on the project.

References

ACSP (Association of Collegiate Schools of Planning), Strategic Marketing Committee. 1997. "Anchor Points for Planning's Identification." *Journal of Planning Education and Research*, 16: 223–225. doi: 10.1177%2F0739456X9701600306.
Bobo, Kimberley, Steve Max, Jackie Kendall, and Midwest Academy. 2001. *Organizing for Social Change: A Manual for Activists*. Newport Beach, CA: Seven Locks Press.
Bradbury-Huang, Hilary. 2010. "What Is Good Action Research? Why the Resurgent Interest?" *Action Research*, 8(1): 93–109. doi: 10.1177%2F1476750310362435.
Checkoway, B. 1995. "Six Strategies of Community Change." *Community Development Journal*, 30(1): 2–20.
DEGC (Detroit Economic Growth Corporation). 2008. *Detroit Fresh Food Access Initiative: Report of Task Force Findings*. Detroit: DEGC.

Drewnowski, Adam. 2004. "Obesity and the Food Environment: Dietary Energy Density and Diet Costs." *American Journal of Preventive Medicine*, 27(3) Supplement: 154–162. doi: 10.1016/j.amepre.2004.06.011.

Forester, John. 1999. *The Deliberative Practitioner: Encouraging Participatory Planning Processes.* Cambridge, MA: MIT Press.

Fung, Archon. 2003. "Associations and Democracy: Between Theories, Hopes, and Realities." *Annual Review of Sociology*, 29(1): 515–539. doi: 10.1146/annurev.soc.29 .010202.100134.

Gallagher, Mari. 2007. *Examining the Impact of Food Deserts on Public Health in Detroit.* Chicago, IL: Mari Gallagher Research & Consulting Group. Accessed March 11, 2020 at http://www.uconnruddcenter.org/resources/upload/docs/what/policy/ DetroitFoodDesertReport.pdf.

Gergen, Kenneth J. 2003. "Action Research and Orders of Democracy." *Action Research*, 1(1): 39–56. doi: 10.1177%2F14767503030011004.

Innes, Judith E. 1996. "Group Processes and the Social Construction of Growth Management." In: *Explorations in Planning Theory*, edited by Seymour J. Mandelbaum, Luigi Mazza, and Robert W. Burchell. New Brunswick: Rutgers University Center for Urban Policy Research, 164-187.

Innes, Judith E., and David E. Booher. 2010. *Planning with Complexity* (Chapter 5). New York: Routledge.

Kretzmann John, P., and John L. McKnight. 1993. *Building Communities From the Inside Out: A Path Toward Finding and Mobilizing a Community's Assets.* Evanston, IL: Institute for Policy Research, Northwestern University.

Meredith, Robyn. 1999. "Black Man's Death Raises Racial Tensions." *New York Times*, May 19. Retrieved January 11, 2020 from www.nytimes.com/1999/05/19/ us/black-man-s-death-raises-racial-tensions-in-detroit.html.

Mies, Maria. 1983. "Towards a Methodology for Feminist Research." In: *Theories of Women's Studies*, edited by Gloria Bowles, and Renate Duelli Klein, 117–139. London: Routledge and Kegan Paul.

Miller, William R., and Gary S. Rose. 2009. "Toward a Theory of Motivational Interviewing." *The American Psychologist*, 64(6): 527–537. doi: 10.1037/a0016830.

Morland, Kimberly, Steve Wing, Ana Diez Roux, and Charles Poole. 2002. "Neighborhood Characteristics Associated with the Location of Food Stores and Food Service Places." *American Journal of Preventive Medicine*, 22(1): 23–29. doi: 10.1016/s0749-3797(01)00403-2.

Pothukuchi, K. 2005. Attracting Supermarkets to Inner-City Neighborhoods: Economic Development Outside the Box. *Economic Development Quarterly*, 19(3): 232–244. doi.org/10.1177/0891242404273517.

Pothukuchi, K. 2015. Five Decades of Community Food Planning in Detroit: City and Grassroots, Growth and Equity. *Journal of Planning Education and Research*, 35(4): 419–434. doi.org/10.1177/0739456X15586630.

Pothukuchi, K. 2016. Bringing Fresh Produce to Corner Stores in Declining Neighborhoods: Lessons from Detroit FRESH. *Journal of Agriculture, Food Systems, and Community Development*, 7(1): 113–134. doi: 10.5304/jafscd.2016.071.013.

Reason, Peter, and Hilary Bradbury-Huang, eds. 2001. *Handbook of Action Research: Participative Inquiry and Practice.* London: Sage.

Rocha, Cecilia. 2001. "Urban Food Security Policy: The Case of Belo Horizonte, Brazil." *Journal for the Study of Food and Society*, 5(1): 36–47. doi: 10.2752/152897901786732735.

Schön, Donald A. 1983. *The Reflective Practitioner: How Professionals Think in Action*. New York: Routledge.

Sengstock, M.C. n.d. *Chaldean Americans*. Retrieved January 11, 2020 from http://www.everyculture.com/multi/Bu-Dr/Chaldean-Americans.html.

U.S. Census Bureau. 2010. 2006-2010 5-Year Estimates. Derived from American Factfinder. Retrieved from https://factfinder.census.gov.

Chapter 12

Green Line Mixed-Use Project Specific Plan in Hawthorne, California

The Green Line Mixed-Use Project Specific Plan case study addresses a controversial 230-unit mixed-use housing development (Project) proposal in Hawthorne, California. The Project was approved through the adoption of a specific plan and supporting policy and environmental documents. This case examines my role in preparing a technical report on parking demand for the developer and provides my interpretation of the review and approval process. I made three practical judgments in conducting the planning assignment: (i) accepting a limited, downstream role, (ii) developing a politically honed analysis rather the ideal solution, and (iii) agreeing to limit the scope of work to parking issues. These are issues that planners in technical consulting roles commonly face.

Local comprehensive plans provide policy guidance for development, but the rules for individual sites are established through zoning and other regulations. The broad nature of comprehensive plans cannot anticipate unique site situations and opportunities. Hence, there are procedures for making changes to plans and zoning based on analysis of a particular site or sites. In most planning departments, staff time devoted to considering adjustments to zoning exceeds that spent on comprehensive planning. These changes are a form of incremental planning as they make land use determinations one at a time.

The Project is a transit-oriented development (TOD) proposed by Blackwood Real Estate (Developer), located within one-half mile of a light rail transit station that is part of Los Angeles County's rail system. TOD is popular because it uses land efficiently, increases housing supply, and generally leads to greater use of transit and active travel modes. Box 12.1 (next page) provides background on the concept. The site provided both rail transit access and workplace opportunities within walking distance; accordingly, the Project was expected to attract residents with lower vehicle ownership than traditional apartments. The approval decision involved changing the land use designation, increasing permitted development intensity, and creating site-specific development regulations on a single parcel of land on Crenshaw Boulevard.

Description of the Planning Episode

While the Project's planning process took multiple years, my involvement was for a six-month period starting June 2017. I was hired by the Developer to provide advice on parking supply and management, write a technical report on the proposed parking supply, and appear at Planning Commission and City Council meetings.

A 274-unit complex was proposed and evaluated, but the City Council approved the Project at a lower density of 230-units. At 91 units per acre, the Project is much higher in density than existing developments in Hawthorne. Construction began in 2018 on the 2.53 acre parcel located at 12540 Crenshaw Boulevard, formally known as the Green Line Mixed-Use Project. The nearby SpaceX headquarters and rocket factory employs approximately 6,000 people. The Project is located in an industrial/distribution district on a major arterial street that has no on-street parking; there are no adjacencies from the Project to existing single-family neighborhoods.

Institutional Setting

The institutional setting for this case is the City of Hawthorne, a community of 86,965 residents located in Los Angeles County. Figure 12.1 shows Hawthorne in the context of southwestern Los Angeles County, near the Pacific Ocean and Los Angeles International Airport.

Box 12.1 The Idea of Transit-Oriented Development

Transit-oriented development (TOD) is considered to be dense, mixed-use development within convenient walking distance of frequent transit service (Cervero 2004). Jamme et al. (2019, 415) identify six characteristics in a review of abstracts about TOD: density, diversity of land uses, pedestrian-friendly design, destination accessibility (transit takes you somewhere you want to go), distance to transit, and travel demand management. Housing-oriented TOD projects respond to housing demand in a way that encourages walking, bicycling and transit use, and generally have lower on-site parking supply. A lower parking supply reduces the costs of housing construction, allows more units on the site, and avoids cross-subsidies from those who don't own cars to those who do (e.g., when everyone pays higher rent to pay for parking costs for those with cars). TODs seek to attract and serve households with lower levels of vehicle ownership and vehicle miles traveled (VMT). Lower VMT, in turn, reduces pollution and greenhouse gas emissions. Walkable destinations and alternative transportation modes benefit those who do not drive because of age or disability, cannot afford a vehicle, or chose not to drive.

TOD has been widely accepted as a wise land use policy, one that serves efficiency, equity, and sustainability. In recent years, however, criticisms of the performance of some TODs have emerged. One concern is gentrifying impacts of rail investment and TOD, and associated displacement of low-income residents to areas with less transit service. TOD units are often more expensive than the existing stock, and current residents worry that a new project will lead to rent increases in their homes. Despite these broader concerns, Chatman et al. (2019, 482) found that "higher income households reduce their VMT more when living in TODs than do poorer households." Despite reducing regional VMT by increasing transit use, TOD may increase local congestion because of higher levels of neighborhood activity.

TOD projects are not always welcomed by local communities. Specifics matter, including unit type and market served, provision of affordable units, parking supply, and the quality of transit service available. TODs built on sites that do not displace existing residents and avoid existing neighborhoods may have less gentrification effect. Those that have lower parking supplies and provide incentives for transit, carsharing, walking, and bicycling have smaller congestion impacts. Also, since transit cannot be expected to serve all trips, TOD locations with walking and cycling access to retail, employment, and other land uses perform well. The Project had all aspects of these characteristics.

Figure 12.2 shows the site in its context, with nearby uses including SpaceX, an Amazon distribution center, and low-scale industrial uses. The underutilized parcel's shallow configuration is not compatible with the site needs of

Figure 12.1 Hawthorne Regional Context. Image source: Goggle, Landsat/Copernicus

industrial/distribution uses. Figure 12.3 provides a street-level view with the Project under construction on the right-hand side of Crenshaw Boulevard, and on the left the SpaceX facility. Figure 12.4 provides an artist rendering of the completed Project.

The following provides a demographic profile. Hawthorne data is listed first; the U.S. data is provided in brackets (U.S. Census 2020):

- More young people: persons under 18 years, 26.0% (22.4%).
- Very diverse: Black or African American alone, 23.9% (13.4%); Hispanic or Latino, 54.8% (18.3%).
- Low share of owner-occupied housing: owner-occupied housing rate, 26.5% (63.8%).
- More risk to social well-being: persons without health insurance 18.2% (10.2%).
- Lower income: 2013–2017 median household income in 2017 dollars, $47,636 ($61,015).

As shown in Figure 12.1, Hawthorne is located four miles east of the Pacific Ocean in a portion of Los Angeles County called the South Bay. The aerospace

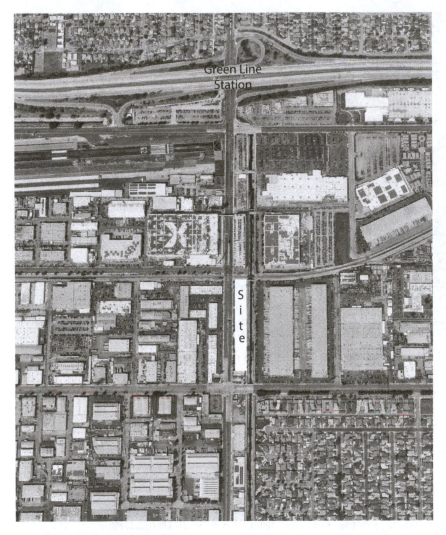

Figure 12.2 12540 Crenshaw Site Context. Image source: Google, Landsat/Copernicus, Author

industry, beach access, and Los Angeles International Airport influence the South Bay's land use patterns and economic activity. The city was incorporated in 1922. It's most famous citizens were Olympian Jim Thorpe and Beach Boy Brian Wilson. Ironically promoted as a city of "good neighbors," Hawthorne was a "sundown town" in the 1930s, meaning that African American people were barred from living there and could not be in the town after dark (Loewen 2018). The town grew as part of the defense industry boom after World War II, and following the Federal Fair Housing Act of 1968, Hawthorne experienced a large influx of Black, Latino, and Asian families. Changes to the power structure of the city lagged the demographic change,

Figure 12.3 Street-Level View of 12540 Crenshaw Under Construction, Showing Central Parking Structure. Image source: Author

Figure 12.4 12540 Crenshaw Project Rendering. Image source: City of Hawthorne, www.cityof-hawthorne.org/s/Green-Line-Mixed-Use-Specific-Plan-final1-yyep.pdf

and the racial legacy of Hawthorne lingers in this now minority–majority community (Meares 2018).

Hawthorne has a five-member City Council, elected at-large. Planning decisions are reviewed and recommended by an appointed Planning Commission. Significant for the case, the Community Development director changed midway through the planning process.

Overview of Planning Process

Development cases involve the planning processes of many entities, including the developer, investors, lenders, the local jurisdiction, other government agencies, technical and design consultants, and advocacy and community groups. While approval authority lies with the local jurisdiction, it is important to recognize the breadth of these multiple, independent processes. This section introduces the planning processes used by the Developer, the local jurisdiction, and me in my particular assignment.

The Developer's planning process started with a search for TOD opportunities in this market area, which led to the subject parcel being identified as having potential for this use. Box 12.2 provides the Developer's perspective

---

Box 12.2 Bludso's with Sam
Gilad Ganish, Blackwood Real Estate (Project Developer)

I was sitting on the patio of Bludso's in Compton having brisket with my friend Sam Hirsch. And by patio, I mean the two wooden picnic benches in the back of the parking lot, near the smoker. Since Sam was based in Los Angeles and I was coming from Newport Beach, this was one of our regular meeting spots. During the conversation, he mentioned that a warehouse Sam's firm had leased was being taken over by SpaceX, and that SpaceX was leasing up space all around their headquarters on Crenshaw (their address says Rocket Road but SpaceX is actually on Crenshaw Boulevard). Although the conversation was not about real estate, I decided that any growth like that deserved further inspection.

My development company was looking for more transit-oriented sites in the Los Angeles area, and this area was also within walking distance to the Metro Green Line. Although a lot of the properties around SpaceX had seen better days, the area looked like it had potential: it had jobs, it had transit within a quarter mile, and it had some shops and restaurants nearby.

There was an empty building across the street from SpaceX that was for sale. We were able to put the property under contract with an extended escrow that would allow us to entitle the property before closing, but given the delays going through the process we ended up buying it before the entitlements were totally completed. I also spent about a year and a half talking with the neighboring property owner before he agreed to sell. This assemblage enabled us to have 2.3 contiguous acres. The site was a fit for us given the proximity to jobs and transit. Initially, this deal came together based more on instinct than financial analysis; our basis was much higher than any recent comps. I remember a couple of other developers literally laughing when I told them we were working on this project.

in selecting the site; he then began discussions with the city and hired a consulting team that designed and analyzed the Project. As the planning process unfolded, the Developer undertook financial analyses to determine if permitted density and development costs yielded the financial performance that met the requirements of investors and potential buyers of the completed rental project.

Approval of the Project required changes to the land use type, building type, density, and development standards. Hawthorne's processes for considering discretionary approvals are guided by state law and procedures. In this case, city officials recommended that a specific plan be used rather than develop numerous deviations from the existing zoning code because that code did not provide development standards suited to this type of development. Although specific plans are normally completed for a multiple-parcel districts, the then-community development director suggested it because a complete new set of standards was required. Hawthorne's past development pattern was suburban style, separated land uses with surface parking, unlike the proposed Project.

The following approvals were required: a General Plan amendment (policy decision that a residential use is allowed), a specific plan, zoning code revisions to recognize the specific plan zone on the parcel, and an environmental impact review (EIR). The guiding policy document, the General Plan, previously designated the parcel as industrial. An EIR was prepared because these actions are considered a *project* under the California Environmental Quality Act.

My assignment was to produce a technical report that was to be included in the package of studies developed for the city's staff report. I followed a process developed in previous assignments for other developers, which involved conducting research about the city, analyzing project characteristics, and applying research and practice knowledge about parking to recommend an appropriate parking supply.

I acted as a consultant to the Developer who approached me regarding parking after it become a critical issue. A traffic engineering firm had completed a parking assessment, but city officials questioned the analysis. My task was to provide an independent, second opinion on the parking demand and associated parking requirements. My role was as a technical expert, drawing on research and other consulting experiences about parking demand and policy.

Being a late addition to the team offered me no opportunity to influence Project scope. I had not worked for the Developer before and did not attend any development team meetings. As a consultant, the work is in the "ask and answer" realm of practice in which the planner's role is highly compartmentalized. It is typical of my consultant practice – cities and developers seek an analytically justified answer to parking questions rather than rely on standards or precedent.

The Core Problem

The broad problem was whether to approve this mixed-use residential development in an industrial zone. Targeted to young professionals, the Project provided needed, dense housing (91 units per acre) in good location. It was proposed on a site that had vacant industrial/commercial buildings, and so did not displace any residents or businesses.

In community deliberations about the Project, questions were raised about land use compatibility, other possible land uses, appropriate density, parking supply, and impacts on traffic congestion. Some residents were opposed to the development of more rental housing and complained that the city had not addressed existing neighborhood problems. During deliberations, the City Council was split on the Project. Planning staff wrote and presented a recommendation to approve the Project and a recommendation to deny it, refraining from favoring either course. They asked the Planning Commission and City Council to decide. The reason given was that the existing General Plan included goals and policies that supported the Project and could be interpreted to oppose it. The core questions were (i) should dense multifamily development be permitted in an industrial zone and (ii) under what conditions?

The core problem for my analysis was to advise on the appropriate parking supply. Parking issues were part of a series of conclusions needed for the "what conditions?" part of the question. To a city that embraces Smart Growth principles, the Developer's parking proposal would not be controversial. It is common to reduce parking requirements for TODs. But the Project's parking plans were controversial because Hawthorne did not have experience with this type of development and residents feared losing suburban lifestyle qualities. Before I became involved, the Developer had already agreed to increase the parking supply over its initial proposal based on negotiations with city officials.

Intended and Actual Outcomes

The Developer asked the city to adopt plan and zoning changes, approve the EIR, and entitle the Project. The Project was approved on October 10, 2017.

During final deliberations, with the City Council split, a council member indicated that they would support the Project if the number of units were reduced from 274 to 230. This change won approval, but there was no analysis of the effects of the change. Links for staff reports and video of City Council and Planning Commission deliberations are listed in the endnote.[1]

After approval, the Developer sold the Project to Houston-based Dinerstein Companies. Construction began in 2018, with completion slated for 2020. The Project has been renamed Millennium Hawthorne. A post-occupancy evaluation would be required to determine if claims made during the entitlement process are realized.

My intended outcome was to provide an analysis to support a city decision concerning Project parking supply. Existing city requirements would have required 841 parking spaces as compared to the proposal for 504 in the 274-unit proposal, a 40% reduction.[2] My analysis concluded that meeting the 841-space requirement would have generated excess, unused parking if built. That possibility was moot, though, because such a supply level would have made the Project economically infeasible due to construction costs and limitations related to the parcel size. The parking structure was already at the practical maximum height. Even the 504-space supply was more than the Developer would have built without the city requirement.

Prior to the Project, residents complained of parking inadequacies in existing neighborhoods, and the city responded by *raising* multifamily parking requirements for new developments. The Project's parking supply proposal, therefore, moved in the opposite direction of recent city policy and made it a flashpoint of controversy.

Examination of the Planning Episode Using Framework Elements

The framework diagram of Figure 5.2 (see Chapter 5) provides prompts that address planner-as-person elements, context, and reasoning and methods used.

Planner-as-Person Elements That Shaped the Approach

My role in the Project was a sideline to my primary job as a professor of urban and regional planning at Cal Poly Pomona, where I have taught since 1986. I have been a member of the American Institute of Certified Planners (AICP) since 1987 and support the aspirational principles and rules of the AICP Code of Ethics.

I have practiced as a consultant since 1989, serving as a subconsultant to larger planning firms or working directly for public agencies, private developers, or nonprofit clients. My first client was the Bay Area Rapid Transit district; parking analysis and policy consulting work expanded as the issue of parking supply and management grew in importance. My expertise in parking analysis began in my practice career, when I worked on parking policy in downtown Los Angeles, and extended through a PhD dissertation on commuter responsiveness to parking pricing and parking consulting for public agencies, developers, employers, and business districts. Seeing the impact of parking requirements from the developer's perspective makes me supportive of reform, but understanding the community controversy the local government planner must address makes me understand why it is often slow to occur.

Personal Framework Elements

I took an evidence-based approach, seeking to use logic and evidence to reform rule-of-thumb approaches to parking requirements. My reform agenda is correcting an underlying bias in favor of private automobile transportation that is found in many plans and codes. In my planning education, an inclination to a truth-seeking form of practice found alignment with professors who employed economic approaches to public policy. Reforming transportation policies and regulations improves efficiency, sustainability, *and* equity.

I hold a view that societal resources are well-allocated when individual choices are based on the price of what is consumed. Practically speaking, those who wish to use parking should pay for it. The caveat to this position is that externalities (e.g., pollution, lower densities) and equity (e.g., accessibility favors those with cars over those without) are accounted for in policies and regulations, which is often not the case. Minimum parking requirements distort the market for parking by forcing developers to supply more parking than they otherwise would. The resulting oversupply means that there is no market price for parking because supply exceeds demand. Oversupplied parking is offered free at most workplaces, and bundled with residential ownership and rental apartments. It is not free, of course, since the cost is reflected in ownership cost or rent, which means those who do not park pay for those who do. The general epistemological position underlying this view is that knowledge is "found" through statistical and economic analyses of travel behavior, such as multinomial logit analyses of mode choice and household vehicle ownership.

The theory of change that shapes my approach in this case is that expert knowledge provides decision-makers and communities with information and frames of understanding to support good decisions. Parking demand modelling under different pricing and supply policies is superior to the flawed practice of establishing parking requirements by copying a neighboring city's requirements or relying on national averages that build in a suburban, auto-first bias. This line of reasoning also supports social justice, because traditional zoning approaches for minimum parking requirements favor the accessibility for those who drive to the detriment of those who do not, and create pollution impacts on vulnerable populations.

Personal Incongruity and Ambiguity

The assignment was clear, and it directly advanced my practice mission. Helping the Project receive approval advanced my intention to facilitate transit-oriented rental housing and parking reform. The Project did not negatively impact a neighborhood or displace existing residents.

Interpretation of Context

My late arrival into the planning episode provided little opportunity to assess context. The Developer briefed me, but other than that, I interpreted the discussion I heard at the Planning Commission and City Council and related it to past experiences in other cities. The lack of direct interaction with local stakeholders posed a risk of missing unique elements of Hawthorne. For example, I did not know at the time that Hawthorne once was a "sundowner city," as previously discussed. Knowing that would not have changed my technical analysis, but I would have better understood the community that was considering and debating the Project. This lack of deep context knowledge is an occupational hazard of time-limited consulting assignments. Consultants are attentive to formal and informal communication in interpreting context, but they know much less than the city's planners.

Context Framework Elements

My primary objective regarding context was getting a quick read on the range of stakeholder positions. Unlike some cases, where arguments all line up on one side, there were varied opinions. The Planning Department's staff report recognized the merits of the Project in supporting the General Plan, but it also had issues with land use compatibility and setting new development standards. On the City Council, some members appeared to be in favor while others appeared to be opposed.

Among community members, more of those who spoke at meetings were opposed to the Project. They were concerned about traffic congestion, negative impacts on the industrial district, the lack of affordable housing, gentrification, and impacts on conditions in their own neighborhoods. Some were opposed to rental housing in general (in a city where most people rent), and others lamented that the Project was intended for young professionals and therefore not of benefit to them or their community. Prior negative experiences with apartments built in previous decades framed some community members' expectations and concerns.

Those who spoke in favor shared a desire that Hawthorne have "nice" TOD developments like other cities, favored economic development, and expressed pride in Hawthorne being the location for SpaceX. The Developer commissioned a public support petition and received 3,100 signatures in favor of the Project and secured letters of support from the Los Angeles County supervisor and the state assemblyperson for Hawthorne.

I learned about context by reading staff reports and listening during meetings, and I then shared and sought an assessment of the validity of my insights with the client. Of course, valuable information can be learned outside of the particular case – in community members' testimony, council deliberations, and departmental interaction about other issues.

Context Uncertainty and Ambiguity

Despite no prior experience with the Developer or the city, the contours of the issue were familiar. I had heard neighborhood arguments against infill housing, dense housing, and lower parking supply many times before and felt that I understood the opposition. Residents who opposed the Project suggested rental housing was not "appropriate," that Hawthorne was "full," that congestion was unbearable, and that new housing would create additional homeless encampments.

My confidence in interpreting context drew from past experience when project opponents seek to prove that parking overspill will occur to scale back or deny a project. Sometimes extra parking is demanded, knowing the cost burden to the developer could kill the project. In this case, I interpreted stakeholders' statements as best I could to determine if they were genuinely concerned about future residents' ability to find parking or were using parking as an opposition strategy.

One additional element of ambiguity was my status as a consultant/academic. The assignment was completed independent from my academic appointment at

Cal Poly Pomona, but my academic affiliation was known. Being a consultant and an academic may have muddied perceptions of my work among stakeholders because I was paid by the client rather than an independent academic researcher.

In sum, I felt little uncertainty and ambiguity about context at the time, despite limited personal experience. The Project supported my mission to improve transportation options and reduce barriers to housing construction. But researching Hawthorne's history in preparing this reflection causes me to reconsider how well I read the community with such little local contact.

The Planning Episode: Reasoning and Methods

The specific questions for my work product concerned parking supply per unit, visitor parking supply, and the sharing of visitor and restaurant parking spaces. The technical report consisted of the following: (i) analysis of the target market, (ii) review of national data sources on parking demand for transit-oriented development, (iii) information about household vehicle availability for rental housing in Hawthorne, (iv) examples of TOD parking requirements in other communities, and (v) application of the Urban Land Institute Shared Parking model to assess peak parking demand.

Logic

This technocratic role I assumed is rooted in deductive logic. I provided multiple types of evidence on parking demand in TOD and made judgments about how these examples apply to the Project. The work is framed by economic theory about utility maximizing behavior in household location and travel, translated to travel and vehicle ownership theories as noted in Box 12.1. Econometric models underpin theories that vehicle ownership and VMT are reduced when TOD features are present. The Project has the previously noted TOD characteristics, but the key question was the *degree* of influence on vehicle ownership and resulting parking demand. The evidence I assembled made the case that the Developer's parking plans were appropriate.

I adopted a technocratic affect in presenting and responding to City Council and Planning Commission questions. I portrayed myself as sincerely seeking truth about the Project's future parking demand and acted in an objective, nonpartisan way. At the same time, my goal was to contribute to parking reform. I was not neutral regarding the decisions of the City Council. This is a covert-activist role, in which the planner adopts a neutral, professional persona but has a reform agenda in mind (Catanese 1974).

Emotion

The small role and short time frame of my involvement in the Project reduced the sense of emotional investment, as it was yet another interesting case. In public meeting environments, I withheld emotional expression when presenting to decision-makers, taking a reasoned and guarded approach. I avoided taking offense at any outwardly or passive aggressive expressions toward me. I sought to present my findings in a way that would not antagonize opponents, to the degree that was possible.

This unemotional role was part of a "you can't get to me" approach to protect myself from shaming by community members who were opposed to the Project. I sought to convince stakeholders that the analysis was technically valid, seeking to head off each possible parking-related reason to deny it. My job was to take the charge of "inadequate parking" off the list of possible reasons for denial. When opponents to a development find that one line of criticism becomes unavailable, they often move on to other areas of vulnerability.

I sought to avoid getting flustered in meetings. At the time, I felt virtuous and believed I was on the side of the "good" because I represented future residents who might live in the development. I perceived impossible aims and illogical thinking on the part of opponents. Of course, some opponents perceived me as a consulting "hack" giving the Developer the answer they wanted. The optics were not good: working in a minority-majority community, I sat in a line at the City Council meetings with mostly male, mostly White consultants dressed in jackets and ties, none of whom lived in Hawthorne. It was easy to cast us as privileged mercenaries from outside the community.

While I did not show emotion, the entitlement case was emotional. Community members expressed deep frustration, anger, and a view that the planning decision-making system was corrupt. Council members accused each other of corruption. Even though the Project was not located in a residential neighborhood, anger about conditions in existing Hawthorne neighborhoods was prominent. At one stage of public comment during a meeting, a community member pointed to the consulting team, and charged that our work in support of the Project would *produce* homeless encampments. He held up a photo of a homeless encampment in Hawthorne neighborhood, pointed at me and the other consultants, and said "you are causing this!" The basis of the claim was that apartments built in the 1970s and 1980s for aerospace employees were not well maintained, and now there were homeless encampments in those neighborhoods. The logic was that apartments degrade communities and lead to homeless encampments. In my view, the claims made had little relationship to Project, and if taken to heart would halt housing production everywhere in Hawthorne.

In playing a "you can't get me" role, I hardened myself and withdrew empathy. I believed the Project was an important contribution to the rental housing supply near an employment hub and a transit station. In my view, the problems community members were raising about neighborhood conditions were valid but not related to the proposed scheme.

An appeal of planning approaches that use markets instead of regulation is their role as a bulwark against political and interest group self-interest and corruption. The market approach in this case is to eliminate parking requirements and let future resident's willingness to pay for a parking space determine the supply.

Hearing classic elements of "not in my backyard" (NIMBY) attitudes expressed intensified the emotional dimensions of my experience – residents who explained that Hawthorne was a "city of good neighbors" opposed market rate rental housing. Claims were made that "we can do better" for a site that sat empty for many years.

Some residents simply did not want their community to change. Seen in a regional context, a "no change" position has produced a housing crisis, leading to high prices, long commutes, and underhoused and homeless populations. I felt discouraged about the poor prospects of hundreds of local governments in Southern California collectively addressing the regional housing shortage by entitling more housing. I sensed the residents' distrust of institutions and planning processes. While I thought the anti-growth positions of some residents were unreasonable, I could understand their frustration. The experience challenged my faith that democratic local planning can respond to the housing challenges that California faces.

Convention

Convention shaped my approach in multiple ways. First, the planning and development approval process is established by California development entitlement law, including land use and environmental law, underpinned by rational comprehensive planning theory and pluralist political theory, and open meeting requirements, underpinned by transparency and good government goals. Political deliberations occurred in the regimented structure of public testimony and City Council discussion, which follows prescribed stages of staff and proponent presentations, public comment, and decision-maker deliberation. The formal decision structure does not allow for a back-and-forth conversation between the public, the Developer, and decision-makers. An alternative is to have this dialogue in publicly noticed workshops to explore issues and alternatives outside the decision environment, but that did not occur.

Convention applies to parking requirements when jurisdictions copy the rates from neighboring or peer jurisdictions or use national averages contained in Institute of Traffic Engineers handbooks. This is common but problematic, as it leads to the replication of excessive requirements that undermine other public goals. At a minimum, those comparisons are used to demonstrate the reasonableness of requirements – that the jurisdiction is not placing itself out of the context of other requirements. This is a common perspective when jurisdictions compete for development. It goes against the evidence-based approach I favor, which argues for local data and parking requirements framed in a city's policy priorities.

Despite my objection to this practice, using parking requirement precedents is so engrained in the thinking of decision-makers that I used a version of it as part of my analysis. I presented "best practice" requirements of cities with more TOD experience. These requirements are far lower than Hawthorne's citywide requirements. I did so for the pragmatic reason that this type of argument is successful in precedent-oriented review and deliberation processes.

Invention

The Project represented invention for the city in terms of the development's characteristics and planning process. It is a denser, taller building with small unit sizes and first-floor retail uses, and the first TOD and workplace-adjacent housing development in Hawthorne. All community members, city planners, local businesses, and the public were dealing with a new approach. And for the issue of parking, the city took a new approach and allowed a TOD project with a lower parking supply than it normally required. Lastly, the specific plan process for a single site was a procedural invention, a way to comprehensively consider all development standards for a new development type.

If there had been an opportunity to invent process, I would have suggested workshops with the City Council, Planning Commission, and the public to discuss parking and transportation issues. This could have had a side benefit of bringing different community stakeholders together with a goal of seeking mutual gain. Mutual gain means that all stakeholders express their vision, values, and concerns, and the planning process searches for solutions that create the largest amount of benefit for all parties. For example, the City Council ended up reducing the density by 44 units, which significantly reduced the financial performance for investors. Box 12.3 provides the Developer's perspective on the last-minute density reduction and what a mutual gain trade might have looked like.

Box 12.3 The Entitlement Process and Unit "Chop"
Gilad Ganish, Blackwood Real Estate (Project Developer)

As part of our due diligence, we met with the head of the Planning Department and discussed our vision for the site. He was very excited and suggested that we could either do our own specific plan or be part of an upcoming specific plan for a larger area that the city was embarking on. Although the second choice would have been less expensive for us, it introduced uncertainty regarding timing and plan parameters that made doing our own specific plan more attractive. This was a good decision because within six months of starting the specific plan process for our project, the local specific plan effort died due to lack of support from City Council. Soon after that, the head of the Planning Department left for another city and we began working with the new Community Development director who unfortunately had a completely different vision of his role in the organization. Rather than present to the City Council what the Planning Department perceived as good planning, his approach was to wait to be told by City Council what should happen and where. In fact, when the project was brought to the Planning Commission after two years of a transparent and open process, the Planning Director was unwilling to include a staff recommendation for approval or denial; this was a first for us. Furthermore, after the Planning Commission recommended approval of the project and adopted a resolution as such, the Planning director was still unwilling to make a recommendation on the project, and we went to City Council without a staff recommendation for approval or denial. Keep in mind that we had been working with staff for two years at this point and had carefully negotiated each part of the project, from parking to setbacks to public art.

When there is no professional guidance from the city manager on down, City Council decisions can become arbitrary and inefficient because there is no analysis of the merits of compromises reached. As an example, one of the most difficult parts of our entitlement process was when the City Council chopped 44 units off the project. Of course the financial impact of losing 44 units was challenging, but what I still think about to this day is how it could have been handled differently. The specific plan process is a legislative process within the city's discretion and, through a development agreement or similar instrument, opens the door for negotiations with the applicant. The unit cut seemed fairly arbitrary to us and didn't really make the project any more appealing to its detractors. It was still a large apartment building with hundreds of units, now five stories instead of six stories. So what? The problem is that if you assume that each "entitled unit" increased the land value by $80,000, then approximately $3,500,000 was lost with

---

Box 12.3 (continued)

that reduction. It was a true lose-lose situation: (i) we as applicants didn't get the value of those entitled units, (ii) the company now building the project didn't get the value of the entitled units, (iii) the project's detractors are still seeing a large building get constructed, and (iv) the city got fewer fees and future tax revenues. But worse than those is that is that if the city had opened a dialogue with us, then an opportunity to create a win-win scenario might have been possible. For example, we could have kept the 274 units but contributed to an affordable housing fund for the city, which we would have certainly agreed to since that would be less of an impact than the unit chop. Instead, $3,500,000 of value basically evaporated.

Discoveries

Despite the delimited nature of this planning assignment, my reflection revealed as rich a set of observations as the climate action plan discussed in Chapter 6. Entitlement decisions are where the action is. My observations include (i) practical judgments made during the planning episode and (ii) take-aways for planning.

Practical Judgments

The direct, on-the-ground impact of project-level entitlement decisions often generate more community engagement, more intense deliberation about goals, and more political negotiation than broad policy plans. In the following, I discuss three practical judgments: (i) accepting a limited role, (ii) tailoring the analysis to political realities, and (iii) ignoring issues outside of my scope of work.

Practical Judgment 1: Accepting a Limited, Downstream Role in a Fragmented Process

Accepting a limited role was the precondition of this assignment. After a few phone conversations with the Developer, I understood what was needed and did not consider proposing a more extensive study or community participation process. Consultants respond to the need, defined scope, and budget of their clients. Not until reflecting back on the case did I consider the degree to which I was accepting a limited downstream role. At the time, I simply wanted to participate in a development project that contributed to transit-oriented housing production; I took the role for granted.

Accepting a fragmented role did not mean that I lacked all opportunity to influence other aspects of the Project, the most notable being the lack of an affordable housing component. Because this work was not my main source of income, I had the luxury of turning down the work, unlike many consultants. Yet pushing for a broader role did not occur to me at the time – the gains of helping a development provide rental units near transit were sufficient. At the time I was retained for the job, I did not think about the broader issue of affordable housing.

Once engaged, I did ask the Developer about affordable housing. He asserted that neither the development team nor the City wanted it included. I accepted the answer and did not question it. My assignment was parking, so pushing for an affordable housing component would have been outside normal consultant practice. But I could have pushed harder – I had the economic freedom to do that and an extra level of authority due to my position as an academic. In hindsight, I wish I had.

Practical Judgment 2: Developing a Politically Honed Analysis Rather Than Recommending the Ideal Solution

My view is that cities should leave it up to developers to decide how much parking to build, following Shoup's (2005) proposal to eliminate minimum requirements, manage and price on-street spaces, and return parking revenues to neighborhoods. But that view was a nonstarter in Hawthorne and many other cities. So I accepted, responded to, and perhaps perpetuated a false problem frame of needing to *prove* that the Project would have "enough" parking. This common approach responds to decision-makers on the basis of where they are.

The AICP Code of Ethics includes two aspirational principles: "(2a) We shall exercise independent professional judgment on behalf of our clients and employers," and "(2b) We shall accept the decisions of our client or employer concerning the objectives and nature of the professional services we perform unless the course of action is illegal or plainly inconsistent with our primary obligation to the public interest" (AICP 2019). This case existed in the tension of those principles. My independent professional judgment was that even less parking should be supplied, but I accepted the Developer's conclusions that pursuing such as course was not politically feasible (or perhaps desirable from a market standpoint). Section 3A says, "We shall protect the integrity of our profession." I delivered a professional opinion that had a greater chance of acceptance. This could be seen as damaging the integrity of the profession among those who claim that professionals should act apolitically, out of a narrow technical base.

Practical Judgment 3: Limiting Professional Recommendations to Parking, Ignoring Land-Use Compatibility Issues

Land use compatibility was a significant issue in Project deliberations. The Specific Plan changed the land use designation from industrial to the specific plan's mixed-use residential regulations. There are four concerns. First, would residents of the development experience excessive levels of noise, vibration, and air pollution, stemming from proximity to industrial uses and the nearby Hawthorne Municipal Airport? The Developer indicated that the Project would have sound-reduction window treatments and disclose the presence of nearby sound-generating uses in leases. Second, would traffic levels associated with the development interfere with truck movements from adjacent land uses? The traffic analysis did not reveal serious congestion issues, but the special nature of truck movements might have been inadequately considered. Third, since the Project reduced industrially designated land, would the loss of industrial land harm the region's diversified economic base? The Developer countered that the site was not suitable for industrial uses because it was shallow and that it represented a small percentage of industrial land in Hawthorne. And fourth, would the presence of about 500 new residents in the neighborhood produce complaints about noise and operations that would lead to the city imposing operational limits on the surrounding industrial uses, thereby diminishing the integrity and efficiency of the industrial district? Whether this happens depends on lease terms and conditions, the nature of the disruption, and the city's response to potential complaints.

The AICP Code indicates that planners "have special concern for the long-range consequences of present actions" and "pay special attention to the interrelatedness of decisions." My scope of work did not include consideration of land use designations or compatibility. City planning staff considered these land use issues in their report, and the Developer's fiscal impact consultant indicated that the small size and narrow configuration of the parcel made it unsuitable for industrial development. Nonetheless, I accepted a role that ignored long-range consequences for the industrial district.

Takeaways for Practice

This case illustrates the evolution underway in land use planning in which public concern for land use compatibility is being changed by two factors: (i) deindustrialization and tighter environmental regulation that reduces industrial impacts; and (ii) new issues and planning challenges, such as providing infill housing near rail transit stops and efficiently using scarce land resources. Three takeaways for professional practice are suggested, speaking to the broad planning issues raised by the case.

Takeaway 1: Recognize the Ways That a Planning Effort Exists in an Ecosystem of Plans and Intentions

The question of where did this development idea come from is complex and multifaceted. In Box 12.2, the Developer describes how his site search plan was influenced by the plans of Metro, the county transit agency. The Project was only conceivable, of course, because of investor interest in mixed-use multi-family housing infill locations. This interest has emerged in response to public plans calling for this type of development and housing demand. Some developers and investors realize that the value of these developments can justify higher development costs than traditional development on vacant land, accepting site constraints and land assembly issues, site remediation requirements, neighborhood opposition, and/or challenging environmental certifications. At the same time, the plans of economic development organizations and local businesses see this land use change as a threat. There is no clear causality in the interactions of these plans and intentions – they reflect the goals of multiple parties influencing one another.

Procedurally, the city General Plan provides the broad goals that should guide the decision, but Hawthorne's goals pulled in different directions. TOD supported housing goals, but goals for a prosperous industrial district suggested denying the proposal. This tension between valid goals is at the center of most planning episodes – not good-versus-bad but good-versus-another-good. This is why comprehensive plans cannot be expected to tightly direct outcomes; rather what they do is direct attention to what matters and require a deliberative process to resolve tensions between goals in specific instances.

Takeaway 2: Reconsider Traditional Forms of Land Use Compatibility Regulation, Shifting From a Hands-Off Post-Approval Approach to Developing and Enforcing Mitigation Agreements That Run with Land

The historical purpose of planning was to control externalities on a collective basis such as managing industrial impacts on residential uses. Euclidian zoning, for example, separated land uses to reduce pollution impacts, and controlled density to address traffic congestion and other forms of crowding. These are crude tools, insensitive to particulars and ignoring the potential of ongoing management to address externalities. This idea has been reassessed by planners who recognize the sprawl-inducing effects of zoning on land-use efficiency, sustainability, and social justice. For example, the Miami 21 form-based code case discussed in Chapter 9 provides an example of the move from Euclidian to form-based regulation.

Environmental regulations and the decreased economic role of heavy industry have made relaxing land use separations possible by reducing the severity of externality problems. Mixed-use infill development fulfills many goals such as increasing housing supply, supporting transit investment, and increasing livability, but it inevitably raises land use compatibility issues in established land patterns. This planning episode highlights the challenges in this transition to mixed uses, not in terms of the Project's internal use mix, but in horizontal mixing among sites. Recognizing nighttime truck operations at the Amazon fulfillment center next to the site, the planning question is this: Should future residents be protected from such impacts by denying housing development in that location, or should they be allowed to trade off the benefits of the new residential location against disbenefits associated with being located next to industrial uses?

The Developer made assurances that operational mitigation strategies would be implemented, such as travel demand management including bicycle parking, carshare parking, first-offer of apartments to nearby employees, and a free transit pass for a trial period. These features are included in development approval conditions and monitoring required for identified mitigation measures. The focus of planners, though, is ensuring compliance during the development period – a "set it and forget it" approach that simplifies the process. A certificate of occupancy certifies that a development is compliant, and once it is issued, planners move on to address other projects. Code enforcement, usually housed in a separate city department, generally deals with violations of health and safety issues rather than the fine points of a travel demand management strategy. This is why planning departments have historically pursued solutions in initial construction, such overbuilding parking, as they do not have later recourse if building occupancy is higher than normal. However, this practice is inefficient, as it requires most developments to build too much parking for the small number of developments that have abnormally high parking demand.

As planning moves to more mixed land uses and new approaches to transportation, public planners need to monitor and enforce the programmatic conditions over the life of the building. This involves contingent approvals so that a development can be better matched to public requirements throughout its economic life.

Takeaway 3: Reform Planning Processes That Privilege NIMBY Sentiments; Use Mutual Gain Negotiation Techniques to Solve Controversies

The land use regulatory system in California is broken, resulting in a housing supply and affordability crisis. A recent study concludes: "The state ranked near the bottom in ... supply of housing relative to population growth, housing affordability, existing single-family home prices, housing cost as percentage of household income for both owner-occupied and renter-occupied households, and overcrowdedness" (Fowler and Chong n.d.). This case shows the problems with the current system of development entitlements, which grants too much power to existing residents and business interests. Reducing the Project density from 274 to 230 units may seem trivial, but when this practice is replicated across the state, it slows housing production. In addition, high parking requirements and regulatory uncertainty discourage future developers from proposing developments, and add to costs. The last-minute density reduction for the Project may deter other developers from doing business in Hawthorne.

Project opponents were correct that the change represented in this development was not intended for them – the target market is younger, more affluent, and likely to be less diverse – the classic story of gentrification. Yet providing new units takes pressure off the existing housing stock. While local government has legitimate interests in managing growth to address issues such as traffic and school crowding, a "local-first" practice creates regional and statewide problems in affordable housing, transportation, and the environment.

Planning emerged as an institutional activity because development was insufficiently regulated, but the pendulum has swung too far toward local control over development. California legislators recognize the problem and new laws are taking small steps to curtail the regulatory power of local government through state preemption, such as excluding developments near transit from environmental review and restricting the scope of certain environmental reviews. A 2019 bill, SB 50 (Wiener), proposed to upzone single-family zoning throughout the state to allow duplexes, triplexes and fourplexes, and upzone even further in "job-rich" or "transit-rich" areas. The bill was held in the 2019 legislative session but was defeated in 2020. These efforts represent the YIMBY (yes in my backyard) movement, supported by employers in the technology sector and local activists for housing supply. Either local governments find ways to increase housing supply or pressure for state preemption will continue (Barth 2019).

The response for local governments seeking to avoid state preemption of zoning powers is to use mutual gain negotiation to address concerns with affordable housing, transportation, and the environment. As noted in Box 12.3, $3.5 million of development value was lost when the unit count was reduced by 44 units at the very end of the process. The Developer would have likely offered millions of dollars for an affordable housing fund as a trade for the 44 units. That win–win did not occur because elected officials made the decision without staff analysis, and because staff did not seek a mutual gain negotiation process.

And Now to You: The Life of a Technical Planner

This case illustrates a common consulting role in providing specialized technical services. Such planning episodes often involved fragmented roles, divided by technical specialty and applied in a specific stage in the planning process. You might be wondering if there are advantages to choosing a fragmented technical role over a broader role of plan-writing. Here are some reasons. First, the limited role allows for specialization to fully understand the nature of the specific problem, the data, models, and the efficacy of solutions. Generalist planners do not have that opportunity. Second, if the topic of specialization is pivotal to a project, the analysis is impactful. Rather than "go through the motions" over a wide variety of less consequential reviews, the specialist planner has a large impact. Third, a specialized career offers varied problem settings – public, private, and nonprofit – and locations. Technical roles in consulting are more likely to involve travel to meet clients and have opportunities for continual learning.

Among the many qualities required for success in this type of planning, two stand out. The first is the ability to quickly read the context for the assignment. Short time frames require an ability to generalize from other experiences in "reading" the planning episode while at the same time not missing valuable local information. And second, consultant planners benefit from refined skills in ethical reasoning that can support them in making good decisions when a client asks for something they do not agree with.

All the professions involved in shaping or creating built form have become more specialized, and planning is no exception. Effective practice requires the technical planner to have an ability to make practical judgments while keeping an eye on the big picture. It also indicates the critical role for generalist planners to synthesize disparate technical analyses to determine how the pieces influence a coherent whole.

Discussion Questions

1. Would you have taken the same approach as Willson if offered the consulting assignment? If yes, what are your reasons? If no, what you would you do differently, and why?
2. Is it appropriate for consultants to push their clients to address issues outside their scope of work? If not, how does this reconcile with the planner's commitment to the broader public good? If yes, under what circumstances? What leverage or forms of argumentation are likely to be successful?
3. Strategies for overcoming NIMBY opposition to otherwise meritorious developments can take many forms: providing technical evidence, reframing, argumentation, convincing, shaming, counterorganizing, building a political coalition, etc. Assume that you are in favor of the Project. What strategy do you think would have worked best in the Hawthorne case?
4. Packed Planning Commission and City Council meetings mean that people care about what is happening in the community. How can planners capture this energy and commitment and engage in longer-term attention to plans and planning issues?

Notes

1 Links to meeting videos and staff reports are available at www.cityofhawthorne .org/council-videos. The key dates for City Council deliberation are September 12, 2017 (Item No. 10); and October 10, 2017 (Item No. 13). The key date for Planning Commission deliberation is August 2, 2017 (Item No. 1)
2 From Hawthorne City Council Staff Report, September 12, 2017, page 13.

References

American Institute of Certified Planners. 2019, September 22. *Code of Ethics and Professional Conduct.* Adopted March 19, 2005; Effective June 1, 2005; Revised April 1, 2016. Retrieved on March 11, 2020 from https://www.planning.org/ethic s/ethicscode/.
Barth, Brian. 2019. "The Double-Edged Sword of Preemption." *Planning,* 2019: 17–23.
Catanese, Anthony J. 1974. *Planners and Local Politics; Impossible Dreams.* Beverly Hills, CA/London: Sage Publications.
Cervero, Robert. 2004. *Transit-oriented development in the United States: Experiences, challenges, and prospects.* Transit Cooperative Research Program Report 102. Washington, DC: Transportation Research Board.

Chatman, Daniel G., Ruoying Xu, Janice Park, and Anne Spevack. 2019. "Does Transit-Oriented Gentrification Increase Driving?" *Journal of Planning Education and Research*, 39(4): 482–495. doi: 10.1177/0739456X19872255.

Fowler, Adam and Hoyu Chong. n.d. *Current state of the California housing market: A comparative analysis*. San Francisco, CA: Next 10. Accessed October 10, 2019 at https ://next10.org/sites/default/files/California-Housing.pdf.

Jamme, Huê-Tâm, Janet Rodriguez, Deepak Bahl, and Tridib Banerjee. 2019. "A Twenty-Five Year Biography of the TOD Concept: From Design to Policy, Planning, and Implementation." *Journal of Planning Education and Research* 39(4): 409–428. doi: 10.1177/0739456X19882073.

Loewen, James W. 2018. *Sundown Towns: A Hidden Dimension of American Racism*. New York: The New Press.

Meares, Hadley. 2018. "Hawthorne's Deceptively Sunny History." *Curbed Los Angeles*. Accessed November 25, 2019 at https://la.curbed.com/2018/1/30/16933546/hawt horne-history-south-bay-racism

Shoup, Donald. 2005. *The High Cost of Free Parking*. Chicago, IL: American Planning Association Planners Press.

U.S. Census. 2020. Accessed March 12, 2020 at https://www.census.gov/quickfacts/ hawthornecitycalifornia.

Chapter 13

Case Comparisons and Implications for Education, Professional Organizations, and Mentoring

The seven case studies show planning to be a varied and complex profession in which practitioners rely on practical judgments about methods and actions. Written after the fact as reflection-on-action, the case authors reveal what they thought, felt, and did. While professional practice inevitably involves habits, norms, and compliance with regulatory procedures, the case authors acted from their own personhood and interacted with an evolving context. Both logic and emotion were employed in making practical judgments about how to proceed. Depending on the nature of the case, the extent of convention and invention varied, but both are present in most cases. This chapter summarizes and compares case study takeaways and discusses reflection initiatives for planning education, professional organizations, and mentoring.

Case Characteristics

As shown, planning practice includes a diverse set of activities and aims. Table 13.1 provides a summary of case characteristics, showing the types of planning addressed and key attributes of each case.

The differences in context and core activity create a challenge for generalization about planning. Planners practice in different settings, have different aims, and use different techniques. I consider this diversity a strength of the profession, but it carries an obligation to communicate across the subfields, to learn from one another, and to find elements of common professional identity.

Planner-as-Person

I was a technocratic planner in the Cal Poly Pomona and Hawthorne cases, and a communicative planner in the Dana Point case – same person, different context and problem. This means that planners develop varied strategies, responsive to context and their evolving view of planning. As well, there is a natural evolution from technical planning at junior career levels to communicative roles in management, leadership, and politics at more senior career levels.

In most cases, the authors report little incongruity between their work and their personal identity, and little ambiguity, because they found forms of practice that fit their values. Most of them are tenured professors and therefore have the freedom to select work that is in agreement with their mission. If cases were based on a random survey of planners, issues of incongruity and ambiguity would likely be more prominent. Not everyone has the good fortune to achieve person–professional alignment, but seeking that alignment is a worthwhile commitment.

Context

The explanations of context reveal many planning settings, including sectoral distinctions (e.g., public, private, nonprofit), and roles as public officials, consultants, and academic community-action planners. Just as it is difficult to generalize about a personal "type" attracted to planning, it is difficult to generalize about context.

In assessing context, case authors often made midcourse corrections as they learned on the go and participants reacted to each step. In some instances,

Table 13.1 Overview of Case Characteristics

	Climate Action Plan (Chapter 6)	Planning for Resilience (Chapter 7)	Inclusionary Housing Policies (Chapter 8)	Form-Based Code (Chapter 9)	Parking Management Deliberation (Chapter 10)	Fresh Produce in Inner-City Corner Stores (Chapter 11)	Mixed-Use Project Specific Plan (Chapter 12)
Type of planning	*Primarily vision and plan-making*		*Combined planning and implementation*			*Primarily implementation*	
Location	Pomona, California	Mamallapuram, India	Portland, Oregon	Miami, Florida	Dana Point, California	Detroit, Michigan	Hawthorne, California
Decision-making body	Public university	Town Council	City Council	City Council	City Council	Multiple	City Council
Subject focus	Environment, climate action planning	Environment, sustainability, resilience	Housing, racial justice, inclusionary zoning	Land use and urban design, form-based code	Transportation, parking management	Community development, healthy food, equity	Land use, transit-oriented development
Core case theme	Economic rationality	Cultural competency	Inside-outside change	Systemic reform	"Talk" processes	Program development	Technical planning
Case-author's role	Consultant/faculty member	Class instructor	City adviser and consultant	Planning director	City consultant	Project manager	Developer consultant
Core activity	Evaluating climate change measures	Managing cross-cultural educational experience	Dual roles as advocate and expert	Managing vision, process, and politics	Listening, framing, and process design	Managing program development and implementation	Analyzing parking demand
Case-author's highest degree	Urban planning	Architecture, environment-behavior studies and research	Urban planning	Landscape architecture	Urban planning	Urban, technological and environmental planning	Urban planning

the planners accommodated context and in others they sought to change it. Levels of uncertainty and ambiguity about that context varied, although no case authors claimed a perfect understanding. As noted earlier, public agency planners have more time to read context, but ambiguity arises when there are unofficial, unstated aims in play. Consultants face greater uncertainty about context because they are with the client for shorter periods of time. For public and private planners, ambiguity is common if clients or decision-makers want plans that do not support the planner's values or those supported by the profession.

Reasoning and Methods

Logic, emotion, convention, and invention were relevant to the practical judgments and outcomes. Table 13.2 reveals that the nature of the case, and the planner's response to it, influenced the framework elements that predominated. In Table 13.2, case authors allocated four votes each across logic/emotion and convention/invention elements to give a sense of the relative importance of those elements to the particular case (the number of votes are shown with a diamond symbol). Across all seven cases, votes for logic and emotion are almost equally divided, but there is significant variation. Votes for invention are almost twice as frequent as those for convention, but that may relate to the cases being innovative planning examples.

Practical Judgments

Practical judgments lie at the core of responsive planning processes. Each case author identified practical judgments that shaped their actions and the way in which they proceeded. Those practical judgments are summarized in three tables. Table 13.3 displays the practical judgments in cases that addressed plan vision and plan-making (Climate Action Plan, Chapter 6; and Planning for Resilience, Chapter 7).

Table 13.4 displays the practical judgments identified for cases that relate to implementation mechanisms, but include feedback loops and consideration of plans and policies (Inclusionary Zoning Policies, Chapter 8; Form-Based Code, Chapter 9; and Parking Management Deliberation, Chapter 10). They reveal the interrelation and interpenetration of planning and implementation in many settings.

Table 13.5 summarizes practical judgments identified for cases that are primarily concerned with implementation (Fresh Produce in Inner-City Corner

Table 13.2 Roles of Logic, Emotion, Convention, and Invention

	Climate Action Plan	Planning for Resilience	Inclusionary Housing Policies	Form-Based Code	Parking Management Deliberation	Fresh Produce in Inner-City Corner Stores	Mixed-Use Project Specific Plan
Logic	◇◇◇	◇	◇◇◇	◇◇◇	◇	◇◇	◇◇◇
Emotion	◇	◇◇◇	◇	◇	◇◇◇	◇◇	◇
Convention	◇	◇	◇	◇	◇◇	◇	◇◇
Invention	◇◇◇	◇◇	◇◇◇	◇◇◇	◇◇	◇◇◇	◇◇

Note: The diamonds shown in each cell represent case authors' allocation of four votes each across the logic/emotion and convention/invention elements to indicate the relative importance of those elements to the particular case.

Table 13.3 Practical Judgments in Plan-Making and Visioning

Climate Action Plan, Cal Poly Pomona, Pomona, California	*Planning for Resilience, Mamallapuram, India*
Proceeding with insufficient technical information and analytic uncertainty.	Facilitating emergence of a plan rather than manage plans tasks toward a predetermined product.
Adopting a rational/analytical role in undertaking cost-effectiveness evaluation.	Creating an engagement in cultural competence at the same time as one devoted to producing a planning project.
Resisting "mission creep" and seeking a narrow definition of plan purpose.	Allowing the experience of disappointment.

Table 13.4 Practical Judgments in Planning–Implementation Hybrids

Inclusionary Housing Policies, Portland, Oregon	*Form-Based Code, Miami, Florida*	*Parking Management Deliberation, Dana Point, California*
Getting political to push equity.	Addressing vision and implementation simultaneously.	Prioritizing talk over technical analysis.
Advancing knowledge and analytic frameworks in an advocacy context.	Using a bottom-up, community-based process that directly addressed disagreement and mistrust.	Focusing efforts on deliberating, "nudging," and framing.
Rebuilding relationships to move equity forward.	Being responsive to political support for action.	Working on a narrow "first world" problem instead of pressing social and environmental issues.

Stores, Chapter 11; and Mixed–Use Project Specific Plan, Chapter 12). Even in these cases, implementation is not separated from plan–making, as the fresh produce case involves program design and the specific plan case involves an entitlement decision that required a change in the comprehensive plan.

Overall, the cases explain planning episodes that are focused on movement from an undesirable present to a better future. They also include significant elements of issue framing, educating stakeholders, and empowering those often disregarded in mainstream planning. Wise navigation of stakeholder and institutional dynamics was important in all cases.

Table 13.5 Practical Judgments in Implementation-Focused Efforts

Fresh Produce in Inner-City Corner Stores, Detroit, Michigan	Mixed-Use Project Specific Plan, Hawthorne, California
Navigating the planning episode step by step rather than seeking to implement a predefined work plan.	Accepting a limited, downstream role in a fragmented process.
Choosing to address a part of the overall problem in focused and limited ways.	Developing a politically honed analysis rather than recommending the ideal solution.
Extending the familiar to develop innovations.	Limiting professional recommendations to parking, ignoring land use compatibility issues.

Planning Takeaways

Each author reflected on their case in terms of broader takeaways for planning, building from the case but also drawing on their wider experience. Consider these points as their "fireside chat" items for planning professionals. Tables 13.6 summarizes those takeaways with the same grouping of cases.

The planning takeaways shown on Table 13.6 emphasize the opportunistic nature of planning action. While regulations and work plans often define the procedural steps to be taken, strategic decisions lie in how to comply with regulations, in planning the episode and in conducting oneself as a professional. The case authors emphasize opportunities for, and the necessity of, building broad support for plan implementation.

These planning takeaways support Hopkins's (2001) notion of planning as paddling a canoe in a moving stream. Planners need to understand the complex flow of stakeholder motivations and determine how to affect them or combine them, change direction, and create reform. We can paddle against the stream but must do so strategically. The case authors employed many abilities and methods beyond technical analysis: cultural competence, emotional intelligence, experimentation, interpretation, moral outrage, narrative, and political and community savvy.

Most experienced planners have their own planning practice takeaways. It is good practice to ask supervisors and other seasoned planners about these questions. In fact, asking about takeaways is an excellent way to initiate a mentoring relationship. As an example, Box 13.1 provides Patrick Siegman's takeaways for consulting practice. Siegman is the transportation planning consultant who wrote commentaries in Chapter 10.

Table 13.6 Planning Takeaways

Type of Case	Title	Takeaways for Practice
Vision and plan-making	Climate Action Plan (Chapter 6)	• Seize windows of opportunity, as change-making is an opportunistic endeavor. Act, even though your effort is insufficient to solve the entire problem. • Create grassroots support, co-benefits, and institutional change to support durable, long-term reform. • Advocate for technical rationality as resistance to "something for everyone" plans.
	Planning for Resilience (Chapter 7)	• Respect and develop the capacities required in order for planning participants to engage in good faith and with open minds and hearts. • Engage in collaboration that is sensitive to the capacity of community hosts, and avoid harm before other objectives. • Develop capabilities for "ground truthing" and simple analytic methods because advanced data and methodological tools are not always available.
Planning–implementation hybrids	Inclusionary Housing Policy (Chapter 8)	• Generate disaggregated analyses and modeling reform to support equity planning. • Focus analysis on trade-offs, and differential benefits and burdens, to bring equity issues to the forefront. • Recognize that change is iterative, political work.
	Form-Based Code (Chapter 9)	• Ground participation in community members' experience of form and place. • Use the tangible nature of implementation tools like zoning to engage questions about vision. • Build a multifaceted base of political, administrative, and community support for reform.
	Parking Management Deliberation (Chapter 10)	• Understand the dynamics of consultant–agency interactions in the process of change. • Discern the opportunities and limits of technical rationality, and use talk processes for "wicked" problems. • Attend to localized problems as a way of helping communities solve bigger issues.

(Continued)

Table 13.6 (Continued)

Type of Case	Title	Takeaways for Practice
Implementation-focused efforts	Fresh Produce in Inner-City Corner Stores (Chapter 11)	• Decipher context and develop responsive planning processes. • Develop deliberative group processes. • Incorporate reflective processes in the midst of planning efforts.
	Mixed-Use Specific Plan (Chapter 12)	• Recognize the ways that a planning effort exists in an ecosystem of plans and intentions. • Reconsider traditional forms of land use compatibility regulation, shifting from a hands-off post-approval approach to developing and enforcing mitigation agreements that run with land. • Reform planning processes that privilege NIMBY sentiments; use mutual gain negotiation techniques to solve controversies.

Box 13.1 A Planning Consultant's Practice Takeaways
Patrick Siegman, Patrick Siegman and Associates

Here are a few of my takeaways from a career in transportation consulting.

1. *Consulting is a good fit for restless souls.* Consulting is an opportunity to visit a community, listen and learn, offer ideas, help build a consensus, and prepare a plan to help a community reach its goals. If your skills and values are a good fit for a community, you can seek repeat engagements. If not, you can move on rather than waiting for a department head to retire or a new council to be elected, as a city's career planners often must do.

2. *Planners should prepare a plan that they genuinely believe has the best chance of achieving the community's stated goals, even if the community is divided.* Where there's significant division, the planner's job is often to prepare a plan that puts the core policy question(s) to the people's elected representatives. "Do you really want to see these particular outcomes in your community? If so, here's what we think is needed to achieve it." Then it is up to elected officials and voters to decide. Avoid "playing it safe" by preparing timid plans that will do little to achieve the community's stated big picture goals.

3. *Don't confuse a process that seems to make most participants happy with actual results.* Drafting a parking plan that restricts housing for people, while requiring housing for cars, may win majority support from local voters.

Box 13.1 (continued)

Maintaining exclusionary single-family zoning (which drives up rents by banning low-cost housing types) may make existing homeowners happy. Using parking regulations to chase away people living in RVs may win local votes. But coldhearted local policies often collide with compassionate federal, state, and regional laws. In my state of California, planners in cities that aim to exclude people often spend their days fighting lawsuits. While planners and lawyers bicker, homelessness grows. So, ask yourself: If your cheerful participatory process results in an exclusionary plan, what have you really achieved? Focus your career on achieving *actual* results. Are rents and home prices readily affordable to regular people? Has homelessness declined?

4. *Propose plans that solve problems that communities may be reluctant to confront and/or don't yet see coming.* In many communities, for example, voters want relief from rising rents and want homelessness addressed, but they also want multifamily housing built somewhere else. In response, state legislatures are passing laws that force every city to allow the construction of more housing. Planners can help cities anticipate trends like these, even if they are crafting a plan that appears unrelated. A curb parking management plan may let fourplexes spring up in (formerly exclusionary) single-family zones, without teeth gnashing over on-street parking shortages.

5. *Sometimes, planners need to let a plan's critics take ownership.* Critics may reject your proposed plan. If the critics are right, their alternative strategies will succeed. If they are wrong, the voters may eventually throw them out. As planners, we have a responsibility to offer honest, thoughtful, evidence-based advice about how we believe a plan will affect a place. But in a democracy, we planners are advisers, not rulers. Ultimately, voters and their representatives decide – and then they get to live with the results.

Implications for Planning Education, Professional Development, and Mentoring

The cases provide a window into practice that has implications for planning education, professional development, and mentoring, adding to other recent case compilations (Lincoln Land Institute n.d., Krumholz and Wertheim Hexter 2018). This section suggests what the planning profession should ask of educational programs, professional organizations, and mentors to support reflective practice.

Planning Education

Returning to Fischler's (2012, 314) point that reflection is "at once popular but marginal," what should planning students expect to learn about reflection in their planning education? Fischler reviews journal articles and finds that Schön's work is frequently mentioned but rarely debated, and that the ideas of reflection are understudied.

Edwards and Bates's (2011) review of the core curriculum in planning programs finds increased interest in planning practice but that the categories of curriculum components studied are primarily knowledge or skill-focused. It seems that "ethics" is a label used to cover a vast range of practice issues, including reflection and many other issues. There is some attention to case-based teaching in planning education, but less than other professional disciplines such as business or law.

Reflection can be taught and practiced in the commonly required capstone workshop or studio. It can occur in internship assignments *if* there is a formal requirement for it. Some programs, such as Cal Poly Pomona's, have professional practice courses that require reflection, but many programs do not. Of course, syllabi may not articulate reflection activities that are a course component or part of the instructor's teaching strategy. Even so, it does not appear to be a significant emphasis. Rather, planning students are expected to figure out reflection on their own.

The profession should ask for broader and deliberate forms of reflection in planning curricula, more than typical practices of asking for reflective papers that comment on a reading or a lecture. Students benefit when asked to reflect on planning *action*, such as team dynamics within a group project, a studio class with stakeholders and decision-makers, or collaborative interactions with allied disciplines. Box 13.2 (next page) provides an example of a course sequence from the University of Cincinnati that creates such opportunities.

Another area where reflection can be advanced is among the planning specialties found within a planning school. Commonly, after completing core courses, students split into groupings of specialists such as spatial analysis, designers, environmental planners, or equity planners. They develop silos in school that continue through practice, even though specialties are highly interrelated.

The academia–practice gap discussed in earlier chapters is complicit in the lack of reflection. In the early days of the profession, the field was less specialized and there were more practitioner–scholars. As academia and practice have specialized, planners commonly identify with a narrow specialty, presenting fewer circumstances that challenge practices and perceptions in ways that require reflection. Practitioners who teach in those programs as adjuncts often do not participate in core curriculum or pedagogy discussions.

Box 13.2 Fostering Reflection in a Course Cluster at the University of Cincinnati

Chris Auffrey, Professor, and Danilo Palazzo, Director and Professor, School of Planning, College of Design, Architecture, Art, and Planning, University of Cincinnati

The Bachelor of Urban Planning (BUP) program in the School of Planning at the University of Cincinnati (UC) is steeped in professional practice. This reflects the long history and importance of the UC co-operative education (Co-op) program and also highlights the school's commitment to engaging communities, local officials, civil society, and other stakeholders. Such engagement is instrumental to the educational success of the BUP's planning and urban design studios. Faculty seek to connect students' studio and classroom experience with professional practice to prepare them for Co-op placements and help students build on their Co-op experience in subsequent courses.

As part of the BUP's year-round, on-campus–off-campus courses–Co-op rotation, fourth-year BUP students spend a summer semester on-campus taking classes. They take an advanced planning studio, Planning Theory and Ethics, Finance and Budgeting, and Urban Planning Law, plus an elective. In 2015, the school integrated all four courses with respect to place, time and topic, scheduling them back-to-back over a compressed seven-week semester instead of the usual fourteen. The goal was to create an educational environment where theoretical, ethical, legal, and financial concepts of planning would be concurrently explored and applied to the real urban problems confronted in a client-based studio.

To this end, we employed flexible scheduling so that material was covered when relevant to the planning issues encountered. For example, for the Planning Theory and Ethics course, materials were applied to specific issues arising in the studio: what information was being considered, how is was being analyzed, and who was making decisions. Studio reviews included faculty from all the summer courses as well as clients (usually communities or redevelopment entities). Final projects explicitly required students to include issues from all the courses.

The response from students and faculty has been positive. Students feel they gained a better understanding of the non-studio course material because they are applied to real-world problems in the context of the studio. In addition, because prior Co-op experience is explicitly incorporated onto coursework, students better appreciate that Co-op is about both learning and preparing to learn. One representative student comment from a Planning Theory and Ethics course evaluation said, "This class was absolutely applicable to our current studio and work outside of class, which made learning easier and much more enjoyable."

Action-research studios in academic planning programs generate reflection opportunities because they create quandaries in which a uni-theory or rule-bound approach usually doesn't work. Action *requires* the reflective synthesis and integration across planning specialties, and the linking of knowledge to action. Here are some ideas for studios:

- Community action-research and client-based studios that explicitly integrate procedural and substantive theories of planning, such as providing core course content in studios, as discussed in Box 13.2.
- Reflection activities that explore differences in the assumptions and methods of planning specialties to help planners work across different bases of thinking and action.
- Interdisciplinary studios that require reflection across disciplines such as architecture, landscape architecture, civil engineering, climate science, or public health.
- Critical evaluation of how new technologies support or threaten broader planning ends, addressing geospatial statistics, big data, and other methods.
- Coursework that teaches and encourages practices of reflection. Professional practice courses can kickstart reflection habits.
- Practitioner–scholar dialogues that promote reflection, such as Cal Poly Pomona's Dale Prize in the Department of Urban and Regional Planning.

The Planning Accreditation Board (PAB) accredits professional planning programs in North America and establishes accreditation standards and criteria to which programs must respond (PAB n.d.). Section 4 of the criteria outlines required knowledge, skills, and values; areas of specialization and electives; instructional delivery and scheduling; facilities; and information and technology. Reflection is not mentioned directly. Professional ethics is mentioned, but as providing *knowledge* about ethics rather than developing students' capacity for conducting reflective, ethical reasoning. Given the importance of reflection in effective practice, the PAB may wish to consider more explicit requirements.

Professional Organizations

Professional planning organizations such as the American Planning Association (APA) offer support activities including publications, conferences, webinars, and the like. They tend to emphasize knowledge and technical skill acquisition, and elevating awareness of the profession, reflecting an impetus to present an outward face of competence and technical expertise.

Organizations like APA must promote the profession in public policy and in relation to competing professions, but that creates an inherent conflict with regard to reflection. Although reflection improves practice, it might also be seen to harm the public face of professions if it reveals uncertainty or a conflict over methods. APA conferences, for example, tend to celebrate success rather than reflect on why things worked or did not work; presentations tend toward manifestos of best practice certainty. There is a disinclination to directly address the lack of a unifying paradigm or to expose planning failures for the sake of learning and reflection.

Interpersonal interactions at conferences mirror this phenomenon. Attendee conversations tend to be with like-minded planners at sessions or meetings of subject-area interest groups. Talking with those having similar subject matter interests, ways of looking at the world, and professional practices does not challenge a planner's fundamental assumptions and axioms. We tend to associate with people who read context in the same way they do and miss out on learning about a different way of understanding a situation. The wide range of planning responses to a given opportunity are more evident when specialists interact, such as when GIS modelers share tips with nonprofit housing developers.

While it is natural to associate with a planning "tribe," reflection benefits are enhanced by going outside that group and looking back in from a different perspective. This is a matter of personal initiative, but it can be encouraged by conference sessions and informal activities built around reflection. For example, local government planners could organize sessions that reflect on the regional transportation consequences of local land use decisions and the tensions between local and regional interests.

There are many opportunities for increasing reflection in the activities of professional organizations. The APA already creates panels that encourage academics to present at their conferences to encourage theory/practice reflection, and it commissions task forces to examine academic–practice connections. The APA's Career Center activities promote reflection on career direction and management roles. Perhaps the best existing conference activities for reflection are ethics sessions that pose scenarios and reveal the variety of valid responses with audience involvement. The following ideas can extend reflection at professional conferences:

• Workshops built around practice reflection using tools such as reflective writing, creative writing, drama, or other art forms, and online reflection forums.

- Sessions that provide opportunities to mourn losses or mistakes in professional practice in a safe environment, and self-care activities that process emotional aspects of planning practice.
- Deliberative forms of learning (e.g., interactive, panel discussion, and storytelling sessions) rather than "sage on the stage" presentations.
- Cross-specialization panel discussions, within planning and with related professions such as architecture, landscape architecture, public administration, real estate development, public health, and law.
- Panels and workshops featuring case studies that use a common reflective framework.

Mentoring

Mentoring is a traditional way that planners reflect on practice (Willson 2018). In order for mentoring to best support reflection, though, dialogues must go beyond mentees complaining and mentors providing too much advice or to many "war stories." Mentoring can support reflection in a number of ways:

- Dialogues that seek a "police report" version of a planning issue a mentee is dealing with (i.e., just the facts, before interpretation). Establishing the facts of what happened, separate from emotional reactions, improves the insights derived from reflection.
- Queries using elements of planner-as-person and context interpretation as the mentee discusses a planning episode.
- Queries about elements of logic and emotion, and convention and invention to examine the efficacy of the approaches used, search for blind spots, and identify new opportunities.
- Mentoring-by-doing activities in which mentor and mentee complete a task together in ways that lead to reflection, such as running a community meeting.
- Interaction with professionals in different subfields of planning, or different professional fields, that provide a perspective that encourages reflection on the mentee's knowledge, skills, and perspectives.

Mentoring can generate a reflective renaissance for the mentor as well, providing meaning and insights into their own career goals and strategies. In Box 13.3 (next page), Tad Widby offers his remembrance of lessons learned from an inspiring public sector supervisor. This example shows that mentor–mentee relationships are often not formal but occur organically in work situations.

Box 13.3 Lessons Learned About the Process of Change
Tad Widby, Retired Planner, formerly with WSP and Parsons Brinkerhoff

Planners often arrive at their first job brimming with the enthusiasm to solve urban or regional problems. That enthusiasm can easily run headlong into complex processes, competing priorities, or disinterested elected officials. And that can lead to the frustration that may send that individual to find a new job. It is healthy to enter that first new job with an understanding of what it takes to get a public policy decision made and what has led to past decisions.

That leads me to reflect on the best director I've had in a planning agency, the late Ray Remy. He encouraged open-minded approaches to large problems but also cautioned that we needed to understand the views, practices, and processes we would encounter. It is well and good, for example, to find ways to meet transit needs and improve air quality, generally accepted goals. However, a set of great ideas is no match for elected officials who don't see the world the same way.

Remy advised to never overestimate the intelligence of an elected official. He explained that many were elected on important, small, local issues (akin to leash laws) and were tasked with tackling complex regional issues. He advised us to make issues understandable and solutions simple, all the while demonstrating why the approach and solutions were in the interests of local governments.

You may feel you are there to bring your insight and enthusiasm to solving big problems. However, if you lead with a sense of "having the answer" you may find that decision-makers are either not ready for that answer or simply don't think things are all that bad.

The *Los Angeles Times* obituary for Remy focused, in part, on his time as deputy mayor to Tom Bradley. It said:

> Remy, known for having an analytical mind, preferred to lay out the pros and cons of a particular position to Bradley, rather than to give his opinion. He once told a reporter that he was a low-profile operator by choice because he could achieve more by staying out of the limelight. He was known as the "issues" man among political insiders for his insight on transportation, water, economic development and other topics.
>
> *(Smith 2019)*

Coming up with a plan is relatively easy. Every citizen has an idea of what should be done for traffic, housing, droughts, and more. What besides education makes a planner different? Certainly, education and exploration of complex issues makes a planner different. However, if that planner does not understand and respect what it will take to have actions taken, frustration will ensue.

Planners should understand complex agency responsibilities and relationships. They should recognize that elected or appointed officials will not see the world as they do – their experiences, beliefs, and motivations are different from yours. If

Box 13.3 (continued)

you can put yourself in their position and develop an understanding of how they see their responsibility, you have the opportunity to create successful outcomes. Sometimes, the best approach is to take more time to develop the issues and solutions. Knowing whether and when to act is just as important as knowing what actions are worthwhile.

And Now to You: There's No One Size Fits All

The case studies provide you with the experience of a series of planning episodes without having gone through them. Becoming interested in case studies provides practical planning wisdom beyond your direct experiences. There is a resurgence in case studies in planning, and more examples are becoming available (Lincoln Land Institute n.d., Krumholz and Wertheim Hexter 2018). One of the best ways to reflect on your practice, of course, is to write your own case, as a factual account or as another form of literature such as a short story or poem.

The case studies offer a window into the variety of planning types. Schön used metaphor to compare professional situations on a "high ground" where research and technique are straightforwardly applied, with "swampy lowlands where situations are confusing 'messes' incapable of technical solution" (Schön 1983, 42). The cases show plenty of swampy situations, but you should note that case authors found theory, technique, best practice, and many other tools were of utility in those situations. They also found ways of reducing blindnesses of various sorts and improving reason. Next, Chapter 14 offers methods to incorporate reflection into regular planning practice, along with question prompts that can get you started.

Discussion Questions

1. Among the cases provided, which one most appealed to you as a form of practice? Why? Do you want to move your career in that direction? Which one did not appeal to you? Why?
2. Given the practice diversity represented in the cases, how would you explain planning to someone who has no exposure to it?
3. Select two cases that appealed to you. Imagine that the two planners who wrote them cases meet in a coffee shop. What would their conversation be like? About what might they agree? About what might they disagree?

4. Find a case study published elsewhere. Review it from the point of view of the Figure 5.2 framework (see Chapter 5). Does the case study provide enough information for you to understand the planner's motivations, their understanding of context, and the practical judgments they made during the planning episode? How can cases be made more useful?

References

Edwards, Mary M. and Lisa K. Bates. 2011. "Planning's Core Curriculum: Knowledge, Practice and Implementation." *Journal of Planning Education and Research*, 31(2): 172–183. doi: 10.1177.0739456X11398043.

Fischler, Raphaël. 2012. "Reflective Practice." In: *Planning Ideas that Matter*, edited by Bishwapriya Sanyal, Lawrence J. Vale, and Christina D. Rosan. Cambridge, MA: MIT Press, 313-332.

Hopkins, Lewis. 2001. *Urban Development: The Logic of Making Plans*. Washington, DC: Island Press.

Krumholz, N. and K. Wertheim Hexter. 2018. *Advancing Equity Planning Now*. Cornell, NY: Cornell University Press.

Lincoln Institute of Land Policy. n.d. "Lincoln Institute of Land Policy Catalog of On-Line Courses and Case Studies." Accessed February 23, 2020 at https://lincoln inst.catalog.insgtructure.com.

Planning Accreditation Board. n.d. "2017 Accreditation Standards." Accessed February 23, 2020 at https://www.planningaccreditationboard.org/index.php?s= file_download&id=500.

Schön, Donald. 1983. *The Reflective Practitioner: How Professionals Think in Action*. New York: Basic Books.

Smith, Dakota. 2019. "Ray Remy, Top Aid to Mayor Tom Bradley and Guiding Force at L.A. City Hall, Dies at 82." *Los Angeles Times*. Accessed April 23, 2020 at https://www.latimes.com/california/story/2019-12-24/ray-remy-obituary-los-a ngeles-mayor-tom-bradley-aide.

Willson, Richard. 2018. *A Guide for the Idealist: Launching and Navigating Your Planning Career*. New York: Routledge.

Chapter 14

Methods and Prompts for Reflection

It is one thing to understand the merits of reflection and another to incorporate it into professional practice. This chapter offers methods and prompts for accomplishing that, organized around the framework elements described in Chapters 3 through 5. In recommending professional reflection, I take encouragement from Terry Eagleton (2003), who argues that "reflecting critically on our situation is part of our situation. It is a feature of the peculiar way we belong to the world. It is not some impossible light-in-the-refrigerator attempt to scrutinize ourselves when we are not there" (60).

The case studies presented in Chapters 6 through 12 provide examples of reflection in hindsight. The passage of time provides a measure of intellectual and emotional distance as well as a chance to consider outcomes over time. This reflection–on–action is an essential professional responsibility and is called for in ethical codes such as those of the American Institute of Certified Planners. As noted, there is a solitary aspect to reflection, but planners should triangulate their reflections with others, learn from them, and obtain a broader view through engagement. Readers who agree with the merits of reflection-on-action might ask: How then do I make wise practical judgments in the moment (reflection–in–action)?

Types of Reflection

This chapter emphasizes reflection-in-action, or thinking about what you are doing and why, *while* you are doing it. But first, some comments on reflection-on-action.

Reflection-on-Action

The cases provide insights that planners can use to improve practical judgments and apply lessons learned. Reflection-on-action provides a feedback loop to current practice. We don't reflect for its own sake, usually, and reflection should not be narcissistic, self-justifying, or self-pitying. It should be appropriately critical of the context in which we plan, ourselves, and our practical judgments. Argyris and Schön's (1974) conception of single- and double-loop learning is useful here. Single-loop learning is a form of error correction, learning from experience, in which the reasons for the error and underlying factors are not questioned. One applies lessons learned from what worked, or didn't work, to the next planning assignment. Double-loop learning asks critical *why* questions about an organization's norms, policies, or objectives as well as one's own motivations, values, habits, or biases. Box 14.1 (next page) provides an example for a current planning setting.

The scenarios offered in Box 14.1 (next page) shows how reflection-on-action may change how a planner acts in interactions with constituents in the future (reflection-in-action). As another example, a planner preparing a new plan may draw on reflection-on-action insights in writing a scope of work and then employ reflection-in-action in making strategic choices during the planning episode. While planners draw on reflection-on-action to refine their practices, the real-time nature of reflection-in-action involves continual adjustments, as described next and shown in many of the cases. Reflection-in-action, done on the fly, is challenging because it does not offer the benefit of reflective distance or time, or the ability to fully understand long-term consequences of practical judgments.

Reflection-in-Action

A good example of reflection-in-action is provided in Chapter 11, in which Pothukuchi adjusted the design of the Detroit Fresh healthy produce program as it was being implemented in response to learning about the community's

Box 14.1 Single- and Double-Loop Learning

Chapter 5 includes a scenario in which a planner responded to a variance request at a city hall zoning counter. That scenario was a positive one in which the planner employed logic, convention, and emotion in resolving the resident's concern (Figure 5.3, Chapter 5). This box considers a scenario that turns out badly – the resident responds in an angry manner upon learning that the zoning code does not permit their proposal. The planner feels that the code is somewhat arbitrary, raising costs and creating time delays without much public benefit. Seeking to be emotionally responsive, the planner empathizes with the resident's frustration, which further emboldens the applicant who broadens their complaint against the city, bureaucrats in general, and demands to see a supervisor. Empathy produced an escalation that resulted in the planner receiving a corrective note on their performance review.

Using reflection on the incident, one takeaway – the single-loop variety – is to never to empathize again. Following that takeaway means that the planner withholds empathy going forward, adopting an emotional disposition of professional distance. Taking the view that their job is to apply the code and inform about procedures, the planner decides to abandon problem-solving with constituents. By showing strong professional boundaries, it is thought, future applicants will be dissuaded from emotional attacks. The weakness of that approach is that withholding empathy and help undermines a sense of good will about local government, potentially making *all* planning business more difficult. In addition, emotional empathy may be an effective response to a different applicant on a different day.

Reflection can support double-loop learning, in which the planner considers *why* empathy produced the angry reaction, in very specific terms, and includes broad factors such as the organization's procedures and norms. Why did the applicant respond the way they did when the planner offered empathy? What was the nature and history of the subject, and did any issues of race, gender, or identity contribute to the interaction? How did agency procedures and ways of dealing with constituents contribute to the interaction? Is the zoning code outdated and causing unanticipated consequences? Considering these factors, a planner can decide on their reactions to applicants in real time and with regard to the specifics of the situation rather than have a default, autopilot approach to dealing with the public. That planner may be more likely to recommend helpful changes to agency codes, procedures, and norms.

and corner store owners' reactions and business practices. Similarly, Bates's Chapter 8 inclusionary zoning housing requirement case in Portland reveals a practice that altered the balance of technical and political roles in response to opportunities and challenges. All the cases report some level of midcourse adjustments, showing the merits of reflection-in-action.

Two dimensions shape the demand for reflection-in-action: the immediacy of the need for practical judgments and the planner's level of mastery. Regarding immediacy, a consultant writing a scope of work proposal has weeks to evaluate different approaches, draw on past experience, and engage in dialogues with subconsultants. A planner facing a deadline for writing multiple staff reports has days or weeks to ponder a recommendation, consult with colleagues, and "sleep on it." At the other extreme, however, a planner facing tough questioning by an elected official must respond in the moment. Similarly, a community organizer must decide in real-time how to respond to a person disrupting civil discourse in a community meeting. Regarding level of mastery, a seasoned planner can draw upon a storehouse of responses based on reflection-on-action. Junior planners, lacking such experience, face greater challenges in reflecting-in-action. This is somewhat counteracted by the nature of their work assignments because procedures and their more specific assignments reduce the demand for reflection. Less-experienced planners may choose more procedural- and analytically based styles of practice, relying on academic coursework, precedent, supervisor guidance, and agency procedures.

Reflection and Intuition

Demand for near-instantaneous practical judgment does not offer time for traditional reflection processes. In those cases, planners employ a variety of processes. For example, they may use instinct, relying on innate characteristics such as a fight-or-flight reaction to an aggressive challenge in a public meeting. They also may draw on habits, developed over years of practice, such as addressing a variance request by conducting a windshield survey of a neighborhood rather than walking the neighborhood and talking with residents.

Many planners say they rely on intuition, which is choosing interpretation or action in ways that are not accessible through senses or rational calculation. Intuition may build on unarticulated moral principles, experiences, or inferences. Dreyfus and Dreyfus (1986) argue that "hunches and intuitions, and even systematic illusions, are the very core of expert decision making" (100). They believe that intuition is fostered with reflection, as one builds a skill.

The nature of the practical judgment shapes the degree of reflection-on-action. Montero (2016, 38) argues the following:

For experts, when all is going well, optimal or near optimal performance frequently employs some of the following conscious mental processes: self-reflective thinking, planning, predicting, deliberation, attention to or monitoring of their actions, conceptualizing their actions, control, trying, effort, having a sense of self, and acting for a reason.

Montero's ideas ring true with my practice: that is why it is so difficult for practitioners to explain their practical judgments. Schön called the process that professionals use in action *theory-in-use*, but that label doesn't do justice to the multiple dimensions noted by Montero. My experience of practice is that planning has a significant creative dimension, including physical design, of course, but also visioning, mutual gain negotiation, process-design, problem-solving, and community engagement. Accepting this proposition means that we can learn from other creative fields. For example, Pohjannoro (2016) studied music composers' intuitive and reflective thinking in composition: "within *intuitive* compositional acts, imagination changed into experimentation and incubation into restructuring, whereas within *reflective* compositional acts, rule-based reasoning changed into contemplating alternatives" (207, italics added). Both are present for music composition and planning. Pohjannoro describes a device called *rational intuition*, which has the following elements: "(i) The guidance of a goal-driven cue … as a determinant and motivational energy; (ii) the selection of intuitive and reflective compositional acts to match the situation; (iii) an expert ability to learn implicitly; and (iv) resilience to abeyance" (207).

Reflection-in-action does not offer the time to consider all elements in the Figure 5.2 framework (see Chapter 5), yet specific elements are of value in the moment. A planner may consider planner-as-person elements such as their core values, and context elements such as the political dynamics of decision-making. They may realize, for example, that logical analysis is overwhelming a neglected dimension of emotion, or that appeals to convention are blocking invention. Such realizations can shape thought, feelings, and action in the moment.

On Doers and Thinkers

Nobody reflects unless they see value in it. As discussed in Chapter 3, people with a wide variety of personality types become planners. Across these types, some are predisposed to reflection and others to action, a basic distinction between "thinkers" and "doers." As well, subfields of planning and different job types may attract particular personality types, each with varying propensities to reflect. For example, a colleague pointed out the following: "Planners who focus on advocacy have a harder time being reflective. Experiences tend to harden views. Planners who see their role as helping to inform good decision-making can build their reflective capability by being engaged with decision-makers and advocates. The two roles tend to attract people with different outlooks" (Tad Widby, personal email communication, December 18, 2019). Yet effective doers reflect on the fly – it just may not be apparent.

Even for those interested in reflection, the pressures of practice can make it seem like a luxury. A common conception is that reflection is something that a tenured professor has time to do, not a planner who is juggling assignments, putting out "fires," whittling down a backlog of variance applications, managing personnel, and navigating local politics. In response to this valid challenge, this chapter discusses easy and quick ways to incorporate reflection into practice.

In some instances, the desired goal or *end* of a planning effort may seem obvious and consensual, and not requiring reflection. The *means* to achieve the end may seem similarly clear. If ends and means are clear, then "getting on with it" is the highest priority. While there are instances where this is true, there is a danger that something is being overlooked when things seem obvious. Planners of urban freeway systems felt those projects represented progress in the public interest. Slum clearance redevelopers believed they were on the right track. Designers of single-family neighborhoods thought curvilinear street design was a good idea but that made bus service difficult. In each case, reflection might have improved outcomes by questioning who wins and who loses, recognizing uncertainty, warning of unanticipated consequences, and critically examining whether the planning process or its goals have bias. Reflection practices examine long-term consequences of alternative approaches, consider alternative futures, and engage ethical dilemmas.

Routine activities and habitual practice require reflection because built-in biases, structural distortions, or unrecognized power imbalances operate behind the scenes. An example of this is unreflective use of standards. In my consulting practice, for example, a 10 spaces per 1,000 square feet parking requirement for restaurants often applies in traditional downtowns, which prohibits entrepreneurs from opening restaurants in historic buildings that lack off-street parking. For many planners, this is "good practice" found in parking generation manuals and other city codes. The consequence of reflecting on the requirement is discovering that it is unknowingly altering the mix of uses in a business district in ways that harm economic development potential, business opportunities, and land use efficiency. This problem may disproportionately affect people of color who may live in older neighborhoods built before parking requirements.

Surprises, failures, resource depletion, organizational change, and any number of disruptions can crack procedural routines and let some light in. A planner who is not normally inclined to reflect may well encounter circumstances that stimulate it, or even require it. As well, the distinction between thinkers and doers may be exaggerated. Box 14.2 provides a commentary on reflective practice by Raphaël Fischler, who is dean of the College of Environmental Design at the Université de Montréal and who wrote his master's thesis under Donald Schön. As a dean, he is a doer, yet the commentary shows how reflection and the demand for action are intertwined.

Box 14.2 Disciplinary and Institutional Factors in Reflective Practice

Raphaël Fischler, Dean, College of Environmental Design, Université de Montréal

The manifesto of the College of Environmental Design speaks of the development among students of human qualities such as humility, empathy, and respect.[1] These qualities are those of the reflective practitioner, a professional who knows the limitations of his or her knowledge and skills and who enters into a true dialogue with others. Although reflective practice is largely a means of improving professional effectiveness, it is also an expression of professional identity, a social and even emotional attitude toward behavior and interaction. It takes humility to accept one's weaknesses or question one's assumptions, empathy with others to recognize their own reflection-in-action, and respect for individuals and institutions to debate values and goals openly.

Not all professionals display these attitudes; some are more humble, others more assertive. At the risk of dealing in stereotypes, one may even say that not all *professions* exhibit the same propensity toward humility and empathy. It is no surprise that the work of Donald Schön has received the highest level of attention in the so-called helping professions of nursing, social work, and teaching, where women constitute a large majority of practitioners. Even in the domain of environmental design, it looks like urban planners, who see their work as eminently dialogical and collaborative, are more prone to engage with Schön's work than architects, where individual creativity is highly valued and a strong ego is not frowned upon. In fields such as business, learning practitioners are often viewed as being in pursuit of excellence and their practice is more likely to be called "deliberate" than "deliberative."

Institutional culture, too, affects the reflexivity one brings to one's work. The university and college where I became dean in 2018 have a culture that is both very egalitarian and rather conflictual: all members of the university community (from students and clerical employees to senior officers) claim to have equal say in decision-making and have, over time, created institutional arrangements and regulations in which they can exercise some power. In this context, deans have little formal authority and do not enjoy a great deal of informal authority either. This can make for a humbling experience that is highly conducive to reflective practice. Also beneficial to reflective practice are the facts that this was my first position as dean and that I was hired from another university with a very different institutional culture. I therefore faced a steep learning curve on my arrival. Two things helped my reflection-on-action: access to a professional coach in my first year and, especially, a relation of trust with my direct collaborators (associate deans and administrators), from which I could seek and receive honest feedback on my behavior and honest answers to my questions. Reflection does not have to occur in isolation; having interlocutors to reflect on one's practice is a great plus.

Fortunately, a wide variety of reflection practices are available to enable planners to match them to their own tendencies and preferences. Whatever the inclination and commitment to reflection, adding *some* level of reflection improves practice. Accordingly, the methods discussed as follows support planners finding the best ways to engage in critical reflection in daily practice, emphasizing ways that do not require a six-month retreat on the top of a mountain.

I ask myself why I have such an interest in reflection. The simple answer is that I have benefited from it in my planning practice. I have become a more responsive and effective planner as I have incorporated reflection-on-action and implemented reflection-in-action. In looking deeper, I find many other influences that lead me in this direction, as shared in Box 14.3 (next page).

Information for "Looking-Inward" Reflection

Looking inward directly supports planner-as-person reflection, but it is also useful in understanding context and making choices during the planning episode. It can occur through purposeful activity, such as keeping a professional reflection diary. Many indirect practices are also available, such as hiking, meditation, or therapy, and group activities such as those focused on professional development. These activities have many effects, ranging from slowing down thought to allow insight, to discovering new frames for interpreting planning episodes, to self-knowledge and healing from disappointment.

Box 14.3 Influences on Inclination to Reflect

As the main body of the text indicates, I recommend reflective practice because it has made me a more effective planner. Going further, however, I identified many factors from my personal life that consistently point to an inclination to reflection. The list that follows explains my perspective:

- Attraction to pragmatist literature in planning theory in works such as Hoch's 2019 analysis of practical judgments in planning practice.
- Literature on reflection practice, in planning and in other professions – works such as Schön's (1983) *Reflective Practitioner* and Bolton and Delderfield's (2018) *Reflective Practice: Writing and Professional Development.*
- The learn-by-doing pedagogy at my university, Cal Poly Pomona, which is influenced by Dewey (1938).
- Existentialist philosophy and its emphasis on the individual understanding oneself in the here and now without the support of dogma – works such as Marino's (2018) *Existentialist Survival Guide,* which takes inspiration from Kierkegaard.
- My religious choice and practice, which seeks virtue, and an approach to religious texts that is interpretive and anti-dogmatic, as exemplified by Zornberg (2009).

I have discussed many of the personal themes in previous chapters. I introduced Myers-Briggs personality types in Chapter 3 but did not indicate my "type," which is INFJ. This grouping describes a tendency toward introversion, favoring intuition over facts, making decisions based on feeling and values, and a slight leaning to judging, preferring structure and order. Of the 16 personality type combinations in the Myers-Briggs system, this type is strongly aligned with reflection.

Planners' types are widely distributed across the spectrum. For example, a planner oriented toward extroversion (versus introversion), observing (versus intuition), thinking (versus feeling), and perceiving (versus judging) may be less inclined to reflect. Any group of planners will have a range of inclinations toward reflection, although certain types may cluster around different planning job categories. My assertion is that planners benefit if they consider the connections between their personality type and their practice approach. It was striking for me to learn that all the aforementioned elements pointed in the direction of reflection.

Looking inward can help resolve interpersonal issues, ethical questions, and career decisions. For instance, it can help a planner understand if their learning style clashes with a collaborator who has a different one, and therefore moving the issue from personality conflict toward understanding. Regarding ethical considerations, looking inward helps a planner articulate and draw on their personal values to inform practice decisions. It also informs the resolution of clashes between personal and professional ethics, or competing ethical mandates, such as serving both scientific understanding and democratic practices (Howe and Kaufman 1979).

There is another level of reflection that engages deeper urgings about purpose and strategy. I use the word soul to represent these deeper urgings, conceiving it as animating principles that exist within a person, often beyond the grasp of direct language comprehension. This is relevant to planning because many people are drawn to it based on a deep sense of purpose. As discussed in Chapter 3, planning work addresses key elements of personal purpose such as love, justice, truth, and beauty.

As Fischler says in Box 14.2, reflection is especially powerful if done collectively with colleagues, advisers, trusted peers, and mentors. Discussions with colleagues from other professions help me understand, for example, the motivations and world views of lawyers, public health professionals, architects, and engineers.

Purposeful Activities

Bolton and Delderfield (2018) provide a comprehensive guide to using writing for professional reflection. This can take the form of a professional diary that helps planners process their about practical judgments and enables looking back in hindsight to pinpoint tendencies and improve future decisions. Bolton and Delderfield also describe other forms of reflective writing including fiction, poetry, and autobiography, as well as other arts and action learning/research. Their book includes creative writing prompts to help process feelings about professional practice and/or allows unexpressed aims to emerge. This type of writing is not intended to create a polished narrative but to find one's voice. It is a means to the end of insight; it is a form of inquiry.

Bolton and Delderfield (2018, 136) argue that reflection can achieve:

- Wider view from a distance.
- Close acute observation: vitally active, not passive, process.
- Perception from significant others, e.g., clients.
- Authority over practice.
- A critical challenging attitude to assumptions.
- Fruitful relationships with professional and academic literature.

Writing about one's practice over time builds a reflective practice journal. It is best to use a password-protected file or writing journal kept in a secure location so that the writer is honest. Knowing that someone else might read the journal leads to self-censoring. A secured journal will help the writer avoid both narcissistic public relations pieces and false modesty. Of course, writing is not the only way to learn about planner-as-person. Discussions with a mentor, conversations with a confidant, letter-writing, thinking while hiking, and many other means are available.

Indirect Activities

Indirect practices produce insights that are not intentionally sought out. Artmaking helps a planner realize deeper urgings related to their purposes, whether through creative writing, theater, visual art, music, dance, film, environmental art, or other forms. Furthermore, artmaking in community planning can have transformative effects for communities. For example, James Rojas's PLACE IT! Workshops (2020) use model-building workshops and interactive models to open discourse, identify dreams and ideas, and translate them to physical form.

For me, making visual art contributed to my evolution from a technically-oriented planner to one who sees an artistry in planning practice. My plein air painting hobby, mentioned earlier, places me in a condition of *not-knowing* just as planning practice does. I accept that I don't know how things will turn out and become more aware of internal processes of selectively not noticing or ignoring certain factors (Willson 2015). Also, artmaking yields intuitive insights on planning projects.

Information for "Looking-Outward" Reflection

Reflection requires a reliable base of information. Faulty data, incorrect interpretation, flawed assumptions, self-deception, or inaccurate assessments can lead a planner's reflection astray. Looking outward serves reading context and making practical judgments about the planning process, the content of plans, and choices in navigating the planning episode.

Information for looking-outward reflection includes everything from legal research to the analytic bases for choices made in the planning episode. A planner can take advantage of information sources that include direct experience, informal conversations, interpretive listening, participant observation, traditional research, and online resources ranging from legislative summaries, to videos of city council meetings, to community blogs. Supervisors, colleagues, and mentors can help identify those sources and the elements of context that are most relevant.

Reporters use triangulation to assemble the *story* from many methods and data sources. In not relying on a single source, the story is heard from different points of view. Triangulation for planners means hearing a variety of perspectives and using multiple investigation methods to test assertions about context. Planners benefit when they employ many methods to learn – community discourse, arts interpretation, the work of activists, or finding nonparticipants and seeking their views.

Context Research in Action

There are many active ways to gain information on community context that go beyond census analyses or community workshops. Planners can engage supervisors, professional colleagues, elected officials, and community members in dialogues that deepen and clarify their understandings. The face value of communications is important – no one likes it when someone says, "You said this, but what you really mean is that." But since coded language is often used, planners also need to read between the lines. For example, claims about neighborhood "character" can mean many things – desirable built-form conditions or exclusion based on class, race, ethnicity, or gender identification.

Non-purposeful community activities often generate valuable information about context and the prospects for plan proposals. For me, live painting in the plein air style takes me outdoors in urban places, where I encounter people, built form, and nature. Children often approach and tell me about their own painting efforts, while others share their responses to my painting and tell me what they think about the neighborhood. I learn about public space and the people in my community through this practice. One afternoon, a rear-end car crash happened in front of my painting location, outside the door of a local bar. When the crash occurred, a gaggle of afternoon drinkers came out the front door, commenting on the crash and on my painting. One drinker explained that a recent road diet and bike-lane project on the street had *caused* the crash. Never mind that road diets generally slow traffic and reduce accidents; they saw it differently. They told the story with absolute conviction, as if sharing a truth. As a transportation planner, it was good to know that perception.

Experiments

Planning reflection requires some information that is only knowable when an idea has been implemented. Unstated factors often affect how professionals, community members, and elected officials will react. Even within a planning office, a planner does not necessarily know how their colleagues will respond to them if they adopt a different way of participating in meetings. Regarding context, a planner does not know if the way the stakeholders think about a proposal will differ after it is implemented. Similarly, a planner does not know how well an alternative planning process would work in a community that has a long tradition of mainstream planning.

Experiments are an effective way of producing information about reactions to change – small interventions that produce responses and reactions such as revealing support or opposition to an idea. For example, Brooks (2002) called for experiments as a part of his feedback strategy planning model, which he describes as floating "trial balloons."

Let's consider a planner developing a housing strategy. Interests opposed to workforce housing may stay in the background during a major study. Later, they may emerge as opposition when the plan is up for adoption, when it is too late to redo the study to respond to their concerns. A planner could feel overconfident as the effort is proceeding because of the opposition strategy of waiting until the end. So how can a planner know if this is the case? One idea is to conduct an experiment: propose a pilot workforce housing project involving temporary reuse of an existing building simultaneous with plan preparation. This has three effects. First, a pilot project is easier to sell than a long-term plan committing to such projects. Second, the opposition may decide to reveal themselves in opposing the pilot, fearing "foot in the door" momentum if it proceeds. Third, knowledge of the arguments made against the pilot project can be used to shape the plan to address reasonable objections and defeat unreasonable ones.

Planners can also experiment with dialogue. If a planning manager seeks a non-authoritative role and consensus in staff meetings, for example, absolute consistency to that intention can allow staff bullies to disrupt meetings in aggressive and passive-aggressive methods. Strategically choosing a different way of behaving in meetings can confuse a bully and produce insight into how the group reacts to the different dynamic. Some meeting environments may require a forceful role while in other situations that role would undermine the formation of a team ethos. In previous work, I have described testing small changes in organizational roles as if playing a part in a play, so as to learn from reactions to showing up differently (Willson 2018).

Interpreting Reflection

Once a planner has gained information upon which to reflect, whether personal or from the world around them, reflection requires interpretation. For example, if a planner observes behavior in a public space, reflection based on knowledge of the literature on human behavior can help them interpret how members of the public perceive those spaces and feel about their personal safety. As well, interpreting community narratives can inform about community members' history, hopes, and fears. Similarly, small talk before a department meeting can provide insight into the psychological dimensions of the organization. The production and interpretation of story is a powerful tool for reflection (Sandercock 2003).

Hermeneutics describes the critical task of interpretation and the procedures for doing so. For example, planners use a hermeneutic approach to seek a deeper sense of the situation and identify underlying meanings hidden beneath the surface. While traditionally applied to interpretation of texts, a hermeneutic approach can also be applied broadly to navigating a planning episode.

A planner might reflect on planning context by asking about the "official" story told about the planning episode. And then about the "unofficial, untold, or suppressed stories." A hermeneutic approach considers relationships between the individual aspects of context and the whole, the entirety of the setting. For example, the agency setting for a planning episode may be emblematic of a common planning problem type, but we may only understand that agency setting in terms of our knowledge of the planning problem type. The interpretation question is how to refine understanding through iterative consideration of details and the whole.

Planners see things in particular ways that relate to their personal qualities and training, often differently than do residents, engineers, developers, social service providers, or elected officials. Rather than seek a simple, objective description, planners should recognize that the story of the planning episode is shaped by a complex set of participants' personal commitments and passions. When exposed to the unfamiliar, we can better understand the story by temporarily suspending our own patterns of belief and interpretation.

The figures of speech used in planning provide windows into theories, frameworks, and mental models that, in turn, reveal context. Metaphor, analogy, and simile are ways of comparing things in which a similarity is used to translate from one element to another element, or one thing stands in for another. Taking metaphor as an example, it is a frame through which we interpret the world in which we have one unrelated thing stand in the place of another, that is "culturally powerful, forming understanding and attitudes, certain elements being foregrounded, others ignored" (Bolton and Delderfield 2018, 122). *Lord of the Flies* includes the following metaphor: "The sun in the west was a drop of burning gold that slid near and nearer the sill of the world" (Golding 1954, 43). Metaphors are widely used in planning, such as Howard's "garden city" or Mumford's city as "theatre for social action" (Setiadi et al. 2017). These figures of speech are required to make sense of the world, and can be either limiting or liberating. Reflection makes them available for critical examination.

Stretton (1978) uses analogy to clarify underlying assumptions in four "city as ..." analogies: city as machine, city as marketplace, city as battleground, and city as community. These are shorthand for expressing sets of understandings and beliefs about cities. Of course, figures of speech can also be used negatively to demonize and harm, oversimplify complex situations, promote pet projects, or stereotype. This occurred in the planning profession when slum clearance planners used comparisons to cancer to describe complex social and physical conditions, which implied the "operation" of slum clearance to remove it.

Each figure of speech corresponds to different expectations about existing conditions, planning process, and the prospects for action. A civil engineer seeing the city as a *machine* may favor modelling and analytical procedures, and infrastructure rather than social programs to fine-tune that machine. They may be disinterested in goal-setting processes, seeing efficiency as self-evident. An analyst who sees the city as a *marketplace* may favor interventions to correct for market failure but otherwise think planning should get out of the way of markets. Residents seeing a neighborhood as a *battleground* expect conflict between property owners and residents, and may disbelieve rational processes that a planner may propose. Lastly, an organizer who understands the city as *community* may practice planning in ways that seek consensus-based decisions.

Planners can examine their own practice through the power of figures of speech. Becoming aware of one's own use of figures of speech may make previously invisible assumptions more visible. For example, when a planner considers their work to be a "balancing act" of finding an agreement between stakeholders, they assume that there is just representation and power among stakeholder groups, a precondition to balancing being a justifiable approach. That is not the case in many instances, as simple balancing will lead to the more powerful groups – business owners, developers, and established homeowners – consistently winning in plan outcomes.

Interpretation is necessarily imperfect. I am not able to read context neutrally because of the interpretive "lenses" I use to understand the world. They shape what I notice and ignore, and what meaning I ascribe to information. An example of a lens is when a planner ignores expressions of emotions by community members because they are considered irrational. Another example is when a planner doesn't see that the organizational structure in which they work stifles innovation, or a planner falls for "nice" political talk about participation and consensus but misses the behind-the-scenes machinations of power.

All planners have blindnesses of certain types, and while we are unable to be free of this, reflection reduces the extent of the blindness. Our interpretive lens is sharper when we reflect ourselves and hear from others, and observe, listen, learn, and engage in dialogue.

Putting the Reflection Framework to Work

The Figure 5.2 framework provides a structure and topic prompts for reflection. Admittedly, it is an extensive and complex accounting. I do not consider all those factors during a planning episode because time is short and many elements are well-established. The key, therefore is determining which elements of reflection have a bearing on the given instance, career stage, and context setting.

The framework's conceptual structure organizes personal, context, and in-episode elements, prompting for considerations that a planner might overlook. Overlooking planner-as-person elements, for example, might impede a planner in understanding an unease they have that stems from a mismatch between who they are and what they are doing. Similarly, a planner who focuses only on the planning episode might not understand certain structural context factors that shape outcomes. And the practical judgments made during the episode itself require explicit consideration of logic, emotion, the application of convention and invention, and any other aspects core to these judgments.

Reflection is simplified by focusing on framework elements that are consequential for a particular episode. If logical claims are well understood but emotions are prominent for a planner or planning constituencies, focusing on the latter will add more insight. Still another way of beginning a reflection process is to ask: What are the systematic impacts of taking a *non-reflective* approach? Would that practice reinforce the status quo, as structural factors are not held up to the light, and power relationships are taken for granted? Likewise, in not reflecting, is a planner avoiding ethical reasoning about whether to reproduce context or seek to change it? Planners are more effective when they engage in the planning episode with eyes wide open.

The next section provides prompts for reflection, organized in the three framework elements. Readers can use the reflection approach discussed in this chapter by making copies of Figure 5.2 and annotating them up for each planning assignment, identifying elements that are important or overlooked, and adding their own prompts.

Planner-as-Person Reflection

Previous chapters introduced the term *reflexivity*, referring to a process of turning back on oneself, an act of self-reference, in which a planner critically considers their position, perspectives, values, and assumptions. Reflexivity assumes that individuals can gain insight on the forces shaping them and their own unique characteristics. Reflexivity is discussed in the literature on reflective professional practice (Bolton and Delderfield 2018) and is useful for planning because practice choices relate to planner-as-person. Self-knowledge means awareness and conscious practice choices, leading to effectiveness and personal resiliency.

Self-knowledge is a lifelong journey that is enhanced by reflection. Discussing soul or psychological concepts can be risky or unpopular in the constrained and gossipy conditions of professional practice, yet connection to essential purposes keeps planners engaged and inspired over long careers. Finding a safe way to address these issues can support reflection on them.

Planner-as-Person Reflection Prompts

Chapter 3 explains planner-as-person elements, as displayed on Figure 5.2. To summarize, the prompts are organized as follows:

- Experiences and identities: nature/nurture/choices, identities, cultural identification, skills and inclinations, personality type, spirituality; unconscious.
- Purposes and assumptions: guiding values and personal ethics; theories of human nature, knowledge, change, and justice.
- Professional style(s): concept of profession, preferred techniques, communication style, professional ethics; sedimented experience; ambition and career stage.

Table 14.1 provides an expanded set of reflection-in-action prompts for selected terms related to planner-as-person. They are intended as examples to help the reader develop additional reflection prompts for other framework elements. The questions are posed in the present tense but can be rephrased in the past tense for reflection-on-action.

Lyles and Swearingen White (2019) advance the idea of personal reflection in conceiving of planning as a caring profession. They provide a list of questions that are also useful for planner-as-person reflection, offering 39 questions that address a planner's vision of leadership, cultural humility, and cultivation of

Table 14.1 Prompts and Sample Questions for Planner-as-Person Reflection

Category	Framework Prompt	Example Reflection Prompts
Experiences and identities	Nature/nurture/choices	• Are there aspects of myself that I keep separate from professional practice? If so, what is the impact of maintaining that separation? What changes are implied by bringing my whole person to my practice? • Have past experiences in planning empowered and/or scarred me? How can I use those experiences to gain insight?
	Personality type	• How does my personality type affect the way I approach planning? What are its strengths and weaknesses? How does it shape my interactions on teams and with stakeholders? • Are there ways to improve my interactions with those having different personality types? • What is the degree of alignment between me as a person and my planning work? Do I need a better alignment?
Purposes and assumptions	Theories of human nature	• Am I approaching participants in the planning process assuming collaborative possibility or a competitive, win-lose circumstance? How does my assumption match reality? • How do my understandings of human nature shape my instinctual responses during a planning episode?
	Theories of change	• What theories of change underlie my work? • Are there benefits to broadening my approach to other theories of change?
Professional style(s)	Concept of the profession	• What primary professional paradigms am I using to shape my practice style? How do they help? Are they limiting? • Do I need to revise my concept of the profession?
	Technique	• What are my preferred planning techniques (e.g., technical analysis, negotiation, or visioning)? How do they respond to context and planning episode? • Are there personal elements that keep me from engaging the full range of planning techniques? • Are there new techniques that would enhance my practice?

compassion. The specific questions concern self-awareness, self-management, awareness of others, working with difference, empowering through relationships, and extending compassion (Lyles and Swearingen White 2019, 296).

Planner-as-person reflection supports practice refinements as well as broader decisions to change jobs or careers. Box 14.4 (next page) discusses a scenario in which planner-as-person reflection leads a planner to the conclusion that their current job is not a good fit.

Context Reflection

Chapter 4 discusses the range of context factors relevant to planning episodes. Surely there are more than those reviewed, but the point is that context matters. Planners are more effective and thoughtful when they explicitly consider context rather than take it for granted. Planners also push back, resist, and seek to change context elements that would lead to harm. The best approach is to be sensitive to the dynamic nature of context throughout the planning episode, including awareness, anticipation, and strategic responses.

It is one thing to have a static understanding of context, but it is another to develop insight and discernment in reading context as it evolves through time, especially when under stress. Believing that context truly *does* matter elicits curiosity about its explicit and unstated elements. With this commitment, planners can craft effective practice strategies and provide a feedback loop to context so they anticipate organizational responses over time, from visioning and study, to plan adoption, to implementation.

Understanding context starts with empathy – for people, groups, organizations, places, stories, limitations, histories, and natural systems. Empathy leads to curiosity, which in turn leads to learning. It is an orientation that does not require time in itself, as a planner can be both busy and empathetic. And of course, understanding another point of view does not mean agreeing with it.

Context Reflection Prompts

Chapter 4 explains the suggested elements of context. To summarize, these elements are organized as follows:

- General setting: society, environment, markets, constitutional law, politics, institutions; planning law and precedent, procedures, professional relationships.

Box 14.4 Reflection and Step-by-Step Responses – A Poor Job-Fit Scenario

Reflecting on planner-as-person can lead to a realization that a particular job is not aligned with a planner's core values and purposes. Sometimes, planners avoid reflection because they have an intuition that it might reveal such a circumstance, which may be inconvenient and/or result in negative financial impacts if they leave their job. Even so, it is better to allow this awareness to reach consciousness than have it operate in the background, leading to poor health or psychological consequences, or to performing poorly at work.

Recognizing a lack of alignment between planner-as-person and a job, one response is to leave the organization and find a new job that is a better fit. For some, the idea of staying in a job that is not a good fit is simply unacceptable. But a resumé with many short job tenures raises red flags among personnel departments and hiring managers.

Reflective planners consider other options to leaving a job. Reflection includes thinking through alternative courses of action, considering likely outcomes and contingencies, and conceiving of ways to change the job they are in. If a particular assignment is in conflict with planner-as-person values, the planner could request a change in work assignments or propose ways of carrying out assignments that addresses their concerns. For example, including a social justice impact section on a traditional staff report format could ensure that important information is placed before decision-makers. Alternatively, a planner frustrated by dysfunction in the organization could propose work process improvements and offer to serve on an interdepartmental team to improve effectiveness and coordination. More broadly, a planner could seek to influence organizational culture and its practices. One planner cannot expect to change an organization on their own, but they could be part of a broader change. Let's say the organization does not provide a supportive culture for staff planners. The planner could organize lunchtime professional development workshops, which could lead to adoption of formal programs and organizational change. Similarly, if a planner works for a city whose elected officials ignore climate change impacts, that planner could propose a briefing from climate change scientists and policy-makers.

It is challenging to address mismatches between planner-as-person and the job. A reflective planner has more awareness, and more specificity about the mismatch than a vague feeling the job isn't a fit. The more specific the awareness, the more likely that a strategic response can be developed. There is no guarantee that any of the aforementioned ideas will lead to a better fit, but it can be beneficial process to seek changes and then assess whether a job change is appropriate.

- Episode setting: issue history, interests, conflict/collaboration; "talk" processes; institutional dynamics; implementation.
- Role(s): job sector, job function(s), charge and level of discretion; professional and interpersonal dynamics.

Table 14.2 provides expanded reflection-in-action prompts for selected terms listed in the context section.

Of course, planner-as-person and context reflection are related. A planner's view of human nature, for example, shapes their interpretation of context. If they view individuals as inherently competitive, they might interpret a messy community conflict as showing the need for systematic regulations, while a planner with a communitarian view might interpret the same conflict as revealing a need for improved dialogue and reconciliation.

Planning Episode Reflection-in-Action

Reflection-in-action for a planning episode can begin with a broad question such as: What is the work that this planning issue calls for? By work, I mean the *lift* – the thing to be done in order to make progress, which would not occur without the planning effort. Also, how will that work be accomplished? There is great variety in answers to these questions. For example, it could be that the lift is getting experimentation started so as to produce better information about feasible approaches. Or, the lift is forging new relationships between departments or agencies so that longer-term, more ambitious planning can be carried out. Or, an issue has lingered unresolved forever and the lift is stakeholders compromising on a "good enough" plan that leaves everyone a bit unsatisfied. Yet another lift is a comprehensive effort that achieves systemic change. Another word for describing this process is generating *movement*. Given the stasis that often exists in public policy, effective planning generates movement toward better conditions. Understanding what lift or movement is needed is critical in determining how the planning episode should be designed, navigated, and managed.

Another simple reflection query is about succeeding and failing, as follows:

- Success: How am I succeeding in the planning episode? What are the natures of the successes, e.g., data and models, decisions, education, empowerment, engagement, outcomes, process, and/or implementation commitment? Why am I succeeding? Is it because of good information and analysis, good decisions, luck, support from others, implementation skill, etc.? How can I extend these successes?

Table 14.2 Prompts and Sample Questions for Context Reflection

Category	Framework Prompt	Example Reflection Questions
General setting	Institutions	• What is the structure, history, and aim of the institution? How do I know what I know about it? How can I learn more about it? • Are reporting lines for staff tightly controlled or loose? Are staff roles fragmented or collaborative? How do others' careerism affect my prospects? • How can I advance planning objectives in the existing structure, either by adapting to it or advocating for organizational change? • Are there social, cultural, and political structures that I seek to change? What should I do if I cannot change them?
	Professional relationships	• What is the level of collaboration and/or competition between staff in my department and other departments? • What is the quality of relationships with other professionals, such as attorneys or engineers? How can I strengthen them? • What level of goodwill have I generated that allows me to seek help from other professionals? How can I generate more?
Episode setting	History	• Does the history of the issue allow moving directly into planning or does it require communication, healing, and reconciliation first? • Are there parties who were aggrieved in the last round of planning who are seeking redress in the current one? How can their grievances be addressed? Should they be?
	Implementation	• What types of support exist for the effort? Is there support for plan adoption only, or do decision-makers care about implementation, or both? • What is the level of implementation capacity available and how can I enhance it in the planning process?
Role(s)	Charge	• Is my mandate clear or fuzzy? Is it written, oral, or an assumed part of agency practices? Does the charge have wiggle room? • Is there an unstated, informal charge? If so, what is it and how can it be addressed? Is there a contradiction between the formal and informal charge? • What room is there to innovate or reframe the problem within the charge?
	Professional dynamics	• What is the capacity for collaboration among colleagues? • How should professional negotiation or problem definition and solutions be organized? • What level of cross-departmental cooperation is possible? • What is the standing of the department or firm in the broader context? • How do others perceive me, personally and in my professional role?

- Failure: How am I failing in the planning episode? What are the natures of the failures, e.g., data and models, decisions, education, empowerment, engagement, outcomes, process, and/or implementation commitment? Why am I failing? Is it incomplete information or flawed analysis, bad decisions, misfortune, undermining by others, lack of upper management support, flawed implementation, etc.? Does my failure serve a larger purpose, and if not, how can I redirect the effort toward a positive purpose?

Reflecting on success can keep the process on track and build a storehouse of experiences for other settings. It also can bring humility if a planner realizes that their role in the success was not the whole story. Reflection on failure is in some ways the more interesting and actionable task. That reflection can help a planner make midcourse correction in process or professional approach.

Reflection-in-action helps a planner recognize their tacit assumptions as they move through the planning episode. It supports discernment about the dynamics of context. It also helps avoid getting stuck with one approach, such as logic without emotion or applying convention without invention. Reflection-in-action naturally undermines doctrinaire approaches that would proceed along a course no matter what happens. In reflection-in-action, planners ask pragmatic questions about what is needed and what works in ongoing moments of the planning episode.

Planning Episode Reflection Prompts

Reflection-in-action supports wise and strategic choices during the planning episode. It could include midcourse corrections to scope of work, decisions on how to address a preferred planning approach, assessing the dynamics of political allegiances, and/or responding to positive surprises and disasters in the process. Tables 14.3 and 14.4 provide example questions for considering the structure of logic, emotion, convention, and invention surrounding critical practical judgments.

Tables 14.3 and 14.4 present a wide range of questions, but those lists are only a beginning. Each planner can develop their own reflection questions and techniques. As an example, planners can use scenario planning to support practical judgments. We normally think of scenarios as part of plan development, such as developing alternative water supply scenarios (Quay 2010). But scenarios can equally serve in-practice deliberations and decisions. For instance, a planner or planning team could create scenarios of how different uses of logic and emotion, and convention and invention inform plan approach and content options.

Table 14.3 Logic and Emotion Elements and Sample Questions for the Planning Episode

Category	Example Reflection Questions
Logic	• How "wicked" is the nature of the planning problem? How am I addressing a lack of definitive formulation, unclear notions of success, or relationships to other problems?
	• Are data, models, and qualitative information of high quality and accessible to the community and decision-makers? Is qualitative information properly integrated?
	• What are my strategies to address politicized decision environments?
	• How am I bringing forward issues beyond the current election timeframe of officials, such as analysis of environmental, social, or financial issues?
	• How well do I understand logical claims of other professionals? How do I portray logical claims based on planning?
	• How am I representing ends/means logical consistency in argumentative processes? How am I dealing with stakeholders who advocate for preferred ends irrespective of broad goals or long-term consequences?
	• Am I representing my technical expertise appropriately, retaining authority in making technical claims and drafting coherent plans and policies, and recognizing the limits or structural elements of that information?
	• Am I considering implementation requirements and their likelihood at the same time as plan-making?
	• Is my participation in mediation and negotiation processes in good faith, relying on reason?
Emotion	• Am I using opportunities to engage emotions to process issues, build resolve, and allow expressions of mutual care?
	• Am I listening well? Am I showing respect for community members, other professionals, or elected officials?
	• Am I using obfuscation, humiliation or shaming to get my way? Have I explained planning terms and processes for those not familiar with them?
	• Am I carrying an appropriate emotional tenor in the planning process, by being open and available, allowing my passions to be known but acknowledging other points of view and life experiences?
	• Am I managing my own emotional reactions, i.e., slowing down, avoiding impulsiveness, or stepping up and reminding myself to reflect-in-action? Do I have appropriate emotional boundaries?

And Now to You: The Reflection Agenda

The pressures of practice may crowd out your time for reflection. You may find reflection uncomfortable because it disrupts the status quo and you sense of self. It is worth it. The key is to find ways to incorporate reflection in ongoing activities, formally by starting a reflective practice journal, or meeting with a mentor, or informally while taking a weekend hike. If reflection becomes a habit, you won't have to remember to reflect and you are on your way to critical reflective practice. If reflection produces realizations that are inconvenient, remember that reflection does not determine action. It is up to you to decide what to do about it.

Table 14.4 Convention and Invention Elements and Sample Questions for the Planning Episode

Category	Example Reflection Questions
Convention	• Am I distinguishing between convention that (i) represents time-tested practical wisdom and (ii) replicates biases and inefficient practices? • Do I have rhetorical strategies to engage with appeals to convention that have negative impacts on others, such as residential exclusion? • Do I have a critical approach to applying best practice lessons in a way that respects local context? • Am I considering appeals to convention in terms of their appropriateness to the specific time and place of the planning episode? • Have I assessed the capacity of the community to absorb change and/or metabolize past setbacks, as well as the positive uses of convention (e.g., caring for your neighbor) in supporting manageable levels of change?
Invention	• Am I bringing new perspectives, frames, methods, and technologies to the planning episode? • Am I questioning existing regulations, protocols, and precedents for their appropriateness to the planning episode? • Have I considered the appropriateness of disrupting the status quo through the planning effort? • Am I searching for community-based invention or invention in other sectors that can be applied to the planning episode? • Have I considered the process of innovation diffusion in creating new ideas and processes? Am I taking advantage of technology in appropriate ways? • Am I considering the role of play, artmaking, workshop, or other creative activities in generating new ideas and insights, and bringing a deeper sense of meaning to planning?

Discussion Questions

1. Identify a metaphor or similar figure of speech that you use in your planning practice. How is it helpful? How is it unhelpful? Are there other metaphors that could reframe the issue for better understanding?

2. Consider an example of single-loop learning that you have experienced, i.e., experience leads to a practice change without asking why. Brainstorm how that example could be transformed into double-loop learning. What would it take?

3. Box 14.3 discusses the influences that lead me to reflect. If you share an inclination to reflect, develop your own map of influences. Examine them critically. If you do not share that inclination, consider what shapes your perspective. For both groups, consider what is lost and what is gained in your preferences.

4. Develop your own version of Figure 5.2 with prompts that are most useful for you to reflect on your practice.

Note

1 The manifesto was written by Myriam Ackad, communications coordinator for the college.

References

Argyris, Chris and Donald A. Schön. 1974. *Theory in Practice: Increasing Professional Effectiveness*. San Francisco, CA: Jossey-Bass.

Bolton, Gillie and Russell Delderfield. 2018. *Reflective Practice: Writing and Professional Development*, 5th edition. Thousand Oaks, CA: Sage Publications, Inc.

Brooks, Michael F. 2002. *Planning Theory for Practitioners*. New York: Routledge.

Dewey, John. 1938. *Logic: The Theory of Inquiry*. New York: Henry Hold and Company.

Dreyfus, Stuart E. and Hubert L. Dreyfus. 1986. *Mind Over Machine*. New York: Free Press.

Eagleton, Terry. 2003. *After Theory*. New York: Basic Books.

Golding, William. 1954. *Lord of the Flies*. New York: Penguin Group.

Hoch, Charles. 2019. *Pragmatic Spatial Planning*. New York: Routledge.

Howe, Elizabeth. and Jerome L. Kaufman. 1979. "The Ethics of Contemporary American Planners." *Journal of the American Planning Association*, 45(3): 243–255. doi: 10.1080/01944367908976965.

Lyles, Ward and Stacey Swearingen White. 2019. "Who Cares? Arnstein's Ladder, the Emotional Paradox of Public Engagement, and (Re)imagining Planning as Caring." *Journal of the American Planning Association*, 85(3): 287–300. doi: 10.1080/01944363.2019.1612268.

Marino, Gordon. 2018. *Existentialist Survival Guide: How to Live Authentically in an Inauthentic Age*. San Francisco, CA: HarperOne.

Montero, Barbara Gail. 2016. *Thought and Action: Expertise and the Conscious Mind*. London: Oxford University Press.

Pohjannoro, Ulla. 2016. "Capitalizing on Intuition and Reflection: Making Sense of a Composer's Creative Process." *Musicae Scientiea*, 20(2): 207–234. doi: 10.1177/1029864915625727.

Quay, Ray. 2010. "Anticipatory Governance: A Tool for Climate Change Adaptation." *Journal of the American Planning Association*, 76(4): 496–511. doi: 10.1080/01944363.2010.508428.

Rojas, James. 2020. "PLACE IT!." Accessed January 29, 2020 at http://www.placeit.org/index2.html.

Sandercock, Leonie. 2003. "Out of the Closet: The Importance of Stories and Storytelling in Planning Practice." *Planning Theory & Practice*, 4(1): 11–28. doi.org/10.1080/1464935032000057209.

Schön, Donald. 1982. *The Reflective Practitioner: How Professionals Think in Action*. New York: Basic Books.

Setiadi, Hafid, Hadi Sabari Yunus, and Bambang Purwanto. 2017. "The Metaphor of "Center" in Planning: Learning from the Geopolitical Order of Swidden Traditions in the Land of Sunda." *Journal of Regional & City Planning*, 28(2 August): 111–128. doi: 10.5614/jrcp.2017.28.2.3.

Stretton, Hugh. 1978. *Urban Planning in Rich and Poor Countries*. Oxford: Oxford University Press.

Willson, Richard. 2015. "Painting the Present: Imagining the Future." *Access*, 46(Spring): 34–37.

Willson, Richard. 2018. *A Guide for the Idealist: Launching and Navigating Your Planning Career*. New York: Routledge.

Zornberg, Avivah Gottlieb. 2009. *The Murmuring Deep: Reflections on Biblical Unconscious*. New York: Schocken Books.

Chapter 15

Building Your Reflective Practice

Planning is a noble profession that makes the world a better place, but planners rarely arrive at definitive answers. We practice with levels of ambiguity, incongruity, and uncertainty. Rather than this being a problem, it makes planning an enterprise worthy of devotion, one that contributes to lifelong learning. The poet Rainer Maria Rilke said it this way: "try to love the questions themselves as if they were locked rooms and like books written in a very foreign tongue. Do not now seek the answers, which cannot be given to you ... Live the questions now" (1938, 27). Reflection is a way to live planning practice questions now, a path to effectiveness and professional fulfillment. The case studies show how reflection-in-action works and the insights that reflection-on-action offers, and Chapter 14 provides ideas on how to incorporate reflection in your practice. Of course, forms of reflection are particular to the individual: reflect in a way that is compatible with your way of thinking and your circumstances, or be bold and use it to move outside your comfort zone.

Taking a step back, we can see that planning involves professional artistry. The case authors found their way through planning episodes, and while they started with certain procedural and technical ideas, they learned and made adjustments as they went. The idea of artistry has many meanings – performance, skill, sensitivity – but the one that resonates strongest with planning is improvisation. Among the musical arts, planning is more like jazz than a marching band (see Schön 1983, 55). Reflection supports the artistry that occurs when jazz players listen and respond to one another in real-time.

As observed in Chapters 1 and 2, planning lacks a single theory or technique, and it generates daunting questions about values: How do you know that you are contributing to the good? How do you choose between different process approaches? How do you determine how much to compromise, or decide what to attend to and what to ignore in the moment?[1] The case authors reflect on how they resolved these questions while seeking personal authenticity in their work.

Reflective practice makes significant intellectual and moral demands that in turn lead to professional growth and effectiveness. It is also a path to personal self-development because reflection improves your capacity for logical thought, emotional understanding, moral reasoning, and choosing under uncertainty. The problem with unreflective planning is that it replicates existing power structures, is stymied by change, and is not creative. Planning by habit, precedent, or superficial best-practice standards hides assumptions and cannot cope with new situations. Moreover, reflection is an important way to test your assumptions and respond thoughtfully in an environment of highly charged claims.

Obviously, reflective practice does not ensure particular processes or substantive outcomes. If you have strong commitments to certain outcomes it may seem like a relativistic, slippery slope. There is no guarantee that another reflective planner will come to the same conclusion as you, and further, in practicing reflectively you might change your mind or realize error. Indeed, reflective practice is destabilizing for the planner as an individual and for their causes, but destabilizing in a good way. The wisdom of fixed positions is questionable in the rapidly changing social, environmental, and economic setting for planning. Reflective planning practice, then, has elements of an act of faith – in your own abilities, in your colleagues, and in decision-making processes.

Fischler (2012) says it this way: "What makes reflective practice a powerful idea is also what makes it difficult to accept and to apply: it holds the promise of improved collective action in the future by *imposing a burden of individual responsibility in the here and now*" (326, italics added). It requires and builds self-confidence and maturity. Reflection is easier for me now that I am nearing the end of my career, with more life experience and less to lose than it was for me at the beginning. I see mistakes I could have avoided with more reflection-in-action early in my career. Plus, a commitment to reflection as planners can have transformative effects on those with whom we plan.

In calling for self-reflection, Eagleton (2003) says the following:

> If knowing the world often enough means burrowing through complex swatches of self-deception, knowing oneself involves this even more. Only someone unusually secure could have the courage to confront themselves in this way without either rationalizing away what they unearth, or being consumed by fruitless guilt.
>
> *(137)*

Can we as planners summon the courage to reflect? And more importantly, can we conduct planning in a way that fosters reflection among the community members and decision-makers with whom we work, and help them find ways to a better future?

Making Sense of Successes and Failures

Let's examine two different planning experiences. In the first, the plan you've been working on is unanimously adopted, you are praised, and the project wins an American Planning Association (APA) award. In the second, the plan you've been working on is ignored for a period of time, and when it reaches decision-makers, it is rejected. You are vilified as an incompetent bureaucrat.

Both scenarios are experiences. Taken at face value, we seek the first scenario and avoid the second one. But experiences, good and bad, don't mean anything without reflection. Reflection turns experiences into practical wisdom, a nuanced form of understanding and interpretation. Reflecting over time, you develop wisdom to draw on in difficult or unprecedented planning situations. This "storehouse" of wisdom doesn't have a lock on its doors, and accepts deliveries in and out. It has windows, too, signifying its social nature.

Reflection helps you interpret why one planning effort was successful while another was not. Was success or failure attributable to your actions, or beyond them? How can you diagnose what happened in order to practice more effectively? By seeking to understand these questions, planners build up reflection-on-action insights to draw on while reflecting-in-action.

Chapter 13 mentioned the role of mentors in the reflection process. One of my mentors is Paul Niebanck. He spurs me to reflect in a decades-long pen pal relationship. Niebanck never suggests what I should do, no matter how much I hope he will. Box 15.1 (next page) provides his interpretation of planning as a field that is comprehensive, collaborative, critical, civil, and committed to constructive change. To my mind, that kind of practice is supported by and requires reflection.

Box 15.1 Come the Peaceful Revolution
Paul Niebanck, Professor Emeritus, University of California, Santa Cruz

Planning is a noun. But it's an unusual noun: it acts like a verb. That kind of noun is called a gerund. The suffix *-ing* gives it away. Gerunds have their own energy, their own urgency, their own agency, even their own intentionality. Plan*ning* doesn't sit still. Planning is active, generative. Planning stirs things, creates things, extends things. Planning is continuous.

As a gerund, planning encourages us to think in abstract and theoretical terms. Meanwhile, life is not theoretical. Life is substantive. So, because of who I am as a person, because of what I have chosen to focus on as a scholar, because of the experiences I've had, and because of the people who have become my closest associates, I have come to call myself an urban planner, a community planner, and a planner who regards planning as part of the democratic ideal.

The conventional definition, the professionally accepted definition, the definition that I learned in a planning theory class in school has three elements:

Goals – Means – Effectuation Or more simply: Ready – Aim – Fire

The rational action model "works" if the society is governed in an exclusively top-down fashion; better yet, if it is a totalitarian state. There's one decision-maker (the autocrat); one set of desires (theirs); one set of instruments (the army, the bureaucracy); and one set of actions (theirs). Presto. I'm not satisfied with that characterization of planning, nor with the requirements for its functioning.

My students came up with alternative conceptions:

Awareness – Appreciation – Concern – Action
Also: Trust – Prepare – Execute – Celebrate

Planning is *comprehensive*. It expands the territory of interest and concern. Planning doesn't seek to zap a problem or dust off an issue. It is willing to wrestle with complexity and wait for the appropriate moment to take action. Planners are broad-minded.

Planning is *collaborative*. Planning is interactive, generative, developmental, and expansive. Planning feeds on the democratic principle and contributes to its realization. Planners are light on their feet.

Planning is *critical*. It takes nothing for granted; rather it seeks to build reliable foundations and to base its actions on understandings that have been subject to scrutiny. Planners hew to a code of ethics that emphasizes self-critique.

Planning is *civil*. It opens itself to the perspectives of whoever has something to say and the contributions of whoever is willing to share in the work. It conducts itself in an orderly and consistent manner. Planners are respectful.

Planning is *committed to constructive change*. Planning is an insistent, relentless, faithful activity. Its ambition is to help build a better world. Meanwhile the world may go nuts, but planning stands firm. Planners aren't quitters. Hope is our byword.

On Being Lost

Given the extent of practical judgments made in the cases, planners naturally feel disoriented or lost at times. You may encounter a bracing difference between your good intentions and the world's indifference or hostility to your ideas. At the workplace, you may experience a gap between your planning mission and the predominant organizational culture. You may also feel lost when facing seemingly irreconcilable values and demands. The case studies provide road maps to this complex, contested terrain – one in which planners use theories as they serve the process, free from unreasonable desire for theoretical canon.

All-encompassing theories offer an apparent escape from a feeling of being lost. A planner adopting an economics framework, as I did, is likely to set about to correcting market failures such as negative externalities, undersupply of public goods, and prisoner's dilemma conditions. A planner embracing a Marxist theory of urbanization will interpret urban phenomena through the lens of capital and seek to rearrange power and economic structure. Alternatively, basing practice on communicative ethics leads to work on improving deliberative processes. Each theory offers explanation and a coherent world view. But in each case, strict adherence to one approach may not be effective.

Seeking an all-encompassing planning theory is seeking an escape from reality. Forcing one approach to address all situations is like following a map when you don't know the starting coordinates. Once lost, those lacking a map may give up, going through the procedural motions in their careers. A more practical tactic is to test different theories for their applicability with an open mind. I've described this approach as principled adaptability in other writings (Willson 2018).

The cases show that theory is useful in action and informs reflection on action. Rather than disparage practice for not following a particular planning theory, we find that planners use it along with their experience and intuition to develop their own styles of practice. Rather than seeing theoretical flexibility as a problem that should be resolved with reference to underlying truths, Richard Rorty (1999) suggests fostering increased awareness of interdependence and considering the implications of practical actions. A pragmatic use of theory can make us more self-reliant as we face difficult questions. We no longer seek to escape from the complex reality of the world. Rorty would replace that quest with a demand for imagination.

The sometimes baffling and unstable nature of planning practice generates anxiety, but it turns out we are not alone. The anxiety of "not-knowing" echoes the concerns of existentialism. Existentialist thought describes the ideas of a wide variety of philosophers who focus on the individual finding meaning. Existentialists describe their anxiety in finding themselves in the world – comprehending it fully, including its joy, love, absurdity and cruelty, considering life and death, and human suffering. Urban planning offers drama that matches that found in the greatest literature.

Existentialism eschews false comfort in the form of dogma. Existentialists reject dualities – putting things in either/or categories in favor of accepting experience and mystery. An example of duality might be separating thinking from feeling, and practicing in only one realm. Existentialists argue that each person's existence precedes any categories or labels applied to them.

Authenticity is a core concern of existentialism (Golomb 1995). The attention to planner-as-person in Chapter 3 suggests that planners seek authenticity and align their practice with it. When authenticity is approached, your practice is more inspired and truer. Knowing yourself also leads to more interest in others, and perhaps an ability to step out of yourself and observe with a level of objectivity. Of course, this means that any old planning job may not be the right one for you.

Both pragmatist and existentialist thought challenge the idea of planning as a technical activity in which professionals straightforwardly identify optimal means (plans, programs, regulations, projects) to achieve desired ends (vision, goals, and objectives). Paying attention to planner-as-person, context, and the demand for practical judgments helps us understand how purely technocratic planning can go wrong. But I admit that I'm not completely convinced of pragmatists' arguments. In some of the cases, technical analysis was essential and must not be interpreted away. For example, pragmatist' ideas have been twisted by climate change deniers to devalue the role of scientific experts when we most need them.

Reflective planning practice is a bit like living on the side of a mountain. You have a perspective on how far you have come, and you can look back and reflect on how you arrived. But you can't see the peak for the trees. The way forward is uncertain and requires exploration. I wrote parts of this book *on* the side of a mountain, in the San Gabriel Mountains north of my home. For me, mountains naturally bring a reflective point of view. Figure 15.1 is a sketch I made during one of my work days.

Some Final, Contradictory Words

I find benefit in allowing contradictions between the types of universalist and relativist conceptions discussed here to carry on in my practice rather than seek

Figure 15.1 Living on the Side of the Mountain. Image source: Author

a refuge in a resolution. The case studies illustrate the complex reality of practice in which the benefits and dangers of all systems of thought can be observed.

Throughout the book, I've made reference to pragmatists such as Dewey and Rorty, and to planning theorists who take up that approach, such a Hoch. Pragmatists are anti-theorists in the narrow sense of theory; they argue that there isn't one source of truth upon which we can rely. Instead, they recommend concepts such as recognizing interdependence (Rorty 1999), developing knowledge in action (Dewey 1938), and "incremental progress toward a more inclusive good based on democratic deliberation" (Hoch 2019, 186). This is out of step with the modernist idea of planning as marching us forward through time toward a common public good.

Pragmatists are criticized for relativism. You may have trouble with pragmatism if you are committed to particular theoretical foundations, values, or positions. It is unsettling to let loose of your moorings, to release your practice into a moving stream. It is natural to seek to build your house on a rock rather on an unstable shore. Theory offers a rock of sorts, an escape from uncertainty.

Apart from giving up the comfort of claims to unassailable theory, I struggle with a deeper challenge to the pragmatist position. For example, I draw on Eagleton in various sections of the book; he is a cultural theorist who is a critic of Rorty and postmodernism. Eagleton's work resonates with existential commitments I have to values of love, justice, truth, and beauty, values that I seek to advance in my planning practice. I cannot prove their veracity but they have changed my existence.

Similarly, I believe that there is a moral standard – again, that I cannot prove – but I act as if there is one. I practice planning as if there are universal, planetwide values such as justice, freedom, human rights, communal meaning, and a right to a sustainable planet. These positions are axioms that stem from my interpretation of psychology, experience, and religion. My conception of justice, for example, is that it is more than the sum of what we think, but rather that it hovers above the human condition. When my work contributes to justice I have the humbling experience of releasing some of its sparks. Accordingly, I am a moral realist who believes that there are better and worse answers to planning questions. The statements of the planning profession, by the way, also imply that there is a moral reality.

I'll end the book with this contradiction: I practice planning as a pragmatist but I live as if there is an ultimate moral reality. Normally, a pragmatist would argue against the notion of a moral reality, claiming there is just "what we do." Normally, one who believes there is a moral reality would argue against the relativism of pragmatism. This contradiction has been with me for decades, and yes, I surely should have worked this out by now. Yet I realize that this is one of many other tensions and contradictions that I and other planners experience such as realism/idealism, efficiency/equity, local/global, technically rational/participation-based, short-term/long-term, and so on. We're in the contradiction business because our profession bridges so many aspects of the human condition. In discussing cultural theory, Eagleton (2003) makes a point that resonates with this condition:

> To be inside and outside a position at the same time – to occupy a territory while loitering skeptically on the boundary – is often where the most intensely creative ideas stem from. It is a resourceful place to be, if not always a painless one.
>
> *(40)*

I deal with my pragmatist/moral realist contradiction with reflection, not to solve it once and for all, but to plan and move forward in its presence. I would like to convince you that living with such contradictions and tolerating ambiguity is a productive way to plan. As Niebanck notes in Box 15.1, this recognizes the verb energy in *planning* as opposed to the noun energy of *plan* (also see Bertolini 2011).

Make practice judgments based on well-thought-out rationale, but discover your path through a planning episode as you move through it. The roots of technocratic planning are a poor fit with present conditions, but some planners wear those garments like an old, moth-eaten overcoat. If that is you, take off the coat. It may feel like it is keeping you warm but it doesn't serve you now. Once coatless, use critical reflection to guide ongoing practical judgments and plan with the support of those judgments.

Planning practice should be animated, alive, and coursing with hope. The way to animate it is with critical reflection in all the ways described here. Reflective planners are clear about the values that have laid a claim on them. These are claims I have made throughout the book. But more important than any claim, I want to make an ask: will you incorporate reflection in your practice?

Here's a theory: care, engage, learn, reason, reflect, act. Repeat.

Tag, you're it!

Note

1 As a plein air style landscape painter, I cannot paint every leaf on a tree I am painting. I have to decide what to pay attention to and what to ignore. Recently, I wrote an essay for *Access* magazine that examines connections between painting and transportation modeling. Transportation modelers must also determine what to pay attention to and what to ignore (Willson 2015).

References

Bertolini, Luca. 2011. Editorial, *Planning Theory & Practice*, 12(2): 175–177. DOI: 10.1080/14649357.2011.586826

Dewey, John. 1938. *Experience and Education*. New York: Macmillan.

Eagleton, Terry. 2003. *After Theory*. New York: Basic Books.

Fischler, Raphaël. 2012. "Reflective Practice." In: *Planning Ideas that Matter*, edited by S. Sanyal, Lawrence J. Bishwapriya Vale, and Christina D. Rosan. Cambridge, MA: MIT Press, 313-332.

Golomb, James. 1995. *In Search of Authenticity: From Kierkegaard to Camus*. New York: Routledge.

Hoch, Charles. 2019. *Pragmatic Spatial Planning: Practical Theory for Professionals*. New York: Routledge.

Rilke, Rainer Maria. 1938. *Letter to a Young Poet*. Translation by M.D. Herter Norton, revised edition. New York: W. W. Norton & Company.

Rorty, Richard. 1999. *Philosophy and Social Hope*. New York: Penguin.

Schön, Donald. 1983. *The Reflective Practitioner: How Professionals Think in Action*. New York: Basic Books.

Willson, Richard. 2015. "Painting the Present: Imagining the Future." *Access*, 46(Spring): 34–37.

Willson, Richard. 2018. *A Guide for the Idealist: Launching and Navigating Your Planning Career*. New York: Routledge.

Index

Page numbers in **bold** indicate tables. Page numbers in *italic* indicate figures.